Beyond Hegel and Nietzsche

Studies in Contemporary German Social Thought (a partial listing)
Thomas McCarthy, general editor

Beyond Hegel and Nietzsche

Philosophy, Culture, and Agency

Elliot L. Jurist

The MIT Press
Cambridge, Massachusetts
London, England

Set in New Baskerville by The MIT Press.
Printed and bound in the United States of America.

Library of Congress Cataloging-in-Publication Data

Jurist, Elliot L.
Beyond Hegel and Nietzsche: philosophy, culture, and agency / Elliot L. Jurist.
p.   cm.—(Studies in contemporary German social thought)
Includes bibliographical references (p.   ) and index.
ISBN 0-262-10087-8 (hc.: alk. paper)
1. Hegel, Georg Wilhelm Friedrich, 1770–1831. 2. Nietzsche, Friedrich Wilhelm, 1844–1900. 3. Culture—Philosophy—History—19th century. 4. Agent—History—19th century. I. Title. II. Series.

B2948.J865 2000
193—dc21

00-038681

for my father, Sumner Jurist,
and for my mother, Hilda Braurman Jurist (in memoriam)

Contents

Contents

Acknowledgements

I would like to take this opportunity to thank all those who have contributed to this book. First, I would like to thank three teachers who guided my interest in philosophy as an undergraduate at Haverford College—Dick Bernstein, Aryeh Kosman, and the late Paul Desjardins. Dick Bernstein continues to be an important interlocutor and remains for me the embodiment of a life devoted to philosophy. I also would like to note my appreciation of two professors who inspired me in graduate school at Columbia University, Arthur Danto and Robert Cumming.

Tony Dardis, Terry Godlove, Bob Holland, and Pat Mann, my colleagues at Hofstra University, gave me valuable feedback on early drafts. I owe a note of special gratitude to Kathleen Wallace for taking time to read and comment upon the manuscript more recently. I would also like to thank Hofstra University for giving me a sabbatical in 1996–97, during which I revised the manuscript.

Early versions of portions of this book were delivered as papers at several meetings of the Social Sciences Seminar in Prague. Thanks to Jean Cohen, Maeve Cooke, Peter Dews, Alessandro Ferrara, Axel Honneth, Martin Jay, and Joel Whitebook for their helpful comments. Kitty Ross's editorial suggestions helped to improve an early version. My friend Cliff Simms and I had many conversations about this book as well as about other pressing issues of life. Both of these sorts of conversations were necessary, and I would like him to know how much I have valued them. Thanks, too, to Dorothea von Moltke for her help. I would also like to thank my family, Andra Jurist, Bruce Stewart, Marney Jurist-Rosner, and Lindsay Jurist-Rosner, for their discretion in the way they probed the question of when this book might be completed. Thomas McCarthy and Larry Cohen have my appreciation for their generous support of this project.

My wife, Ruth Ben-Ghiat, contributed enormously to the successful completion of this book. Her fearless but gentle determination—as we both completed books—deserves more than an enthusiastic thank you. I feel grateful for her love and intellectual companionship.

This book is dedicated, with love, to my parents, Sumner Jurist and the late Hilda Braurman Jurist. Sadly, my mother died before I was able to complete the book. I know that she would have enjoyed seeing it. Her memory remains a strong presence in my life.

Editor's Note

The abbreviations used to cite works are shown in boldface in the bibliography.

Beyond Hegel and Nietzsche

Introduction

From the perspective of mainstream philosophical culture, Hegel and Nietzsche both exemplify the superfluousness of nineteenth-century philosophy. Within the Continental tradition, on the other hand, Hegel and Nietzsche are typically juxtaposed as opposites in terms of their basic philosophical commitments, their styles, and even their life experiences. Indeed, one could argue that Hegel and Nietzsche are the two foundational figures of Continental philosophy, and, furthermore, that their legacy endures in that twentieth-century Continental philosophers can be classified, more or less, as Hegelians or Nietzscheans.[1]

One can discern the opposition between Hegelians and Nietzscheans by comparing critical theory, which has a strong Hegelian influence, and poststructuralism, which has a strong Nietzschean influence. Critical theorists and poststructuralists alike, however, affirm the juxtaposition of Hegel and Nietzsche as philosophical opposites. For instance, Habermas (1987, p. 120) claims that Hegel is Nietzsche's "great antipode" and warns against "Nietzscheanisms of all kinds" (1983, p. 253), while Deleuze (1983, pp. 8–9, 195) asserts that "there is no compromise between Hegel and Nietzsche" and Derrida (1985, pp. 23, 59) refers to "hand-to-hand combat between Hegel and Nietzsche."[2] The ready acceptance of a fundamental difference between Hegel and Nietzsche constitutes, ironically enough, a rare point of agreement between Habermas and these contemporary French thinkers.

This book has its origins in a certain uneasiness with the conception of Hegel and Nietzsche as philosophical opposites. There are clearly grounds for contrasting Hegel and Nietzsche, but this should not lead us to neglect the areas of consensus between them. Nor should we ignore the possibility, where their views seem to be at odds, of finding a way to render their views as complementary. My aim, simply stated, will be to place Hegel and Nietzsche in conversation with each other. This will entail paying attention to where they disagree as well as to where they agree, though the business of establishing differences and likenesses is not what is ultimately important. Resisting the customary antinomy, I aspire to probe their deepest philosophical motivations and to reassess their relationship in a way that preserves rather than diminishes its complexity. To a large degree I will be immersed in the exploration of nineteenth-century texts, yet I will be mindful of how the works have been read and used. Therefore, I will be as concerned with interpretations of Hegel and Nietzsche as with specifying their views.

Before articulating my perspective further, let me briefly describe some of the reasons why Hegel and Nietzsche have been perceived as opposites.

A major divide between Hegel's and Nietzsche's philosophies is found in the legacy of the Enlightenment: whereas Hegel valorizes reason and knowledge, Nietzsche gives primacy to the irrational and exhibits some skepticism toward knowledge.[3] A closely related issue is whether modernity is worth salvaging, as Hegel believed, or whether it is to be despaired about, as Nietzsche contended. Hegelians assess modernity as problematic and oppressive but not hopeless; Nietzscheans tend to see it as dislocating and pathological, and thus to raise the specter of a new (postmodern) era.

Another perceived contrast between Hegel and Nietzsche has to do with Hegel's communitarian sympathies and Nietzsche's preference for an "aristocratic radicalism" in which individuals hold themselves above any community and have the strength to create values for themselves. All Hegelians—regardless of whether they are in the tradition of right or left Hegelians—exhibit serious concern about society and its institutions. Nietzscheans gravitate to the edge of society and are tempted by what lies below and beyond. Nietzsche's perspectivism is designed in part to undermine or at least to question the value of any kind of communitarian vision.

Hegel and Nietzsche are often understood, too, as holding contrasting views about the relation between philosophy and art. Hegel defends philosophy as a superior form of articulation, devaluing art for its reliance on an external and sensuous medium. While Hegel acknowledges that art and philosophy are both valid as human efforts to represent Spirit [Geist], he does not hesitate to conclude that philosophy accomplishes its end in a way that has rendered art less necessary. Nietzsche celebrates art as providing justification for life itself, condemning philosophy as clumsy and intrusive in comparison. In *The Birth of Tragedy*, Nietzsche illustrates the harmful effect philosophy had on art, especially on tragedy. Yet Nietzsche does not simply reject philosophy. He seeks to transform philosophy to have a new, playful incarnation. Therefore, it is most perspicuous to think of Nietzscheans as attempting to remake philosophy in the image of art.

Certainly, Hegel and Nietzsche exhibit radically different philosophical styles. Hegel beckons us to endure "the strenuous labor of the concept" in order to complete the journey to knowledge (PhS, p. 35).[4] Nietzsche hypothesizes that the best way to deal with the deepest philosophical problems is like taking a cold bath: "quickly into them and quickly out again" (GS #381; BGE #295). There is something predictable and obsessive about Hegel's philosophy: propagated in systematic form, it shows the subject struggling, but marching inexorably to attain certainty. Nietzsche invites philosophers to become followers of Dionysus and to learn how to dance (GS #381). His aphoristic style is marked by spontaneity, unconventionality, and even contradiction: it is an appropriate vehicle for displaying the decentered subject.

Hegel does not speak of himself in his philosophical works. He excludes himself as a matter of discretion, but also because of his wish to identify with the ideal of a universal subject. No doubt, too, Hegel, the person, might have diminished the system, revealing, so to speak, the Wizard of Oz behind the curtains. Nietzsche maintains that the realm of the personal is present, but usually concealed, within a philosopher's work. He argues, therefore, that we ought to contend with the personal (more precisely, the relationship between the personal and the theoretical) as a bona fide philosophical topic. Nietzsche's last work, *Ecce Homo*, is unnerving in part because of how intensely personal it is. As Nietzsche declares in one of his *Nach-gelassene Fragmente*: "My writings speak only from my own experiences [Erlebnissen]—happily I have experienced [erlebt] much—: I am in them with body and soul." (SW 12, p. 232)

The notable contrast in the styles of Hegel and Nietzsche has a parallel in their respective lives and careers. Hegel's career got off to a slow start; he was considered inferior to the younger Friedrich Wilhelm Joseph von Schelling, and he spent a number of years without a university position. Eventually, Hegel became a renowned philosopher, occupying Johann Gottlieb Fichte's chair of philosophy in Berlin, growing more conservative politically, joining the company of the elite in Prussian society, and enjoying his family and a large circle of friends and students. Nietzsche, on the other hand, began his career in a blaze of glory, becoming a professor at the age of 24. Nietzsche's work as a philologist became controversial with his first book, *The Birth of Tragedy*, and as his health problems mounted he began to remove himself from his academic position at the University of Basel. Nietzsche's fate was to become a lonely, itinerant philosopher. When he went mad, his philosophical works were just starting to become known throughout Europe; however, Nietzsche was deprived of recognition such as Hegel ultimately received in his lifetime.

In one of the most influential writings on the contrast between Hegel and Nietzsche, the 1941 book *From Hegel to Nietzsche*, Karl Löwith concludes that Hegel was the last great metaphysician and Nietzsche the first anti-metaphysician.[5] According to Löwith, Christianity is the crucial divide between Hegel's affirmation of the metaphysical tradition and Nietzsche's new beginning. This point of view is plausible, but it does not necessarily allow for the most fruitful exploration of their respective philosophies. Other scholars, including Walter Kaufmann, Daniel Breazeale, and Stephen Houlgate, have made valuable contributions to our understanding of the relationship between Hegel and Nietzsche by articulating parallels in their metaphysics and epistemology.[6]

My treatment of the relationship between Hegel and Nietzsche builds on these predecessors, but I pursue a new direction. I focus on the psychological sensibility that informs Hegel's and Nietzsche's philosophical projects, and I pay especially close attention to the theme of agency, which is crucial in their respective attempts to imagine satisfied human lives. In taking this angle, I have been inspired by those philosophers who have shown reluctance to accept Hegel and Nietzsche as opposites. On the critical-theory side, Horkheimer and Adorno (1986, p. 44) argue that "Nietzsche was one of the few after Hegel who recognized the dialectic of enlightenment." Even though Hegel and Nietzsche might occupy different poles in the dialogue of reason and unreason, Horkheimer and Adorno appreciate that both thinkers engage that dialogue. Indeed, they try to incorporate both Hegel and Nietzsche in arguing against vindicating rationality by forsaking irrationality. For Adorno in particular, philosophy must benefit from the example of psychoanalysis, which affirms the inescapability of irrationality without dismissing rationality

On the French side, Georges Bataille (1985, p. 219) writes that "Nietzsche is to Hegel what a bird breaking its shell is to a bird contentedly absorbing the substance within." Bataille's point, it would seem, is that Nietzsche is an advance over Hegel—quite literally, a birth takes place with the shattering of the protective but enclosed and confining (metaphysical) egg. Yet, in intimating that Nietzsche's philosophy represents progress over Hegel's, Bataille acknowledges the period of gestation as well as the birth, thus confirming a developmental, organic link between Hegel and Nietzsche.[7] I infer that it is misguided to look back to Hegel by displacing Nietzsche (as Adorno emphasizes), but that it is equally undesirable to embrace Nietzsche by ignoring that his philosophy unfolds from Hegel (as Bataille reveals).[8] This insight serves as a guide for my study.

In chapter 1, I develop the idea that according to Hegel and Nietzsche philosophy is integrally related to culture. More specifically, I contend that both thinkers agree that philosophy is a product of culture and also that philosophy ought to be a response to culture. Hegel and Nietzsche distance themselves from the foundational myth of modern philosophy, the Cartesian myth, which (unwittingly or not) places a wedge between philosophical culture and the rest of culture. Although Hegel does not revile philosophy, as Nietzsche does, we can uncover a parallel between them in terms of what I call "the psychology of knowledge." The psychology of knowledge offers an alternative paradigm to epistemology in demanding that we concern ourselves with the confluence between knowledge and human well-being.

In chapter 2, I engage the philosophical conceptions of culture in Hegel and Nietzsche. I delineate three senses of culture: as customs, as Bildung, and as self-fathoming. Hegel and Nietzsche concur that customs represent an antiquated sense of culture that is at odds with individual self-expression, although Hegel is characteristically less vehement than Nietzsche on this subject. Both thinkers also use the nature/culture distinction in order to affirm that culture ought not be regarded simply as the negation of nature; culture moves beyond nature by being inclusive of it. Hegel and Nietzsche regard Bildung as a necessary form of training which is directed to our subjective experience. They distinguish true and false versions of Bildung, endorsing the former in terms of fostering a dynamic kind of agency. Yet both philosophers also express reservations about the ideal of Bildung. As they see it, there is a need to conceptualize a new meaning of culture, which I term "self-fathoming." While the first two senses of culture are well-grounded in Hegel's and Nietzsche's writing, the third sense is admittedly more speculative on my part. Self-fathoming denotes our particular plight in modernity where a disparity opens up between the objective space of customs and the subjective space of Bildung. This places a new and difficult burden on us. Self-fathoming is not a matter of looking within; it involves a more elaborate inquiry regarding how we have come to think of ourselves in the way we do. In particular, self-fathoming requires that we face up to self-misunderstanding, self-deception, and self-thwarting. Self-fathoming is prompted by the wish to confront the dissatisfaction of modern culture and coincides with the philosophical challenge of embracing the psychology of knowledge.

In chapter 3, I address Hegel's and Nietzsche's views of ancient Greek culture. As they see it, Greek culture represents a contrast to modern culture in being healthy and providing satisfaction to its citizens. Yet neither Hegel nor Nietzsche is content with idealizing the Greeks. Both affirm that we can and should learn from the Greeks but warn against nostalgically looking to the past as a way to absolve ourselves from dealing with the present. My chapter turns upon Hegel's and Nietzsche's distinct perspectives on Greek tragedy as a means of grasping Greek culture. Hegel sees tragedy as affirming the institutions of society, whereas Nietzsche views tragedy as affirming life in the face of the abyss of meaningless. For Hegel, the spectator is addressed qua citizen; for Nietzsche, the spectator is addressed qua human being. Nonetheless, both Hegel and Nietzsche regard tragedy as the means by which Greek culture raised fundamental questions about itself. Tragedy is equally compelling for Hegel and Nietzsche; not only do both see it as a source for the psychology of knowledge and self-fathoming, but they incorporate it in their respective philosophical projects.

In chapter 4, I examine Hegel's and Nietzsche's critique of modern culture and consider their influence on Horkheimer, Adorno, Habermas, and Heidegger. I argue that there are some significant points of convergence between Hegel and Nietzsche in the analysis of what is wrong with modern culture: the failure to provide satisfaction is a result of a division in self-identity, and the corresponding premium that comes to be placed on subjectivity leads to the devaluing of what lies outside it. Furthermore, Nietzsche follows Hegel in noting the ascension of usefulness as a dominant criterion of value in modern culture. For Nietzsche, though, usefulness is linked to the ascendance of science as a cultural ideal. This reminds us that any account of the differences between Hegel and Nietzsche must acknowledge changes that took place in their respective eras. Nietzsche's conclusions about modern culture are more negative than Hegel's: alienation has turned into despair. Yet his despair must be contextualized. It is true that Nietzsche refrains from any global solution to the crisis of modern culture. His sense of disappointment is keener, and he is more insistent that we ought not avoid negative affects, such as anger and sadness, that are generated by modernity. Nietzsche assesses modern culture as hopeless, but he is not hopeless about agency as a means of resisting it. Like Hegel, Nietzsche offers a rescription of agency as a way to overcome the dissatisfaction of modern culture.

In part II of the book, Hegel and Nietzsche have more of an opportunity to speak without interruption. The main focus is on their respective understandings of human agency. The chapters in this part are shorter than those in part I. In chapter 5, I begin with some general reflections on the meaning of human agency. I distinguish between persons and agents, and I turn to Charles Taylor's genealogical account of the latter. I pay special attention to how Hegel and Nietzsche fit within Taylor's schema. Using Taylor's terms, I argue that Hegel attempts to integrate both "self-objectivation" (the scientific project of self-investigation) and "self-exploration" (the artistic project linked to expressivism), whereas Nietzsche affirms the latter but is ambivalent about the former. Although Nietzsche is dubious about utilizing the language of science and objectivity, he does value "self-control." In subsequent chapters, I explore in more detail what Hegel and Nietzsche mean by agency: in chapters 6–9 I take up Hegelian agency, and in chapters 10–13 I pursue Nietzschean agency.

Chapter 6 concerns Hegel's concept of recognition. The concept of recognition serves as Hegel's proposed solution to the crisis of modern culture; it also provides a basis for clarifying his theory of agency. Recognition is conceived as specifying a bond that deepens the sense of connection among members of society and thereby heals the split between the individual and society. Recognition harks back to the bond fostered by the polis, although it sustains rather than eclipses individuality. I distinguish the socio-political and epistemological functions of recognition, and I demonstrate, in particular, that recognition must be linked to the main theme of the *Phenomenology of Spirit*: self-knowledge. As I see it, it is crucial to appreciate that recognition includes self-recognition. Two specific aspects of self-recognition are distinguished: the self as socially constituted and the self as self-identical. The latter contains a further distinction between "being-for-itself" and "being-for-another." Hegel's theory of agency hinges on the integration of our self-concern (being-for-itself) with our concern for others (being-for-another). Borrowing psychoanalytic terms, one could say that human agency entails an integration of narcissism and relatedness. For Hegel, such an integrated sense of agency is a prerequisite for social integration. In that chapter I also discuss the relation between recognition and several other basic Hegelian concepts: cognition, satisfaction, experience, and desire.

In chapters 7 and 8, I offer a close reading of Hegel's concept of recognition in the *Phenomenology of Spirit*. Hegel's declaration in the Self-Consciousness chapter that self-consciousness attains "satisfaction" only in relating to another (PhS, p. 110) is a demand for a fundamental revision of epistemology and thus of modern philosophy itself. I trace the failed initial attempt at modernizing the concept of recognition in the Self-Consciousness chapter to the "internal" recognition in the Reason chapter, and then on to socio-historical developments, such as "natural and ethical" recognition in ancient Greece, "legal" recognition in ancient Rome, and the hope for "mutual" recognition that emerges from the Enlightenment and from Kant's moral philosophy. I show that Hegel's psychological discourse is sustained throughout PhS, coexisting with the louder voices of science, system, and the authority of reason. Hegel revises philosophy in order to contend with the dissatisfaction he detects in modern culture; the project of recollecting the vicissitudes of agency culminates in an ameliorated sense of agency that is designed to foster satisfaction in the future.

In chapter 9, I explore Hegelian agency more broadly. I reflect on Alexandre Kojève's appropriation of recognition, which distorts Hegel's actual view but which encourages us to reflect on what Hegel means by satisfaction and agency. In particular, Kojève's reading highlights desire as the backdrop to the concept of recognition. Next I examine recent reinterpretations of Hegel in the works of Axel Honneth and Jessica Benjamin, both of whom recast recognition to emphasize the intersubjective basis of agency and introduce psychoanalysis in this connection. Finally, I offer my own reading, which is indebted to Honneth and Benjamin but which gives more expression to some of the tensions between narcissism and mutual recognition. A psychoanalytic reading of Hegel brings out the crucial intersubjective element in his conception of agency and helps us to discern what remains viable in his thinking about recognition.

In chapter 10, I begin to unpack Nietzsche's idea of agency. I argue that his regarding agency as comprising multiple components does not negate the possibility of integration. I maintain that four factors delineate what Nietzsche means by integrated agency: accepting narcissism as the source of motivation, acknowledging the demands of the body (especially instincts), avowing affects, and defining oneself in relation to the past. Ultimately, Nietzsche regards integrated agency as entailing coherence and determination, but not transparency or unity. Since it is obviously controversial to ascribe to

Nietzsche a commitment to integrated agency, it will be important to acknowledge the limits he places on agency and to take due notice of comments that suggest a position of anti-agency. As I see it, Nietzsche is ambivalent but not necessarily inconsistent in the way he conceives of agency. One can value integration without achieving it in a perfect sense, and one might enjoy being released from agency without being prepared to abandon it entirely.

In chapter 11, I consider the will to power. Focusing on both the concept of 'the will' and the concept of 'power', I investigate whether Nietzsche uses 'power' to mean mastery or domination. Siding with neither the proponents of mastery nor those of domination, I argue that, for better or worse, there is evidence for both points of view. In being consistent with narcissism, instincts, and affects, the will to power helps us to understand Nietzsche's understanding of integrated agency. I also reflect on the will to power as a recasting of the Hegel's notion of being-for-itself and as a challenge to his notion of being-for-another.

In chapter 12, I delve into an aspect of Nietzsche's philosophy that has been little explored: how he conceptualizes our relations to others. I argue that, while Nietzsche's approach to agency deepens and complicates Hegel's interest in self-concern, it is less evident how he thinks about concern for others. I begin by examining Nietzsche's comments about the relation between self and other. I then take account of his numerous reflections about friendship. I conclude that, though Nietzsche fails to acknowledge basic aspects of human relationships, such as mutuality, he is far from indifferent to considering our relation to others. Nietzsche's struggle with others in his own life is, no doubt, a clue to his view of relationships.

In chapter 13, I branch out to look at current perspectives that can be understood as outgrowths of Nietzschean agency. I begin with Jacques Derrida, emphasizing the influence of Emmanuel Levinas on his thought. I also introduce Jacques Lacan, who is not directly influenced by Nietzsche but whose psychoanalytic theory expounds the notion of decentered agency in a way that constitutes one vision of Nietzschean agency. Lastly, I consider Judith Butler, whose theories about gender and agency borrow from Nietzsche via Michel Foucault's emphasis on the body as culturally constructed. Butler's recent turn to "the psychic life of power" confirms the plausibility of connecting her perspective to Nietzschean agency. Derrida, Lacan, and Butler all extend Nietzschean agency by resorting, at least in part, to psychoanalysis. In the final section of chapter 13, I offer my own version of Nietzschean agency, stressing the importance of affects— an aspect of his philosophy not taken up by Derrida, Lacan, or Butler.

In the epilogue, I summarize the conclusions of my study of the relationship between Hegel and Nietzsche. My attempt to work through their relationship is meant to exemplify their shared commitment to working through all allegedly opposing concepts, to thinking beyond what is easy to take for granted. Insofar as I bring Hegel and Nietzsche together, I am seeking to disburden us from an outmoded and useless antinomy. To fix a contrast between these two thinkers without acknowledging the changes that occurred during the nineteenth century is tantamount to refusing to accept precisely what Hegel and Nietzsche claim about the relationship between philosophy and culture. To internalize Hegel's and Nietzsche's claim about philosophy and culture, on the contrary, raises questions that reach well beyond the interpretation of the nineteenth century.

My reading of Hegel, which highlights the ideal of satisfied agency and his overall attention to psychology, brings him closer to Nietzsche. Thus, it is evident that I am partial to the anthropological reading of Hegel. Although the ontological reading preserves what has primacy for Hegel himself, it is corrupted by his grandiose and self-serving fantasy about the fulfillment of Geist within his own culture. There are hermeneutic questions to face once one departs from Hegel's own self-understanding. At the same time, there are Hegelian reasons that might justify the choice to dwell on anthropology rather than ontology. Hegel claims that philosophy "provides satisfaction [Befriedigung] only for those interests which are appropriate to their time" (Hegel's introduction to LHP, p. 106). In this context, Hegel observes that Plato and Aristotle no longer satisfy us as they satisfied the Greeks; correspondingly there should be no need for us to seek our own satisfaction according to Hegel's standards. To be sure, it is important not to obscure what Hegel believed and to try to understand Hegel within his context, but this not docs not require present-day philosophers to disregard what is pressing to them.

By highlighting Hegel's concept of recognition, I make my sympathy for the tradition of left Hegelianism apparent. Yet, as I see recognition, it is not only a socio-political vision that promotes our sense of connection to others; it also contains a notion of agency that demonstrates how constitutive others are in the formation of identity. There are good reasons to be suspicious about the seamless web of self-recognition, recognition of others, and social reconciliation that Hegel offers. However, this ought not hinder our appreciation of his insights into agency, which are developed in an illuminating way in the theory and the practice of psychoanalysis. Hegel shows us that a theory of agency must account for both narcissism and relatedness, and also for their interrelation. Indeed, Hegel's brilliance as a psychologist deserves more acknowledgement than it usually receives.

Paying attention to Hegel as a psychologist is an antidote to the simplistic, "sound bite" view of Hegel as the philosopher of totality. Hegel is not the philosopher of totality any more than Nietzsche is the philosopher of exploitation. Paying attention to Hegel as a psychologist deepens our appreciation of the uniqueness of his philosophy. In his depiction of the live drama of modern agency, Hegel shows a psychological astuteness that is not matched by Kant, Fichte, or Schelling. Undoubtedly, it is important to explore Hegel's Kantian roots and to try to contexualize his relation to early German Idealism. One might wonder, though, about the implications of the current tendency to dwell on Hegel's relation to Kant. It is tempting to read this tilt back to Kant as a substitution for Hegel's tilt forward to Marx. Perhaps the current tendency is not as neutral a scholarly development as it might seem. I raise this point not in the name of advocating an older and better Hegel, but as a reminder of the complex interaction of culture and memory that contributes to the construction of the Hegel of our own time.

If my reading of Hegel brings him closer to Nietzsche, it is also the case that my reading of Nietzsche brings him into closer proximity to Hegel. My reading of Nietzsche emphasizes his psychological approach to modernity and agency. I think that it is one-sided to view him exclusively as an advocate of self-invention. While I appreciate how Nietzsche anticipates postmodernism, I also think it is important not to ignore that his focus on the quest for individual self-realization through integrated agency and his aesthetic elitism (particularly his disdain for popular culture) situate him within modernist thinking. Nietzsche departs from Hegel in registering despair about modernity; yet this despair is best understood as a radicalization of the alienation that Hegel describes. Of course, it is a mistake to assimilate Nietzsche too readily to the philosophical tradition; at the same time, one should avoid the opposite extreme (as do proponents of the "wild and freaky" Nietzsche, who obscure his rethinking of modern agency). Dionysian experience, however compelling, can occupy us for only part of our lives. Nietzsche was well aware that it does not offer a complete vision of a satisfied life.

Nietzsche's ambivalence toward agency means that it is difficult to specify with any confidence what he really thinks. This can be frustrating, especially in comparison to Hegel. Yet, as I see it, this is also what makes Nietzsche an extraordinarily honest and realistic thinker. Nietzsche's view that the body, instincts, and affects cannot be expunged from human agency counterbalances many philosophical conceptions of agency. His appreciation of the limits of agency is also important; it anticipates and is fully consistent with psychoanalytic notions of decentered agency. Although Nietzsche does not give us an adequate picture of our relation to others, his idea of the will to power is more profound than Hegel's notion of being-for-itself.

Hegel's notion of recognition postulates the intersubjective basis of agency, yet this does not mean that one has to endorse Hegel's expectation that self-recognition will produce social reconciliation. Nietzsche's notion of the will to power and his emphasis on the body, instincts, and affects contribute to decentered agency, but this does not require one to accept his idiosyncratic view of our relation to others. Intersubjectivity and decentering can be understood as complementary as long as one does not imagine that this automatically dissolves the deep and abiding tensions between the will to power and recognition. My title, *Beyond Hegel and Nietzsche*, indicates that we can now see through the artificiality of demands that we choose between what these two thinkers offer. It is meant to suggest "both Hegel and Nietzsche" as well as "after Hegel and Nietzsche."

I
Philosophy and Culture

1

The Culture of Philosophy

We too must observe and interpret past thought within the horizon of a particular thinking: that is to say, our own. No more than Nietzsche or Hegel can we step out of our history and "times" and, from an absolute standpoint, without any definite and therefore necessarily one-sided point of view, observe what-has-been in itself. The same limitation holds for us as it did for Nietzsche and Hegel, with one additional factor; namely, that perhaps the compass of our thinking does not even have the essentiality—and certainly not the greatness—of the questions posed by these thinkers. . . .
—Martin Heidegger, *Nietzsche*

The relationship between philosophy and culture is an enormous and vexing subject. In order to address it properly, one would have to steer a path between overestimating or underestimating its significance. One ought to refrain, for instance, from assuming that the content and validity of philosophy can be reduced to the ideas of a culture. Yet, at the other extreme, one ought to avoid rendering the relationship in trivial terms: although it is indisputable that philosophy is rooted in a particular cultural context, the acknowledgement of such a cultural context does not automatically help us understand and/or evaluate that philosophy. As we will see in this chapter, Hegel and Nietzsche uphold the view that there is a profound relationship between philosophy and culture, and they do so in a way that is neither reductive nor trivial.

Philosophy is a product of culture, according to Hegel and Nietzsche, and this means that we should be attentive to how philosophy bears the influence of the culture in which it originates. Yet

Hegel and Nietzsche also defend a stronger thesis: that philosophy bears the obligation to observe culture and also to respond to culture. They regard it as a challenge, therefore, for philosophers to take account of their relation to culture, particularly during times of cultural crisis. Hegel and Nietzsche suppose that it is beneficial to understand our own beliefs as being mediated by culture. They presume that the nature of our beliefs can be clarified further, and that this contributes to the possibility of enhancing our lives.

Before refining the claim that philosophy and culture are integrally related, and in particular before undertaking an examination of the similarities and the differences between Hegel and Nietzsche, I would like to say something about the title of this chapter, "The Culture of Philosophy." It has a polemical ring, and it should not be taken too literally. My intention is less to assert that philosophy is a culture than to maintain that it has some features that make it like a culture, and that it is illuminating to think from such a perspective.

1.1 The Cartesian Myth

In this section I shall describe the "Cartesian myth," which will help me to develop the notion of the culture of philosophy and to clarify the background of Hegel's and Nietzsche's conception of the relationship between philosophy and culture.

Descartes provides mainstream philosophical culture with a kind of foundational myth. This myth tells of a protagonist who faces and overcomes the challenge of skepticism.[1] The Cartesian myth is an armchair odyssey wherein the rational examination of one's own mind secures epistemological victory. The path offers justification for philosophers to proceed afresh—unconstrained by the past, yet armed with faith in a new methodology. The Cartesian myth is striking in the way that it encourages and rewards a self-imposed withdrawal from the surrounding world. This narrative conforms to other foundational myths, insofar as its hero survives travails and at long last finds what "he" is seeking.[2] Yet, unlike many foundational myths, the Cartesian myth seems to demand social isolation, not only as a means, but as end in itself. The Cartesian myth promotes the quest for certainty in knowledge, and, especially, the monumental turn to subjectivity. Yet it is just as significant, I believe, to emphasize the wedge that

Descartes places between philosophical culture and the rest of culture.[3] The Cartesian myth beckons us to trust our rational selves by registering a muted yet unambiguous distrust of the world of culture. Safety is found through retreat. The culture of philosophy—ironically put—is to be cultureless.

Let us consider the Cartesian myth from a contemporary standpoint before turning to the nineteenth century. Very few philosophers today, of course, would be inclined to proclaim their allegiance to the Cartesian myth, but this does not mean that we cannot discern the remnants of its influence. In the philosophical culture in which I was raised (that of the late 1970s and the early 1980s), many philosophers regarded the world of culture either as contaminating (and hence to be ignored) or as only a minor component of philosophy (and thus of marginal importance). During its ascendance in the postwar period in American universities, Analytic Philosophy—enamored with science, defining itself adamantly as without precedent, and adopting an indifferent attitude toward the philosophical past and toward vast areas of culture—unmistakably affirmed a commitment to the Cartesian myth.[4]

Analytic Philosophy, of course, has changed over the years. In one sense, it has been superseded as a paradigm by the Cognitive Science movement, thereby fulfilling the ideal of moving philosophy closer to science. In another sense, the Analytic movement simply has widened its scope, becoming more responsive to issues formerly regarded as belonging to Continental philosophy and the tradition. Some of its proponents readily would concede that Analytic Philosophy exists only in the sense that there remain philosophers who practice a certain style of doing philosophy, which values rigor and preciseness. The main shortcoming of the interpretation of Analytic Philosophy as simply a style of doing philosophy is that it minimizes the fact that the Analytic movement itself has a history and that it has evolved over time.[5] Perhaps the most striking development that has occurred in Analytic Philosophy is the renaissance of scholarship in the history of philosophy. The philosophical past is now accorded much greater respect, although the meaning of this rejoining with the tradition is far from obvious.[6]

Although blatant disregard for the philosophical past is out of fashion, only selected parts of the philosophical past have been regarded as valuable resources for the present. The seventeenth and eighteenth centuries are respectable in a way that the nineteenth century is not—precisely, I would argue, because of the nineteenth century's concern with the relationship between philosophy and culture. Although a growing number of philosophers are at work on nineteenth-century philosophy, some of them even adopting an Analytic style, the stigmatization of the nineteenth century in mainstream philosophical culture persists. It seems improbable that this stigmatization is simply a matter of style, or that it merely shows a lack of rigor and preciseness.

There remains a conspicuous neglect of culture in mainstream philosophical culture. One sphere in which this can be glimpsed is in the Analytic literature on agency, which I will discuss in part II. The neglect of culture in philosophy is all the more remarkable when one ponders the spreading of the Cultural Studies paradigm throughout the academy. Whatever one thinks of that paradigm, it would be difficult to dispute how much it derives from Hegel and Nietzsche, who have been marginal to mainstream philosophical culture.[7]

The argument that Hegel and Nietzsche regard philosophy as having an integral relation to culture will require us to investigate their respective views about philosophy itself as well as to consider their differing responses to the Cartesian myth. The subject of the interdependence of philosophy and culture is a natural starting point for the rethinking of the relationship between Hegel and Nietzsche that I undertake in this book. However, that philosophy and culture are integrally related is a rather preliminary and general claim. It does not necessarily presume an intention to debunk philosophy.[8] It suggests only that Hegel and Nietzsche are restless under the dominant sway of the Cartesian myth, and that they share the wish to create alternative perspectives.

1.2 Hegel's Actual Knowers

According to Hegel, philosophy expresses the "spirit of the age." In the introduction to the *Lectures on the History of Philosophy* (volume I, p. 53), he explains:

Philosophy which arises among a people, and the definite character of the standpoint of thought is the same character which permeates all the other historical sides of the spirit of the people, which is most intimately related to them, and which constitutes their foundation . . . their institutions, and forms of government, their morality, their social life and the capabilities, customs and enjoyments of the same.

This statement is meant to convey certain limits for philosophy, as Hegel clarifies in the 1820 introduction to the *Lectures on the History of Philosophy* (p. 49), where he observes that a philosophy "belongs to its own time and is caught in that time's restriction." Later (p. 112), he adds that "no one can escape from the substance of his time any more than he can jump out of his skin."

The following well-known statement in the *Philosophy of Right* (1821) is consistent with Hegel's view of 1820:

To comprehend *what is* is the task [Aufgabe] of philosophy, for *what is* is reason. As far as the individual is concerned, each individual is in any case a *child* [Sohn] *of his time;* thus, philosophy, too, is *its own time comprehended in thoughts.* It is just as foolish to imagine that any philosophy can transcend its contemporary world as that an individual can overleap his own time or leap over Rhodes. If his theory does indeed transcend his own time, if it builds itself a world *as it ought to be,* then it certainly has an existence, but only within his opinions—a pliant medium in which the imagination can construct anything it pleases. (PR, pp. 21–22)

This passage affirms the idea that philosophy necessarily exists within a particular cultural context; in addition, it specifies that individuals are to be regarded as children of their culture. However, Hegel locates the "chief task" of philosophy in a general enterprise: the comprehension of what is. This plea for the primacy of metaphysics is typical of Hegel's mature perspective on philosophy. But Hegel also warns against the kind of speculation that indulges itself in a flight away from culture. It seems, then, that Hegel conceives of culture as a part of "what is." Yet, a different sense emerges if we compare Hegel's perspective from an earlier era to the above passage. In his farewell lecture at Jena in 1806, Hegel declared:

We find ourselves in an important epoch in world history, in a ferment, when Spirit has taken a leap forward, where it has sloughed off its old form and is acquiring a new one. The whole mass of existing ideas and concepts, the very bonds of the world have fallen apart and dissolved like a dream. A new product of the Spirit is being prepared. The chief task of philosophy [Die Philosophie hat vornämlich] is to welcome it and grant it recognition [anzuerkennen], while others, impotently resisting, cling to the past and the majority unconsciously constitute the masses in which it manifests itself. Recognizing [Erkennend] it as the eternal, it falls to philosophy to pay it reverence. (Rosenkranz 1844, pp. 214–215; also quoted by Lukàcs (1976, p. 454)

In this context, Hegel affirms that philosophy is a response to culture, not just a product of culture. He clearly argues in favor of giving philosophers a role to play in the face of cultural change. Although he acknowledges the eternal nature of Spirit, his main point is to urge philosophy to rise to the challenge presented by the cultural present. In the passage from the *Philosophy of Right,* he dwells on the relationship between philosophy and culture within the large context of comprehending "what is." In the passage from the Jena lecture, he urges a dramatic response to the immediate state of culture. In the first passage, he notes the danger of metaphysical zeal; in the second, he warns of the danger of passivity and inhibition in relation to culture.

Throughout his works, Hegel comprehends philosophy as mediated by its cultural context. Philosophy is linked to culture in that the latter encompasses, in Hegel's evocative phrase, "the seriousness of fulfilled life" [dem Ernste des erfüllten Leben].[9] Hegel wants to encourage philosophers to define themselves anew in light of their relation to culture. This does not mean that philosophy is imprisoned or that it cannot move forward. Up through the time of the *Phenomenlogy of Spirit* (1807), Hegel had hopes for philosophy to play a transformative role in relation to culture as well as to politics. The preface to PhS describes the present as a "time of transition" characterized by "that lost solid and substantial sense of being" (p. 4). Hegel declares dramatically: "By the little which now satisfies [genügt] Spirit, we can measure the extent of its loss [Verlustes]" (p. 5). Only philosophy, according to Hegel, offers satisfying cognition.

The introduction to PhS, in contrast to the preface, portrays the project more conventionally as epistemology. Yet Hegel reiterates the theme of philosophical cognition as satisfying. His notion of cognition is not concerned with justification alone; it also engages the question of what it means for a human being to know. The sense in which cognition is tied to satisfaction is crucial; I will explore it in chapter 2 in connection with Hegel's notion of Bildung and in chapter 6 in connection with what Hegel has to say in PhS about the nature of cognition and recognition.

In reformulating epistemology, Hegel suggests a new direction for philosophy. The move from consciousness to Geist in PhS testifies to the limitations of monological subjectivity, divorced from culture as it appears to be.[10] Hegel's claim that a relationship exists between philosophy and culture clearly is not meant to cast doubt on the possibility that philosophy can achieve knowledge and truth. Hegel agrees with Descartes, of course, that philosophy can attain knowledge through rationality, and, in particular, that rationality ensures evolution from a personal to a universal standpoint. I shall have more to say about Hegel's response to the Cartesian myth and to Descartes himself in the last section of this chapter.

It is important to appreciate that, when he invokes rationality, Hegel is defending an expanded notion of rationality that does not restrict itself to the thinking mind of the individual. Indeed, Hegel's phenomenological approach in PhS reveals that the experience of consciousness is much broader than an account of thinking. For example, it is important to understand that the concept of "recognition," introduced in the Self-Consciousness chapter, is itself a form of cognition. At the same time, Hegel's description of the dialectic of recognition has its source in desire, a motivational state that is hard to fit within the framework of modern epistemology. In view of the weight Hegel places on how the enslaved consciousness is transformed through the activity of work and the affect of fear, it is apparent that he is concerned with a broader terrain than knowledge.

In PM #471, Hegel specifically warns against the "arbitrarily imposed" separation between thinking and feeling that philosophers have propagated. Although there can be no question that Hegel values thinking over feeling, he is less dismissive of feeling than one might suppose. Hegel regards rationality as a superior guide to action, although he does not imagine that this entails ridding ourselves of emotion. It is fair to claim that, according to Hegel, rationality and emotion can coincide and are not necessarily in opposition. Hegel is not prepared to reject the enterprise of epistemology, but he does wish to reform it to be more rooted in human life and culture.

As we have seen, Hegel's early view registers hope that philosophy can be instrumental in fostering cultural change. His mature view becomes more sober, as the famous "owl of Minerva" passage in the *Philosophy of Right* reveals: philosophy has a role only after the fact; it cannot serve to transform culture.[11] Although the way Hegel conceives of the relationship between philosophy and culture does become subsumed within the terms of his system of philosophy, he never loses interest in fathoming their relationship. In the *Lectures on the History of Philosophy*, Hegel wrestles with how philosophy is both eternal truth and determined by culture. On the one hand, he maintains that philosophy is the logical derivative of the Idea: it is immutable and must be realized in a system in development. On the other hand, he shows that philosophy is bound by its cultural specificity.

Hegel resolved the tension between ontology and anthropology by claiming that his own era was the culmination of the development of humanity to be fully rational. However much one might argue that Hegel's ultimate intention was to vindicate ontology, the philosophical past and the cultural present remained vital aspects of his philosophical project. Although Hegel's views about the potential impact of philosophy on culture changed, he retained a lively and persistent interest in the history of philosophy and in contemporary social and political issues.[12] Hegel's letters provide a window into the vicissitudes of his thinking about the role of philosophy. In addition, they reveal a candid and human side, supplementing what we know from his philosophical work.

Inspired by the French Revolution, the young Hegel was enthusiastic about the possibility that philosophy could serve to help transform culture. It is well known that Hegel initially welcomed the spread of Napoleonic influence through Germany. During his time in Jena, as he began his academic career and first experimented with a system of philosophy, he still planned to found a journal that would focus on *culture générale*, emulating French literary reviews. It is also worth recalling Hegel's praxis as an educational reformer. Under the guidance of his older colleague and friend, Friedrich Immanuel Niethammer, Hegel became an advocate of classical neo-humanism during his tenure as rector of the gymnasium at Nuremberg. Even much later in his career, Hegel voiced reservations about the ivory tower, fretting that *Jahrbücher für wissenschaftliche Kritik*, the state-supported journal begun in 1826 for Hegelian criticism, had "turned out almost too scholarly in relation to our earlier plans." He added: "Yet we German scholars . . . are not easily weaned away from erudition, thoroughness, and mere shop-talk." (*Hegel: The Letters*, p. 529)

Nevertheless, a growing pessimism can be discerned in Hegel's thinking about the relationship between philosophy and culture. By 1822 he regarded philosophy with a world-weary posture: "And if philosophy as well fully comes [only] with age, one accommodates oneself all the more easily to the fact that nothing much becomes of the world anymore." (*Hegel: The Letters*, p. 473) What he meant is perhaps amplified in another letter written around his fiftieth birthday: "I have spent thirty of these fifty years in these ever-unrestful times of hope and fear. I had hoped that for once we might be done with it. Now I confess that things continue as ever. Indeed, in one's darker hours, it seems that they are getting ever worse." (ibid., p. 451)

The extent of the change in Hegel's attitude toward philosophy is evident in an 1822 letter to Karl August von Hardenberg (a Prussian government minister who instituted many reforms) in which he argues that "philosophy warrants the protection and favor allotted to it by the state. Moreover, philosophy in its own sphere of action— which, though limited, nonetheless enters into the inner [nature] of man—may give immediate support to the Government's beneficent intentions." (*Hegel: The Letters*, p. 459) It is evident that Hegel has amended his view about the relation of philosophy to influence culture. He has become unambiguous about the limited appeal of philosophy: ". . . a deeper interest in the great spiritual concerns of our age—as well as earnestness in their thoughtful study—is typically restricted to the few" (ibid., p. 542).[13]

The disparate strands of Hegel's thinking about philosophy are captured in a letter he wrote to his friend Christian Gotthold Zellman around the time of PhS: "Philosophy is a lonely thing; indeed, it does not belong on the streets and in the marketplace, but it is still not far removed from the actions of men."[14] The tension here between the simultaneous pulls to accept philosophy as solipsistic and to see it as related to broad human concerns is striking. More specifically, the reference to philosophy as a lonely thing seems to be a nod to the Cartesian legacy.[15] That philosophy does not belong on the streets or in the marketplace intimates both that philosophy requires quiet contemplation and that there is no going back to Socrates's style of philosophy. That it is still not far removed from the action of human beings means, however, as Hegel confirms in the preface to PhS, that philosophy must aim for "actual knowing" rather than for "love of knowing."

1.3 Nietzsche's Philosophical Physicians

Like Hegel, Nietzsche acknowledges the powerful influence of the "spirit of the age." In *Human, All Too Human* (II, part 1, #382), he observes that the spirit of the age "does not only lie upon him but is also within him" [nicht nur auf ihm liegt, sondern auch in ihm ist]. Yet, pointing out the reclusive and anti-social nature of most philosophers, he mocks the idea that philosophers embody the spirit of the age. It should, however, be kept in mind that by the middle of the nineteenth century the phrase "the spirit of the age" had undergone a shift in meaning. As Karl Löwith has pointed out (1967, p. 216), the young Hegelians construed Hegel's notion of how the present is shaped by the past in terms of how the present would shape the future. As was often the case, Nietzsche was responding to interpretations of Hegel as much as to Hegel himself. Nietzsche upheld the view that philosophy and culture are integrally related, but his understanding of the relationship was affected by his greater ambivalence toward philosophy. Let us pause to consider Nietzsche's relationship to Hegel before inquiring further into the former's view of the relationship between philosophy and culture.

Nietzsche is wary of the extent to which Hegel dominated German philosophy. He notes that the students of Hegel have served as the educators of Germans throughout the nineteenth century (HAH II 1 #170). In *On the Uses and Disadvantages of History for Life* (#8), Nietzsche rails against "the enormous and still continuing influence of this philosophy, the Hegelian." What particularly offends Nietzsche is Hegel's presumption of having the God-like vantage point of grasping world-history in completed form. Nietzsche wryly notes the convenience that "for Hegel the climax and terminus of the world-process coincided with his existence in Berlin" (ibid.). Yet Nietzsche also pays homage to Hegel, noting in *The Gay Science* that Hegel's emphasis on becoming and development constitutes a distinctively German kind of self-understanding. Nietzsche then delivers the extraordinary judgment that "we Germans are Hegelians even if there never had been any Hegel" (GS #357).[16] Despite the apparent irony in this tribute, in no way does Nietzsche exempt himself.

It is not clear how familiar Nietzsche was with Hegel as a philosopher. In his application for the professorship in philosophy at the University of Basel, Nietzsche named his main philosophical interests as Kant and Schopenhauer.[17] The Deleuzean assumption that Nietzsche saw Hegel as his great antagonist must contend with the lack of much evidence of Nietzsche's reading Hegel and with the generic nature of the majority of Nietzsche's comments about Hegel. Furthermore, one must reconcile such an assumption with passages in which Nietzsche praises Hegel and credits him with cosmopolitan taste.[18]

Nietzsche presents Hegel as a forerunner to other major cultural figures, including Darwin and Wagner (GS #99, #357; BGE #244). He also associates Hegel with Goethe's neo-Hellenism (SW 7, p. 80; SW 12, p. 443; WP #95). Hegel is commonly paired with Schopenhauer, sometimes as an opponent but sometimes as a brother.[19] For Nietzsche, who was acutely aware that his era lacked such a single, dominant philosopher, Hegel exemplified the era in which German philosophy reigned supreme.[20]

At the same time, Nietzsche wants to distance himself from aspects of the idealist tradition of German philosophy, such as its system making and (especially) its pretense to absoluteness. The shadow of Nietzsche's opposition to the philosophical tradition thus falls on Hegel, despite the greater antipathy he reserves for Kant and other moralists. In *Beyond Good and Evil* #6, Nietzsche argues strenuously that philosophers have gone to great lengths to conceal and deny their own prejudices, which are in fact moral ones. Nietzsche's main point is that philosophy is inevitably an expression of personal and cultural values: ". . . the personal confession of its author and a kind of involuntary and unconscious memoir" (ibid.). This frequently quoted statement deserves close inspection. In part, Nietzsche intends to expose the hypocrisy of philosophers. He chides their aspiration to stand on lofty ground, which they can do only at the expense of ignoring themselves. Yet he also urges philosophers to become more self-conscious about the relationship between their ideas and their lives.[21] He wants philosophers to strive to become more aware of and more honest about the personal underpinnings of their ideas. Apart from his ridiculing of the tradition, Nietzsche can be understood as attempting to sketch a new direction for philosophy. This new direction requires us to begin from a personal standpoint and to reflect on ourselves; to what extent he imagines that it might be possible and desirable to go beyond ourselves remains unclear.

Although Nietzsche can be vituperative about philosophy, he does not simply attack it. In a revealing passage (HAH II 1 #201), he articulates the ongoing struggle of philosophy to develop itself:

> The philosopher believes that the value of his philosophy lies in the whole, in the building: posterity discovers it in the bricks with which he built and which are then often used again for better building: in the fact, that is to say, that that building can be destroyed and *nonetheless* possess value as material.

This is a comment on the pretensions of philosophers; indeed, the aphorism in which it appears is titled "Error of Philosophers." In particular, Nietzsche seems to be postulating an alternative, and he seems to have the building metaphor from Descartes's *Meditations* in mind. Although Nietzsche wishes to cast doubt on the system-making aspirations of philosophers, his insight here coincides with Hegel's appreciation of the disparity between intentions and results in philosophy. Moreover, Nietzsche implies in this passage an acceptance of the possibility of progress in philosophy—an acceptance that he will later modify. Nietzsche wants to direct philosophers to recognize themselves and the contribution of their own experience in their work. The psychological underbelly of philosophy claims special attention.

The relationship between philosophy and culture is a persistent concern throughout Nietzsche's writings. In early writings, Nietzsche argues rather baldly that "culture is a unity" and "the philosopher only seems to stand outside of it" (PT, p. 57). He also states that, despite the attempt by philosophers to fight against the age, philosophy "has no existence at all of its own" and "is colored and filled according to the age" (ibid., p. 71 (1873)). In the fourth lecture of *On the Future of Our Educational Institutions*,[22] the companion of the philosopher exclaims: "And when it occurred to me that I could save myself by flight from all contact with the spirit of the time [mit dem Zeitgeiste], I found that this flight itself was a delusion [Täuschung]." In "On the Uses and Disadvantages of History for Life" (UM #3) Nietzsche notes that the idea of freeing oneself from the present is "always a dangerous attempt," and in "Human, All Too Human" he avers that "the best in us has perhaps been inherited from the sensibilities of earlier ages to which we hardly any longer have access by direct paths" (HAH I #223). This last statement is admittedly inconsistent with some of Nietzsche's anti-historicist tendencies. Still, it makes us appreciate the psychological complexity of his view of how the philosophical past influences the present.

In the preface to *The Case of Wagner*, Nietzsche describes in a personal way how culture dwells within the philosopher:

What does a philosopher demand of himself first and last? To overcome his time in himself, to become "timeless." With what must he therefore engage in the hardest combat? With whatever marks him as a child of his time. Well, then! I am, no less than Wagner, a child of this time; that is, a decadent: but I comprehend this, I resisted it. The philosopher in me resisted. . . .

Nietzsche defines philosophy as constituted by the pursuit of timelessness, and here he does not revile this impulse; he identifies with it. He also acknowledges that, no matter how much he might wish to escape it, he is shaped by the spirit of the age.

How feasible, according to Nietzsche, is the ideal of timelessness? In one way, it is doubtful that he would endorse such a possibility. In another way, he does wish to promote the effort to overcome the spirit of the age, and the general tone of this passage is celebratory— as if he has, at least, succeeded in distancing himself from his own age. In book V of *The Gay Science*, Nietzsche notes the importance of asking whether one can escape the values of European culture. He goes on to recommend trying to distance oneself from one's own time, as he had done in earlier works, but he adds that such "overcoming" can serve to affirm what is most valuable about one's own time. There is a dialectical quality here: Nietzsche sees himself as untimely, but not timeless. Though he does not identify with the spirit of the age, he is hardly dismissive of it.

Nietzsche's reservations about philosophy far exceed Hegel's desire to reform the tradition. In the *Birth of Tragedy*, for example, Nietzsche inveighs against philosophy's decadent influence on tragedy, questioning the value of its cherished ideal of rationality and asserting that life can only be justified aesthetically. Around the same point in his unpublished writing, however, Nietzsche emphasizes that, although philosophy cannot serve to develop culture, the philosopher has an important role as a "cultural physician" (PT, pp. 74 and 102).[23] In a letter to his fellow philologist Erwin Rohde, Nietzsche notes his intention to write a book titled *The Philosopher as Physician of Culture*, stressing that it will concern "a fine general problem, not merely one of historical interest" (Nietzsche, *Selected Letters* #50). In the second preface to *The Gay Science*, Nietzsche lauds the "philosophical physician" and specifically links the concern for philosophy and health to psychology. The language of health and pathology underscores Nietzsche's wish to inject a psychological element into philosophy.

An excellent statement of how Nietzsche conceives of the relationship between philosophy and culture occurs in a passage from his early writing (1873) titled "Can Philosophy Serve as a Foundation of a Culture?" (PT, p. 123). Nietzsche's response to this question is mixed. At first, he seems tentatively affirmative. Then he clarifies: although it might have been possible in the past, philosophy can no longer serve as a foundation. His explanation stresses that modern philosophy's focus has become diminished and too restricted. There is a parallel in *Philosophy in the Tragic Age of the Greeks*, where Nietzsche begins by stressing that philosophy is beneficial to a healthy culture but then goes on to state limits for philosophy in modern culture, specifically that it is not able to aid in the reintegration of the individual into the group (PTG #1). In contrast to Hegel's mature view, Nietzsche unambiguously argues against official recognition of philosophy by the state (SE #8): "A union of state and philosophy can therefore make sense only if philosophy can promise to be unconditionally useful to the state, that is to say, to set usefulness to the state higher than truth."

Nietzsche's ambivalence toward philosophy is constant throughout his writings. It is too strong, in my opinion, simply to assert that he opposed philosophy in his early writings, as he clearly places hope in the ideal of the philosopher as cultural physician. In the middle works, Nietzsche begins to formulate an alternative vision of the philosopher—as a free spirit. In the preface to *Human, All Too Human*, for example, Nietzsche imagines free spirits on the horizon, noting that this is a way for him to compensate for the absence of contemporary kindred spirits. Free spirits are described multifariously, in ways that are difficult to reconcile—for example, as anarchistic, as abiding by moderation, and as valuing thought and inquiry.[24] Nietzsche also suggests that the ultimate criterion for determining free spirits is their attitude toward Christianity (HAH II 2 #182).

In his later works, Nietzsche links free spirits to the "new philosophers" he envisions on the horizon (BGE #44). He is not specific about the relation of these new philosophers to culture; to some extent, they seem to be defined by their total opposition to everything that modern culture represents. The new philosophers are characterized in terms of creating their own values, living beyond good and evil, and firmly distinguishing themselves from the many (BGE #211, #212, #284).[25] Nietzsche suggests that their sole virtue will be honesty (BGE #227). However, he endorses the capacity to dissemble and to be cruel—although he qualifies this to mean a kind of intellectual severity in the name of "profundity, multiplicity and thoroughness" (BGE #230). Yet Nietzsche also observes that, according to free spirits, the philosopher is "the man of the most comprehensive responsibility who has the conscience for the overall development of man" (BGE #61). Indeed, it makes sense to regard Nietzsche himself (at least, the character that he portrays in his writings) as the prototype of the new philosopher, who is preoccupied with sorting out his relationship to the legacy of culture.

The "new task" that Nietzsche repeatedly invokes for future philosophers entails description and diagnosis of culture. This is consistent with the attitude implied in an early (1875) piece: "Philosophers strive to understand that which their fellow men only live through. By interpreting their own existence and coming to understand its dangers, the philosophers at the same time interpret their existence for their people." (PT, p. 141) Nietzsche describes the philosopher as a "rare plant," thus asserting philosophy as a kind of elite praxis (WP #420). He champions a model of the philosopher as an activist—as one who refuses to be restricted by book learning.[26] He plaintively notes in FEI (p. 130) that "philosophy itself is banished [verbannt] from universities: wherewith our first question as to the value of our universities from the standpoint of culture [Bildungswerth] is answered."[27] Though Nietzsche is uninspired by traditional philosophy, he upholds the possibility of a different kind of philosophy, which can be "the most spiritual will to power" (BGE #9). In contrast to "philosophical laborers" (a category in which Nietzsche explicitly places Hegel), Nietzsche urges the philosopher to indulge in play and to revel in what he sees as life-affirming activities.[28]

Nietzsche is not optimistic about a public role for the philosopher, and he is adamant about his identity as an "untimely man." He emphasizes, for example, that "the greatest thoughts" are not experienced contemporaneously—sounding very much like the Hegel of the "owl of Minerva" passage (BGE #285). Nietzsche frequently stresses that the philosopher keeps himself separate from others:

We new philosophers, however, not only do we start by describing the actual order of rank and differences in the value of men, we also desire precisely the opposite of an assimilation, an equalization: we teach estrangement in every sense, we open up gulfs such as have never existed before, we desire that man should become more evil than he has ever been before. In the meantime, we are still strangers to and from one another. We have many reasons to be hermits and to put on masks—we shall therefore be poor at looking for those like us. We shall live alone and probably suffer the torments of all seven solitudes. But if we should come across one another, one may wager that we mistake or mutually deceive one another. (WP #988 (1885))

The image of the philosopher depicted here fits Nietzsche's self-image, particularly the description of the hermit's isolation."[29] Yet the celebration of aloneness is pitched in the voice of "we."[30] Nietzsche's portrayal of the philosopher's isolation is not necessarily at odds with Hegel; his description of the compulsory misrecognition of others, though, constitutes a rupture with Hegel's commitment to the possibility of mutual recognition in the modern world.

It is helpful to read the above passage in the context of a passage in *Philosophy in the Tragic Age of the Greeks* (1873):

The philosopher is a philosopher first only for himself, and then for others. It is not possible to be a philosopher completely for oneself. For as a human being a person is related to other human beings, and if he is a philosopher, he must be a philosopher in this relationship. I mean that even if a philosopher strictly separates himself from others, even if he is a hermit, he thereby provides others with a lesson and an example and is a philosopher for them. Let him conduct himself however he pleases, as a philosopher he still has a side which faces other men. (PT, pp. 108–109)

Here Nietzsche affirms and extends Hegel's recognition that philosophy requires us to distance ourselves from others, and he follows Hegel's pessimism about the relevance of philosophy. Like Hegel, too, Nietzsche recognizes the impossibility of the philosopher's turning his back on others. Regardless of the philosopher's social isolation, it would be a mistake to infer that Nietzsche concludes that the philosopher is unable to contribute to culture. "Untimely" does not mean "without regard to time" or "a-timely." It is also misleading to assume that Nietzsche means "anti-timely," although in some passages he defines himself against his own time. For Nietzsche as well as for Hegel, the solitude required to do philosophy must be distinguished from the content of philosophy, and in both men's writings the content of philosophy manifests and engages cultural concerns.

1.4 The Psychology of Knowledge

So far, my aim has been to establish that both Hegel and Nietzsche regard philosophy as integrally related to culture. Both defend the notion that philosophical ideas bear the discernible influence of culture and that thinking in this way improves our philosophical interpretations and our self-understanding. As I have maintained, Hegel's and Nietzsche's views are intended to be stronger than the rather inconsequential view that philosophy cannot help but be a product of culture. They wish to stress, in particular, that philosophy does not arise *ex nihilo*; nor is it influenced only by other philosophy.

Although Hegel and Nietzsche see philosophy as a response to culture, both thinkers acknowledge that philosophy demands solitude. Although it is impossible to escape entirely from culture, one can acquire a better vantage point by positioning oneself at its periphery. Hegel and Nietzsche flirt with the idea that philosophers might influence culture directly, but they decide that this is unrealistic. It would be erroneous, though, to surmise that either Hegel or Nietzsche concludes that philosophy is irrelevant to culture. In acknowledging limits to philosophy's influence on culture, Hegel and Nietzsche affirm the value of rethinking what philosophy is and (as we will see in the next chapter) the value of offering a philosophical understanding of culture. In the rest of this chapter, I shall pursue the question of Hegel's and Nietzsche's respective reactions to the Cartesian myth (including their reactions to Descartes), and I will introduce a new description of the alternative they present—the psychology of knowledge.

Consider the following passage from Foucault's "The Subject and Power" (Dreyfus and Rabinow 1983, p. 216), which sets up a contrast between Hegel and Nietzsche—both of whom were influenced by Kant—and Descartes:

When in 1784 Kant asked, Was heisst Aufklärung? he meant, What's going on just now? What's happening to us? What is this world, this period, this precise moment in which we are living?

Or in other words: What are we? As Aufklärer, as part of the Enlightenment? Compare this with the Cartesian question: Who am I?, as a unique, but universal and unhistorical subject? I, for Descartes is everyone, anywhere at any moment?

But Kant asks something else: What are we? in a very precise moment of history. Kant's question appears as an analysis of both us and our present. I think this aspect of philosophy took on more and more importance. Hegel, Nietzsche. . . .

Foucault locates the source of Hegel's and Nietzsche's rejection of the Cartesian myth in the Enlightenment. In emphasizing Kant as the crucial predecessor for both Hegel and Nietzsche, he seems not to give much credence to earlier challenges to Descartes. In Spinoza, for example, we find a protest against the disconnected, disembodied nature of the Cartesian hero. Vico's rejection of the Cartesian myth in this connection should also be acknowledged.[31] Foucault's perspective is valuable in that it draws attention to the contextual backdrop of Hegel and Nietzsche, although it is strange that he implies that Kant does not share Descartes's view of the subject as "everyone, anywhere at any moment." It is possible, in fact, to contrast Kant and Hegel to Nietzsche on this point. Still, one can appreciate the frame that Foucault provides without sharing all its premises. Indeed, this study can be understood as an attempt to specify the aspect of philosophy that, according to Foucault, "took on more and more importance" in Hegel and Nietzsche after Kant.

A closer look at how Hegel and Nietzsche respond to the Cartesian myth reveals some important disagreements. This is especially true of their respective views of philosophy. Hegel defines himself as part of the philosophical tradition in a way that Nietzsche never did and never would care to do. Hegel seeks to alter the trajectory of modern philosophy; Nietzsche is more radical in conjuring an alternative. At times, Nietzsche sounds as if he is prepared to disregard or overturn the tradition. Directly comparing Hegel's and Nietzsche's responses to the Cartesian myth will help us attain a sharper elucidation of their linkage of philosophy and culture.

The Cartesian myth implies that philosophical progress begins when the world of culture is left behind. According to the Cartesian myth, progress in philosophy depends on making epistemology the central focus. Both Hegel and Nietzsche distance themselves from the abstract and narrow limits of such philosophical concern. Both question the kind of knowledge that is divorced from the end of living well. Both register discontent with the way that modern philosophy has abdicated any role for itself in addressing the state of modern culture. Both would redirect philosophy to engage the world in a more active way.

Tensions between Hegel's and Nietzsche's thought are evident in their views on knowledge. Hegel, critical of the idea that one can determine knowledge from an external criterion, emphasizes that knowledge must be tested in actuality. However, he does not question the value of knowledge itself, and he regards skepticism as self-contradictory. Hegel is unequivocal about the possibility of "a fully developed, perfected cognition [Erkenntnis]," although he also highlights the long and error-prone journey toward "scientific cognition" (PhS, p. 43). Furthermore, Hegel argues in favor of philosophical knowledge as unique—that is, as distinct from knowledge in mathematics and other fields.

The uniqueness and the specificity of philosophical knowledge lead Hegel to quarrel with the Cartesian myth. Hegel criticizes Descartes for not appreciating the independence of philosophy from other kinds of scientific knowledge; at the same time, he credits Descartes with moving philosophy away from subservience to religious authority (LHP III, pp. 221, 248). Hegel identifies with the turn to the subject's own justification of philosophical knowledge, yet he is not content with understanding knowledge only in terms of securing the external world. Hegel repeatedly observes how naive he finds Descartes (ibid., pp. 224, 225, 233, 248). What he sees as lacking in Descartes, and what he provides in his philosophy, is an exposition of how knowledge makes its appearance. This requires an investigation into the nature of cognition itself, which, it turns out, requires a historical sensibility. As we will see in chapter 6, Hegel explicates cognition through the concepts of "experience" and "satisfaction." For present purposes, it is sufficient to claim that knowledge entails negative moments in which what we know turns out to be false, and that knowledge is motivated by a desire for well-being. Hegel upholds a commitment to knowledge, but rather than define this in terms of confirming the existence of the external world he regards justification as a means and knowing as requiring actualization.

Nietzsche's view of knowledge is, characteristically, more conflicted than Hegel's. In the middle-period aphorism "Pleasure in Knowledge" (HAH I #252) he writes: "Why is knowledge, the element of the scholar and philosopher, associated with pleasure [Lust]? Firstly and above all, because one here becomes conscious of one's strength." Yet both before and after the middle period he also expressed doubt and even cynicism about the value of knowledge. In the early, unpublished essay "On Truth and Lies in an Extra-Moral Sense," Nietzsche exclaims that the invention of knowledge is "the haughtiest and most mendacious minute of 'world history'—yet only a minute" (Kaufmann 1954, p. 42). In later writings he remains critical of the overvaluation of knowledge, but his real concern lies with defining the appropriate sphere of knowledge, not asserting its fraudulence. In BGE #15, Nietzsche emphasizes that it is our instincts that underlie the desire for knowledge, and that we ought to think about knowledge as constituted through our senses, and especially the body. In GS #333, he expresses frustration that philosophers mistakenly have restricted 'knowledge' to mean conscious thinking. Although it is fair to claim that Nietzsche's intention is to challenge our conception of knowledge, rather than simply reject it, there are moments—

even in the later writings—when we find Nietzsche endorsing the "Yea and Amen of ignorance" (BGE #230).

Nietzsche engages in a polemic against the philosophical tradition as governed by dogmatism. His rejection of dogmatism, however, does not betoken an acceptance of skepticism. In BGE #2, Nietzsche opposes the dichotomy between dogmatism and skepticism as a fiction promulgated by the philosophical tradition. In BGE #208, he specifically distances himself from skepticism—at least, from the negative kind of skepticism that he detects in the modern world. Thus, although Nietzsche registers his discomfort with epistemology as it is conventionally conceived, he does not disavow knowledge. He often includes himself in the category "we seekers of knowledge" (e.g., in GS #380 and GM III #12). For Nietzsche, the pursuit of knowledge means that philosophers ought to be more honest about the hidden assumptions underlying their views of knowledge (particularly moral and religious assumptions), and that knowledge is predicated on mistakes and false starts. According to Nietzsche, genuine philosophers accept and understand that knowing is a creative endeavor (BGE #211).

In his doctrine of perspectivism, Nietzsche articulates the creative aspect of knowledge. Perspectivism entails reversing customary views—". . . to see differently . . . to *want* to see differently." In this crucial passage (GM III #12), Nietzsche describes perspectivism as a new and fruitful way of knowing, not just a foil against philosophical knowledge. Nietzsche even sanctions the notion that perspectivism is open to the possibility of convergence toward objectivity, although he offers the qualification that he does not mean "disinterested knowledge" but a capacity to adjust perspectives flexibly and to make use of affects. This emphasis on affects is important. Nietzsche imagines that affects contribute to, rather than detract from, knowledge.[32] To look within oneself is to take account of how one feels. In the *Nachlass* (SW 12, p. 190), Nietzsche asserts: "Who interprets? Our affects." He challenges the desirability of adopting a point of view that seeks to be impersonal. An impersonal point of view serves to disguise the personal; hence, according to Nietzsche, it lacks a useful function.

What is Nietzsche's response to Descartes? In UHDL #10, Nietzsche remarks: ". . . perhaps I still have the right to say of myself *cogito, ergo sum*, but not *vivo, ergo cogito*. Empty 'being' is granted to me, but not full and green life; the feeling that tells me I exist warrants to me only that I am a thinking creature, not that I am a living one, not that I am an *animal* but at most a *cogital*." The neologism 'cogital' spotlights Nietzsche's concern that Descartes valorizes thinking over life. In BGE #16, Nietzsche again mentions the *cogito* argument, closely analyzing the numerous presuppositions it entails about the I who thinks and what it means to think. Nietzsche questions the basis of the *cogito* as an "immediate certainty," declaring: "we really ought to free ourselves from the seduction of words." According to Nietzsche, then, the *cogito* represents a retreat from life that is supported by questionable and unexamined needs.[33]

Following Hegel, Nietzsche credits Descartes for affirming the independence of the will, but concludes that he is "superficial" and "not radical enough" (BGE #191; SW 11, p. 632). Nietzsche sees Descartes as not quite liberating philosophy from morality and religion, whereas Hegel focuses on the inordinate influence of science on Descartes (which, he argues, interferes with an appreciation of philosophy as an autonomous discipline). Hegel and Nietzsche share the sense that the abstractness of Descartes's project—its removal from an actual human standpoint—is an evasion of philosophy's most demanding task. Nietzsche differs from Hegel, however, in questioning the value of aspiring to have an impersonal view.

Nietzsche is dubious both about a universal standpoint and about an impersonal standpoint. It is, according to him, as unlikely that we can escape a personal view as that we can escape the influence of our culture.[34] In contrast, Hegel sees an impersonal view as desirable: the philosopher strives to make his first-person perspective objective, and ultimately he recognizes the value of rendering our shared views concrete. Philosophy is defined, according to Hegel, by its adoption of such a universal standpoint, which allows us to expunge what he sees as the arbitrary, idiosyncratic elements of the realm of the personal.

For Nietzsche, the personal is a kind of bedrock truth; for Hegel, the motivation to escape the personal is connected to the crucial role of others in allowing us transcend the personal. Nietzsche never squarely faces whether there might be something desirable about incorporating the views of others and thereby transcending the personal. It is fair to wonder what Hegel means by the impersonal. To what extent does Hegel endorse the impersonal in the sense of meaning "beyond the personal" or the "non-personal"? As I see it, the latter position, which would resemble Thomas Nagel's idea of "the view from nowhere," is not an aspiration for Hegel. Although Hegel occasionally implies that valuing the impersonal requires disregarding the personal, he does not always take such a hard line.[35] It is not likely that either Hegel or Nietzsche would be receptive to the other's view. Yet this should not stop us from asking whether their views must be construed as inconsistent. One might argue, for instance, that upholding the value of the personal in no way commits one to rejecting the desirability of the suprapersonal. This is especially the case insofar as the latter is mediated by the views of real others.

Although both Hegel and Nietzsche are critics of epistemology, Hegel is less hostile to the Cartesian myth.[36] *The Phenomenology of Spirit* is, of course, a story about a journey to unconditional, certain knowledge. Hegel has faith in knowledge in a way that Nietzsche does not, even though Nietzsche countenances knowledge in a new form (perspectivism). Ironically, however, it is Nietzsche's life, rather than Hegel's, that conforms to the image of the solitary figure writing philosophy in a room. In emphasizing the role of the other and introducing us to the paradigm of intersubjectivity, Hegel articulates a new way to think of knowledge.[37] Although Hegel's and Nietzsche's views about knowledge diverge, a significant parallel has been uncovered, insofar as both thinkers wish to construe knowledge as a fulfilling endeavor.

According to the Cartesian myth, knowledge guarantees the connection between our minds and the world; this rescues us from terror and anxiety, but it would be far-fetched to suggest that it bestows well-being. Hegel and Nietzsche insist that well-being is a legitimate concern for philosophy, and that we ought to entertain questions about what it means to know. Both thinkers are sensitive to the struggle that knowledge requires; both emphasize the inevitability of failure and the need for continual revision. Finally, both displace knowledge as a matter of verisimilitude to reality, conceptualizing it instead in terms of the wish to achieve satisfaction in life.

Hegel and Nietzsche ask basic questions about knowledge in relation to human beings—questions rarely raised by epistemologists. In one sense, epistemology as a project is rejected; in another sense, the domain of epistemology is expanded beyond the "thinking mind." The notion of "living well," which has its source in Greek culture—especially in Greek tragedy—is adopted as a preferable ideal. The echo of Hegel's claim in the preface to PhS that philosophy ought to replace its aim of "love of knowing" in order to become "actual knowing" resounds in Nietzsche's work. However, one can discern an impatience in Nietzsche—a tilt toward actual living that does not necessarily heed or depend on knowledge. Whereas Hegel expands rationality to include affects, Nietzsche makes affects central to his concern for living well. It remains to be specified, of course, what each thinker has in mind about the ideal of living well. Although Hegel and Nietzsche share this ideal, it is unwarranted to presume that they concur or that we know much about what it really means until we consider their notions of agency.

The parallel between Hegel's and Nietzsche's redescriptions of epistemology can be characterized in terms of the "psychology of knowledge." Nietzsche's attraction to psychology is obvious: he urges us to think of him as a psychologist, and he presses philosophy to be more sensitive to psychology.[38] It is more questionable to ascribe an interest in psychology to Hegel, especially if one recalls Hegel's circumscribed pejorative meaning: psychology as subjective experience.[39] My use of 'psychology' is meant to reflect Hegel's concern with human motivation and human flourishing in general. Hegel adopts an expanded sense of rationality that is inclusive of the irrational; thus, his focus is on the intersection of psychology and philosophy. It is fair to say that for Hegel psychology is incorporated into the project of rationality, whereas for Nietzsche psychology supersedes but does not negate the project of rationality. I shall use "psychology of knowledge" to denote a shared sphere in which Hegel and Nietzsche reflect on knowledge and affirm the confluence of knowledge and human flourishing.

Hegel challenges epistemology in a way to which Nietzsche is sympathetic, although Nietzsche takes this in a direction that from Hegel's perspective would be extreme. Hegel and Nietzsche negotiate the Cartesian myth by reorienting epistemology, exploring the motivation of knowing and its real benefits for living. This leads to a new task for philosophy: understanding culture in a philosophical way, which will be the subject of chapter 2. In chapters 3 and 4, the focus will be on Hegel's and Nietzsche's immersion in evaluating their own culture by means of comparing "ancient culture" to "modern culture."

2

The Philosophy of Culture

That culture so far has failed is no justification for furthering its failure.
—Theodor Adorno, *Minima Moralia*

To establish the claim that philosophy and culture are interrelated for Hegel and Nietzsche, I have focused primarily on their respective views of philosophy. In this chapter, I will address their views of culture. This will allow us to illuminate their rejection of the Cartesian myth, and it will also clarify their embrace of the psychology of knowledge. As we will see, the psychology of knowledge takes on a heightened significance for agents in modern culture who no longer can rely on tradition.

The absence of a single, well-defined concept of culture in either Hegel or Nietzsche's thought complicates the assessment of their views on the subject.[1] To begin, we must turn to Johann Gottfried Herder, who influenced many nineteenth-century thinkers. As Geuss has observed (1996, p. 155), Herder claims that "there is a plurality of different, nationally specific ways of living, each with its own particular way of viewing the world, its own characteristic virtues and achievements, its own desires, ambitions, ideals, and each in principle of equal value." Construing culture in terms of its "internal coherence," Herder anticipates the neutral sense of the concept that emerges in anthropology, especially in his appreciation of the differences that exist across cultures (ibid., p. 155).[2]

It is commonly assumed that Hegel simply displaced the concept of culture from the centrality it was given by Herder and replaced it with

Geist.[3] Although Geist does subsume culture, it does so in an inclusive way, and it is clearly not intended to establish a concept that opposes material life. Moreover, Hegel occasionally uses the word 'Kultur' in an overall way to characterize a particular social group (for example, the French or the Germans). To grasp the full implications of how Geist replaces culture, it will be necessary to explore Hegel's understanding of Bildung. Let us also note that Hegel does follow Herder in one important respect: he depicts the unfolding of culture in developmental stages.

Herder's influence on Nietzsche is readily apparent. In *The Birth of Tragedy*, Nietzsche enumerates types of culture and thus approximates the anthropological sense of culture. In his later work, however, Nietzsche moves away from this point of view and is notably judgmental about cultures, reserving the greatest criticism for German culture.[4]

Nietzsche mainly uses 'Kultur', and sometimes the older form, 'Cultur'. Yet 'Bildung' also can be found in his work. For Nietzsche, 'Bildung' has connotations of philistinism and thus is often regarded with disdain. There are times, however, in which Nietzsche expresses hope for a rejuvenated form of Bildung. It is most perspicuous, therefore, to say that Nietzsche distinguishes between a kind of Bildung that he likes and admires and a kind that he criticizes and condemns. Generally speaking, Nietzsche seems to have a preference for 'Kultur' or 'Cultur', but there is overlap in meaning between these terms and 'Bildung', and they are often used without precision. Nietzsche tends to use 'Kultur' or 'Cultur' to refer to the values of particular social groups. Nietzsche also uses it to refer to the aesthetic realm, especially when he wants to render qualitative judgments. In both Nietzsche and Hegel, 'Bildung' can refer either to the process of becoming cultured or to the state of being cultured.

My approach in this chapter will be to delineate three distinct senses of 'culture' in the work of Hegel and Nietzsche: culture as customs, culture as Bildung, and culture as self-fathoming.[5] Culture as customs points to the objective realm, traditions, rituals, and values—that which binds humans together in groups. This sense of 'culture' overlaps with 'civilization', particularly insofar as it is juxtaposed to nature. Culture as Bildung denotes the subjective realm—more precisely, how the objective realm is internalized by individuals, including how one becomes a cultivated person and what it is like to attain such a state. The term "self-fathoming" requires careful consideration, as it is a notion that I am inferring; it is not explicitly used by either Hegel or Nietzsche. Culture as self-fathoming denotes the realm of how we think of ourselves, a mixture of the subjective and objective realms. For both Hegel and Nietzsche, self-fathoming is at issue only in a culture (such as modern culture) in which a disparity exists between culture as customs and culture as Bildung.

A historical relationship exists among the three senses of 'culture'. Hegel and Nietzsche regard customs as an antiquated form of culture, and they both construe Bildung as an attempt to achieve an adequate form of culture in the modern world. Both postulate a dynamic sense of agency as necessary in order to achieve satisfaction in modern culture. There is some disagreement between them, and to some extent it should be understood as a product of the differences in their respective eras. Problems with Bildung lead to its reformulation; the result is culture as self-fathoming.

For both thinkers, culture is the medium through which one is bound to fathom oneself. For Hegel this points in the direction of affirming one's relation to the whole, but he also believes that one must be prepared to choose and craft a life for oneself—an idea that Nietzsche develops and expands. It is no longer possible to look to culture to provide answers for the individual, nor can culture simply be displaced and disregarded. Self-fathoming entails self-determination, but this does not occur in a vacuum. Engaging in self-fathoming requires us to form ourselves in relation to what has formed us. As we will see in this chapter, some genuine differences between Hegel and Nietzsche emerge in connection with the telos of Bildung and self-fathoming. This chapter culminates with a comparative discussion of the philosophical methods they deploy to comprehend culture: phenomenology and genealogy.

2.1 Customs

Hegel and Nietzsche use the first sense of 'culture' to refer to the customs [Sitten] that organize and bind specific social groups. In this sense, the concept of culture is closely related to social ethics [Sittlichkeit]. There is obviously a connection between culture and tradition, although this does not preclude customs from changing over time and varying across societies. This sense of culture denotes external space, the sense of belonging to something that pre-exists and is outside of oneself. What underlies it is the distinction between nature and culture: the latter alter the former.

According to Hegel, customs are produced by and for human beings. In the first part of the Geist chapter of the *Phenomenology of Spirit*, "The True Spirit. The Ethical Order [Die Sittlichkeit]," customs are specifically associated with "human law" (as opposed to "divine law"). Customs are values that provide the individual with certainty; they gain their authority through being "openly accepted and manifest to all" (PhS, p. 268). Hegel identifies customs with a specific kind of social world: the world of Sittlichkeit (or Greek culture), in which individuals are content to subordinate themselves to the universal.

As Hegel reiterates in the "Religion in the Form of Art" section of the Religion chapter of PhS (p. 425), where he returns to the topic of Greek culture, Geist is "the free Nation in which hallowed custom constitutes the substance of all, whose actuality and existence each and everyone knows to be his own will and deed" [das freye Volk, worin die Sitte die Substanz aller ausmacht, deren Wirklichkeit und Daseyn alle and jeder einzelne als seinen Willen und That weiss]. He proceeds to clarify that at this stage in its development Geist "lacks the principle of the pure individuality of self-consciousness" and "has not yet withdrawn into itself from its contented acceptance of custom and its firm trust therein" (ibid.) [hiermit darauf dass dieses noch nicht aus seiner ruhigen Sitte und seinem festen Vertrauen in sich gegangen ist]. Customs restrict us; thus, as culture evolves, a greater ambivalence about acceding to them arises naturally. This does not mean that customs can or should be eradicated, although in the modern world our reliance on them diminishes. For Hegel, customs guide us before we are able to guide ourselves.

In later works, Hegel confirms that customs constitute an initial stage of culture in which the universal dictates to individuals.[6] Through customs, human beings move away from nature; customs are thus described as "second nature" in PR #151. In this same passage, he suggests that "habits" can be counterproductive and even cause death. Hegel also notes that barbarians are immersed in customs without awareness, but that we no longer find satisfaction in customs (PR #211, Zusatz). As Wood explicates in his commentary (1991, pp. 427–428), "the decline of an ethical life founded on custom is inevitable, because subjective reflection on the ethical life of custom is inevitable and because such reflection inevitably finds this ethical life limited and hence unsatisfactory."[7] Customs reign in cultures before Geist becomes self-conscious.[8]

In the introduction to *Lectures on the Philosophy of History*, Hegel contrasts customs, which are concrete, with the abstract notion of "the good" in a society. Customs are associated with the "everyday contingencies of private life" [gewöhnlichen Fälle des Privatlebens] (LPWH, p. 80). Hegel reiterates the point that customs are dominant insofar as subjective needs do not assert themselves. It is not surprising, then, that Hegel describes the world-historical individual as someone who flouts customs.

Nietzsche regards customs with greater suspicion than Hegel. In *Daybreak* Nietzsche reflects extensively on customs. After defining customs in terms of "traditional ways of behaving and evaluating," he locates them within the framework of the "morality of mores"—a morality that requires the individual to "sacrifice himself" (D #9). Nietzsche cites no historical era that corresponds to the morality of mores; however, he clearly indicates that the morality of mores is antiquated and not binding in the modern world. In *On the Genealogy of Morals* Nietzsche is more vociferous about customs, thundering against "the oppressive narrowness and punctiliousness of custom" (GM II #16). Here custom is blamed for "taming" humankind through "forcible sundering from [its] animal past."

In "Custom and What Is In Accordance with It" [Sitte und Sittlich] (HAH I #96), Nietzsche proposes that to be in accordance with custom is "to practice obedience towards a law or tradition established from old." He suggests that customs often get detached from their original meanings, become habits, and garner prestige as their origin becomes remote. Nietzsche argues that the primary purpose of customs is to preserve community; the individual who fails to heed them, he explains, must be condemned as evil. In the later aphorism

"Custom and its Sacrifices" [Die Sitte und ihr Opfer] (HAH II 1 #89), Nietzsche describes customs more bluntly, stating that their two sources are that the community is worth more than the individual and that an enduring advantage is to be preferred to a transient one. Customs thrive, Nietzsche suggests, under a morality in which "the individual outvotes [majorisiert] himself" (ibid.). According this perspective, to choose willingly to adhere to customs is paradoxical. Nietzsche makes it abundantly clear that "free spirits" are defined, in fact, by their refusal to be so fettered (HAH I #225). Yet Nietzsche does not portray customs in entirely unfavorable terms. For example, in "Pleasure in Custom" [Lust in der Sitte] (HAH I #97) customs are described as "a union of the pleasant and the useful." Although Nietzsche argues that customs require compliance, it is not as if he expects us to live entirely without them. This is apparent in his summary statement that "one does not know that the same degree of well-being [Wohlbefinden] can also exist under different customs or that even higher degrees are attainable" (ibid.). Still, it is clear that Nietzsche presumes that the free spirit seeks well-being without subordinating himself or herself to customs.

Although customs do not satisfy the individual in modern culture, Hegel does not depict them as harmful, as Nietzsche does (except in the passage in PR in which Hegel refers to the lethality of habits). As we have seen, Hegel mainly wants to link customs to an earlier era. Nietzsche's approach to customs echoes Hegel in presenting customs as part of an antiquated form of culture. Nietzsche also concurs with Hegel that the power of customs has weakened in the modern world (D #9). He introduces the concept of the "morality of mores" in order to capture how customs coercively direct our conduct and interfere with our individuality. As Nietzsche emphatically states in GS #46, the morality of mores regards our inner life as "attached to iron necessity with eternal clamps."

Although he follows Hegel in maintaining that customs restrict individuality, Nietzsche does not identify the Greeks with the reign of customs, as Hegel does in PhS. On the contrary, Nietzsche suggests that the Greeks had begun to move away from the morality of mores and were "hovering in an interesting intermediate position" (GS

#149).[9] The perniciousness of customs, which Nietzsche detects, is absent from Hegel's account of Greek culture. To further explicate both thinkers' perspectives on customs, we must turn to what they say about the nature/culture distinction.

Nature and Culture

Both Hegel and Nietzsche question whether nature and culture are pure opposites. Nietzsche challenges the nature/culture distinction in two ways. First, he rejects the distinction itself by conflating the pair. In *Philosophy and Truth* (p. 123) he proposes a definition of culture as "improved physis."[10] Second, he sides with nature against culture. He argues repeatedly that it as impossible as it is undesirable for humans to abandon their natural endowment. In GS #109 he speaks of the need to "naturalize humanity." In GM II #2 he invokes the natural as the necessary antidote to the conformism inspired by customs. This reinforces the well-known passage (BGE #230) in which Nietzsche describes the "task" of translating man back to nature, thereby overcoming the "scrawled and painted over . . . eternal basic text of homo natura" and notes that this task requires us to reject "old metaphysical bird catchers" who urge humanity to believe "you are more, you are higher, you are of a different origin." An implication here is that nature is, in fact, superior to the seductive, but false consolation offered by culture.[11] And with his contrast between master morality and slave morality, Nietzsche affirms the notion that nature fosters strength and health.

Yet Nietzsche registers doubts about the ideal of going back to nature, and he questions the valorizing of nature that one finds in the Stoics and in Rousseau.[12] We can never leave nature behind, Nietzsche avers in *The Future of our Educational Institutions*. A true form of Bildung not only allows but will encourage a relation to nature, cultivating our "contemplative instincts" and aiding in achieving "calmness, unity, consistency and harmony" (FEI, p. 97; SW 1, p. 716). In *Twilight of the Idols* ("Expeditions of an Untimely Man," #48) Nietzsche offers an insightful gloss on his position: "I too speak of a 'return to nature' [Rückkehr zur Natur], although it is not really a going-back [Züruckgehn] but a going-up [Hinaufkommen]."

How can Nietzsche identify himself with one side of the nature/culture distinction while rejecting that distinction? A part of the answer lies in his resistance to how the Greek distinction between physis and nomos was appropriated by Christianity. Nietzsche examines the Pauline distinction between the natural and the spiritual in connection with the advent of slave morality, which rejects revenge and other forms of instinctual gratification in favor of a spiritualized kind of gratification. He repudiates such vicarious gratification and is drawn to celebrate the natural. Nietzsche also maintains that the metaphysical tradition has derived its value from religion. He is adamant that culture must concern itself, as the Greeks realized, with the body as much as with the soul (TI, "Expeditions of an Untimely Man," #47).

Hegel addresses the nature/culture distinction in the Culture section of the Geist chapter of the *Phenomenology of Spirit*. He makes the assumption that culture is an overcoming of nature: it requires "the setting aside [Aufheben] of the natural self" (p. 298). This is not a demand to reject the natural self; on the contrary, Hegel stresses that the cultured self must include the natural self. This point is made clearly in the *Philosophical Propaedeutic* (p. 43): "The freedom of man, as regards natural impulses, consists not in his being rid of such impulses altogether and thus striving to escape from his nature but in his recognition [anerkennt] of them as a necessity as something rational. . . ." Hegel emphasizes the importance of temperance for satisfaction and health in describing what he terms "practical Bildung."

The context of Hegel's remarks about nature and culture in PhS is important, since "mutual recognition," sought by Geist, does not exist in the modern world. In the modern world the integrity of the individual is defended in relation to the community; yet, because the bond among individuals in the community has weakened, the modern world is constituted by "self-alienated Spirit." Moreover, Hegel is wary of the persistent demand in modern culture for the individual to sacrifice his or her natural self.

The relationship between the natural and the spiritual stands at the center of Hegel's entire philosophy. Hegel attempts to reconcile nature and spirit by arguing that nature stands in relation to spirit as the immediate to the mediate; in this sense, Geist is a development from nature. Geist is nature that is aware of itself. It would appear from this that Nietzsche would oppose Hegel—at least that side of Nietzsche that grants primacy to nature over spirit. Nietzsche's vehemence toward what he sees as the Christian misappropriation of the nature/culture distinction marks his distance from Hegel.

According to Hegel, a relation in which spirit is granted primacy over nature is superior to a united relation of spirit and nature. For example, in the *Lectures on the History of Philosophy* Hegel assigns the unity of spirit and nature to the Oriental world, which he sees as a less advanced stage of consciousness. "Therefore," he emphasizes (LHP, p. 166), "they all err who assume that the unity of spirit with nature is the excellent mode of consciousness." Hegel's approval of the primacy of the spiritual over the natural is, nonetheless, only one side of the story. As with Nietzsche, there is an important sense in which Hegel wants to reject the opposition between nature and spirit.

In Nietzsche, the renunciation of the natural (espoused by Christianity) and the coerciveness of customs cause unhappiness. Nietzsche is distinctly hostile to the kind of morality that is governed by the demanding and arbitrary expectations of customs. Hegel is less opposed to customs, which he sees as belonging to the past but not as culpable for severing us from our nature. Hegel is hopeful that mutual recognition, which in its ultimate instantiation has connotations of agapaic love, might transform our unhappiness.

Hegel's and Nietzsche's language concerning how culture overcomes but does not negate nature is revealing: whereas Nietzsche uses 'hinaufkommen', Hegel uses 'aufheben'. Though both words indicate upward movement, 'hinaufkommen' is more qualified. It is as if Nietzsche is looking up while remaining within nature, whereas Hegel is looking down from the position of transcendence.[13] Nevertheless, Hegel and Nietzsche share a commitment to work through opposing concepts, challenging the false nature/culture antinomy. In Hegel, the determination to work through opposing concepts entails moving from the immediate to the mediate: Aufhebung preserves as it surpasses. Nietzsche discountenances the possibility of such transcendence, though he is no less committed than Hegel to demonstrating that opposing concepts inherited from the past must be examined anew.

2.2 Bildung

The second sense of the concept of culture employed by Hegel and Nietzsche is Bildung. Culture is conceived as a process of self-cultivation whereby one develops oneself to be cultured intellectually, morally, and aesthetically. Here the focus is on culture as it is subjectively experienced and internalized by an individual. This sense of culture entails becoming and development; it specifies both a process and a state. As a process, Bildung has the aim of satisfaction, and it is particularly relevant when customs no longer are fully adequate. As an actual state, Bildung is expressed in character and is specifically manifested through judgment.

Hegel and Nietzsche wrote in different eras, and any comparison of their views on Bildung must be sensitive to this fact. Bildung was originally conceived broadly as depicting the ideal development of a young person; however, as mass culture unfolded in the nineteenth century, knowledge of the arts and philosophy—that is, the acquisition of high culture—took on a heightened significance in defining the concept. At first, Bildung was distinct from but closely allied with education. For example, Hegel, during his time as an educator, was involved in implementing a humanist model of education that distinguished between gymnasium students (who were to receive a traditional, universal education) and other students (who were to receive a practical and technical education). Bildung was never intended as education for the masses, though the spread of education to a broader segment of society in the Napoleonic era was appealing to Hegel.[14]

Nietzsche was an elitist, and throughout his work culture is regarded as the domain of the few. In *On the Future of Our Educational Institutions*, Nietzsche lays down the theme that true culture is aristocratic; his later view remains fairly consistent (FEI, p. 34, 75, 89). In *Human, All Too Human* (1 #439), Nietzsche avers that a higher culture is defined by the presence of two castes: the workers (those who are "compelled to work") and the idle ("those capable of true leisure . . . [the caste] that works if it wants to"). One change in Nietzsche's thinking is that, instead of indulging the fantasy of a triumphant "German Geist," as he did at first, he eventually becomes quite hostile to German culture. Nietzsche clearly opposes what he sees as dual tendencies in modern culture: to extend culture to everyone and to dilute it by allowing the state to administer it (FEI, introduction, pp. 12–13; SW 1, p. 647). Nietzsche associates Hegel with a commitment to subordinating culture to the state—a subordination that Nietzsche opposes (FEI, pp. 87, 89). It is not clear how aware Nietzsche was that in mourning the demise of the Greek notion of paideia he was following Hegel. As we will see, Hegel advocates a true kind of Bildung as a synthesis of modern and ancient culture. Though Nietzsche also invokes a true kind of Bildung, he is partial to an aestheticized reading of Bildung that, unlike Hegel's, does not identify itself with the philosophical tradition.

Goethe, a main source of the idea of Bildung, influenced both Hegel and Nietzsche. Indeed, the structure of Hegel's *Phenomenology of Spirit* seems influenced by the Bildungsroman tradition.[15] Nietzsche, on the other hand, tends to be skeptical toward Bildung on the ground that it easily degenerates into philistinism (the bourgeois notion that a little bit of culture is good for everyone). Nietzsche also worries that Bildung contains latent theological connotations, portending a kind of redemption. Nevertheless, as we will see, the truth is more complicated: Hegel has reservations about the concept of Bildung, and Nietzsche is sympathetic toward a modified version of Bildung that avoids philistinism. Indeed, both Hegel and Nietzsche distinguish between true and false forms of Bildung. This does not mean that they agree, but it does suggest that we must be cautious making inferences about how they differ. Indeed, in accounting for differences between them we should not lose sight of their shared commitment to satisfaction as the goal of culture.

In the following subsections, I will attempt to clarify what each of the two thinkers saw to be the nature of a true form of Bildung. This will help me to refine the claim I made in chapter 1 that Hegel and Nietzsche embrace the psychology of knowledge.

Hegel-Bildung

Hegel lived in the era in which the idea of Bildung flourished. Harris (1972, pp. 18–19) tells us that in his youth Hegel took the trouble of copying a long passage from Moses Mendelssohn that divides Bildung into Kultur (having to do with aesthetics) and Aufklärung (having to do with science or the use of reason in general). It is tempting to see Hegel's early philosophy as motivated by an attempt to integrate these two components, and particularly tempting to regard the *Phenomenology of Spirit* as the fulfillment of this attempt.

In PhS, Hegel develops the idea of Bildung in an original way, presenting it in both a general and a specific form. In the introduction, he claims that the work will present "the detailed history of Bildung of consciousness itself to the standpoint of Science" (p. 30), Bildung being ultimately linked to the unfolding of Geist.[16] The most extended specific discussion of Bildung occurs in connection with French culture in the chapter titled "Der Reich der Bildung" (p. 265).[17] Here Hegel conceives of Bildung as representing progress since the Greeks in the direction of achieving satisfaction, but as being inadequate as a way to overcome the self-alienation of Geist.[18]

Hegel's double use of 'Bildung'—as a description of the entire process of development and as a specific moment that falls short of realizing the ideal of mutual recognition—is confusing. Indeed, the confusion is magnified in that the general sense affirms the ideal of satisfaction, whereas the specific sense seems to imply dissatisfaction. Perhaps some of the confusion can be lessened if we think of Bildung in the general sense as a many-staged journey at the end of which an abiding satisfaction is realized and Bildung in the specific sense as one of the stages.

It will be important to take a closer look at the notion of satisfaction, a notion which is most commonly linked to the stage of desire but which also is connected to the notion of cognition (PhS, p. 51). In chapter 6 I shall focus on satisfaction, which is such a basic aspect of Hegel's philosophy that it has not been a subject of much inquiry by Hegel scholars.

For the moment, however, let us try to make sense of the relationship between the general and specific senses of Bildung by clarifying what Hegel means by the notion of true Bildung. In PhS, true Bildung occurs at the end of the journey, and thus it has religious connotations for Hegel. In his early work *The Spirit of Christianity*, Hegel introduced Bildung in the context of interpreting Christianity as embracing this world rather than being focused on the world beyond. Hegel juxtaposes the true Bildung found in Christianity to the

"Missbildung" of the Jews.[19] On November 3, 1810, around the time of his stint as an educator, Hegel wrote in a letter to a friend: "You yourself know better than anyone how highly the Protestants esteem their scholarly educational institutions, how these institutions are as dear to them as the churches. . . . Protestantism does not so much consist in any special creed as in the spirit of reflection and higher rational education [Bildung]." (*Hegel: The Letters*, p. 227) The fulfillment of Bildung, as Hegel sees it, occurs through Christianity.

Yet, other dimensions besides religion figure prominently in Hegel's thinking about Bildung. The *Philosophical Propaedeutic*, written in conjunction with Hegel's involvement with educational reform, contains a detailed discussion of Bildung. Hegel argues that Bildung is the means of educating oneself as an individual "into conformity with universal nature" (PP, p. 41). Bildung, he emphasizes, denotes "what we ought to be": not mere animals, but spiritual, rational beings. This must include the self-understanding of being "universal spiritual essence." Hegel also makes a crucial distinction between theoretical and practical Bildung in this context: theoretical Bildung trains us to see objects from "points of view" [Gesichtspunkte]; it enables us to judge without the impediment of subjective interest. This coincides with Hegel's determination to overcome the personal. Theoretical Bildung achieves this through "attentive study," rather than "sensuous intuition." "An educated [gebildeter] man," Hegel summarizes (ibid., p. 43), "knows at once the limits of his capacity for judgment." Theoretical Bildung trains the mind to expand itself as well as to recognize its limitations. Practical Bildung, in contrast, concerns the gratification [Befriedigung] of our desires.

Thus, Hegel does not conceive of Bildung exclusively in intellectual and spiritual terms. Practical Bildung is regulated by prudence [Besonnenheit] and temperance [Mässigung]; its end is health and satisfaction. This is significant, as it is easy to assume that Hegel's attachment to rationality means that he was not concerned with the well-being of the body.

Hegel goes on to prescribe "following the mean" as the ideal course:

Health is an essential condition for the use of mental powers in fulfilling the higher vocation of man. If the body is not preserved in its proper condition . . . then it obliges its possessor to make of it a special object of his care and, by this means, it becomes something dangerous, absorbing more than its due share of the attention of the mind. Furthermore, excess in the use or disuse of the physical and mental powers results in dullness and debility. (PP, p. 44)

Hegel introduces prudence in this context, perhaps with Aristotle in mind. Prudence, he notes, means "reflecting upon what one is doing" in order to do what is necessary, rather than becoming too absorbed in any one endeavor.

Theoretical Bildung raises us to the level of rational will; practical Bildung aids us to realize satisfied embodied lives. The two aspects come together by means of the acquisition of judgment. As Gadamer has maintained (1975, pp. 10–19), Hegel's notion of Bildung features a return to the self from alienation that is accomplished by keeping oneself open to others. Gadamer emphasizes that, according to Hegel, Bildung promotes us to the universal. Gadamer proceeds to connect Geist and Bildung, concluding that the Geisteswissenschaften constitute and contribute to Bildung (ibid., pp. 10–19). Despite Gadamer's interest in what Hegel has to say about practical Bildung (which is hardly surprising in view of the importance of the Aristotelian notion of phronesis in his thinking), his interpretation of Hegel dwells more on theoretical Bildung than on practical Bildung.

Overall, Hegel regards Bildung as a means for individuals to internalize the universal without the self-sacrifice of customs. Bildung enhances one's sense of self, fostering connection to others in society. In PR #187, Hegel describes Bildung as a liberation: ". . . the absolute transition from an ethical substantiality which is immediate and natural to the one which is intellectual and both infinitely subjective and lofty enough to have attained universality of form." Bildung renders our subjective will objective (ibid.). By virtue of the process of Bildung, one attains a new state of mind. One becomes a "universal person," and one then views others as universal too—no longer as "a Jew, Catholic, Protestant, German, Italian, &c." (PR #209).[20] Here Hegel modifies his earlier religious prejudice in order to sustain the Enlightenment ideal. A Kantian dimension rises to the fore: that one ought to regard others as one regards oneself (i.e., as an end and never as a means).

In the *Philosophy of Right* Hegel dwells on the danger of misconstruing Bildung as the satisfaction of particularity. Yet, even though he adjusts the meaning by moving away from practical Bildung, he does not abandon the link between Bildung and satisfaction.[21] For example, in PR #20 he describes Bildung in terms of the "cultivation of the universality of thought," which he connects to "satisfaction" [Befriedigung]. Satisfaction usually refers to the body (PR #189, Zusatz), but we must not overlook that Hegel uses the concept more broadly to refer to our relation to others (PR #182) and to successful action in general (PR #121). Thus, in PR, as in PhS and PP, Hegel affirms that the achievement of true Bildung brings satisfaction.

As Hegel sees it, Bildung can be attained only by discipline. In the introduction to the *Lectures on the Philosophy of World History*, Hegel argue that Bildung requires the "throwing off" [abschütteln] of nature—a view that is distinct from his view (discussed in the previous section) of how Geist transcends nature by including it. Hegel goes on to assert (LPWH, p. 50) that "man can only fulfill himself through education and discipline" [Der Mensch ist, was er sein soll, nur durch Bildung, durch Zucht]. Ultimately (PR #57), Hegel maintained that Bildung is fulfilled by the state—a clear-cut change from his position in PP.[22] This is also a change from PhS, which shows Bildung functioning in alliance with religion and as a vehicle to absolute knowledge (Lauer 1983, pp. 103–113).[23] In Hegel's remarks about the dynamic evolution of consciousness culminating in the self-knowledge of Geist, the PhS clearly shows the influence of the Bildungsroman tradition. As Bakhtin has noted (1986, pp. 20–23, 43), the Bildungsroman itself constructs a continuity of becoming and a totality of meaning within a particular framework of time: entelechic development.

Forster (1998, p. 293) detects dual tendencies in Hegel's PhS: a "law and purpose historicism," wherein history follows a teleological process of development aimed at a final goal, and an "intellectual historicism," wherein history is revealed as a succession of human perspectives that differ from one another in fundamental ways. Forster believes that the former is untenable; thus, he sees it as unfortunate that Hegel "marries" the two tendencies in PhS. He proceeds to argue (ibid., p. 294) that "law and purpose historicism" is more evident in Hegel's later works, although "intellectual historicism" informs PhS in a way that it does not inform any of Hegel's other works. Intellectual historicism seems consistent with Nietzsche's perspectivism; however, as will be evident in the next subsection, Nietzsche's understanding of Bildung resolutely opposes law and purpose historicism.

Nietzsche-Bildung

Nietzsche conceives of Bildung as an ideal belonging to an earlier era. Its "Schiller-Goetheschen Basis" (SW 7, p. 506) entails naive and idealistic assumptions from which he wishes to distance himself. In contrast, Nietzsche (D #195) derides "a so-called classical Bildung."[24] Yet Nietzsche does not reject the idea of Bildung altogether.

When Nietzsche raises the concern that the German has "no culture [Cultur] because his education [Erziehung] provides no basis for one" (UDHL #10), he is not simply being negative. His assessment of the state of German culture is intended to get the reader to appreciate the need for cultural transformation. He is warning against cultural philistinism (a term that, in letter #164 and in EH, "The Untimely Ones," #2, he brags of having invented). He wants to defend the idea of a noble culture.

Although Nietzsche regards Bildung as an antiquated concept, he is, for the most part, favorably disposed toward Goethe. This in itself ought to condition our response to Nietzsche's view of Bildung. Nietzsche proclaims, for example, that Goethe is the last German for whom he has reverence, stressing that he represents a European rather than a German event (TI, "Skirmishes of an Untimely Man," #51). Schopenhauer, Hegel, and Heine are also included in this good company (ibid., #21).[25] Nietzsche even goes so far as to claim that Goethe is himself "an entire culture" (HAH II 2 #125). Yet Nietzsche avers that Goethe's appeal is "only for the few, for contemplative natures in the grand style, and is misunderstood by the crowd" (SE #4).

According to Nietzsche, Rousseau, Goethe, and Schopenhauer offer contrasting images of humanity for the modern world. Nietzsche sees Goethe as reacting to the turbulence and excessiveness of Rousseau, who seeks liberation through the glorification of nature: ". . . the Goethean man is a preservative and conciliatory power—with the danger . . . that he may degenerate to a philistine" (SE #4). Thus, even though Nietzsche claims that Goethe's appeal is limited, he sees that Goethe is easily appropriated by middlebrow taste. Nietzsche goes on to register his support for Schopenhauer, whose anguish knows no moderation: ". . . to speak frankly: it is necessary for us to get really angry for once in order that things shall get better" (ibid.). The Schopenhauerean human being is radical in being willing to suffer in order to uphold truth; indeed, such a person stands heroically outside "the institutions which have produced him" (ibid.).

Though Bildung is an impossible task for most people, Nietzsche implies here that it can be achieved by a few noble individuals. As Nietzsche explains it, the "idea of culture" has one task: "to promote the production of the philosopher, the artist and the saint within us and without us and thereby to work at the perfecting of nature" (SE #5). He adds that the true goal of culture is to produce genius (SE #6), although later he will amend this view and criticize his own fetishizing of genius (EH, "Human, All Too Human," #1). Nietzsche's elitism is a function of his concern about the dilution and diminution of culture. Culture must be protected, he believes, from philistinism—the embourgeoisement of culture. When Nietzsche considers popular and mass culture—as in his scathing comments in the preface to BGE about newspaper reading—it is with disdain.

Nietzsche repeatedly condemns the state of German culture, labeling it a "so-called culture" and a "pseudo-culture" dominated by philistines (DS #11; BT #20; GS #86). In EH, "The Untimely Ones," #1, he expands on his "ruthless contempt" for German culture by describing it as "without meaning, without substance, without aim: mere public opinion." He looks elsewhere—to France—for a culture that he might respect.[26] Nietzsche also celebrates the exuberance of Greek culture, crediting it with being more than "a kind of knowledge about culture" (UDHL #10). He expresses hope that a "higher culture" might be achieved, but he is dubious about it occurring in his own time.

In SE #4, Nietzsche describes the philosopher's relation to modern culture rather stunningly:

Now how does the philosopher view the culture [Cultur] of our time? Very differently, to be sure, from how it is viewed by those professors of philosophy who are so well contented with their new state. When he thinks of the haste and hurry now universal, of the increasing velocity of life, of the cessation of all contemplativeness and simplicity, he almost thinks that what he is seeing are the symptoms of a total extermination and uprooting of culture. The waters of religion are ebbing away and leaving behind swamps or stagnant pools; the nations are again drawing away from one another in the most hostile fashion and long to tear one another to pieces. The sciences, pursued without any restraint and in a spirit of the blindest laissez faire, are shattering and dissolving all firmly held belief; the educated [gebildeten] classes and states are being swept along by a hugely contemptible money economy. The world has never been more worldly, never poorer in love and goodness. The educated [gelehrten] classes are no longer lighthouses or refuges in the midst of this turmoil of secularization; they themselves grow daily more restless, thoughtless and loveless. Everything, contemporary art and science included, serves the coming barbarism. The cultured man [Der Gebildete] has degenerated to the greatest enemy of culture [Bildung], for he wants lyingly to deny the existence of the universal sickness and thus obstructs the physicians.

There are a number of significant points here. First, Nietzsche lays down the gauntlet to those he sees as academic philosophers (like the mature Hegel) who serve the state. Second, he locates the failure of modern culture in its relation to time—specifically the frantic, perpetual wish for progress. Third, he criticizes Bildung as a middlebrow aspiration that actually leads to sickness and to the degeneration of culture. Bildung, he argues, can do nothing to fend off the dawning barbarism; in fact, it is opposed to culture—a part of the problem, not a solution. Regardless of how negative Nietzsche seems to be here about Bildung, it would be mistaken to ignore that he is introducing—if only by way of contrast—the prospect of a true form of Bildung. Philosophical physicians diagnose sickness; presumably they also can hasten cures.

Although Nietzsche does not spell out what a true form of Bildung would be like, he does prescribe "hopes" and "tasks" for culture (EH, "Twilight of the Idols," #2). Perhaps a clue to Nietzsche's own notion of Bildung can be found in EH, "Why I Am So Clever," #9, and in other works where he suggests that becoming is a matter of self-overcoming. Nietzsche stresses independence of judgment, amor fati, and playfulness (EH, "Why I Am So Clever," #10; BGE #43). Nietzsche's approach to Bildung differs from Hegel's in its attention to play and in its rejection of the fantasy of attaining complete development.[27] For Nietzsche, Bildung in the positive sense is connected to the notion of the will to power. As I noted above in connection with how culture transcends nature, Bildung must contend with and nourish the body[28]; otherwise, culture will doom us to unhappiness. In this sense Nietzsche anticipates Freud's worry about the danger of completely renouncing our instincts in order to live within society.

Reconstructing Bildung

Hegel and Nietzsche seem to have conflicting perspectives on Bildung. For Hegel, Bildung is a process that is worth articulating and trying to emulate for the resulting state of mind it produces. Nietzsche subjects the process of Bildung to ridicule because of its bourgeois connotations, yet he leaves room for a more authentic, elitist variety. Early on, Nietzsche views Bildung as a state reserved for the genius; later, he gives this up, although the cultivation of an aesthetic sensibility continues to appeal to him. According to GS #76, an aesthetic sensibility (not circumscribed to artistic creation) enables a person to live aesthetically—that is, in a stylized and tasteful manner.[29]

Nietzsche, unlike the mature Hegel, shows no interest in Bildung as administered by the state. One would be mistaken, however, to suppose that he is indifferent to its social implications. As Warren (1987, p. 61) insightfully notes, Nietzsche "fully acknowledges the deep interdependence of the individual and society even while he speaks on behalf of the individual." Warren finds support for his view in the following passage from Nietzsche: "Collective self-esteem is the great preparatory school for personal sovereignty." (WP #773) When reading this passage, though, one should be aware of the next sentence: "The noble class is that which inherits this training." In other words, what Nietzsche means by "collective self-esteem" applies only to the elite members of society. Warren is right that Nietzsche exhibits some concern for the relationship between the individual and society; yet Nietzsche also urges us to regard culture as "unpolitical, even antipolitical" (TI, "What the Germans Lack," #4).[30]

Hegel and Nietzsche also differ on Bildung because of Hegel's assumption of entelechic development. Necessity and finality govern Hegel's conception of Bildung. This is most obvious in PhS, where Hegel equates consciousness's unfolding path to Bildung with science. Nietzsche beckons us to venture on a spontaneous and unpredictable path, open to new perspectives. Moreover, it is anathema to Nietzsche to regard the state of Bildung as a resting place—recall his wry comment on the world-terminus coinciding with Hegel's life in Berlin. For Nietzsche, valuing Bildung positively ought not obscure the ceaseless and chaotic flow of life, nor can it mitigate our awareness of living in a Godless world.[31]

Can we conclude that Nietzsche and Hegel's views of Bildung are mainly opposed? As Löwith proposed, Hegel is the philosopher of the bourgeois-Christian world, and his conception of Bildung exemplifies this. Hegel is primarily concerned with Bildung as mediating between the individual and the community, and between what society was and what it could be. He is also concerned with defending the German Idealist project of self-determination. However, Hegel anticipates Nietzsche in expressing concern about the danger of philistinism. In the *Aesthetics*, Hegel offers some amusing observations that parody the Bildungsroman and implicate it as a form of philistinism.[32]

Nietzsche is especially concerned with protecting Bildung from being infected by bourgeois-Christian values; in this sense, as Löwith suggests, Nietzsche represents a new era in philosophy. Yet we must be wary of too easily accepting such a generalization. For one thing, Hegel saw his own era as one of ferment and transition, and so the idea of his era as a culmination is at odds with his self-understanding. Rightly or wrongly, each thinker regards his own era as caught between the old and the new. Furthermore, as much as Nietzsche protests the usual assumptions about Bildung, he does not repudiate all connection between Bildung and Geist.[33] Nor does he construe Bildung as an arbitrary and radically individual matter. For example, in GS #86 he emphasizes that being cultivated does not countenance the free expression of emotions. It remains difficult to be specific about what true Bildung could mean for Nietzsche; he is particularly vague about its implications for human relationships. For Hegel, Bildung is obviously connected to our relations to others; this is less true for Nietzsche.

Nietzsche's skepticism toward institutions leads him to conclude that Bildung must be realized outside the social order—a conclusion that has no counterpart in Hegel. Yet Nietzsche follows Hegel in acknowledging the discipline and training that Bildung entails, adopting the word 'Zücktung' from him.[34] Like Hegel, Nietzsche is drawn to Bildung as compensation for the absence of paideia in the modern world. Bildung is a standard that one imposes on oneself in light of the absence of a credible outside standard. Nietzsche also follows Hegel in construing Bildung as a form of becoming. More precisely, Bildung requires a process of training and breeding that involves the acquisition of judgment. There is a tension between Hegel and Nietzsche, however, in that Nietzsche offers a counterdiscourse, opposing limits to judgment and even reveling in transgression. What Hegel and Nietzsche hold in common is that Bildung prescribes a dynamic kind of agency which is grounded in the desirability of health and satisfaction.

Hegel's description of the method of transforming substance into subject (PhS, p. 10) is echoed in Nietzsche's proposal that redeeming the past is a matter of transforming "it was" into "thus I willed it" (*Thus Spoke Zarathustra* II, "On Redemption," p. 251). Caution must be exercised in interpreting this passage because of Nietzsche's ambivalence toward the will. Nevertheless, it provides a lens through which Nietzsche's view of Bildung can be glimpsed together with Hegel's.[35] For both Hegel and Nietzsche, Bildung is at once a new project and a remedial one. Bildung exists as an attempt to compensate for what is missing in modern culture.[36] Certainly there are moments of profound suspicion in Nietzsche concerning Bildung, satisfaction, dynamic agency, the will, and even modern culture, and I do not mean to underestimate or minimize them. Yet such moments ought not lead us to embrace the false antinomy that Hegel affirms Bildung whereas Nietzsche denounces it. It is worth continuing to articulate a perspective from which we can glimpse how both thinkers affirm a dynamic sense of agency.[37]

2.3 Self-Fathoming

Beyond true Bildung, for Hegel and Nietzsche, lies what I will call "self-fathoming." This third sense of the concept of culture in Hegel and Nietzsche is more difficult to ground textually and thus must be regarded as speculative.

Both thinkers formulate self-fathoming as a way to ground true Bildung and to distance themselves from false Bildung. The etymological appeal of 'self-fathoming' is that it conveys depth and breadth together. Depth is appropriate insofar as Hegel and Nietzsche venture beyond the surface of immediate conscious experience; breadth is also connoted by the embrace that both thinkers offer to the formative influence of culture.

The notion of self-fathoming anticipates the notion of culture as a symbolic realm of representation; thus, Hegel and Nietzsche are important forerunners to contemporary ideas about culture as the realm of how we think about ourselves (as opposed to the social and political realms, which concern how things really are). Culture is not defined here by artifacts or practices, but by a realm of meaning that is psychological. Although it is not quite explicit, both Hegel and Nietzsche seek to reserve a specific designation for the sphere of humans actively engaged in trying to understand themselves. More precisely, Hegel and Nietzsche include in this sense of culture the need to reflect upon and question our shared self-understanding.

The understanding of culture, according to this third sense, is a matter of interpretation. This has important ramifications for how philosophy understands itself and for how it understands its relation to culture. The interpretive function of philosophy means that philosophy sees itself as part of culture: philosophical works can be understood as manifestations of the self-understanding belonging to that culture. The interpretive function of philosophy also means that philosophy is responsible for interpreting culture—that is, for interpreting the interpretations of a culture. For Hegel, of course, we need to add a qualification: interpretation does not exhaust what philosophy is, since philosophy, expounded as science, can be equated with rationality.

This third sense of the concept of culture provides a way to think about culture that occupies the ground between the objective and the subjective. 'Culture' designates a space that serves to confound too strong a distinction between what is external and what is internal to us. It is akin to the psychoanalytic notion of psychic reality, which is neither unrelated to external reality nor exclusively determined by it. This sense reveals an awareness that our thinking is a product of how we interpret our experience: our experience itself is, in an important sense constructed, rather than being a result of passively imbibing the external world. This sense of culture gives expression to the need to rethink knowledge in the direction of living well, or what I am calling the psychology of knowledge. The psychology of knowledge gives us a framework in which to understand what philosophy is; self-fathoming is the specific form that is required in modern culture.

Hegel and Nietzsche emphasize that this third sense of the concept of culture is produced under certain conditions. It would seem that these conditions occur when the first sense of the concept (culture as customs—the objective realm) and the second sense (culture as Bildung—the subjective realm) are no longer adequate and are in friction with each other. Therefore, not all cultures require the third sense of culture. It is especially germane in cultures that have come to the point where their self-understanding (and the examination of it) reveals a disparity between culture and society. The highest purpose of culture, according to both Hegel and Nietzsche, is to provide satisfaction. There is a need for philosophy to articulate this and to cope with and perhaps redress any disparities. Self-fathoming demands that we recognize how culture influences us, but it does not influence us in the sense of preventing us from altering our relation to it. Unlike customs or Bildung, self-fathoming builds a critical posture into our understanding of culture.

As we saw in chapter 1, Hegel was more optimistic than Nietzsche about a role for philosophy in fostering cultural change, particularly in his early years. His view of culture as self-fathoming emerges most clearly from the *Phenomenology of Spirit*, a work that moves phenomenologically from the past to the present. In the preface to PhS (p. 3), Hegel stresses that culture must "pass serious judgment" on life. In the *Lectures on the History of Philosophy* (I, p. 356), Hegel affirms that culture must not only be "believed but investigated [untersucht]."[38]

In his early writings, Nietzsche tended to view culture in terms of "unity of style" or "melody" (PT, p. 109). It is only when he adopts the method of "genealogy" that culture acquires a critical dimension. Genealogy assesses the immediate state of culture and also assumes responsibility for a new task—a higher culture (EH, "The Untimely Ones," #1).[39] Nietzsche is unabashed in welcoming a critical and even hostile stance as part of culture itself. He suggests that a high culture, in order to liberate itself, must be characterized by "the ability to contradict, the attainment of a good conscience when one feels hostile to what is accustomed, traditional and hallowed" (GS #297).

Foucault's reflections on Nietzsche emphasize the uniqueness of genealogy as a form of philosophical inquiry: only genealogy opposes the assumption of origins as essential identity and adequately contends with the absence of continuity in tracing the path from the past to the present. According to Foucault, only genealogy forsakes a "supra-historical perspective." Alluding conspicuously to Hegel, Foucault (1977, p. 152) claims that genealogical inquiry is not guaranteed by a "totality closed upon itself" or a "completed development"; it does not arrive at "the end of time."

Although Foucault is justified in emphasizing Nietzsche's anti-Hegelian commitment to historical contingency, his view obscures the shared commitments Hegel and Nietzsche have. Both phenomenology and genealogy are guided by the assumption that the best way for the present to position itself in relation to the future is to understand how the past dwells unacknowledged in the present. Both want to specify how the present has come into being, arguing that we can do this only by disentangling ourselves from the false self-understanding of the past, particularly the acceptance of opposing concepts. As projects of the psychology of knowledge, both phenomenology and genealogy direct us to our boundedness to the past and attempt to free us from the illusion of the Cartesian myth.

Phenomenology and genealogy both hinge on the process of examining the self-understanding of the past and revealing in what way it departs from reality. In particular, both phenomenology and genealogy try to work through forms of understanding that faithfully adhere to traditional opposing concepts. In Hegel and Nietzsche, there is a determination to push beyond antiquated distinctions. Hegel terms this process of working through "experience." Nietzsche does not spell out the tools of his methodology; instead, he utilizes his philological training to propose that we must read culture as a text. Nietzsche also adds a physiological dimension to this the task in his demand that we pay attention to the body and to affects. Nietzsche's attraction to the future is clearly not at the expense of interest in the past; for better or worse, his affirmation of the value of forgetting exists alongside his commitment to memory.

Finally, both phenomenology and genealogy function by means of performance: the reader measures himself in relation to what happens "on stage" and comes to understand his or her implication in this process. The reader's own self-understanding must be faced—an unsettling and challenging aspect of confronting such a work. Ultimately, I would argue that phenomenology and genealogy work according to a standard of what is plausible in a psychological sense— that is, a standard of what supports and sustains satisfaction in the lives of human beings. These methods share the process of leading us to face how the past is recapitulated in one's own identity, especially the negative effects of concealing this.

The task of seeing oneself as a product of the past must be counterbalanced by the need to distance oneself for the sake of critical reflection. This is an obvious and deep theme in Hegel's *Phenomenology of Spirit*. In Nietzsche, there is a rejectionist tone which advocates that we distance ourselves from culture. At other times, though, Nietzsche sounds surprisingly similar to Hegel:

There is great advantage to be gained in distantly estranging ourselves from our age and for once being driven as it were from its shores back to the ocean of the world-outlooks of the past. Looking back at the coast from this distance we command a view, no doubt for the first time, of its total configuration, and when we approach it again we have the advantage of understanding it better as a whole than those who have never left it. (HAH I #616)

This passage from Nietzsche's middle period (sometimes called his positivist stage, because of his attention to knowledge) is difficult to interpret. I would concede that it may not be representative of Nietzsche. Nevertheless, in this context Nietzsche refutes interpretations that one-sidedly portray him as relentlessly opposed to Hegel. On the basis of this passage, it would seem that Nietzschean perspectivism does not necessarily oppose the aspiration of grasping the whole or at least striving for an enlarged vision. Moreover, it confirms that Nietzsche does not embrace self-invention at the expense of defining ourselves in relation to culture.

The concern that motivates both Hegel's and Nietzsche's thinking— the morass of modern culture—can be transformed only by referring to the past and by tracing how we have arrived at the present from the past. To better explore this, I will shift in the next two chapters from the abstract focus on philosophy and culture to a more specific account of the dialectic between ancient and modern culture. The most prominent distant contours of the coast are, for both Hegel and Nietzsche, Aegean; thus, in chapter 3, I shall explore ancient Greek culture. In chapter 4, I shall turn to examine the nearer contours: Hegel's and Nietzsche's understanding of modern culture.

3

Ancient Greek Culture

Remember that Periclean Athens had no museum of antiques.
—Christian Gauss

Like many other German philosophers and poets of the nineteenth century, Hegel and Nietzsche greatly admired the ancient Greeks. It is neither mere adulation nor nostalgia, however, that governs their response to ancient Greek culture. Rather, they regard it as a counterpoint to modern culture. According to Hegel and Nietzsche, ancient Greek culture provides a standard. Hegel declares: "It is necessary that we appropriate the world of antiquity not only to possess it, but even more to digest and transform it." (ETW, p. 327) And Nietzsche proclaims: "To get past Hellenism by means of deeds: that would be our task. But to do that we must first know what it is." (Notes on "We Philologists," SW 7, p. 25) Both Hegel and Nietzsche affirm the value of mastering ancient Greek culture so that it may serve the present. In this chapter I will render the claim that philosophy and culture are integrally related more concrete by examining Hegel's and Nietzsche's dialectical comparison between ancient Greek culture and modern culture.

Hegel's view of ancient Greek culture evolved from unbridled enthusiasm (when he was young) to a mixed appraisal (as he formulated his own system of philosophy). At first, Hegel looked to the polis as a model of social harmony and integration. By the time of the *Phenomenology of Spirit*, however, he had come to feel that the model of the polis failed to offer an adequate safeguard for individuality. In PhS, ancient Greek culture is presented as the original stage of Spirit—the first culture that deserves serious consideration. Hegel credits ancient Greek culture as the source of culture; however, he asserts that it is deficient from a modern standpoint because it makes the untenable demand that the individual subordinate himself or herself to society. Ultimately he claims that, although his own culture still has something to learn from the Greeks, that culture has become outmoded as a realistic alternative for modern culture.

The early Hegel saw ancient Greek culture as providing the basic framework of how the individual ought to bond to society. In *Natural Law* (p. 123), Hegel compares the relation between the individual and ethical life in ancient Greek culture to the lesser relation found in (modern) contract theory: "The form of an inferior relation as the contractual one has forced its way into the absolute majesty of the ethical totality." Hegel criticizes contract theory, especially Fichte's version, for its reliance on constitutional law based on moral principles that "belong only to the sphere of the finite and the individual" (ibid., p. 124). He contrasts this to "ethical vitality," wherein "the people has a shape in which a specific character [Bestimmtheit] is present" (ibid., p. 126). Individuals are not merely bound to ethical life formally but are "united [vereint] with universality and animated [belebt] by it" (ibid.). Hegel invokes the word 'recognition' in order to conceptualize this relation.

The achievement of ancient Greek culture, thus, lies in its emphasis on the profound connection of the individual to society. In Hegel's words: "As regards ethical life, the saying of the wisest men of antiquity is alone true, that 'to be ethical is to live in accordance with the ethics [Sitten] of one's country.'" (ibid., p. 115) Insofar as one is not a citizen, the individual is "only an unreal impotent shadow (ibid., p. 270). Hegel suggests that Greek tragedy grapples with how to reconcile an individual's needs along with the needs of society, a problem that he sees as continuing to resonate with us. Although ancient Greek culture lays out this problem, we can longer accept the solution it provides.[1]

Like Hegel, Nietzsche encourages us to think about ancient Greek culture as a contrast to modern culture, and he also flirts with the idea of integrating them together. However, his view is strongly equivocal. Trained as a classical philologist, the ancient Greeks were at the center of Nietzsche's interests from his first writings. At the same time, Nietzsche does not always conceive of the relation between ancient and modern culture as subject to mediation. For example, he declares in a *Nachlass* entry from 1875 that he wishes to "produce complete hatred between our present 'culture' and ancient culture" (SW 8, p. 33). In the foreword to *On the Uses and Disadvantages of History for Life*, the point is stated more moderately: "I do not know what meaning classical studies could have for our time if they were not untimely—that is to say, acting counter to our time and thereby acting on our time and, let us hope, for the benefit of a time to come." Indeed, Nietzsche is explicit that the present is intertwined in our inquiries into the past: "Greek antiquity provides the classical set of examples for the interpretation of our entire culture and its development. It is a means for understanding ourselves, a means for regulating our age—and thereby for overcoming it." (PT, p. 127)

Nietzsche's mature view is less preoccupied with the past, but he never abandons the view that we can learn from the Greeks. Indeed, Nietzsche's affinity to ancient Greek culture, though shifting in focus, is one of the most consistent themes in his oeuvre. In his first book, Nietzsche describes the Greeks as our "luminous guides" (BT #23) and as charioteers who reign over "our own and every other culture" (BT #15). In *Twilight of the Idols*, he proclaims: "the Greeks remain the first cultural event in history: they knew, they did, what was needed" ("Skirmishes of an Untimely Man," #47). These statements suggest that Nietzsche would not disagree with Hegel's conceptualization of Greek culture as the first stage of Spirit. Let us take a closer look at the evolution of his view of the Greeks.

Nietzsche's own evaluation of his hopes about ancient Greek culture is evident in BT #4, where he acknowledges that "everything in this essay points to the future: the impending return of the Greek spirit." It is clear that Nietzsche harbored the hope that Wagnerian opera could play the role in his culture that tragedy had played in ancient Greek culture (BT #19). But it is difficult to judge how serious Nietzsche was about the prospect of such a return. In the unpublished 1875 notes on "We Philologists," Nietzsche warns: "It is not true that we can attain culture through antiquity alone." (SW 8, p. 19) His respect for the Greeks must be weighed against his belief that a genuine culture must be created; it cannot simply be imitated. Nietzsche was always attuned to the complex needs that are played out in our representations of the Greeks. On the one hand, Nietzsche is critical of the neo-classical view of the Greeks, drawing our attention to their courage in facing the terror and horror of existence. On the other hand, in D #195 he raises doubts about anyone's access to the past:

> Nothing grows clearer to me year by year than that the nature of the Greeks and of antiquity, however simple and universally familiar [weltbekannt] it may seem to lie before us, is very hard to understand, indeed is hardly accessible at all, and that the facility with which the ancients are usually spoken of is either a piece of frivolity or an inherited arrogance born of thoughtlessness. We are deceived by a similarity of words and concepts: but behind them there always lies concealed a sensation which has to be foreign, incomprehensible or painful to modern sensibility.

Nietzsche's stance here is one of hermeneutic modesty; he even ponders the incommensurability between ancients and moderns. Nonetheless, at the conclusion of the passage, a contrast between ancient and modern culture is affirmed.

Nietzsche never offers approval for the entirety of ancient Greek culture. In *The Birth of Tragedy* he differentiates between a healthy aspect of Greek culture (which he names "tragic culture") and an unhealthy aspect characterized by the overvaluation of reason ("Socratic/Alexandrian culture"). In fact, Nietzsche offers an even more differentiated characterization of ancient Greek culture, and I shall return to it later in this chapter. His interpretation stresses the point that it was the influence of the "deity" who spoke through Euripides—viz., Socrates, who harmed tragedy, and, in effect, all of Greek culture (BT #12).[2] It becomes evident that Nietzsche associates modern culture with Alexandrian culture (BT #18). Indeed, Socrates's pernicious influence on tragedy has ongoing ramifications: it fosters a love of knowledge in intellectuals that serves as a defense against strong affects.

For Nietzsche, as well as for Hegel, ancient Greek culture provided genuine satisfaction for those who lived within that society. The disparity between culture and society that exists in modernity did not exist for the Greeks: to put it ironically, the Greeks were so cultured that they did not need culture. Perhaps Nietzsche sums up the appeal of Greek culture for both thinkers in his claim that the Greeks were "superficial out of profundity" (GS, preface to second edition). They managed to attain a joyousness of spirit that contrasts with the "hunger" and "thirst" of modern culture.

In one convoluted passage in *The Will To Power* (#419), Nietzsche discusses the "homesickness" he detects in the attitude of German philosophy toward the Greeks. Aligning himself with Leibniz, Kant, Schopenhauer, and Hegel, Nietzsche argues for giving up the kind of retrospection propagated by German philosophy.[3] The wish to connect with the Greeks by means of a "rainbow bridge" is a fantasy, yet, it turns out, that is not necessarily impossible. "To be sure," Nietzsche remarks, "one must be very subtle, very light, very thin to step across theses bridges!" Nietzsche then reverses himself and expresses hope for the rejuvenation of German philosophy and culture through Greek culture:

A few centuries hence, perhaps, one will judge that all German philosophy derives its real dignity from being a gradual reclamation of the soil of antiquity, and that all claims to 'originality' must sound petty and ludicrous in relation to that higher claim of the Germans to have joined anew the bond that seemed to be broken, the bond with the Greeks, the hitherto highest type of man. (WP #419)

This passage is clearly offered in a different spirit from the above-quoted passage from *Daybreak*, which stipulates our remoteness from the Greeks. It is consistent, though, with Nietzsche's goal of bringing the ancient and the modern together. This goal, however worthy, must confront the fact that, as Nietzsche speculates, "the German Reformation" may have fatally injured the prospect of achieving it, having "perhaps rendered the complete growing-together of the spirit of antiquity and the modern spirit impossible forever" (HAH I #237). Whereas in *The Birth of Tragedy* Nietzsche embraces the hope that the Apollonian and the Dionysian can be reunited, in his later work he insistently pits the joyousness of the Dionysian spirit against the hostility to life he finds in Christianity.

In his later work, Nietzsche is dubious about the prospect of reclaiming ancient Greek culture for the present because of his adamant opposition to German culture. As he becomes preoccupied with imagining a future liberated from Christianity, he is less inclined to distance himself from any models from the past. Thus, for independent reasons, Hegel and Nietzsche eventually move away from claiming that it is possible to actualize what they admire about the ancient Greeks. Still, for both thinkers self-fathoming is at stake in articulating a contrast between ancient and modern culture. More specifically, Hegel and Nietzsche focus on Greek tragedy in order to ground their understanding of ancient Greek culture. Thus, tragedy occupies a privileged position from which the Greeks can be glimpsed reflecting on themselves.

3.1 Reconciling Hegelian Tragedy

In Hegel's earliest writings, Greek tragedy is of fundamental importance. Tragedy provides a model of reconciliation between the individual and the community that is linked to Christian reconciliation. In *The Spirit of Christianity* (1798–1800), Hegel presents tragedy as offering a model of reconciliation in a social, political, and religious sense that is allied with, and even supplements, that of Christianity; both tragic and Christian reconciliation are juxtaposed with the alleged harshness of Judaic law. In *Natural Law* (1802–03), tragedy plays an even more significant role. "Tragedy in the realm of the ethical" is invoked as a description of the negative element in tragedy, transgression, which Hegel uses to explicate the dilemma of modern society, where conflict interferes with the individual's sense of bonding to others in society.[4] Both moments of conflict and reconciliation are integral to Hegel's view of tragedy in PhS.

Before examining Hegel's definition of tragedy, I want to make a few brief comments about its place within PhS. As consciousness embarks on its journey to self-knowledge, Hegel's philosophical project expands from the domain of epistemological inquiry to the explicit inclusion of socio-cultural concerns. The Geist chapter denotes a crucial moment in Hegel's project away from the depiction of "shapes of consciousness" (which are abstract) to "shapes of the world" (which are concrete and historical) (p. 265). In its actual embodiments, Geist engages in the pursuit of mutual recognition. Greek tragedy is one such embodiment—the first that Hegel contemplates. In the background, we should keep in mind that the preface outlines the absence of mutual recognition that characterizes modern culture. Greek tragedy is introduced in the first section of the Geist chapter, The Ethical Order, which concerns the ancient world.[5] It is subsequently treated in the second section of the Religion chapter, Art-Religion.[6]

Tragedy, according to Hegel, can be defined in terms of a collision that passes into reconciliation via pathos. Collision is a result of conflicts involving pairs of opposites: the human and the divine, the male and the female, the ethical and the natural, the universal and the individual, and the state and the family. Tragedy exhibits a special concern for conflicts of an ethical and social dimension, revealed in the opposition between right and right (or wrong and wrong), as opposed to the more simplistic formulation of right versus wrong. By portraying collision in terms of "powers," Hegel magnifies the sense in which tragedy involves opposing principles. Thus, he has often been criticized for minimizing the significance of the role of character in tragedy.[7] There is some basis for this criticism, as is evident when Hegel argues that "it is not this particular individual who acts and is guilty; for as this self he is only the unreal shadow, or he exists merely as a universal self, and individuality is purely the formal moment of the action as such" (p. 282). It is quite misleading, however, to overlook that Hegel sees the collision as taking place within the protagonist as well as, more abstractly, between the demands of the state and the demands of the family.[8]

Antigone is the paradigmatic example throughout Hegel's discussion of tragedy in PhS.[9] The character of Antigone embodies the "natural" recognition between brother and sister that is seen as a foundation of ethical order [Sittlichkeit]. The collision is generated after Polyneices is killed by Eteocles, his brother. Antigone, their sister, resolves to bury Polyneices despite the state's edict, issued by Creon, that prohibits her doing so. "Ethical" recognition, which describes a bond among citizens, is seen as a higher stage that stands opposed to the "natural" recognition, which describes a bond among family members. Tragedy dwells in the movement from natural to ethical recognition. As the first stage of Spirit, tragedy represents an initial attempt to achieve mutual recognition, where the self struggles to know itself as well as to adhere to external norms.

In Hegel's view of tragedy, pathos ensues from the collision. Pathos is a result of tragic error (hamartia), which belongs to the protagonist, and is abetted by guilt (stemming from hamartia) and destiny. What is tragic in Greek tragedy, according to Hegel, is the paradox of voluntary acknowledgement of guilt on the part of the protagonist—despite the arbitrary force of destiny. Acknowledgement of guilt by the protagonist heightens the importance of self-recognition.[10] Self-recognition, according to Hegel, precipitates reconciliation on the social level for the protagonist.

Reconciliation, in the most complete sense, is achieved only with the aid of the spectator via the dramatist. This becomes evident because of Hegel's insistence on a negative outcome for the protagonist regardless of his or her self-recognition. In contrast to his later view in the *Aesthetics*, Hegel declares here (p. 258) that "only in the downfall of both sides alike is absolute right accomplished, and the ethical substance as the negative power which engulfs both sides, that is, omnipotent and righteous Destiny, steps on the scene."[11] The protagonist must be destroyed, despite the fact that confrontation with death, as Hegel observes, is a formative experience. Reconciliation in Greek tragedy means that the universal (that is, both the social and the cosmic order) prevails over the individual. While Hegel sees the subordination of the individual as the essential characteristic of ancient Greek culture, he also appreciates that tragedy hints at the emergence of the individual as an individual. In emphasizing conflict and the destruction of the protagonist, we can also observe that Hegel's attraction to the Greeks departs from the placidly beautiful, neo-classical image.

Pöggeler (1973, p. 91) argues that by the time of PhS tragedy has receded in importance for Hegel, occupying a position of merely historical significance. He maintains that tragic reconciliation is supplanted by the image of the Golgotha of Spirit, which is explicitly introduced at the end of PhS. Correspondingly, Pöggeler notes that Hegel's tragic archetype changes from Aeschylus's *Oresteia* in the early writings, where reconciliation is clearly affirmed, to Sophocles's *Antigone*, where reconciliation is mixed and must be measured against the protagonist's death (ibid., p. 91). There is no doubt that by the time of PhS Hegel has moved away from his youthful homage to the

Greek polis as a viable model for modern society.[12] In addition, it is true that Hegel's discontentment with the invocation of destiny in tragedy increases as he becomes committed to the explanatory power of philosophy. Yet this does not mean that tragedy assumes a position of merely historical importance. As Menke (1996, p. 73) has maintained, the conflict between Recht and the individual anticipates the very problem that Hegel finds in modern culture.

The formulation in *Natural Law* of the problematic relationship between the individual and society, conceptualized as "tragedy in the realm of the ethical," does not fully account for Hegel's interest in tragedy. It becomes evident in PhS that what is paramount for Hegel about tragedy is self-recognition, whereby self-knowledge is achieved. The overall project in PhS, which will be explored in chapters 6–8, depicts the experience of consciousness as it comes to know itself as Spirit. Thus, Hegel's understanding of Greek tragedy must be appreciated contextually as a moment within this journey to self-knowledge.

Hegel's discussion of Greek tragedy does not ignore self-knowledge. He describes the tragic hero in terms of "the antithesis of knowing and not knowing" (PhS, p. 446) and maintains that tragedy presents consciousness which has "followed its own way of knowing and concealed from itself what was openly revealed" (p. 448). The collision ensues, at least in part, as a manifestation of this self-division within the protagonist. Oedipus is as relevant here as Antigone:

Actuality therefore holds concealed within it the other aspect which is alien to this knowledge, and does not reveal the whole truth about itself to consciousness: the son does not recognize his father in the man who has wronged him and whom he slays, nor his mother in the queen whom he makes his wife. In this way, a power which shuns the light of day ensnares the ethical self-consciousness, a power which breaks forth only after the deed is done, and seizes the doer in the act. For the accomplished deed is the removal [aufgehobene] of the antithesis between the knowing self and the actuality confronting it. (PhS, p. 283)

It is clear that tragedy depicts a struggle within the protagonist for self-knowledge, not simply a struggle between the protagonist and others. The protagonist must overcome a lack of self-knowledge in order for tragic reconciliation to occur. Self-knowledge means that one is no longer self-divided and that one affirms the knowledge of oneself as bound to others in society.

An explication of Hegel's view of tragedy, however, supplies only a partial basis upon which to evaluate the influence of tragedy in PhS. It is evident that the Sittlichkeit of the Greek world is regarded as outmoded in the modern world. It is also clear that Art-Religion is regarded as inferior to Revealed Religion (Christianity). Yet tragedy in PhS has a significance that is both subtle and pervasive. Szondi (1986, p. 54) astutely suggests that "the *Phenomenology* places the Tragic (though without calling it by that term) in the center of the Hegelian philosophy." Szondi emphasizes the ethical and social problems presented in tragedy; he also stresses the collateral influence of Schelling and Hölderlin on Hegel. Indeed, during the early period of German Idealism tragedy was not comprehended from a purely aesthetic perspective. It was viewed from a metaphysical perspective as a means of representing truth, from a social perspective as a vision of a good society, from a religious perspective as disclosing the divine presence in the world, and from a moral perspective as offering a model of freedom through struggle that serves as an alternative to Kantian morality.

By the time of PhS, Hegel had distanced himself from Schelling and Hölderlin in the name of expounding philosophy systematically as science (Szondi 1974).[13] Yet Hegel describes the goal of PhS in the preface as "actual knowing" as opposed to "love of knowing." It would be extravagant to imply that the goal of Hegel's project resembles the goal originally articulated by Herder and Schiller of creating a comparable form of drama for one's own culture that might have the same impact that Greek tragedy had in ancient Greece. Nor can one maintain that Hegel was attempting to write for "future festivals of the Fatherland," as Hölderlin hoped to do.[14] Nevertheless, as both Menke and Szondi emphasize, the transgression that is inherent in tragedy represents an abiding thorn in the side of negotiating a balance between the individual and the legitimate demands of society. Tragedy provides a glimpse of how self-thwarting is necessarily a part of self-fathoming, although self-fathoming only comes into existence in modern culture. Hegel regards tragedy as an outmoded form of reconciliation for the modern world; nonetheless, it resonates throughout PhS, reminding us of the threat of conflict and failure. PhS is a compelling work because its defense of philosophy is not contained within the usual limits of philosophical exposition. As I shall argue in an excursus at the end of this chapter, one can understand PhS on a deeper level by reflecting on how it incorporates Greek tragedy.

3.2 Living with Nietzschean Tragedy

Nietzsche's view of tragedy is similar to Hegel's in that it entails conflict and then reconciliation via pathos. Here the conflict is between two opposing artistic impulses, which spring from nature and are named after gods: the Apollonian and the Dionysian. The Apollonian is associated with dreams and illusion—the realm of appearance in general. It affirms beauty, defends individuation, and provides order to tragedy. The Apollonian sets limits; in seeking moderation, it has a ready connection to wisdom and philosophy. The Dionysian introduces an element that is not accounted for in Hegel's view of tragedy. It is associated with ecstasy and intoxication—with the realm of primitive instinct. Its function is to examine "the innermost heart of things" by directly facing what is painful and contradictory in life. The Dionysian embraces a primal unity in which one is liberated from individual will. The Dionysian represents limitlessness; it seeks out and revels in excess.

According to Nietzsche, tragedy thrives when the Apollonian and Dionysian impulses can compete and flourish. It forges the healthy "tragic culture" celebrated in *The Birth of Tragedy*. In addition to the main contrast between tragic culture and Socratic/Alexandrian culture, referred to earlier in this chapter, Nietzsche makes several more distinctions concerning the evolution of Greek culture. He delineates four distinct stages of art: Titanic culture, where the Dionysian spirit first led the Greeks to portray the gods (the Titans) as a way of coming to terms with barbarism and the horror of existence; Homeric culture, where the Apollonian spirit prevails, organizing and celebrating the radiance of the Olympian pantheon; Dionysian culture, where the Dionysian spirit from outside of Greece returned in the form of festivals with the purpose of glimpsing the abyss through intoxication and excess; and Doric culture, where a "permanent military encampment of the Apollonian" occurs, which Nietzsche rejects as the pinnacle of artistic achievement (BT #3 and #4).[15] In each of these four stages, either the Dionysian or the Apollonian prevails. Each stage is one-sided—a reaction to the previous stage.

Only tragic culture manages to bear the weight of both the Dionysian and the Apollonian at the same time. The "fraternal union" of the Dionysian and the Apollonian results, not in agreement, but in a reciprocal mutuality: "Dionysus speaks the language of Apollo; and Apollo, finally the language of Dionysus." (BT #21)

Let us take a closer look at how Nietzsche conceives of the relationship between the Apollonian and the Dionysian. First of all, they form a delicate balance, which is easily undone. Second, although they condition each other, this does not imply a synthesis.[16] At one point, Nietzsche does inform us that the "antithesis" between the Apollonian and the Dionysian is "sublimated [aughehoben] into a unity," yet this statement occurs in his reflection on *The Birth of Tragedy* in *Ecce Homo*, where Nietzsche self-consciously parodies the Hegelian leanings that he detects in his first book. Coexistence between the Dionysian and Apollonian impulses is fragile; integration can occur, but the two impulses remain unstable.

Nietzsche suggests that the distinction between the Apollonian and the Dionysian embodies the contrast between the old Chthonic gods and the new Olympian gods. The older gods, including Dionysus, emerged from a rural folk religion that had a more intimate connection to nature. The Olympians, including Apollo, represent an aristocratic world and hence signify the reign of culture over nature. As was noted in chapter 2, Nietzsche wants to stress that culture includes natural forces as well as civilized ones; being cultured does not have to mean leaving nature behind. Although Nietzsche's representation of the ancient meaning of these two figures is, for the most part, fair-minded, Silk and Stern (1981) point out that the association of Apollo with appearance and illusion is somewhat of a projection on Nietzsche's part. They suggest (p. 171) that this allows for a clear-cut contrast with the Dionysian, which reveals the underlying truth of life. May (1990, p. 4) adds that there is not much evidence for Nietzsche's link between the Apollonian and the *principium individuationis*.

Nietzsche uses the distinction between the Dionysian and the Apollonian not only as a way to characterize tragedy but also in an attempt to fathom art and all of culture. He elevates the distinction as the key to understanding the achievements of the ancient Greek culture and, by way of contrast, the deficiency of modern culture.

Nietzsche's hope for the rejuvenation of art in his own world hangs on the distinction between the Dionysian and the Apollonian. The distinction allows Nietzsche to press his case that tragedy, which has its source in music, conveys deeper truths than philosophy, which restricts communication to words and rationality. In contrast to Hegel, Nietzsche does not think that tragedy aspires to be philosophy. Nor does Nietzsche agree that philosophy is superior to art as a form of articulation. "Perhaps," he exclaims, "there is a realm of wisdom from which the logician is exiled." (BT #14) For Nietzsche, tragedy represents wisdom, and wisdom demands that we accept the limitations of knowledge.[17]

Nietzsche dwells on conflict and pathos in tragedy, and especially on the element of transgression. Transgression is understood as an expression of the Dionysian love of excess; it is part of life, and not merely a negative experience. The suffering of the hero inspires us to have the courage to glimpse the truth of life in all its horror and terror. Reconciliation takes place by virtue of the "metaphysical comfort" derived from tragedy (BT #7). Yet Nietzsche warns against inflated, moralistic interpretations of reconciliation. He is dismayed by the encroachment of philosophy upon tragedy, which he traces to Euripides's having smuggled the views of Socrates into his plays. Committed to rationality and to the fantasy of understanding everything, the Socratic influence leads tragedy to commit suicide. Euripides's introduction of a Socratic influence is specifically located in the notion that the beautiful can be defined in terms of the intelligible (BT #11, #12). Since the beautiful belongs to the aim of the Apollonian impulse, the Apollonian is displaced, and tragedy becomes a competition between the Socratic and the Dionysian—whose opposition ruins the delicate tension that had existed and undermines wisdom.

What Nietzsche finds interesting about tragedy is that it frames mystery and horror in such a way that a radical self-confrontation can take place for the protagonist and for the spectator. This experience is not really a matter of self-knowledge. Nietzsche affirms the limitations of rationality; he even raises the suspicion that reason has a deleterious effect on all of culture. Rationality as espoused by Socrates is hostile toward myth. According to Nietzsche, myth is crucial for the well-being of culture: ". . . without myth, every culture loses the healthy natural power of its creativity" (BT #23). Myth transports us beyond the everyday world of experience. Euripides's use of the chorus especially disturbs Nietzsche because it brings the ordinary citizen up on stage and thereby strikes a blow against the elevated status of tragedy.

The democratizing tendency that Nietzsche detects in Socrates's philosophy contributes to the undoing of tragedy. Intelligibility, Socrates's central commitment, must be open to anyone who can exercise the capacity to reason. To borrow the terminology Nietzsche uses in *On the Genealogy of Morals*: aristocrats suffered no such inhibitions in their elitist valuation, simply believing that the good ought to be defined in terms of themselves—the good is us (GM I #2). Philosophy, under the banner of love of truth, ushers in a universal valuation that attempts to disguise that it too is a moral valuation. Originally, Nietzsche maintains, tragedy was free of the preoccupation with morality.

Does this mean that Nietzsche neglects the social and political relevance of tragedy in the life of the city? Silk and Stern (1981, p. 284) suggest that Nietzsche downplays this element because his interpretation dwells so much on the experience of the individual. McGinn (1975, pp. 90–91) has argued, however, that Nietzsche at least points to the political implications of tragedy. One example of how this is the case is found in Nietzsche's assertion in BT #21 that "it is the people of the tragic mysteries that fights the battles against the Persians; and the people that fought these wars in turn needs tragedy as a necessary potion to recover." In this passage, tragedy is seen as a function of a particular social and political climate: as both the source and the product of Athens's strength. Nonetheless, it remains awkward for Nietzsche to handle the social and political elements in tragedy, as he concedes in his self-critique in *Ecce Homo*. The lawless intensity of the spirit of Dionysus shows no deference to the social and political order.

A perplexing aspect of Nietzsche's account of Greek tragedy is its lack of attention to specific examples. It is the categories of the Dionysian and the Apollonian that guide his interpretation. Yet the figures Nietzsche does mention, Antigone and Cassandra, are telling. Cassandra, the barbarian (i.e., Trojan) prophetess who is brought back by Agamemnon from Troy and murdered by Clytemnestra, can be identified with the Dionysian spirit. She gives voice to the irrational in Aeschylus's *Agamemnon*, speaking an affective language that sounds like nonsense. Significantly, too, she is the enemy of Apollo. Nietzsche counterbalances Hegel's view of tragedy, which focuses mainly on Antigone, by adding the Dionysian character of Cassandra. It is probable that Nietzsche would assess the Hegelian account of tragedy as mainly Apollonian, urging us to abide by limits and to seek self-knowledge. Although Hegel does pay attention to the element of transgression, his affinity for the Socratic legacy is troubling to Nietzsche.

Nietzsche's reflections on *The Birth of Tragedy* in *Ecce Homo* include the amusing comment that it "smells offensively Hegelian." One can hypothesize that Nietzsche is referring to the dialectic of opposing principles that guides his definition of tragedy. Perhaps he also is alluding to the threefold dialectical schema he uses to trace the origins, the development, and the decline of tragedy. Nietzsche praises his work for showcasing a "psychological analysis" of Dionysian experience that focuses on the experience of the individual who willingly abandons individuality in order to affirm a bond to life itself. Thus, Nietzsche departs from Hegel's view of tragedy, especially when he associates affirming rationality with undermining life.

The death of Greek tragedy, according to Nietzsche, is tragic: Euripides's appropriation of Socratism results in suicide. Nietzsche's own later assessment of *The Birth of Tragedy* reveals a tragic side to his self-interpretation, as if the influence of Hegel on Nietzsche had repeated the deleterious influence of Socrates on tragedy. The Dionysian and the Apollonian are forces within Nietzsche's work, not just forces that operate in tragedy. Indeed, just as tragedy calls the spectator to acknowledge Dionysus, *The Birth of Tragedy* calls upon the reader to do the same.

Nietzsche's musings about the Hegelian smell of *The Birth of Tragedy* must be placed alongside his comments about his having been too influenced at the time he wrote the work by the "cadaverous per-fume" of Schopenhauer's un-Greek pessimism (EH, "The Birth of Tragedy," #1). Philosophy is regarded, on this account, as obstructing and distorting tragedy. Appropriately, the haunting and diffuse Hegelian influence is smelled; it is not manifest to our eyes or to our touch. In his later assessment of *The Birth of Tragedy*, Nietzsche men-tions smell again in connection with Dionysus's opposition to deca-dence. In his later work in general, Nietzsche adopts the symbol of Dionysus to describe his own philosophy, banishing the countervail-ing force of the Apollonian as well as that of Socrates.

Nietzsche passes over the idea that recognition is constitutive of tragedy, and he does not see tragedy as providing justification for the moral and social order. Tragedy concerns the individual qua individ-ual, who, gaping into the abyss of meaninglessness, opts to affirm the value of human life.[18] It is through aesthetics that this metaphysical experience occurs. This is the basis of what Nietzsche terms "tragic culture." Although Nietzsche believes that tragedy exemplifies Greek culture, he does not pay much attention to the function of tragedy as a social institution—precisely what is of major importance to Hegel.

3.3 Antigone vs. Cassandra?

To some extent, the differences in Hegel's and Nietzsche's respective eras help to account for the different emphases in their assessments of Greek tragedy. Hegel lived under the shadow of neo-classicism, but at the same time his friend Hölderlin was moving to articulate a more original interpretation of ancient Greek texts.[19] Nietzsche was con-scious of being an epigone, and as much as he rejects neo-classicism, he muses that after Goethe, Schiller, and Winckelmann "the endeavor to attain to culture and to the Greeks on the same path has grown incomprehensibly feebler and feebler" (BT #20). Nietzsche under-takes a more radical interpretation of ancient Greek culture than Hegel, yet his deconstruction of the neo-classical image of the Greeks is anticipated to a degree by Hegel.

Despite their different emphases, Hegel and Nietzsche concur that the truth of ancient Greek culture can be grasped in tragedy. They

find in tragedy a commitment to human flourishing that has no counterpart in modern culture. Both are fascinated by how tragedy func-
tioned as a religious ritual that, at the same time, was about the
culture. They disagree, however, as to whether tragedy is addressed to
the spectator qua citizen (Hegel) or qua human being (Nietzsche).
Indeed, Hegel tends to ignore what Nietzsche highlights: that tragedy
forces humans to face the deep, uncomfortable questions about contingency and meaninglessness. Hegel is uncomfortable with the role
that destiny plays in tragedy precisely because it suggests that there
are limits to our capacity to understand and control the world.
Bernard Williams puts it eloquently (1993, p. 164): "Greek tragedy
precisely refuses to present human beings who are ideally in harmony
with their world, and has no room for a world that, if it were understood well enough, could instruct us how to be in harmony with it."
Hegel's main concern is with the socio-political implications of
tragedy. This does not mean that he overlooks the individual as an
individual, but he does not treat the human dimension of tragedy
adequately. He does not show much interest in how tragedy engages
our emotions, both in the sense of moving us to feel and in the sense
of encouraging us to be familiar with our emotions.

Correspondingly, Nietzsche fails to grapple with the implications of
tragedy as an actual social institution—precisely what is most important for Hegel. Current theories of tragedy lend support to Hegel by
warning against viewing tragedy in aesthetic terms and thereby underestimating its socio-cultural function. As Longo (1990, p. 16) puts it:
"The dramatic spectacle was one of the rituals that deliberately aimed
at maintaining social identity and reinforcing the cohesion of the
group." Nietzsche's aestheticizing of tragedy is due, I suspect, to his
failure to distinguish sufficiently between what it means for us to
receive tragedy and what it meant to the ancient Greeks. As Nietzsche
came to understand, the fantasy of a Wagnerian resuscitation of
German culture had interfered with his view of tragedy.

There is a certain one-sidedness to both Hegel's and Nietzsche's
views of tragedy.[20] Moreover, their views seem to counterbalance each
other, and, thus, one might well consider that an ideal theory of
tragedy would manage to integrate both of them. Though this is an

interesting possibility, I shall only offer a few reflections here.[21] I do not think that the alleged one-sidedness of Hegel's and Nietzsche's views can be fully accounted for in terms of the former's Apollonian leanings vs. the latter's Dionysian leanings. As I have maintained, although it is true that Nietzsche does not pay sufficient attention to the socio-political aspects of tragedy, he does acknowledge that this is a lack in his theory. And although Hegel endorses reconciliation, there are glimpses that he appreciates the tragic wisdom that Nietzsche favors. Hegel vindicates philosophy over tragedy, but he borrows from tragedy; Nietzsche vindicates tragedy over philosophy, yet he does speculate about the prospect of "an artistic Socrates" [eines künstlerischen Sokrates]—that is, a new kind of philosophy that might combine the tragic and the philosophical (BT #14).

Although there are important differences between Hegel and Nietzsche, both judge modern culture's lack of a counterpart to Greek tragedy unfortunate. Tragedy offers a contrast as well as a challenge to modern culture. Both Hegel and Nietzsche try to incorporate tragedy in their philosophical responses to their own culture. As I will discuss in the excursus at the end of this chapter, in many ways Hegel's PhS resembles a tragedy. Nietzsche carries out his own enactment in BT #3; the extent of his investment in tragedy is evident from his self-designation as "the first tragic philosopher." Greek culture furnished satisfaction for the Greeks in a way that inspires respect. For Hegel, the satisfaction provided by Greek culture is unworkable for modern culture; for Nietzsche, the eternal value of Dionysian experience must be reclaimed.

Both thinkers openly acknowledge that their narrative accounts of how "we" differ from "them" marks the gravity of the problems of modern culture. At the same time, this contrast serves to offer a place to begin to think through this difference. The dialogue between ancient and modern culture, as we will see in the following chapter, is meant to contribute to healing modern culture; it contributes to the formulation of an alternative model beyond the Cartesian myth. To imagine that culture can be excluded as irrelevant to philosophy condemns philosophy to be only about itself—a manifestation of the problem that both Hegel and Nietzsche sought to overcome.

Excursus on the Phenomenology of Spirit and Tragedy

The *Phenomenology of Spirit* resembles Greek tragedy in a number of ways. This does not mean that Hegel intended to write a tragedy; it means only that Hegel borrows from tragedy and appropriates it for his own (philosophical) purposes. In this excursus, I shall investigate and specify the resemblance between PhS and tragedy, although in doing so, I would not dispute that there are also many ways that PhS differs from Greek tragedy. Tragedy is "digested and altered" by Hegel; its pervasive influence in PhS is not necessarily transparent. In conceiving of PhS in terms of this pervasive influence, I will extend the argument I made in the chapter: that it is mistaken to assume that tragedy is reduced to having merely a historical importance for Hegel.

The general arc of movement in PhS, as in tragedy, is from ignorance to knowledge, where knowledge is a matter of self-knowledge. Self-knowledge in Hegel is based on self-recognition (a concept that will be explored in detail in chapter 6) and, more generally, self-fathoming (introduced in chapter 2). Self-knowledge through recognition has a dual connotation just as it does in tragedy: self-identity (where there is no longer a disparity between the knower and what is known) and the acknowledgement of the self as socially constituted (where the self is defined as fundamentally related to others in society). Self-knowledge in PhS, as in tragedy, heals self-division and moves toward a reconciliation, whereby an abiding connection to society is affirmed.

Just as Orestes, Antigone, and Oedipus all are social outcasts at some point, PhS depicts several stages of consciousness in which the individual asserts himself and ends up in an alienated state, cut off from a connection to the universal order. "Unhappy Consciousness" (as this stage is called in the chapter on Self-Consciousness) occurs after the initial experience of failed recognition as consciousness first confronts an object that is itself another consciousness. "Deranged Consciousness" in the chapter on Reason and "Lacerated Consciousness" in the chapter on Geist can be understand as variations on Unhappy Consciousness. Hegel describes Unhappy Consciousness as "the tragic fate of the certainty of self that aims to be absolute" (p. 455).

Hegel regards self-knowledge as a harmonious and peaceful state characterized by "supreme freedom" and "assurance" (p. 491). He elaborates (p. 492): "The self-knowing Spirit knows not only itself but also the negative of itself or its limit: to know one's limit is to know how to sacrifice oneself." Self-knowledge can be achieved only by passing through the entire movement of PhS, including the stages of Unhappy Consciousness. Hegel's notion of self-knowledge suggests the ideal of the tragic hero who has pushed past limits and has sacrificed himself—which results in the need to establish and abide by limits.

Self-knowledge for Hegel is a distinctively human endeavor, enabling us to demarcate, for example, the human world from the animal world. More precisely, self-knowledge serves a dual function. On the one hand, it belongs to the experience of the single individual and aids in the process of acquiring self-determination and individuation. On the other hand, it fosters a bond between the individual and others. As Hegel writes in the preface (p. 43): "For it is the nature of humanity to press onward to agreement with others; human nature only really exists in an achieved community of minds. The anti-human, the merely animal, consists in staying within the sphere of feeling, and being able to communicate only at that level." Hegel conceives of self-knowledge in a way that distances itself from the Cartesian myth, which is based on abstract, single agency—dirempted from the social realm and apparently indifferent to satisfaction. Yet, insofar as Hegel thinks of self-knowledge as fostering autonomy, we can observe a difference between his own view and the view that he ascribes to tragedy. According to Hegel, tragedy requires the subordination of the individual to society and thus cannot satisfy the modern demands of freedom.

Structuralist interpretations of tragedy suggest that it both defines and celebrates the human, and that being human is defined by overcoming the danger of two extremes. The extremes are the *pharmakos*, an animal-like being filled with potent irrational desires that threaten the social order, and the *tyrannos*, a god-like being who is filled with hubris, making him a threat to both the social order and the gods.[22] Both the pharmakos and the tyrannos are at odds with "human nature" and "an achieved community of minds." In PhS, self-knowledge cannot be achieved when consciousness operates as "being-for-itself" (Hegel's phenomenological language describing a consciousness that is motivated by its own self-interest—a state that corresponds especially to the pharmakos).[23] This threat is first presented as implicit in Desire (at the beginning of the chapter on Self-Consciousness), where consciousness attempts simply to devour its objects. Consciousness then confronts another consciousness for the first time. Not surprisingly, this encounter evolves into a full-fledged conflict—the life-and-death struggle.[24]

Nor can Hegelian self-knowledge be achieved when consciousness purports to be something more than human—e.g., as the master who rules over the slave and places himself over the quintessentially human activity of work. For Hegel, the god-like pretension of the master is especially evident in the case of the Roman emperor—"the lord of the world" (p. 293). Perhaps the threat of being tyrannos can be discerned in all the postures of self-certainty in PhS. By contrast, progress toward self-knowledge is made in PhS when mediation occurs; consciousness faces itself and chooses to place limitations on its omnipotence—in particular, that it includes being-for-another in its self-understanding, as well as being-for-itself.

The resemblance of PhS to Greek tragedy is not simply a matter of a common denouement—self-knowledge. It is also be located in the process of achieving it. To be more specific, self-knowledge in PhS occurs through a process of interaction and struggle. Interaction signifies that consciousness's self-understanding is necessarily transformed in encountering other consciousnesses. In this connection, it is worth recalling Aristotle's belief (*Poetics*, 52a35f) that it is preferable for tragic recognition (anagnorisis) to occur through interaction with others, rather than through interaction with inanimate things or facts. One also should not overlook how defining the interactions are for Oedipus's self-knowledge in *Oedipus Tyrannos*—with Creon, Tiresias, the Corinthian messenger, the shepherd, and, of course, Jocasta. What Oedipus does alone, answering the riddle of the sphinx, may be contrasted to his search for the murderer of Laos, which requires the aid of others.[25]

Struggle is manifest at every stage in PhS, especially in consciousness's first traumatic encounter with another consciousness. The struggle that emerges highlights consciousness's willingness to risk itself in death, which, as has been mentioned, is featured in Hegel's interpretation of tragedy. The struggle in PhS has a destructive aspect, indicated by the life-and-death struggle. Although death is a possible outcome, it does not occur in Hegel's scenario. Instead, the struggle yields the master-slave relationship—a distorted form of recognition. In general, the positive value of struggle is manifest as consciousness propels itself on the way to greater self-knowledge. In the language I introduced in chapter 2, self-fathoming is impossible without self-thwarting. Steadfastness is required as consciousness proceeds along a path that is as winding as it is long.

PhS resembles tragedy on a structural level, where the elements of narrative and performance join with the process of interaction and struggle to promote self-knowledge. Narrative guides consciousness, not merely to move forward when a given stage proves inadequate, but it also helps consciousness to comprehend how each stage is related to what came before.[26] The element of performance is introduced in the beginning, where Hegel draws attention to PhS as a self-enacted journey, insisting that consciousness will move itself along the way. Four structural elements can be distinguished in PhS: consciousness (the abstract designation for the subject of experience in the work), the we (a voice differentiated from both Hegel's own voice and consciousness, which is never precisely defined), the author (Hegel), and the reader (us). These four elements can be compared to the four elements of tragedy: consciousness as the protagonist, the we as the chorus, the author (Hegel) as the dramatist, and the reader as the spectator.

Consciousness, like the protagonist, is the featured presence on stage—the subject of the ostensive "aboutness" of the work. It is consciousness, for example, whose experience most obviously culminates with self-knowledge. The we of PhS, like the tragic chorus, interacts with the featured presence; yet, its role is probably best understood in terms of a mediating function in two senses: between consciousness and Hegel and also between consciousness and the reader. Hegel utilizes the introduction, before the "performance" begins, to vow to remain at a distance and not interfere with the experience of consciousness ("all that is left for us to do is simply to look on" (p. 54)). Consciousness and the we share something in appearing on stage and are thus distinguishable from both Hegel and the reader.

One cannot assume, however, that consciousness and the we are identical. The latter often functions as observers to the main action. At least sometimes, the we does not undergo experience at the same time as consciousness. Some have gone so far as to identify the we and the author, just as Sophoclean choruses have been accused of serving as the mouthpiece for Sophocles's own views. Hegel commentators Hyppolite and Kroner have argued that the best way to understand the we is as inclusive of Hegel and any other phenomenologists, i.e. those who have successfully accomplished the journey of consciousness (Hyppolite 1974, p. 290f; Kroner 1921, volume 2, pp. 369–370).

Both the we and the reader are in a position of reacting to consciousness. The we and the reader are removed from the main action, although the we cannot actually exempt itself as it is a part of the work. Moreover, the we has the function of helping to direct the reader to his or her own implication in the work. The we and the reader can also be identified in terms of their plurality as witnesses, in contrast to the singularity of consciousness. Of course, as consciousness develops, it redefines itself to be both singular (an I) and plural (part of a We). As a specific illustration in tragedy, it has been suggested that in Euripides's plays, the role of the chorus and the spectator are fused. Among Hegel commentators, Lukàcs (1976, pp. 46–54) and Findlay (foreword to PhG, p. viii) have identified the we with the reader, interpreting the former as "phenomenological students."[27]

The most important aspect of the structural parallel between PhS and tragedy is revealed in the role of the reader-spectator, and, more specifically, in the relationship between consciousness-protagonist and the reader-spectator. Through the means of narrative and performance, the subject of both PhS and Greek tragedy is transformed—shifting from what happens "on stage" to incorporate what happens "off stage." Let me elaborate on how this works in Greek tragedy and then return to PhS.

In its capacity as a social institution, tragedy requires the spectator to measure himself or herself against the experience of the protagonist (Vernant 1981, pp. vi–x). The success of the tragedy depends on the degree to which the spectator can see himself in the experience of the protagonist. This does not have to be taken too literally. Given that Oedipus's actions are extremes, the spectator probably does not need to identify with him in the sense of imagining himself committing the same crimes. Perhaps it is sufficient if the spectator identifies with Oedipus in the sense of affirming that a bond is shared (viz., being human), regardless of how atrocious Oedipus's crimes are. For the purposes of tragedy, being human means avoiding the extremes of sub-humanity (pharmakos) or supra-humanity (tyrannos).

It is possible, therefore, to ascribe recognition to the spectator; that is, to see it as following upon and being prompted by the recognition of the protagonist.[28] This is especially true if katharsis is understood to include a cognitive aspect: where the spectator does not merely feel for what the protagonist has experienced, but has some understanding of it as well (Else 1957, p. 439).[29] The spectator's recognition has its source in his or her inevitable familiarity as a Greek with the protagonist's story. The spectator is, initially, one step ahead of the protagonist. Consequently, a kind of detached self-confidence characterizes, not only a protagonist like Oedipus, but also the spectator. Yet the action of the drama implicates the spectator as much as it does the protagonist, reversing the advantage, as the spectator comes to terms with the truth that, in reality, he or she is just as human as Oedipus and no less impervious to fate

To affirm oneself as a human being means to know oneself as necessarily related to the human community. This is a challenge for both the protagonist and the spectator. Here the protagonist leads the way, although it must be acknowledged that not all tragedies work in the same way. Even if one sees Oedipus's recognition as coinciding with his self-blinding, when he symbolically takes on the punitive function of the community, the ending leaves Oedipus as an outcast. Perhaps it is precisely the role of the spectator to restore Oedipus to the community. As Kuhns (1970, p. 11) has urged: ". . . what the audience must do, where the best tragedy is concerned, is to confer upon the protagonist the resolution his situation cannot confer upon him." Nevertheless, there are examples of tragedy in which this is not necessary, as the fruit of recognition is manifest on stage. At the conclusion of the *Eumenides*, Orestes is invited to become a citizen of Athens. In *Oedipus at Colonus*, Oedipus's self-knowledge is rewarded, as he is restored to the community by Theseus, the legendary Athenian law-giver, who recognizes him and makes him an honorary citizen of Athens.

The spectator's recognition consists of his readiness to recognize the protagonist in himself and thereby to affirm a bond to others in society. In tragedy, the social bond is strengthened by virtue of being tested through transgression. Moreover, the spectator enacts his or her chosen participation in society. In being like Oedipus, the spectator is better able, in reality, not to be Oedipus. Tragedy questions and then seems to defend and uphold social integration. A paradigm emerges, therefore, to the effect that self-knowledge is a prerequisite for the achievement of social integration.

In PhS also, the reader is required to measure himself or herself against the experience of consciousness. This means, first of all, being able to see himself in the experience of consciousness, and, secondly, being able to follow consciousness on this journey. The reader has an advantage over the vague abstraction "consciousness," at least in having read the preface and the introduction, which describe what is to come, but also in being an actual, self-aware human being. A shift takes place eventually in PhS, however, whereby the reader begins to emulate consciousness. (At what particular point this occurs is, perhaps, determined by variations in the awareness of the reader.) As Geist, consciousness knows itself in a way the reader might resist or deny. However, by the chapter on Morality, an identity among consciousness, the we, and (Hegel presumes) the reader has been reached:

> Here, then, knowledge appears at last to have become identical with its truth; for its truth is this very knowledge and any antithesis between the two sides has vanished, not only for us or in itself, but for self-consciousness itself. . . . Now, however, the object is for consciousness itself the certainty of itself, viz. knowledge. . . . [It] is pure knowledge. (p. 364)

At this stage, finally, self-knowledge arrives on the scene. Moreover, it is at this stage that Hegel explicitly equates knowledge and truth. It is revealing that, historically, Hegel is describing the era virtually contemporaneous to his own.

The reader's experience of recognition is supposed to occur as a response to reading PhS. This recognition resembles the recognition of the spectator of tragedy in that it is constituted by a resolve to know oneself as necessarily belonging to society, to define oneself as such, and to be willing to act accordingly in the world. Clearly, Hegel follows tragedy in taking up the idea of recognition and in adhering to the paradigm that self-knowledge is a prerequisite for social integration. He differs, however, in devaluing the element of fate and elevating our capacity to act autonomously and freely.

It is crucial to keep in mind that according to Hegel social integration eludes modern culture. PhS presents a narrative, which is especially designed to address the absence of mutual recognition in the modern world.[30] The unhappiness of the narrative refers, not only to the persistent forms of Unhappy Consciousness, but to the fact that Hegel sees the actual consciousness of nineteenth-century Germany in this light. Hegel diagnoses the reader as unhappy, and while he does not promise to leave the reader happy, he does believe that he is equipping us to face and potentially transform our unhappiness.

It is interesting to wonder whether the resemblance of PhS to tragedy might be due in part to the parallel circumstances in their respective historical eras. It has been argued that tragedy is a response to the social upheaval of Athens in the fifth century B.C.[31] As a measure of the mounting disorder, tragedy ultimately offers validation for social order. It does this, however, in a radical way: by directly confronting the perversion of order and thus leading the spectator to an appreciation for the need for order. Although Hegel might not have conceived of tragedy in these terms, he does regard tragedy as a form of cultural self-representation that necessarily reflects social life.[32]

In conclusion, the claim that PhS resembles Greek tragedy is based on the general movement from ignorance to knowledge, on their culmination in self-knowledge, and on their similar processes of interaction and struggle to self-knowledge. In addition, the claim is based on the structural parallels that rely on narrative and performance, and on their paradigm of self-knowledge as a prerequisite for social integration—which is perhaps offered in part as a response to contexts of social upheaval.

4
Modern Culture

The essence of modernity as such is psychologism, the experiencing and interpretation of the world in terms of the reactions of our inner life and indeed as an inner world, the dissolution of fixed contents in the fluid element of the soul, from which all that is substantive is filtered and whose forms are merely forms of motion.
—Georg Simmel, "Rodin"

Both Hegel and Nietzsche seek to capture the self-understanding of modern culture. They wish to offer a mirror reflection of modern culture, and, in particular, to inspire the reader to acknowledge the deficiencies of modern culture. They abandon the Cartesian myth in favor of the compelling task of facing squarely the contrast between the unity of the ancient world and the dividedness of the modern world. For Hegel and Nietzsche, philosophy must examine the lack of satisfaction in modern culture and explore the prospects for reversing this.

Culture as customs denotes the objective realm. For Hegel, this is an legitimate although outmoded aspect of culture.[1] Hegel emphasizes that Greek tragedy is concerned with conflicts about the validity of customs. Nietzsche is more negative about customs, viewing them as unnecessarily restrictive.

Culture as Bildung arises when customs no longer satisfy us; it directs us to the subjective realm. Bildung is associated with modern culture. Nietzsche has greater reservations than Hegel about the concept of Bildung and is particularly wary of linking Bildung to the state. However, both thinkers endorse a version of Bildung that entails a dynamic sense of agency: Bildung as a contemporary version of paideia.[2]

Culture as self-fathoming denotes an intermingling of the objective and subjective realms. This sense emerges when the objective no longer can define us (as with customs) and the subjective threatens to dominate the objective (as with Bildung). Self-fathoming makes us aware of our subjective freedom, but it also forces us to grapple with how the culture lives within us. Like Bildung, self-fathoming is a strictly modern phenomenon. As much as Hegel and Nietzsche regard this as a new development, though, it contains elements from Greek tragedy. Greek tragedy provides an image of a healthy culture reflecting on itself. Self-fathoming, then, is both a liberation from the other two senses and a means of reclaiming them (insofar as that can be done in the modern world). Both thinkers exemplify self-fathoming, thus breaking free from the philosophical past as well as offering responses that are directed to their own culture. Their philosophical works resist the state of modern culture by means of performance: phenomenology and genealogy both address the reader in a way that is self-implicating. These creative philosophical methods hark back to Greek tragedy in implicating anyone who partakes in experiencing them.

I begin the first section of this chapter with Hegel's description of the problem of modern culture and what he sees as a possible solution. The point of entry will be the Culture section of the *Phenomenology of Spirit.* This will lay out the problem, as Hegel sees it, and prepare the way for clarifying his solution to the problem of modern culture. The topic of "modern culture" is, of course, an immense one. My aim in this chapter will be to introduce Hegel's solution to the problem of modern culture, which I will continue to explore in chapters 6–8. In the first section of the present chapter I introduce Hegel's critique of modern culture and then consider some responses to it by the critical theorists Horkheimer, Adorno, and Habermas. In the second section I present Nietzsche's critique of modern culture. I also introduce Heidegger's critique of modern culture, which was inspired by Nietzsche. In the third section I highlight some parallels between the views of Hegel and Nietzsche as well as some of the differences. I suggest that some of the differences can be accounted for in terms of changes in culture that occurred over the course of the nineteenth century, and that therefore it makes sense to locate Hegel's and Nietzsche's views on a continuum. I also reconsider Horkheimer, Adorno, and Habermas in light of my account of Nietzsche's view, since Habermas specifically voices concern about the Nietzschean influence on Horkheimer and Adorno. Ultimately, I wish to argue that, in spite of the differences, Hegel's and Nietzsche's respective accounts are not contradictory and even supplement each other. I would add that, in order to account for the changes in modern culture in the twentieth century, we ought to try to incorporate and integrate both of their views insofar as that is possible.

4.1 Unsatisfied Yearning: Hegel, Horkheimer, Adorno, and Habermas

In his early works, Hegel expresses concern about the lack of satisfaction in modern culture. In an essay on the German Constitution written in the period 1799–1803 (*Hegel's Political Writings*, p. 146), Hegel emphasizes the fragmentation of German culture: "Every centre of life has gone its own way and established itself on its own; the whole has fallen apart. The state exists no longer."[3] In the *Fragment of a System* (1800),[4] Hegel explicates the difference between happiness and unhappiness in terms of psychic unity and inner/outer disharmony. In *Difference between the Systems of Fichte and Schelling* (1801), Hegel suggests that the division in modern self-identity is a spur for philosophy: "The need for philosophy arises when the unifying power has disappeared from the life of men, when the contradictions have lost their living interrelation and interdependence and assumed an independent form." A similar theme is reiterated in the preface to PhS, where Hegel voices his concern about the exigency of need for philosophy in view of his culture's lack of "solid and substantial being." Hegel adds the mournful assessment: "By the little which now satisfies [genügt] Spirit, we can measure the extent of its loss." The task of philosophy, Hegel maintains in the preface to PhS, is "recovery" [Herstellung], not merely knowledge of what is.[5]

Hegel discusses culture at length in the middle section of the chapter on Geist in PhS. 'Geist' denotes the inherent sociality of the human mind. It occurs as a moment in the development of consciousness in which one becomes aware of oneself as universal—that is, as a part of a living ethical world [sittliche Welt]. This moment can be juxtaposed against the mainly epistemological orientation of the first half of PhS, where consciousness regards itself abstractly as a singular subject. The change is from "mere shapes of consciousness" to "shapes of a world" (p. 265). The first section in the "Geist" chapter, on Greek culture, is titled "Sittlichkeit." The next section, titled "Culture" [Bildung], bears the subtitle "Self-Alienated Spirit." Here Hegel focuses on French culture during the Enlightenment and its aftermath, which leads directly into his own cultural world.

In the "Culture" section, something is wrong. Geist is at odds with itself: "double, divided and self-opposed" (p. 295). On the one hand, Spirit clings to Faith, a traditional and religious form of consciousness; on the other hand, it establishes Insight, a form of consciousness that affirms a commitment to reason and is associated with the Enlightenment. The dialectic that unfolds between Faith and Insight vindicates neither side. Hegel demonstrates how each is one-sided, misconstruing and failing to appreciate the other. The individual is seduced by the promise of autonomy, wherein subjectivity becomes the measure of all things. The individual endures the feeling of being cut off from Sittlichkeit. This feeling is intensified by the crisis in meaning that results from the loss of religion. Hegel comments that Faith, at least, included a longing for something beyond itself (p. 337). He is concerned about the implications of a world without religion, but he does not entertain the existential issue of meaninglessness that will come to preoccupy Nietzsche and many other twentieth-century philosophers.

Insight's apparent victory over Faith is only a partial victory, since "usefulness" is elevated to the level of the highest concern. Although this might seem to indicate a new pragmatic turn for the unfolding of Geist, it lays the basis for disenchantment with the world. The flourishing of usefulness is also suggestive of what might be called a narcissistic side of consciousness, which can be glimpsed in Hegel's description that "everything exists for his pleasure and delight" (p. 342). Hegel emphasizes the grandiosity of this consciousness (ibid.): ". . . he walks the Earth as in a garden planted for him. He must also have plucked the fruit of the tree of the knowledge of Good and Evil."

Indeed, the threat of narcissism can be seen quite clearly in Hegel's observation that "for consciousness, qua pure insight, is not a single self which could be confronted by the object as equally having a self of its own, but is pure Notion, the gazing of the self into the self, the absolute seeing of itself doubled; the certainty of itself is the universal subject, and its conscious Notion is the essence of all actuality" (p. 356).[6] The discussion of Insight concludes as Hegel reveals that the alleged satisfaction of Enlightened consciousness is more tenuous than it appears.

The attempt to repress the need for a relation to the infinite comes back to haunt the Enlightenment: ". . . we shall see whether Enlightenment can remain satisfied [Befriedigung]; that yearning of the troubled Spirit which mourns over the loss of its spiritual world lurks in the background. Enlightenment itself bears within it this blemish of an unsatisfied yearning [unbefriedigten Sehnens]." (p. 349) The crisis that ensues from Insight's apparent victory is shown to lead to the Reign of Terror that followed the French Revolution. In the Reign of Terror, culture is not merely self-divided but self-destructive: it explodes in a kind of narcissistic rage. In this context, Hegel, the great rationalist, shows an unexpected sensitivity to the limits and even dangers of the misappropriation of "pure reason." The crisis of modern culture is profound, and agency must be renewed if empty subjectivity is to be overcome. This renewal of agency occurs through rational self-understanding and through mutual recognition with others—which, for Hegel, will prove to be related.

A shift occurs in Hegel's view of modern culture in his later work. Consider this key passage from the introduction to the *Lectures on the Philosophy of History* (p. 66)[7]:

It is easier to perceive the shortcomings of individuals, states, and the course of world affairs than to understand their true import. For in passing negative judgments, one looks down on the matter in hand with a superior and supercilious air, without having gone into it thoroughly enough to understand its true nature, i.e.. its positive significance. . . . To see only the bad side in everything and to overlook all the positive and valuable qualities is a sign of extreme superficiality. Age, in general, takes a milder view, whereas youth is always dissatisfied [unzufrieden]; this is because age brings with it maturity of judgment, which does not simply tolerate the bad along with the rest out of sheer lack of interest, but has learnt from the seriousness of life to look for the substance and enduring value of things.

Here a general appeal to common sense is contrasted with the harshness of immature judgment. This passage can also be read, however, as self-justification for the change in Hegel's own evaluation of modern culture. Notice how Hegel distances himself from the theme of dissatisfaction. In his later work he fashions a more optimistic reading of modern culture and social reconciliation. He comes to believe that despite the flaws in modern culture, it has the institutions (in the form of the family, civil society and the state) to achieve such reconciliation (Hardimon 1994, pp. 102–108).[8] In particular, he celebrates the development of the state in the form of a constitutional monarchy as the "achievement of the modern world" (PR #273).

Some further reflection about the *Phenomenology of Spirit* in relation to the *Philosophy of Right* on modern culture is in order. The former claims that the present is a time of transition. Borrowing from Hegel's own standard, it does not seem that this view is unduly colored by youthful excess; if anything, anxious anticipation is as evident as disgruntled posturing. There is an ardent, passionate tone in PhS, augmented perhaps by Hegel's rush to complete the work. Like some other scholars, I am attracted to the live drama about human agency that is at the heart of PhS. Others rightfully stress that PR represents the fulfillment of Hegel's vision, and that PhS is downgraded in importance precisely on the basis that Hegel deems it an inadequate introduction to his system of philosophy.[9] It will not possible in this context to resolve the issue of the relationship between these two works. One should not underestimate the consistency between the two works—more specifically, the fact that the principle of construing the modern world in terms of the "freedom of subjectivity" (articulated in PR #273, Zusatz) is as valid for PS .[10] Yet it is difficult to escape the underlying tension between the two works concerning the nature of dissatisfaction in modern culture; in the later work, the extent of this problem is reassessed and downgraded.

Horkheimer and Adorno's *Dialectic of Enlightenment*, which interprets modern culture as dissatisfied from a mid-twentieth-century standpoint, is particularly relevant because it reinterprets Hegel's mixed assessment of the Enlightenment, especially the theme of the self-destructiveness of the Enlightenment. For Horkheimer and Adorno, the self-destructiveness unleashed in the fascist era confirms the hypocrisy of the Enlightenment. In detecting concealed irrationality within the ideal of rationality, Horkheimer and Adorno present a severe indictment of the Enlightenment—an indictment that far exceeds what Hegel has in mind. Nevertheless, Horkheimer and Adorno follow Hegel in important respects—for example, in defining the modern world in terms of the ascendance of usefulness as the ultimate criterion of value and the corresponding peril of disenchantment. Their reading of usefulness focuses attention on the glorification of technology: the mentality of the "calculability of the world" (Horkheimer and Adorno 1986, p. 7). Usefulness implies domination (ibid., p. 4): "What men want to learn from nature is how to use it in order wholly to dominate it and other men." Horkheimer and Adorno develop Hegel's view in a particular direction beyond Hegel, ultimately portraying Hegel's dialectic of the Enlightenment as foundering, itself a victim of the mythology of the Enlightenment (ibid., p. 24). Horkheimer and Adorno assert that, despite its self-assured stance of superiority to mythology, the Enlightenment is itself a mythology. Its self-understanding—or self-misunderstanding—results in alienation.

Hegel's depiction of the dialectic between Faith and Insight reveals that Insight embraces finitude and thus cannot sustain an abiding sense of satisfaction. In Horkheimer and Adorno, this same dialectic occurs between Enlightenment and mythology (or, in other terms they use, between "ratio" and "mimesis"). They are suspicious about the Enlightenment's conviction that ratio has an absolute value; they praise mimesis for the way it fostered meaning in mythology. Mimesis creates a relation that brings us into closer connection to the object it represents, whereas ratio entails distancing. Like Nietzsche in *The Birth of Tragedy*, Horkheimer and Adorno appreciate that mythology successfully provides emotional comfort for humans. Magicians, for example, imitate demons in order to frighten and/or appease them; thus, even animism is to be valued as offering meaning in contrast to ratio, which, in their view, simply murders meaning. In the view of Horkheimer and Adorno, ratio's wish to dominate nature is emblematic of Western culture.

In comparison with the ready parallel between the function of Insight in Hegel and the function of ratio (accentuated by usefulness) in Horkheimer and Adorno, it is less obvious how Hegel's notion of Faith compares to Horkheimer and Adorno's notion of mimesis. Horkheimer and Adorno turn the longing for the beyond (that is, what Hegel sees as the need to be part of something infinite) to connote a longing for the meaning and the well-being that mythology provided. Horkheimer and Adorno emphasize how the Enlightenment contributes to the disenchantment of the world by "the extirpation of animism" (p. 5). In other words, according to their interpretation, the Enlightenment abets rather than tames nihilism.

According to Horkheimer and Adorno, the Enlightenment is bound to fail in its attempt to repress "mythic fear." There is an implied contrast here to the Dionysian element of tragedy, wherein the Greeks withstood the absence of meaning in order to affirm meaning. Indeed, Horkheimer and Adorno (p. 44) clearly acknowledge Nietzsche as an important predecessor: "Nietzsche was one of the few after Hegel who recognized the dialectic of Enlightenment." For Horkheimer and Adorno, the Enlightenment's self-destructiveness becomes manifest in anti-Semitism and can be understood through the psychological mechanisms of projection and the disavowal of mimesis. As we will see, Horkheimer and Adorno turn to psychoanalysis in order to bolster their concern with the fragility of civilization and its vulnerability to narcissism and aggression.

Habermas's portrait of the dialectic of Enlightenment, like that of Horkheimer and Adorno, has its source in Hegel. As Habermas explains in the *Philosophical Discourse of Modernity* (1987, p. 21), Hegel relies on the dialectic of Enlightenment in order to embrace a "critical concept of modernity." According to Habermas, Hegel was "the first philosopher to develop a clear concept of modernity" (ibid., p. 4). Later (p. 43) he adumbrates this point: "Hegel is not the first philosopher to belong to the modern age, but he is the first for whom modernity became a problem." Habermas credits Hegel with understanding modernity to be the central problem for philosophy and defending the promise of completing modernity.[11] Thus, Habermas uses Hegel in order to reach more optimistic conclusions about modern culture than the first generation of critical theorists.

Habermas is fully sympathetic to Hegel's choice to regard modernity as a main concern for philosophy, and he is especially drawn to the complex and mixed assessment of modernity that is found in Hegel's discussion of Insight. Nevertheless, Habermas argues that Hegel failed to provide a solution to the problem of modernity because he was wedded to a monological notion of self-knowledge— the philosophy of the subject, rather than the intersubjective communication model that Habermas advances. It is revealing that Habermas's interpretation of Hegel on modernity is silent on the longing for the beyond (that is, Hegel's concern for the preservation of Faith)—precisely what Horkheimer and Adorno take up, albeit in a transformed way, with their idea of mythic fear.

Looking back to Hegel, Habermas finds a defense of the Enlightenment that properly values rationality. Moreover, Habermas scores a polemical point in his own favor by tracing Hegel's evolution beyond the aesthetic solution to modernity that tempted him in his youth to his tentative embrace of intersubjectivity with the concept of recognition in the Jena writings. The opposition, for Habermas, is Nietzschean-inspired attacks on the Enlightenment, which he sees as nihilistic and as bound to mere aesthetic solutions. Either of these attitudes is predicated on skepticism toward rationality. This provokes Habermas to distance himself from what he fears is an dangerous tolerance for irrationality. Indeed, Habermas (1987, p. 106) is clearly put off by the tone he finds in Horkheimer and Adorno's work: he suggests that it is "their blackest book," and he harps on its oddness.[12] As Habermas sees it, Horkheimer and Adorno "oversimplify" the achievement of the Enlightenment, which in his opinion must be carried forward.[13] In particular, Habermas regards the notion of mimesis primarily as an aesthetic concept that constitutes a separate and inferior realm to ratio. Habermas emphasizes that Horkheimer and Adorno fail to do justice to the accomplishments of the Enlightenment because they conceptualize rationality inadequately; their critique, in his view, lacks adequate grounding.

Habermas's interpretation of Horkheimer and Adorno turns on the point that they were tempted by the influence of Nietzsche. He argues that they are trapped by the mutually exclusive needs of affirming and rejecting (rational) critique. Dubious about their claim that Nietzsche was "one of the few after Hegel who recognized the dialectic of the Enlightenment" (1987, p. 120), Habermas makes the pointed response that "they cannot overlook that Hegel is also Nietzsche's great antipode." What Horkheimer and Adorno share with Nietzsche, according to Habermas (p. 121), is a "certain lack of concern in dealing with the (to put it in the form of a slogan) achievements of Occidental rationalism." Is it really surprising, though, that, as the Holocaust raged, Horkheimer and Adorno felt the impotence of critique so sharply? What would it mean to affirm rational critique in the face of such irrationality? In the best light, we might read Habermas as urging us to appreciate that we no longer have to be so despairing. Still, his reading of Horkheimer and Adorno does not meditate on the contrast between his own positionality and the context in which the *Dialectic of Enlightenment* was written.

Viewed from the present, the negativity of Horkheimer and Adorno appears extreme. Yet it remains open to debate whether the destructiveness of modernity has abated in the postwar era, as Habermas believes. As I will suggest in the last section of this chapter, it is significant that Habermas overlooks Horkheimer and Adorno's penetrating psychological insight into modernity. Before exploring the views of Horkheimer, Adorno, and Habermas further, let us probe the history of modernity by clarifying Nietzsche's view of modern culture.

4.2 Agitatedness and the New Barbarians: Nietzsche and Heidegger

Nietzsche's assessment of modern culture contains elements from Hegel, but he also pursues new avenues, and he is much harsher in his evaluation. Like Hegel, Nietzsche believes that there is something wrong with modern culture, and at times he uses similar language, such as referring to "our unsatisfied [unbefriedigten] modern culture" (BT #23). Nietzsche also concurs with Hegel that modernity represents a special challenge and a special opportunity for philosophy. "Philosophers," he proposes, "appear during those times of great danger, when the wheel of time is turning faster and faster." (PT, p. 6).

Nietzsche departs from Hegel, though, in ascribing pathology to modern culture and in finding little reason to be hopeful about the future. Indeed, he warns of a coming "catastrophe" in European culture (WP #2). As a philosophical physician, he makes the diagnosis that there is "a disorder in the modern soul which condemns it to a joyless unfruitfulness" (SE #2). The result is a "general decrease in vitality" (TI, "Skirmishes of an Untimely Man," #37). Our weakened condition is manifest in modern ideas about equality and altruism, which, according to Nietzsche, are merely secularized forms of Christian values (D #132). Modern culture, according to Nietzsche, perpetuates sickness: "Hence each helps the other; hence everyone is to a certain extent sick, and everyone is a nurse for the sick." (TI, "Skirmishes of an Untimely Man," #37) Moreover, Nietzsche is emphatic about condemning modern culture as "not a real culture" and as a "bogus culture" (UDHL #4; RWB #4).[14] Modern culture is depicted again and again as inferior to ancient Greek culture. But what, precisely, is so wrong about modern culture?

Like Hegel, Nietzsche detects a division in self-identity in modern culture that results in a lack of satisfaction. Both thinkers see the schism in modern identity as widening and deepening. Following Hegel, Nietzsche argues that modern culture is characterized by an inner/outer dichotomy, and that the outer is thereby devalued in meaning (UDHL #4). Nietzsche specifically notes that this is "an antithesis unknown to peoples of earlier times." Modern culture is "essentially subjective" [wesentlich innerlich]; it can be summed up, according to Nietzsche (ibid.), by the title "Handbook of Subjective Culture [innerlicher Bildung] for Outward Barbarians." Nietzsche traces the crisis of objective meaning in modern culture back to the loss of religion. In particular, as we have seen, he expresses concern about the absence of myth in modern culture. The death of God raises the specter of nihilism. Although Nietzsche is not sentimental about the demise of religion, he sees such a loss as having ongoing consequences.

As Nietzsche sees it, science is responsible for the absence of myth in modern culture. The ascendance of science as a cultural ideal has the effect of diminishing humans to be useful and herdlike. For the most part, Nietzsche regards the impact of science on culture as deleterious:

As long as what is meant by culture [Kultur] is essentially the promotion of science [Förderung der Wissenschaft], culture will pass the great suffering human being by with pitiless coldness, because science sees everywhere only problems of knowledge [Erkenntnis] and because within the world of the sciences suffering is really something improper and incomprehensible [Ungehöriges und Unverständliches], thus at best only one more problem. (SE #6)

Nietzsche's account here is a mixture of prophecy and hyperbole. It anticipates the supreme value that science (especially natural science) has attained in our own cultural milieu, yet it is not a balanced view of science. For example, no attempt is made to acknowledge that, though science shares some responsibility for causing suffering, it also has contributed to the alleviation of suffering. Nietzsche's reflections are important because they help us to appreciate the extent to which natural science flourished over the course of the nineteenth century. Though this is important to Nietzsche's account of modern culture, it is less of a concern for Hegel.[15]

Nietzsche agrees with Hegel that modern culture is characterized by an empty subjectivity. For Hegel, a subjectivity that is detached from having a social identity risks narcissism, the doomed effort to evade and deny one's own inherent sociality. Nietzsche is virtually Hegel's opposite when he asserts that subjectivity is empty because it is caused by the spread of social conformism rather than by detachment from society. Modern culture, Nietzsche writes, fosters mediocrity; it produces "a useful, industrious, handy, multi-purpose, herd-animal" (BGE #176). The slave mentality, which Nietzsche traces from its source in Judeo-Christian values, is deeply entrenched in modern culture.

This tension between Hegel and Nietzsche concerning our bond to society is sharp. Nevertheless, the issue of narcissism raised by Hegel is germane to Nietzsche, too, as narcissism does not only entail self-involvement but includes inordinate dependence on others for the maintenance of self-esteem.[16] Hegel and Nietzsche might agree that the problem of modern culture lies its failure to promote a genuine subjectivity in which the self is not subject to extreme vicissitudes of self-involvement or dependence on others. Both thinkers believe that, in the absence of an adequate notion of agency, satisfaction will be missing in modern culture.

Tension between Hegel and Nietzsche can be found, too, in Nietzsche's protest about the extent to which subjectivity has become wedded to epistemology in modern culture. Defining subjectivity in terms of knowledge is an error that has its source in the Cartesian myth. According to Nietzsche, such an overreliance on knowledge is an indication that the culture is in trouble. He is emphatic that it is "impossible to build a culture upon knowledge," and he concludes that "knowing is probably even a substitute for culture" (PT, pp. 29, 32). In the unpublished early essay "On Truth and Lies in a Nonmoral Sense" (PT, p. 80), Nietzsche suggests that the overvaluation of knowledge amounts to a form of self-deception.

Caution must be exercised in interpreting Nietzsche's objections to knowledge. In his middle period, as we know, he held knowledge in high esteem (HAH I #36 and #37). Also, as I have emphasized, Nietzsche does not intend to condemn the desire to have knowledge per se; rather, he is urging us primarily—as he does with morality—to question the value of knowledge. Furthermore, he raises the possibility of revising our conception of knowledge no longer to be an absolute value determined by rationality alone. Nietzsche's perspectivism directs us to be open to knowing in different ways, rather than condemning and discouraging the wish to know (Clark 1989, pp. 127–158).[17] He defends thinking itself as an instinctive activity: "To this day the task of incorporating [einzuverleiben] knowledge [Wissen] and making it instinctive is only beginning to dawn on the human eye and is not yet clearly discernible [erkennbare]." (GS #11) Nietzsche accords respect to knowing in a psychological sense—what I have termed the psychology of knowledge. But his reservations about knowledge mark his view as different from Hegel's.

It is clear that Nietzsche is more thoroughly negative about the prospects for modern culture than Hegel. Nietzsche's attack on modern culture has a vociferous and unyielding tone: "The whole of the West no longer possesses the instincts out of which institutions grow, out of which a future grows: perhaps nothing antagonizes its 'modern spirit' so much." (TI, "Skirmishes of an Untimely Man," #39) According to Nietzsche's later work, there is no end to the crisis of modern culture, no hope for transcending the paradigm of master and slave. "The notion of an 'age of transition,'" Megill points out (1985, p. 6), "entails a limited crisis, a crisis contained by a unifying dialectic or by some similar promise of return. Nietzsche and his successors find no such promise."

Nietzsche's evaluation of modern culture went through some significant changes. In *The Birth of Tragedy*, Nietzsche is committed to making a contribution to the resolution of the crisis of modern culture. In his middle period, there are moments when he continues to hold onto the prospect of transforming modern culture. In "Our Age's Good Fortune" (HAH II 1 #179), he even acknowledges a positive element in modern culture: the ability to observe and enjoy past cultures. Tentatively affirming hope for modern culture, he writes:

> In respect to the future there opens out before us, for the first time in history, the tremendous far-flung prospect of human-ecumenical goals embracing the entire inhabited Earth. At the same time we feel conscious of possessing the strength to be allowed without presumption to take this new task in hand ourselves without supernatural assistance; indeed, let our undertaking eventuate as it may, even if we have overestimated our strength; there is in any case no one to whom we owe a reckoning except ourselves: henceforth mankind can do with itself whatever it wishes.

In this description, the fate of modern culture seems to depend on whether we humans can assume the burden of autonomy. Yet elsewhere in the same work (HAH I #285) Nietzsche takes a more sober tone, warning of certain tendencies in modern culture that interfere with the evolution of a higher culture:

> Modern agitatedness [moderne Bewegheit] grows greater the farther west we go, so that to the Americans the inhabitants of Europe seem one and all ease-loving and epicurean creatures, though in fact they are swarming among one another like bees and wasps. This agitatedness is growing so great that higher culture [höher Cultur] can no longer allow its fruits to mature[18]; it is though the seasons were following upon one another too quickly. From lack of repose our civilization is turning into a new barbarism [neue Barbarei].

Setting contemplation against modern agitatedness, Nietzsche traces the transformation from the dysphoria of "unsatisfied yearning" to something more disturbing. According to the metaphor he employs, modern culture brings about a distortion of nature.[19] Nietzsche's reference to a new barbarism eerily foreshadows events of the twentieth century.

Indeed, Nietzsche's conclusion that modernity is propelled by a momentum that is beyond anyone's control leads him to be pessimistic about the future.[20] He offers little hope for collectively forging a solution for modern culture. However, he never abandons the idea that it is the task of philosophy to diagnose modern culture, nor does he give up the ideal of a healthy culture. Despite modernity's woes, Nietzsche believes that facing up to cultural decline can help us to "prevent it from occurring" (HAH I #247). Throughout his work, Nietzsche remained attracted to the idea that a few extraordinary individuals can escape the fate of the general culture.

Nietzsche's later writings exclude the possibility of altering modern culture by means of philosophical intervention. There are some passages in which grandiosity leads Nietzsche to come to another judgment, as when he suggests that "it is only beginning with me that there are hopes again, tasks, ways that can be prescribed for culture [Cultur]" (EH, "Twilight," #2). However, Nietzsche refrains from committing himself to lay out a solution to the problems of modern culture. These competing impulses in Nietzsche's philosophy—one that is in the direction of cultural critique, another that advocates estrangement from modern culture—are never resolved. Instead, they are embodied in the figure of Zarathustra, who is both a hermit and a charismatic leader of humanity.

Megill makes the point that Nietzsche proposes myth as providing the only escape from the malaise of modern culture. Indeed, in *The Birth of Tragedy* Nietzsche dwells on Greek myths, and later he seeks to invent his own myths. Nietzsche regards myth as forming and preserving culture.[21] Still, Nietzsche has a restrictive view of what a communal solution for modern culture could be like. Myths, in Nietzsche's interpretation, are promulgated by and for an elite; for the masses, they are directives to obey. Nietzsche does not hold human community in high esteem—for example, in BGE #284 he exclaims that "all community makes men—somehow, somewhere, sometime 'common.'"

Insofar as Nietzsche ever envisioned improvement for modern culture, it was fundamentally aesthetic rather than political improvement.[22] For example, in "Richard Wagner in Bayreuth" he asserts that "the redemption of art" is "the only gleam of light to be hoped for in the modern age" (RWB #6). In an important passage in *Twilight of the Idols* ("What the Germans Lack," #4), he positions culture and the state as "antagonists" and argues that culture must be realized independently. "All great ages of culture are ages of political decline," he asserts. "What is great culturally has always been unpolitical, even antipolitical." This claim can be deployed to justify the view that Nietzsche intended to offer an aestheticized, apolitical reading of modern culture. It is clear, however, that Nietzsche does not regard culture as immune to the "great politics" that he forecasts for the future (BGE #208). There are good reasons, which will be discussed in the next section, to avoid making the precipitous conclusion that Nietzsche is apolitical.

Wary as Nietzsche is of proposing solutions, he does offer an astute and illuminating psychological analysis of modernity. Indeed, it is fair to say that psychology is a crucial tool in Nietzsche's understanding of modern culture. In BGE #23 he asserts that "psychology is now again the path to fundamental problems," and in GM he stresses his vocation as a psychologist. Psychology leads Nietzsche to diagnose moderns as disliking themselves and to single out the man of "modern ideas" as especially "dissatisfied [unzufrieden] with himself" (BGE #222). He turns to psychology in order to differentiate health and sickness. Underlying this distinction, as Nietzsche sees it, is the distinction between those who affirm life and those who reject it. Affirming life has to do, first and foremost, with recognizing rather than rejecting our affects, instincts, and body.[23] We must not forget, however, that Nietzsche imagines that only an elite truly want and can tolerate health. There is no utopian strain in Nietzsche, as there is in critical theory.

Heidegger is one of the most important interpreters of Nietzsche, and his view of modernity is particularly indebted to Nietzsche. Like Hegel and Nietzsche, Heidegger locates the problem of modernity in the empty subjectivity that it produces. However, Heidegger's bleak assessment seems to follow Nietzsche more than Hegel. In his *Introduction to Metaphysics*, Heidegger dramatically voices concern that the "spiritual decline" he sees as haunting Europe has advanced so far that awareness of this decline is in jeopardy. Although Heidegger's description of "the darkening of the world" hardly leaves room for hope about the future of modern culture, he insists that his view is distinguishable from Kulturpessimismus, and he mocks the patent absurdity of labels such as 'optimism' and 'pessimism'. He articulates a range of four phenomena associated with this darkening: the flight of the gods, the destruction of the Earth, the transformation of men into a mass, and the hatred and suspicion of everything free and creative (Heidegger 1959, p. 31). Each of these phenomena can be traced back to Nietzsche[24]: the emptiness of the divine realm to Nietzsche's theme of the death of God, the destruction of the Earth to Nietzsche's concern about the harmful effect of science and technology, the emergence of mass culture to Nietzsche's analysis of the growing trend toward herd-like behavior, and the negative response engendered by freedom and creativity to Nietzsche's concept of ressentiment.

Heidegger is especially concerned that modernity is increasingly affected by science and technology. His critique of technology is complex and warrants separate treatment.[25] For present purposes, let me simply highlight that Heidegger follows Nietzsche in regarding science as eclipsing other values in modern culture. Both Nietzsche and Heidegger wish to defy this trend in their writing. In this regard, there are interesting parallels to be observed between Heidegger and Horkheimer/Adorno.[26] First, what Heidegger has to say about mythos and ratio coincides with the dialectic of Enlightenment. Heidegger sees mythos as revealing truth, not as a form of irrationality; he also protests against the identification of ratio with "thinking." It is a consistent theme in Heidegger's work that feelings and moods are open to Being in a way that ratio is not, and he distinguishes this from an embrace of irrationality (1971, p. 25). Furthermore, there is a close connection between the centrality of anxiety in Heidegger and the notion of mythic fear in Horkheimer and Adorno. When he observes "Not logical—hence mystical; not ratio—hence irrational," Heidegger (1980, p. 143) actually anticipates Habermas's (1987, p. 184) charge that his philosophy is mystical.

Perhaps the most significant commonality between Heidegger and Horkheimer/Adorno is the underlying assumption that, although the destructive tendencies manifesting themselves in modern Western culture might be gathering momentum and force, they have been latent all along. As these philosophers see it, these destructive tendencies are attributable to the human need to use reason to dominate nature. More precisely, these philosophers understand modern culture's problematic relation to nature as essential to Western thinking, rather than as an outgrowth of modern existence. Indeed, these philosophers detect a hubris that comes back to haunt humanity in modernity. For Horkheimer and Adorno, this can be glimpsed in fascism; for Heidegger, the threat of nihilism is less specific.

Like Nietzsche, Heidegger registers despair about the future because of nihilism.[27] In the context of discussing Nietzsche's philosophy, Heidegger (1987, volume 3, p. 178) suggests that the essence of modernity is "consummate meaninglessness." Ominous pronouncements accompany this worry, as when Heidegger tells us that "there is no room for halfway measures in the present stage of the history of our planet" (ibid., p. 6). Heidegger's belief about the dimness of modernity's future prospects escalated after his disappointment with the Nazis, in the wake of World War II itself, and during the Cold War; he became more skeptical about the interaction of philosophy and politics. In view of his involvement with the Nazis and his scorn for democracy, it would be wrong to imply that Heidegger was uninterested in politics. However, for the most part, his view of modernity, like Nietzsche's, lacks a specific political valence. Heidegger often voiced anti-modern sentiments, and he was prone to parochialism.[28] Although Nietzsche too was capable of spouting disturbingly bad political ideas, he remained dedicated to the cosmopolitan ideal of being a good European.

Heidegger's investigation of Nietzsche centers on the claim that Nietzsche was the last metaphysician of subjectivity—the culmination of the modern Western tradition that began with Descartes but which really goes back to the Protagorean notion that "man is the measure." This interpretation of Nietzsche is controversial, partly because Heidegger relies so heavily on unpublished material from *The Will to Power* and partly because, as he is well aware, his view is at odds with Nietzsche's self-understanding of his having emancipated himself from the tradition. Heidegger's strong identification with Nietzsche begins with the acknowledgement that Nietzsche wished to overcome the tradition, but it culminates with a disidentification: he sees himself succeeding where Nietzsche failed. There is something obviously self-serving in this interpretation, particularly in the supposition that Nietzsche ought to have concerned himself with Being. Even if we grant Heidegger the point that Nietzsche fails to grapple with Being, that does not justify his lack of interest in the kinds of issues that do concern Nietzsche. Heidegger dismisses the question of values, which is pressing for Nietzsche and which follows directly from his commitment to the integral relation between philosophy and culture. Nevertheless, Heidegger's interpretation is insightful in exploring Nietzsche's attachment to the idea of subjectivity. For Heidegger, overcoming the subject requires that we open ourselves to non-agency. This is especially true of his later work, where he challenges us to "will non-willing" (Heidegger 1966, pp. 59–60). As we will see, Nietzsche is ambivalent about agency; he believes that we need to reconceptualize the will, affirming the idea of amor fati. However, he remains committed to the challenge of "becoming who one is." Heidegger, in stressing the trajectory from Nietzsche to Descartes in volume 4 of *Nietzsche*, obscures the fact that culture, not a fundamental concern for Descartes, is a fundamental concern for Nietzsche.

Heidegger's attention to Nietzsche as a psychologist has not been appreciated enough. In *Nietzsche*, Heidegger closely examines a passage from WP #12 in which Nietzsche invokes three reasons (having to do with the loss of the categories of purpose, unity, and Being) for thinking of nihilism as a psychological state. Focusing on the emergence of psychology as a response to the demise of cosmological values, Heidegger stresses the originality of Nietzsche's understanding of psychology:

For Nietzsche, 'psychology' is not the psychology being practiced already in his day, a psychology modeled on physics and coupled with physiology as scientific-experimental research into mental processes, in which sense perception and their bodily conditions are posited, like chemical elements, as the basic constituents of such processes. Nor does psychology signify for Nietzsche research into the 'higher life of intelligent mind' and its processes, in the sense of one kind of research among others. Neither is it 'characterology,' as the doctrine of various human types. One could sooner interpret Nietzsche's concept of psychology as 'anthropology,' if 'anthropology' means a philosophical inquiry into the essence of man in the perspective of his essential ties to beings as a whole. In that case, 'anthropology' is the 'metaphysics' of man. But, even so, we have not hit on Nietzsche's 'psychology' and the 'psychological.' Nietzsche's 'psychology' in no way restricts itself to man, but neither does it extend simply to plants and animals. 'Psychology' is the question of the 'psychical'; that is, of what is living, in the particular sense of life that determines becoming as 'will to power.'

On the verge of admiring Nietzsche as a psychologist, Heidegger recoils from the humanist bias he detects. His criticism of Nietzsche is not easy to follow. Heidegger equivocates as to whether Nietzsche restricts psychology to humanity, and he simply ignores how crucial it is for Nietzsche to affirm the connection between the human and animal worlds. Who knows what to say about Heidegger's apparent interest in the psychology of plants?

For Heidegger, Nietzsche's psychology appears to be a disguised form of metaphysics, and Nietzsche is apparently guilty of forgetting Being. Heidegger is not moved by the things that have primacy for Nietzsche: immanence, satisfaction, and well-being.[29] Although Heidegger is well aware of the attention Nietzsche gives to affects, instincts, and the body, he fails to plumb the depths of Nietzsche's psychological thinking about agency.[30] Heidegger deserves to be recognized for establishing the connection between psychology and the will to power, yet he is largely insensitive to the subtlety and the light-footedness of Nietzsche's psychology. Heidegger's own boundedness to the philosophical tradition leads him to be reductive about Nietzsche's psychology; he fails to realize how daring it is.

Heidegger's attack on metaphysics keeps him from thinking seriously about culture. When he addresses the concept of culture (1987, volume 4, part 1, p. 17), he emphasizes that it is often arbitrarily applied to past eras. Of course, there is good reason to refrain from thinking that the Greeks were conscious of possessing a notion of culture like that of us moderns. Missing in Heidegger, however, is any deeper consideration of culture. This is all the more problematic because of Heidegger's despair about modern culture and his rather passive conclusion that there is nothing to be done.[31] Nietzsche too registers a sense of despair, but, like Hegel, he imagines that an active stance in relation to modern culture is possible. Nietzsche is hopeless about modern culture as a culture, but he is not hopeless about agency as a means of resisting such a culture.

4.3 Alienation vs. Despair?

Hegel and Nietzsche give new meaning to Schiller's famous declaration that "it was culture itself that inflicted this wound upon modern humanity" (Schiller 1974, p. 39). Their work urges us to assume responsibility for our fate. To take this one step further: If it is the case that culture renders harm to us moderns, perhaps it is culture that provides the path toward healing. In this context, healing would denote the fulfillment of satisfaction. Hegel would be especially wary of such language if it were used to weigh against rationality; nevertheless, I would like to suggest that he anticipates Nietzsche's psychological analysis of modern culture. Hegel argues that we must come to terms with the lack of satisfaction in modern culture in order to achieve the kind of social and political rapprochement to which he commits himself with mutual recognition. Although Nietzsche despairs over the future of modern culture, he explicitly embraces psychology as the key to understanding modern culture. Nietzsche's belief in contingency means that there is nothing inevitable about the direction of modern culture.

Initially, the main hope that Nietzsche extends to modern culture is the idea of the genius. Genius is identified with true culture, and Nietzsche even suggests that "the procreation of genius . . . is the goal [Wurzel] of all culture" (SE #3). It is, he notes, impossible to predict when a genius might arrive and impose order and rank on culture. This new master could overturn the slave-dominated morality of modern culture. Nietzsche does not seriously envision mutual recognition (Hegel's solution to the problem of modern culture). Nietzsche's justification of autocratic behavior suggests that there is no escape from the master/slave paradigm. Thus, Nietzsche is scathing toward socialism and other modern social movements, and for the most part he is hostile to democracy.

Hegel and Nietzsche differ profoundly on whether the master/slave paradigm can be resolved. Furthermore, Hegel sees that paradigm as a means to a new end; Nietzsche does not. However, there is some overlap between Hegel's and Nietzsche's diagnoses of what is wrong with modern culture. In particular, Nietzsche, following Hegel, worries about the empty subjectivity fostered by modern culture. Both thinkers see danger in the emergence and valorization of "usefulness" in modern culture. Nietzsche senses in a heightened way the potential for self-destruction in modern culture, and he is also more concerned than Hegel about science and technology. Like Hegel, however, Nietzsche directs our attention to the theme of agency.

Among the changes that took place between Hegel's era and Nietzsche's were political events such as the revolutions of 1848, wars, nationhood for Germany, the growth of nationalism in general, and the abolition of slavery; social changes such as the expansion of the bourgeoisie and of mass culture; and scientific developments such as the theory of evolution and the growth of industry and technology. Nietzsche's more pessimistic assessment of modern culture must be understood, as with Marx, as reflecting the magnitude of these changes. That Hegel's and Nietzsche's critiques of modern culture are distinct does not mean that Nietzsche entirely rejects Hegel. The critique of modern culture from Hegel to Nietzsche shifts from alienation to despair, but their views ought to be located on a continuum.

The shift from alienation to despair is evident in the contrast between Hegel and Nietzsche on the issue of the split in self-identity and the prospect of reconstituting it. The split in self-identity that Hegel describes might be on the increase and might be painful, but it is not characterized by the violence that Nietzsche detects. For Nietzsche, the split in self-identity means rupture: identity is torn apart rather than merely sundered. The result is fragmentation into multiple parts. As we will see when we turn to the theme of agency, Hegel imagines the prospect of unity and transparency, whereas Nietzsche defends the multiplicity that admits the possibility of integration, but not unity or transparency. For Hegel, the split in self-identity yields to a new kind of identity; for Nietzsche, the split in self-identity can be mitigated but non-identity prevails.

In summary, Hegel and Nietzsche define modern culture in terms of its lack of satisfaction. The lack of satisfaction, which is due to division in self-identity and which is manifest in a disharmony between inner and outer, results in an empty subjectivity.

Finally, there is in the work of each of these thinkers a sense of longing for unity with the world. For Hegel, this unity means that Insight should not transcend Faith in an undialectical way. For Nietzsche, there is a need for myths in order for culture to flourish. Each of them hoped in his youth for a restoration of myth and then moved to a position of accepting the call to invent myth for the present.[32] Each offers an astute psychological account of the problem of modernity, though Nietzsche is more explicit than Hegel.

Insofar as Nietzsche offers solutions to the woes of modernity, they are primarily aesthetic, with some political content. Hegel provides a solution—mutual recognition—that is rooted in rational self-understanding, which has direct links to society and politics.[33] Nietzsche's politics support the desirability of order and hierarchy; he defends the right of authority and is disdainful of equality. A major concern for him is the conformity that is encouraged in modern culture. Characteristically, it is easier to see what Nietzsche is against than to see what he favors.

One can take Nietzsche's view that culture is apolitical at face value, yet it also may not indicate the irrelevance of politics to Nietzsche. Detwiler (1990, p. 59ff.) makes a strong case for the latter possibility. He maintains that Nietzsche intends to offer a political solution to modern culture—a solution that opposes democracy and which promotes an elitism that not only defends inequality but at times even applauds slavery (ibid., chapter 5, especially pp. 100–108). Detwiler (ibid., p. 113) emphasizes Nietzsche's fascination with the aestheticization of politics, labeling Nietzsche's position "aristocratic radicalism."[34] The oxymoronic tone of this epithet is appropriate: Nietzsche speaks from an aristocratic posture and shows disdain for the ordinary realm of politics, yet he hardly refrains from proffering political opinions. Of course, one should never underestimate the degree to which Nietzsche self-consciously wants to be provocative.[35] Still, Nietzsche associates himself—if only in fantasy—with "men of prey" (BGE #257) who subjugate others in the name of forging a higher culture. One would be hard pressed to find a passage in which Nietzsche takes notice of a downside of autocratism. Ultimately, Nietzsche looked to culture as capable of serving as a shelter from politics, but this does not mean that he embraced an ideal of culture as a sphere separate from politics.

Mark Warren too has argued that Nietzsche's understanding of modern culture has political ramifications. In his view, there are two competing political tendencies in Nietzsche: cultural aristocracy (which coincides with the "aristocratic radicalism" described above) and an implicit model of culture that identifies "the individual and the collective on the basis of the interests individuals share in subjective identities" (Warren 1987, p. 67). There is a side to Nietzsche that sees culture as fostering individuation, as we saw in connection with his idea of true Bildung in chapter 2. Warren (p. 73) attributes to Nietzsche the belief that "recognition" exists in a healthy culture, and notes the parallel to Hegel.[36] Warren's interpretation puts the best face on Nietzsche's politics. Although he does not ignore the predominant strain of aristocratic radicalism, he goes too far in elevating the second model in Nietzsche's work to compete with the first model.[37] There is in Nietzsche's later work a cynicism that has only disdain for the second model.

There is good reason to be skeptical about Nietzsche's politics, but this does not doom Nietzsche's frustration, anger, and sadness with modern culture to irrelevance. In regarding modern culture with despair, Nietzsche does not emphasize defeat; rather, he issues a call to face up to the emotions that emerge from witnessing the disparity between modern culture's promise and reality. Nietzsche's belief in the unexpungeability of irrationality in human life is more an affirmation of the importance of affective experience than an attack on rationality.[38] His philosophy corresponds to a moment of accelerated change that was at once impossible to assimilate and too readily assimilated. No matter how distasteful his politics may be, Nietzsche provides a legacy of uncompromising resistance to modern culture. As I see it, however, Nietzsche's attraction to the right of the master is grandiose; his insistence on the inevitability of the master/slave paradigm is too gloomy.

My criticism of Nietzsche is not meant to imply an endorsement of Hegel's critique of modern culture, which is further removed from us in time than Nietzsche's and which is based on a model of a relatively small and homogeneous world. Hegel's notion of recognition suggests that the path from alienation must be conceived in terms of our relation to others. Recognition remains a valuable concept, although (as I will argue in part II) it must be qualified in certain respects. There is something appealing, too, about the mixed assessment of modern culture that Hegel presents in PhS. Hegel portrays modernity's possibilities and its liabilities. That he did not envision the nihilism described and confronted by Nietzsche ought not be held against him.

So far, my conclusion is that the dialectic of modernity must accommodate the ambivalence of Hegel's assessment (particularly his hope for resolution through human relationships), the negativity of Nietzsche's later assessment (particularly his accurate prediction of barbarism), and, in a more positive vein, Nietzsche's attention to affects, instincts, and the body. It is not possible now to understand the state of culture by looking to Hegel and bypassing Nietzsche. With this in mind, let us again consider Horkheimer's, Adorno's, and Habermas's perspectives on the dialectic of modernity beyond Hegel and Nietzsche.

We are now in a better position to evaluate Habermas's concern about Nietzsche's influence on Horkheimer and Adorno's *Dialectic of Enlightenment*. Habermas is correct to observe that Horkheimer and Adorno pick up from Nietzsche the notion that the Enlightenment was hostile to myth. Furthermore, we can glimpse the influence of Nietzsche in Horkheimer and Adorno's criticism of modern culture as conformist and in their criticism of science as instrumental and as glorifying only the useful. When he characterizes Nietzsche's aristocratic radicalism as conservatism, Habermas overlooks the possibility of being more inclusive of Nietzsche within critical theory (Jay 1973, p. 256).

As I have mentioned, Habermas claims that, as a consequence of their rejection of the Enlightenment, Horkheimer and Adorno are left without the grounding of critique. He observes that Adorno's aestheticized solution for modern culture is already implied by the notion of mimesis. But Habermas's account of Horkheimer and Adorno is conspicuously silent on the issue of anti-Semitism and the dialectic of Enlightenment.[39] It is in the context of analyzing anti-Semitism that Horkheimer and Adorno propose mimesis as constituting a relation to the other that is opposed to the false projection of fascism. In false projection, one attributes to the other what one dislikes about oneself. Horkheimer and Adorno suggest (DE, p. 168) that "the portrait of the Jews that the nationalists offer to the world is in fact their own self-portrait." Mimesis here becomes a bond between self and other that can be seen as resembling what is called 'identification' in psychoanalysis; false projection resembles a disorder of the self that is characterized by the lack of boundaries between self and other (that is, narcissism). Horkheimer and Adorno's contrast between mimesis and false projection is a fruitful attempt at integrating Hegelian recognition and Nietzschean will to power. In mimesis, the self respects the other as an other; in false projection, a kind of master-slave relationship prevails— with potentially lethal consequences.

Horkheimer and Adorno's discussion of the psychological dimension of mimesis prevents us from reading mimesis as simply an aesthetic notion.[40] This psychological dimension is also important because it suggests that Horkheimer and Adorno are not as negative as Habermas implies. In *The Philosophical Discourse of Modernity*, Habermas obscures the psychological dimension of mimesis, although he does mention it in *The Theory of Communicative Action* (1981, pp. 290–291). In the latter, he notes that mimesis is implicitly used by Horkheimer and Adorno to denote a bond between individuals in which selfhood is ensured rather than eclipsed. Thus, Habermas affirms the broader meaning of mimesis insofar it can be viewed as bolstering his own position: intersubjectivity as the basis of abetting the development of autonomous selfhood.

A complete reading of Horkheimer and Adorno would have to take account not only of the Nietzschean influence but also of the related influence of psychoanalysis. As Jay has pointed out (1986, p. 93), and as Rabinbach (1997, p. 184ff.) also documents, the influence of psychoanalysis grew as the Frankfurt School began to give more attention to anti-Semitism. Habermas's exclusive focus on the influence of Nietzsche on Horkheimer and Adorno has the effect of creating too easy a target for him. What is not rational conjures up the specter of fascism for Habermas—especially Nietzsche's proto-fascism and Heidegger's complicity with fascism.[41]

Habermas's zealous support for the Enlightenment attenuates the conflictual aspect of the dialectic of the Enlightenment. Owing to his anxiety about the danger of irrationality, Habermas has little interest in considering the emotional sustenance that mythology provides.[42] It is as if Habermas confirms Horkheimer and Adorno's warning that the Enlightenment conceals its own mythic fear. It is worth emphasizing in this connection that Horkheimer and Adorno are hardly champions of irrationality. In the fascinating response to questions that follows his paper "The Meaning of Working Through the Past" in *Critical Models*, Adorno elucidates his position on irrationality. He acknowledges the danger of irrationality, but he maintains that repressing irrationality is equally dangerous. In particular, Adorno expresses concern about how instinctual impulses and affects can appear in "distorted, twisted and altered forms as aggression, as projection, as displacement." He specifically credits Nietzsche's work as the place where this under-standing of irrationality was "first wonderfully described" and Freud's corpus as the place where it was subsequently "thoroughly analyzed" (Adorno 1998, p. 299). Habermas's neglect of depth psychology in his later work is a loss for critical theory.

In *Modernism as a Philosophical Problem*, Robert Pippin focuses on the tension between Horkheimer/Adorno and Habermas with regard to the "dialectic of modernity"—a tension which Pippin explicates as fol-lows (1991a, p. 77): although the promise of reconciliation for modernity seems out of reach, we cannot simply abandon it. Like Habermas, Pippin attributes the dialectic of modernity to Hegel. However, he also maintains that Nietzsche's critique of modern cul-ture embodies aspects of modern culture itself: it reveals that moder-nity's aporia has intensified (ibid., pp. 104–105). On the one hand, Pippin concurs with Habermas that Horkheimer and Adorno's per-spective on modern culture is one-sidedly negative. On the other hand, Pippin is critical of Habermas for leaning one-sidedly in the direction of endorsing modern culture. I am sympathetic with the general direction of Pippin's argument. However, it is unfortunate that neither Pippin nor Habermas lingers to address Horkheimer and Adorno's notion of the Enlightenment as a falsely self-satisfied or nar-cissistic consciousness—a theme that can be traced back to Hegel and that is also articulated by Nietzsche. This theme emerges clearly in Georg Simmel's analysis of modern culture, which highlights the psy-chological experience and interpretation of a fluid inner world. According to Simmel (1978, p. 481), an "exaggerated subjectivism" unfolds in modernity; it is characterized by having no center and the relentless pursuit of fresh stimulation.[43]

It is greatly to their credit that Horkheimer and Adorno refuse to be encumbered by the false antinomy between Hegel and Nietzsche.[44] From the friendly environment of Santa Monica, they smelled death—mass death—and forged their admittedly despairing inter-pretation of modern culture accordingly. They document for us that, despite its comforts, the smoldering dissatisfaction of modern culture had exploded. They provide concrete proof that self-division had turned into self-destruction.

II

Culture and Agency

5

On the Concept of Agency

Modern Inwardness is not a simple phenomenon but at least double. Modern self-exploration is in some senses at odds with self-control. Self-objectification tends to occlude what self-control tries to articulate. The one seeks to grasp us in the general categories of science, the other to allow our particularity to find expression.
—Charles Taylor, "Inwardness and the Culture of Modernity"

Although in the first part of the book I heeded fundamental differences between Hegel and Nietzsche—differences in regard to their views of knowledge (chapter 1), the aims of Bildung (chapter 2), the meaning of Greek tragedy (chapter 3), and the prospects for modern culture (chapter 4)—the very project of comparing Hegel's and Nietzsche's views lends itself to overestimating what they share. This is not to retreat from the idea that there has been a tendency to contrast the figures of Hegel and Nietzsche reflexively without appreciating patterns of agreement. As I concluded in chapter 4, both philosophers look to a rejuvenated sense of agency in order to come to terms with the dissatisfactions of modern culture. The conclusion of part I thus leads us to part II, where I shall undertake an inquiry into Hegel's and Nietzsche's notions of agency. Here, however, mutual dialogue will be subordinated to the aim of investigating their respective views more fully.

In the present chapter, I consider the word 'agency', locate it historically by borrowing from Charles Taylor's work, and derive a rough outline of a way to conceptualize Hegel's and Nietzsche's views of agency.

5.1 Persons and Agents

It is difficult to draw a line between the concepts of *person* and *agent*. On the one hand, it would be strange if the concepts were not overlapping; on the other hand, they have had separate lives, and it is not clear how to think about their interrelation.

As a starting point, I propose to distinguish the concepts in the following way: all agents must be persons, but not all persons are agents. To be an agent is an achievement; to be a person is less obviously so. Traditionally, a person is defined as a unit of legal and theological responsibility; an underlying sense of identity goes along with this supposition. The identity of a person is often a kind of generic category, its meaning fixed as much by how others regard one as by how one regards oneself. The identity of an agent as I am thinking about agents is more complex, with fluid and varying boundaries. Because it includes how one thinks of oneself, it is a richer concept than personhood. At the risk of oversimplification, I might venture to say that agents have more interesting selves than persons do.

The vast philosophical literature on "personal identity" focuses on continuity and reidentification.[1] Although personhood is sometimes conceived as an achievement (which would mean that it is possible for some human beings to fail to be persons), the problems associated with this concept tend not to challenge that personhood is a basic status that most human beings possess.

Personhood lacks the exemplary status that goes along with agency.[2] The kinds of cases conjured by imaginative analytic philosophers are especially relevant to persons. The infamous brain in a vat, and anecdotes about Jones's finding himself with Smith's body, though stimulating, are removed from the concerns that are most germane to agency. Metaphysical issues raised through hypothetical cases about whether personhood is linked to one's psychological continuity or to one's body can be profound, but they can also interfere with getting around to questions that arise once we assume that persons normally have bodies and that bodies are an essential part of what it means to have personhood.

A dog fancier might be troubled by the anthropocentrism of the assertion that personhood is a basic human capacity. One might not want to exclude the possibility of dog personhood, even if one is prepared to regard human personhood as special. Yet this line of thought takes us down a slippery slope—what could one say about ant personhood? Criticism from another direction might come from someone who infers that, given what I have stated, that a dead human is no longer a person—indeed, that the phrase "a dead person" would be oxymoronic or perhaps unintelligible. There are metaphysical puzzles here too, but I would have no trouble mourning a dead human as a former person. Anticipating a further rebuttal, I would add that there is no reason not to extend to former persons the same respect that one extends to other persons.

Introducing respect requires the qualification that, though being alive may well be a necessary condition of (actual, not former) personhood, it is not sufficient condition. Personhood, as I have suggested, is a generic category, but it is often linked to the idea that humans ought to be accorded respect. No evaluation is required, as personhood is an attribute of humans—even bad and crazy humans. An implicit way to draw the line in distinguishing persons from agency arises from the fact that agency is inescapably determined by content. To be an agent, I believe, one must understand something about one's relation to oneself, as Kantians have emphasized. However, for Hegel and Nietzsche agency requires that one understand one's relation to oneself within a context of cultural meaning. The notion that conveys this commitment is self-fathoming, which I described in chapter 2.

A few more general observations about the concept of agency are in order. An agent is, in the most literal sense, one who acts, and it may be contrasted to being a *patient* (i.e., one who is acted upon). From experience, I know that if, in describing my work at a social occasion, I mention the word 'agency', I will likely be met with blank stares or overt perplexity. 'Agency' is a technical term used by philosophers and social theorists. Indeed, the philosophical use of 'agent' virtually is the opposite of many of the everyday associations that accompany the word: FBI agents, insurance agents, and sports agents are engaged in representing others, not themselves.

Traditionally, philosophers have been drawn to the word 'agency' in connection with the problem of free will. Agency is thus predicated on our intentions, particularly the capacity to engage in second-order reflections on our own desires and beliefs. The philosophical meaning of 'agent' is not confined to the realm of action, though action is never alien from the concept of agency. Charles Taylor's work on agency emphasizes that agents must engage in "strong evaluations," but certainly Taylor wishes to connect this reflexivity to living a good human life.

There is a large gap between philosophers who are inclined to think of agency in terms of the link between beliefs and action and philosophers who are seeking to capture something further—something like self-realization. It is possible to distinguish what we might call a thin and a thick sense of agency. The thin sense of agency denotes efficaciousness—success measured in terms of the commensurability of one's beliefs and actions. The thick sense of agency is in search of something more—being satisfied is often linked to having a good or worthy character. Efficacious agency is more abstract and, thus, bears an affinity to many conceptions of personhood. This thin sense of agency has the merit of presuming less, but it also means less.

Self-realizing agency implies both cultivation and the challenge of pursuing a worthy ideal. Such a qualitative kind of pursuit ordinarily supposes background values that support and sustain the ideal. At the same time, at least in Western culture, self-realizing agency requires independence. With the thick sense of agency, determining agency shifts from a yes/no assessment to a continuum. The thick conception of agency opens the door to tough questions about sorting out the private and public aspects of agency. It also forces us to ponder the universality of the concept. Nonetheless, 'agency' is appealing precisely because it is less ethnocentric than 'selfhood', which is predicated on an autonomous sense of self. Every culture has some notion of what is required for a desirable human life, but not all cultures share the Western view that the proper telos of development entails an individuated self.

Having acknowledged different perspectives on agency, I shall proceed without trying to settle questions about the merits of the thin vs. the thick sense of agency. Admittedly, the thick sense gets us into the muddy waters of culture, which advocates of the thin sense have the common sense to try to avoid. In the end, however, the thin sense of agency is no freer of culture in its conception. One gains access to a certain range of problems with the thin sense of agency or personal identity, and these problems are well worth contemplating; but one does not thereby escape the factor of culture. The thick sense of agency raises alternative considerations. Invariably, they lead us to reflect on the history of the concept.

5.2 Taylor's Genealogy of Agency

Taylor gives sustained attention to the concept of agency. In a number of books and articles he has emphasized the centrality of agency for being able to come to terms with modernity, tracing the concept and its derivatives historically. Yet Taylor's work is by no means just historical; his exploration of history is designed to help us understand the unarticulated and implicit aspects of how we conceive of the concept of agency. As a result, Taylor has developed one of the most ambitious and engaging models of agency.

An important source for Taylor is Harry Frankfurt's 1971 work on the human capacity to engage in second-order desires. For Taylor, agency is grounded in the quality of our motivation—in the capacity to make "strong evaluations." Strong evaluations are distinguished by their "articulacy and depth." Taylor adds that strong evaluations contribute to a sense of responsibility in a way that weak evaluations do not. The strong evaluator, according to Taylor, has recourse to a "richer language." Weak evaluations entail a "simple weighing of alternatives"; thus, they lack the "vocabulary of worth" that characterizes strong evaluations. Thus, language is intrinsically related to human agency. Moreover, according to Taylor, emotions are important for the constitution of agency, and emotions ought to be connected to language. It is a distinctive aspect of Taylor's model of agency that feelings are regarded as a crucial to evaluations and self-understanding: "Language articulates our feelings, makes them clearer and more defined; and in this way transforms our sense of the imports involved; and hence transforms the feeling." (Taylor 1985, volume 1, p. 71) There is a reciprocal effect: words express feelings, and feelings are thereby altered and rendered into new forms.

My comments about agency in the first section of this chapter dovetail with Taylor in emphasizing agency as an achievement. Yet the line between personhood and agency that Taylor draws differs from the one I have proposed.[3] In "The Concept of a Person," Taylor maintains that personhood is a subclass of agency, thereby reserving the former to describe a bearer of rights, while construing the latter as a more generic category—an inversion of the relationship between personhood and agency that I have sketched. What is confusing in Taylor, though, is that, while he clearly regards the word 'agency' as exemplary, he suggests that animals can be agents but not persons.

To be appreciated fully, Taylor's model of agency must be examined within the context of the history of the concept. It becomes more intelligible once we take account of his genealogy of agency in connection with his (re)formulation of the concept.[4] As is evident from the epigraph at the beginning of the present chapter, Taylor sees the idea of inwardness as setting the concept of agency in modernity apart from the concept of agency that existed in earlier epochs. Inwardness is connected with the notion that we are defined by our interior life and ultimately by our sense of self (Taylor 1992, pp. 93–94).[5] The trajectory I discerned in chapter 4 is evident in Taylor's account.

Although Taylor sees agency as a modern phenomenon, he draws attention to traces and remnants that have a much older lineage. Indeed, Taylor stresses that there is much that adheres to the concept of agency that we fail to recognize. He explains: "We all too easily assume that people have always seen themselves as we do" (ibid., p. 93). Taylor produces a specific example for us to consider: the dichotomy between inward and outward that we take for granted in our self-understanding. Taylor's approach shows a sensitivity to self-thwarting as constitutive of self-fathoming.

Modern inwardness, according to Taylor, can be analyzed into two components: self-control and self-exploration (ibid., p. 94). Both self-control and self-exploration have convoluted histories that need to be unearthed. He suggests that self-control is a persistent theme in the Western philosophical tradition from Plato onward, and that it is defined by the idea that the good man is "master of himself" (p. 95). This mastery is achieved by reason's ascending to its proper place over desires. From Plato, Taylor leaps to the seventeenth century, where he sees a shift in how reason is understood and in its perceived relation to passions. Whereas Plato understood reason as "clear vision" that disclosed the "order of things," Descartes construes reason in terms of instrumental control, wherein the subordination of the passions is less of an issue (pp. 95–97).

Taylor stresses that Descartes's conception of reason is procedural rather than substantive—a property of subjective thinking, not a vision of reality. Corresponding to this change in the nature of reason, according to Taylor, is a transformation in the notion of agency: "Reason and human excellence require a stance of disengagement" (p. 98). This emphasis on disengagement, which represents a crucial turn in the concept of agency, is germane to the Cartesian myth, as I noted in chapter 1. Taylor's primary focus is on disengagement from our bodies and from the cosmos (p. 98). However, he also discusses disengagement from traditions or habits (p. 101). Although Taylor acknowledges that disengagement has an antecedent in Stoic philosophy, he argues that it opens up an uncharted and specifically modern path: the path of a "human agent who is able to remake himself by methodical and disciplined action" (p. 99).

From Descartes, Taylor moves on to Locke, whose idea of the mind as a tabula rasa further contributed to disengagement by dramatizing the ideal of self-shaping. Locke's suggestion that identity is determined by self-consciousness (i.e., awareness of one's own continuity) is a determinative basis for the Anglo-American literature on personal identity. Taylor is especially interested in tracing the pull toward self-examination that occurs as a result of the expectation to scrutinize and remake ourselves—what he terms "reflexivity." In particular, modern agency requires "self-objectivation"—a first-person point of view that is not found in the ancient world. Though Taylor's assertion that the ancients did not concern themselves with self-objectivation might be questioned, his account is persuasive in showing how self-objectivation emerged as the source for a uniquely modern kind of discomfort with the world.

Taylor's narrative then turns to the strand of modern inwardness that is linked to the second component, self-exploration. Augustan (Saint Augustine) is the figure who is associated with a turn inward that utilizes a first-person perspective. Augustan's turn inward occurs, of course, as a way to discover God; in Montaigne, the turn inward becomes an end in itself. Interestingly, Taylor notes that self-exploration is to some degree "antithetical" to disengagement (p. 105). He claims that self-objectivation removes us from our own identity, whereas self-exploration directs us to it. Self-exploration, according to Taylor, is based on the assumption that "we don't already know who we are" (p. 105). This latter theme, prominent in Montaigne, is even more so in expressivism, where fulfillment and creativity are seen as the sources of agency.

Taylor's tour de force culminates with some reflections about the duality of modern inwardness. Although his choice of philosophers is fairly representative, one wonders whether the coherence of this narrative would have been affected if he had considered additional, perhaps lesser-known thinkers. It is also fitting to wonder how Hegel and Nietzsche fit into this story—a question that will be the main focus of the next section of the present chapter. To his credit, Taylor does acknowledge the fundamental tensions that inform his account. Two key observations emerge: that "modern self-exploration is in some senses at odds with self-control" and that "self-objectivation tends to occlude what self-control tries to articulate" (p. 107). The kind of self-control that Montaigne seeks has to do with expression; it can be juxtaposed to self-objectivation as Descartes conceives of it, which restricts itself to following scientific method. In other words, Taylor acknowledges that the integrity of modern inwardness as a concept is threatened by the deep chasm that opens up between what we might call an aesthetics of the self and a science of the self.

However debatable some of the details of Taylor's genealogical account may be, his work is successful in dislodging monolithic assumptions about agency. What Taylor aspires to do, and what he accomplishes well, is to challenge conceptions of agency that are indifferent to history. In particular, Taylor deftly directs us to reflect on some ideas that have been dragged along from the past and on some that had been displaced and forgotten. From Taylor's perspective, this is bound to help us choose better and more wisely in the future.

5.3 Hegel and Nietzsche in Context

Although Taylor's narrative extends from Plato to the present, expressivism represents a decisive moment in the genealogy of agency.[6] 'Expressivism', a term that Taylor takes over and develops from the work of Isaiah Berlin, captures the new mentality of the post-Enlightenment era, in which the loss of external meaning results in the adoption of a heightened focus on inwardness. This transformation entails a turn away from humans as rational animals to an entirely new point of view: a human "comes to know himself as expressing and clarifying what he is and recognizing himself in this expression . . . self-awareness through expression" (Taylor 1975, p. 17). More specifically, Taylor explains that expressivism affirms that the process of pursuing inwardness means that before pursuing inwardness one lacks determination and cannot be fulfilled in the same sense. The aim of modern inwardness is individuation—that is, creating oneself as a unique individual.[7]

Taylor emphasizes the importance of Herder's work in the unfolding of expressivism, specifically the idea that language was an "expression," not just a referential sign as Enlightenment thinkers had maintained. This notion of expression was linked to the idea that emotions have primacy in human life, and it also was extended to the nature of art. Expressivism was born out of a spirit of affirming the potential of humans to forge an integrated way of living. Let us look more closely into Taylor's understanding of expressivism.

Taylor delineates four wishes that underlie expressivism: for unity and wholeness, for freedom, for union with nature, and for union with other humans (1975, pp. 23–28). The first wish arose during the Enlightenment as a protest against the dissection of humans, which fostered false dichotomies such as soul/body and reason/feeling. Freedom, Taylor suggests, is the central value of humanity; it coincides with self-realization as the goal of human life. The wish for union with nature upholds the connection between the body and living nature and seeks communion. The wish for union with others is a wish for a deeper bond of connection within human community.

In view of the two trends of modern inwardness described in the preceding section, it is apparent that expressivism follows the trajectory of self-exploration rather than that of self-control—especially insofar as self-control is conceived as self-objectivation. Indeed, Taylor specifically notes that "the expressivist revolution constituted a prodigious development of modern post-Augustinian inwardness, in its self-exploratory branch" (1989, p. 389). Taylor is aware of tensions within expressivism—in particular, that the wish for unity and wholeness, the wish for union with nature and the wish for union with others seem to be at odds with the ideal of individuation. However, he does not grapple with the implications of such seemingly contradictory impulses.

As I have noted, Taylor acknowledges that there are tensions between self-exploration and self-objectivation. This is a particularly important point, as he understands the motivation of Hegel's philosophy precisely in terms of an attempt to resolve and embrace both aspects of modern inwardness. As Taylor elaborates (1989, pp. 24–27), Hegel adheres to the expressivist tradition in embracing unity and wholeness and being anti-dualist, in celebrating freedom as the principle of the modern world, in seeking union with nature, and especially in affirming union with others through Sittlichkeit. Recall that the early Hegel was immersed in an intellectual atmosphere that was enamored with remaking philosophy as expressivistic. The influence of self-exploration can be seen in Hegel's assertion that "mind . . . is already mind at the outset, but it does not yet know that it is" (PM #385). It can also be discerned in passages where Hegel defends the value of human emotion—for example, where he suggests that the educated person feels more deeply than the uneducated one (PM #448, Zusatz).

As Hegel begins to develop his own philosophy, however, he is unambiguously influenced by Kant and by the modern philosophical tradition. Although Hegel offers an expanded version of rationality, he never abandons rationality, and he is earnest about elevating philosophy to the status of science. As I noted in chapter 1, although Hegel rejects the Cartesian myth, he clearly has sympathies with it: he adopts self-objectivation as a part of a first-person perspective that aspires to be universal and impersonal. His allegiance to self-

objectivation is most evident in his affirmation of the need for justification in philosophy.

Therefore, one cannot assimilate Hegel into the expressivist camp
without qualification. At the same time, it would be a mistake to
emphasize his allegiance to self-objectivation at the expense of
acknowledging his investment in self-exploration. Hegel rejects the
paradigm of epistemology in favor of the psychology of knowledge.
He preserves a commitment to the kind of justification that only rationality can provide, but not as an end in itself, apart from a concern
about well-being. Hegel remained influenced by ancient Greek ideas
about self-control as well as the modern idea of self-objectivation.
Recall from chapter 2 that Hegel was fully dedicated to self-fathoming, to the ideal of a dynamic sense of agency. Taylor's work provides
us with a broad framework in which to understand this: its confluence
with the expressivist ideal. There is a twist, however: for Hegel, individual self-understanding leads to an appreciation of humanity as a
vehicle for Geist.

Taylor's view of Hegel highlights the background of expressivism
and modern inwardness in general. Taylor clearly admires Hegel for
his attempt to integrate the different strands of modern inwardness,
and he goes on to make a number of interesting points about the presuppositions that limit the relevance of Hegel today.[8] The focus on
modern inwardness is particularly insightful in illustrating the seriousness of Hegel's concern with culture. Still, it is equally important
not to minimize Hegel's affirmation of knowledge, which signals his
allegiance to the philosophical tradition and, in his eyes, provides the
path for solving the problems of modern culture. Although Hegel's
intention is to integrate self-exploration and self-objectivation, a commitment to the latter prevails in his work.

Let us pause to consider Hegel in language closer to his own terminology. He uses 'person' to refer to the external status that each
subject has. In the *Phenomenology of Spirit* he traces the notion of
personhood to the Romans, characterizing it as a universal category;
however, he also sees it as an "empty unit" requiring a split between
public and private (p. 292). In the Master/Slave section of the Self-
Consciousness chapter, Hegel juxtaposes the superior status of being
"an independent self-consciousness" to being a person (p. 114). Hegel

also discusses personhood in the *Philosophy of Right*, where he suggests that 'person' designates a subject that is self-aware and for-itself (PR #35, Zusatz). He alludes to the Kantian idea of personhood, which is defined in terms of rights and respect. He also observes (ibid.) that "the highest achievement of a human being is to be a person," yet he proceeds to qualify this point, since the concept encompasses so much. He expresses reservations about defining oneself in terms of formal right: only "emotionally limited people" [einem beschränkten Herzen und Gemüte] do so in contrast to those "of nobler mind" (PR #37, Zusatz). Although Hegel values the concept of personhood, he implicitly recognizes the need for a more exemplary category of self-identity. As I shall demonstrate in the next chapter, there are reasons that it is appropriate to utilize the word 'agency' in conjunction with Hegel.

Nietzsche does not pursue the integration of self-objectivation and self-exploration. Though his commitment to self-exploration is evident, his opinion of self-objectivation is less clear. Nietzsche does not figure as importantly in Taylor's writings as Hegel. In *Sources of the Self* (p. 63), Taylor suggests that Nietzsche is the philosopher who first opposes what Taylor terms 'hypergoods'—those "higher-order goods . . . which not only are incomparably more important than others but provide the standpoint from which these must be weighed, judged, decided about." Taylor sees Nietzsche (in contrast with subsequent philosophers of this ilk) as accepting the hypergood of "yea-saying," which has roots in Romantic expressivism (ibid., pp. 102, 445). Taylor discusses Nietzsche primarily in the course of explicating the views of Foucault, Derrida, and other neo-Nietzscheans, and he makes a point of claiming that the French interpretations of Nietzsche are sometimes one-sided (ibid., p. 488).[9]

In *Philosophical Arguments*, Taylor locates Nietzsche's work within expressivism. Nietzsche, relative to Hegel, is portrayed as representing a radical version of expressivism. Whereas Hegel takes expressivism to mean bringing to light that the self can be defined by self-expression, Nietzsche challenges this idea in the name of self-invention, which tips the balance from "finding" to "making" (ibid., p. 117f.). Taylor reads Nietzsche as reveling in the aesthetics of existence, wherein the self becomes a work of art (ibid., p. 16). This dramatizes Nietzsche's allegiance to self-exploration as opposed to self-objectivation.

Let us consider where Nietzsche stands in relation to the four wishes of expressivism. Nietzsche endorses anti-dualism, yet he is suspicious about unity and wholeness as unrealistic and as fraudulent projections. He embraces the wish for freedom in his conception of the free spirit, although he is dubious about the notion of free will (which he sees as an invention of philosophers). He allies himself closely with the wish for union with nature—especially through Dionysian experience. He is not responsive to the expressivist wish for unity with others—a wish highly valued by Hegel. As was established in chapter 2, Nietzsche is concerned with self-fathoming; however, his emphasis is on making, rather than finding, and it lacks the Hegelian premise of self-enclosed development.

Nietzsche's interest in self-exploration outweighs his concern with self-objectivation. The aim of self-exploration is evident in the subtitle of *Ecce Homo*: "How One Becomes Who One Is." Indeed, Nietzsche goes on to proclaim in *Ecce Homo* that "to become what one is, one must not have the faintest notion of *what* one is" (EH, "Why I Am So Clever," #9). This exemplifies Taylor's point that with self-exploration it is assumed that one must explore oneself because one does not already know who one is. Nietzsche's praise of the idea of giving "style to one's character" (GS #290) further confirms his commitment to self-exploration.[10]

What about Nietzsche's relation to self-objectivation? Nietzsche is clearly not friendly to the idea of disengagement, viewing it as a posture to which philosophers have felt the need to aspire. He insists that underlying postures of disengagement are inescapably personal needs of human beings. In GS #15 Nietzsche muses: "Perhaps you know some people near you who must look at themselves only from a distance in order to find themselves at all tolerable or attractive and invigorating. Self-knowledge is strictly inadvisable for them." This idea can be linked to the opening passage in the preface to the *Genealogy of Morals*, in which Nietzsche argues that "men of knowledge" lack knowledge of themselves: "We have never sought ourselves—how could it happen that we should ever *find* ourselves?" It would seem, then, that according to Nietzsche the inclination to objectify oneself is opposed to the openness that is required in order to explore oneself.

Although Nietzsche is wary of self-objectivation, he does not necessarily disavow the other component of modern inwardness, self-control. In numerous passages, especially from his middle period, he praises self-mastery and moderation (see, e.g., HAH I, preface and #464; HAH II, #326). There are passages in book V of *The Gay Science* in which he praises self-determination and connects it to being a free spirit. In *Twilight of the Idols* ("Skirmishes of an Untimely Man," #38), Nietzsche proposes that freedom is grounded in responsibility for oneself.[11] In a number of passages in *The Will to Power*, Nietzsche defends self-control in terms of control of affects. Consider, for example, the following:

> Blind indulgence of an affect, totally regardless of whether it be a generous and compassionate or a hostile affect, is the cause of the greatest evils. Greatness of character does not consist in not possessing these affects—on the contrary, one possesses them to the highest degree—but in having them under control. (WP #928)[12]

Thus, Nietzsche's commitment to self-exploration in no way precludes the value of self-control. For Nietzsche, self-control organizes and restrains affects, but it does not expunge them. Self-control is construed in line with the expressivist attachment to emotion. The influence of the ancient Greeks (especially the Aristotelian notion of megalopsyche) is also evident here.

Nonetheless, one must be careful not to misinterpret Nietzsche as siding with Apollo against Dionysus. Along with the many passages that praise self-control, Nietzsche encourages us to let go, to forget, and to revel in the absence of regulating oneself. A revealing example is found in the conclusion to "Self-control" (GS #305): "For one must be able to lose oneself occasionally if one wants to learn something from things different from oneself." In this sentence Nietzsche seems to be proposing that it is not inconsistent with agency to abandon agency. His defense of the desirability of losing oneself occurs in the context of asserting a specific claim about exposing oneself to "things different from oneself." The qualification "occasionally" may save Nietzsche from contradicting himself.

We might read Nietzsche as claiming that self-control is desirable except when it is preferable to open ourselves to displace such control. However, interpreting "losing oneself" in terms of a kind of reasonable exception still might fail to register a full appreciation of the Dionysian impulse. Nietzsche values an overflowingness of character that refuses to be harnessed and that is modeled on sexual passion. From even a cursory look at what Nietzsche has to say about self-control, it is evident that his view of agency is complicated and rife with potential contradictions.

Let me reiterate a few points. Taylor, though he acknowledges the tension between self-exploration and self-objectivation, does not ponder the relationship between self-exploration and self-control. He discusses self-control in connection with Plato and the Stoics; he has relatively little to say about the Aristotelian paradigm in which affects are shaped to be appropriate.[13] There is an argument to be made, then, that self-exploration supersedes but does not necessarily replace ancient Greek ideas about self-control. My point is a criticism of Taylor only in the sense that there is more to say—a point that I suppose he would be prepared to concede.

Taylor's description of expressivism offers an important background for understanding the philosophical projects of Hegel and Nietzsche. In particular, Hegel's concern about attaining unity with others is not matched by Nietzsche, and Nietzsche's interest in affects and drives are subordinate in Hegel because of his commitment to rationality. Moreover, we have ascertained that Hegel attempts to embrace both self-objectivation and self-exploration, whereas Nietzsche regards them as in tension and opts to value self-exploration over self-objectivation. Hegel and Nietzsche appreciate self-control, although Nietzsche does so more ambivalently. Framing the views of Hegel and Nietzsche in these ways is helpful, but it is also rather general. This introduction to the theme of agency can only conclude, then, with a promissory note to plunge more deeply now into the question of what Hegel and Nietzsche mean by 'agency'.

6

Agency and Recognition in Hegel

Whenever and wherever it is possible to speak of recognition, there is *eo ipso* a prior hiddenness.

—Søren Kierkegaard, *Fear and Trembling*

In this chapter, I shall specify further the meaning of the concept of agency in Hegel. A number of themes that emerged in earlier chapters will be revisited: the psychology of knowledge, self-fathoming, tragic self-knowledge, the problem of modern culture, the need for a renewal of agency, and preliminary ideas about Hegel's understanding of agency as self-objectivation and self-exploration. As will become evident, Hegel's concept of recognition provides a key for integrating all of these themes.

There is considerable overlap between the themes of agency and recognition. For Hegel, agency is embedded within the concept of recognition; thus, the latter will claim my attention as I prepare the way to clarify the former. I shall begin, therefore, with a general discussion of recognition; then I shall move on to self-recognition, an aspect of recognition that has special importance in my account. In the third and final section of this chapter, I shall locate self-recognition in relation to other important concepts in the *Phenomenology of Spirit*: cognition, satisfaction, and desire.

6.1 Socio-Political and Epistemological Functions of Recognition

The most obvious function of recognition is socio-political: Hegel proposes it as a solution to what is wrong in modern culture. Yet, as I shall demonstrate, the concept has another function, which is episte-mological. Indeed, in order to appreciate the concept of recognition fully, we will have to think about it in relation to some other impor-tant notions in the *Phenomenology of Spirit.* It will be important to clar-ify, too, in what sense the socio-political and epistemological functions are related.

At its most basic, recognition prescribes a bond among the mem-bers of society that surpasses the minimal and superficial bond speci-fied by social contract theory.[1] Hegel intends the concept of recognition to reflect a deeper bond that is meant to be reminiscent of the polis. Unlike in the polis, however, the bond specified by recog-nition is intended to respect, rather than eclipse, individuality. Recognition stipulates a social and political model that is appropriate for modern culture, wherein individuality is valued. This function of recognition has served as a basis of communitarian thinking and remains a vital part of contemporary social theory.

A second function of recognition in PhS is epistemological. Hegel understands recognition as a stage on the path to knowledge. Recognition [Anerkennen] must be understood as a form of cogni-tion [Erkennen]. Like cognition, recognition has a double structure: as a relation between a self and object and as a relation between a self and itself. As a relation between self and object, recognition denotes a special kind of object, an object that itself is a subject. According to Hegel, this involves mutuality, and each subject learns something about itself from the other. As a relation between a self and itself, recognition feeds into the overall project of PhS: the achievement of self-knowledge. The epistemological function of recognition reflects Hegel's commitment to rational justification and sustains the ideal of expounding philosophy as science.

At first glance, it is perplexing that Hegel relies on the concept of recognition to work in such different ways. Recalling Hegel's interest in the psychology of knowledge, however, helps to provide a bridge between the socio-political and epistemological functions. For Hegel, human satisfaction depends on our comprehension of the deep nexus between our knowledge of ourselves and our actual relation to others. The concept of recognition specifies the bond between self and others that ought to exist in modern culture; yet it is also intended to spawn a new kind of rational agency, which might help to rectify modernity's woes. Thus, a proper notion of agency is a prerequisite for better social integration; in turn, social integration allows agency to thrive in a freer way.

Satisfaction is the aim of recognition in both of its functions. It combines the bond of the socio-political function and the rational justification of the epistemological function. Of course, we need to understand precisely what Hegel means by 'satisfaction'—a term that is widely, but not consistently used. As we know, Hegel contrasts cultures that provide satisfaction with those that fail to do so, and he maintains that modern culture can achieve satisfaction only by means of a transformation of agency. Although it is one-sided to focus on the concept of recognition solely in terms of offering a model of agency, I shall argue that the full implications of this particular aspect of recognition have not been adequately articulated and thus ought to claim our attention. To that end, I shall now sharpen my own approach to recognition as agency, investigating the reciprocal influence between the recognition of others and self-recognition. Self-recognition will be the main focus here. Two aspects of self-recognition will be distinguished: the self as socially constituted and as self-identical. I suggest that Hegel's phenomenological terms "being-for-another" and "being-for-itself" are crucial for understanding how he sees self-recognition, and I also discuss these notions in terms of the psychoanalytic themes of relatedness and narcissism.

6.2 Self-Recognition

So far, I have proposed that recognition has two main functions, one socio-political and the other epistemological, and that both are mediated by satisfaction. In this section, I pursue this point, with particular attention to the sense in which the concept of recognition overlaps with agency. Recognition does not merely concern the relation between self and other, and agency is not exclusively determined by the relation of a self to itself. Rather, recognition entails both a relation to an other and a self-relation. Moreover, the epistemological side of this self-relation means that recognition feeds into the fundamental theme of PhS: self-knowledge.

Through self-recognition, which ultimately culminates in self-knowledge, the self comes to know itself in two ways: as socially constituted and as self-identical. Just before the Master/Slave section, Hegel spells out the concept of Geist as "We that is I and I that is We" (p. 110). Although this concept is not realized until later in the work, what happens here prompts a reformulation of the starting point of the work. Initially, consciousness explores the content of its own mind in a vacuum. There is something lacking in such solipsism, as it overlooks the existence of others and obscures their fundamental importance. The major discovery at the next juncture in consciousness's journey is that "self-consciousness achieves its satisfaction [Befriedigung] only in another self-consciousness" (p. 110). This discovery is about understanding oneself as related to others, and it must be held distinct from the discovery (which emerges later in the Spirit chapter) that the self is socially constituted. At the stage of self-consciousness, consciousness comes to appreciate that there is a lack of satisfaction in ignoring and/or withdrawing from others.[2]

The second aspect of self-knowledge is that the self comes to know itself as self-identical. This phenomenological experience involves a dialectic of revealing what has been concealed. As we will see in the next two chapters, self-identity is attained and lost numerous times in consciousness's journey. Self-identity, like self-fathoming, is predicated on facing and overcoming self-division. Hegel uses phenomenological language in describing the struggle to attain self-identity: "being-for-itself" and "being-for-another." This terminology is intended as an original and precise way to capture the internal experience of being a subject.

"Being-for-itself" has a range of meanings. It indicates the actualization of potentiality—that is, of "being in-itself." Actualization means that consciousness alters its own self-understanding through experience. As Hegel tells us in the preface, being-for-itself emerges through the externalization of being in-itself (p. 15). He proceeds to suggest that being-for-itself is produced in the process of the recollection of being in-itself (p. 17). Yet being-for-itself has connotations that go beyond the actualization of being in-itself: the term reflects that consciousness is motivated by "desire" and by the pursuit of its own self-interest. One even might argue that being-for-itself is the engine that propels consciousness in the direction of self-knowledge.

This hypothesis raises interesting questions. Since Hegel begins his discussion of self-consciousness with desire, it is fair to wonder how to reconcile such an irrational motivation with consciousness's pursuit of rational self-knowledge. One might press the question of whether Hegel opens himself up to the interpretation that irrationality underlies rationality. The last section of this chapter will focus on the implications of desire as the prelude to recognition. For now, it is sufficient to observe that Hegel departs from the Kantian approach that founds agency on restricting the ever-present danger of the "dear self." It is evident that Hegel regards satisfaction as a legitimate human pursuit.

Being-for-itself can be plausibly conceived as the source of a sense of agency. Hegel describes being-for-itself in terms of independence. Being-for-itself, thus, is an affirmation of freedom achieved through self-determination. At the same time, though, Hegel stresses that self-consciousness "does not see the other as an essential being, but in the other sees its own self" (p. 111). Even more pointedly, he informs us that "self-consciousness is, to begin with, simple being-for-self, self-equal through the exclusion from itself of everything else" (p. 113). In other words, being-for-itself in its initial form is predicated on the denial of being-for-another.

In PhS, all the connotations of being-for-itself overlap with independence. Ultimately, Hegel claims that being-for-itself is an "invisible unity" (p. 479). This aspect of being-for-itself is made especially clear in a sketch for the Logic of 1808 in which Hegel asserts: "What has being-for-self is numerical one [das numerische Eins]. It is simple, related only to itself, and the other is excluded from it. Its otherness is manyness [Veilheit]."[3] Although it is possible to read this statement as intimating that being an I excludes being a We, that would be mistaken, since Hegel defines the concept of Geist in PhS in terms of the identity of I and We. Once again, Hegel wishes to emphasize the self-enclosed nature of being-for-itself; it is not sufficient to account for being-for-itself merely in terms of the actualization of being in-itself or in terms of independence.

As I see it, being-for-itself coincides with narcissism and thus has a psychological dimension.[4] Hegel shows that narcissism is at the source of consciousness's oscillations in self-esteem; narcissism can also be discerned in consciousness's impulse to see itself as a self-enclosed unity and to reduce others to parts of itself. Narcissism explains the tendency to obscure that we are also constituted as being-for-another. For Hegel, however, being-for-itself is not necessarily antithetical to being-for-another. In particular, there is no reason to assume that narcissism, in and of itself is pathological. It becomes pathological only insofar as it pushes consciousness to disregard being-for-another.

Hegel conveys the narcissistic side of humans in equating the desire for recognition with the desire for prestige.[5] Psychologically speaking, Hegel shows the need to be admired and honored by others to be prompted by an even more fundamental wish: to feel good about oneself, to enjoy a positive sense of self-esteem. This raises another aspect of being-for-itself: that the need to feel good about oneself and to be able to comfort oneself is a specifically modern need.[6]

Being-for-itself varies according to different historical and cultural contexts. In modern culture, being-for-itself has a heightened importance, since it is no longer possible for us to find comfort in customs and tradition. Correspondingly, being-for-itself must bear more weight. This is a hardship, but also an opportunity for a new kind of fulfillment. Being-for-itself, from Hegel's standpoint, in no way dooms us to be self-enclosed atoms. In trying to conceptualize agency, he urges us not to focus on being-for-itself to the exclusion of being-for-another.

Being-for-another is Hegel's way of affirming that human agency is defined by relatedness. The word 'relatedness' gives expression to the desire to be connected to others. As an agent, one interacts with others, one depends upon others, and one comes to see that others offer insight to oneself. As a result, one becomes acquainted with being-for-another as a part of oneself. This realization is distinct from, and ought not be equated with, the discovery of one's own sociality. Although being-for-another can be understood as the basis of sociality, there is a difference worth preserving between the quality of this early interaction and later, self-conscious stages of development. Hegel is describing an elemental awareness that is implicit and must unfold. Being-for-another affirms intersubjectivity, but it does so initially at a level of experience that is interpersonal.[7]

Just as being-for-itself can negate being-for-another, being-for-another can negate being-for-itself. Hegel regards the latter as the more likely danger: we are more likely to err in the direction of being selfish as opposed to being selfless. The struggle between being-for-itself and being-for-another reveals Hegel's appreciation for the depths of conflict that are inherent to human agency. Hegel affirms the legitimacy and desirability of integrating being-for-itself and being-for-another; yet, one should not underestimate the difficulty of this challenge.

From a Hegelian point of view, it is misguided and unhealthy to define oneself strictly in terms of narcissism or relatedness. The pursuit of either of these alternatives to the exclusion of the other might seem to offer the promise of satisfaction, but, in truth, dissatisfaction will be the result. By emphasizing that being-for-another is a part of self-identity, Hegel claims that the two aspects of self-knowledge are not opposed. Self-knowledge is not bifurcated in being composed of self-identity and the socially constituted self. Instead, the self as socially constituted means that the individual accepts that the universal dwells within him or her as an individual. The self as self-identical embraces being-for-another and being-for-oneself as potentially complementary. The former is a matter of one's relation to others, and the latter is a matter of one's relation to oneself. Thus, as will soon be apparent, recognition mirrors the double relation of cognition itself. Put another way, being-for-another has ramifications for both one's external relation to others and one's internal relation to oneself. Moreover, being-for-another clarifies that the project of self-fathoming cannot be carried out in isolation from others.

Indeed, consciousness's encounter with another consciousness proves to be momentous, as each must come to fathom what first is resisted—that the other conceives of itself as a subject and not merely as an object. Self-consciousness marks the turning point in which consciousness itself is transformed: self-consciousness makes itself the object of consciousness as well as other objects. This can be understood as the dawning of a new sense of agency. The word 'agency' conveys Hegel's wish to describe an honorific category of selfhood. 'Agency' serves as an umbrella term that is inclusive of self-recognition, self-identity, and self-knowledge. Hegel does not explicitly use 'agency' in this way, although he does refer to the "subject who acts."[8]

Pippin and Pinkard use 'agency' in connection with Hegel. Pinkard (1994) claims that agency is a crucial idea in PhS, but he does not reflect on or try to justify its appropriateness to Hegel.[9] Pippin (1991b, pp. 532–541) argues that Hegel follows Kant in conceiving of agency in terms of freedom and self-determination and concludes that both Kant and Hegel are fully committed to equating free agency with rational agency. Yet Pippin also observes a contrast in the views of Kant and Hegel: Hegel believes that we are immersed in history and culture, whereas Kant adopts the "anytime, anyplace" ideal. Hegel's commitment to "self-fathoming" distinguishes his view from Kant's and, in my reading, renders their corresponding notions of agency quite different. Pippin maintains that Hegelian agency is an extension of the idea of personhood in Kant. It is important to acknowledge, however, that Hegel sees a tension between personhood and agency; he sees the former concept as being limited, and, thus, we may infer, he might be especially receptive to reserving a place for the latter concept.

Hegel's notion of agency is not merely an assertion of the rational truth that humans are, by nature, related to others and social. Self-thwarting and the ineluctability of struggle between being-for-another and being-for-itself are too prominent. Genuine satisfaction hinges on the challenge of integrating being-for-another and being-for-itself. Although Hegel concurs with Kant that true contentment is possible through rational agency, he differs from Kant in the extent of his engagement with the pressing dissatisfaction of modern culture. Indeed, Hegel's perspective can be expressed in the form of a slogan: Satisfaction is impossible without fathoming dissatisfaction. Hegel's depiction of agency moves through a dialectic of satisfaction and dissatisfaction. Over the next two chapters, I shall examine Hegel's actual text in order to substantiate the web of connection between recognition and agency.

6.3 Cognition, Satisfaction, and Desire

Let us now consider some prominent features of the *Phenomenology of Spirit*. My aim here is not to try to settle large textual questions, nor will I strive to offer a full commentary.[10] Rather, my intention will be to follow out the strands of the work that have to do with the theme of recognition and agency. This will require a clarification of the relation of recognition to ideas that at first glance might appear unrelated: cognition, satisfaction, and desire.

In general, PhS can be divided into two main parts: the human as single individual and the human as universal individual [Geist]. There are three main discussions of recognition: one at the midpoint of the human as single individual (the Self-Consciousness chapter), one at the midpoint of the transition between the human as single individual and the human as universal individual (the Reason chapter), and one at the midpoint of the human as universal individual (the Geist chapter).[11] Habermas offers a general way to distinguish the two parts (1971, p. 32): ". . . the self-reflective relation of the isolated subject to itself and the intersubjective relation of a subject that knows and recognizes a subject in the other just as the latter does with regard to the former."[12] This is a helpful way to approach the text, but I would add the qualification that the second part does not replace the first part. The limitations of the first part are enacted and produce the need for the second part; the addition of a new perspective, however, does not mean that the first part is abandoned.

Whereas the preface to PhS touts philosophy as a rigorous science and voices concern about the state of modern culture, the introduction focuses exclusively on epistemology. There is no mention in the introduction of the need for consciousness to define itself historically and culturally; instead, Hegel turns to explicate the nature of cognition. Still, the introduction serves to verify the transformation of "love of knowing" into "actual knowing" (p. 3). The discussion of cognition lays the basis for grasping the sense in which recognition is a form of cognition. Hegel never explicitly defines cognition as a concept; rather, he approaches it by specifying what it is not. Any definition offered would have to come from the standpoint of the phenomenologist (i.e., one who has completed the very journey that consciousness is about to embark upon), and Hegel emphasizes that the project will proceed from the standpoint of the experience of consciousness. Consciousness proceeds through a process of self-examination: testing whether its notions correspond to its objects.

Cognition requires testing within consciousness itself; the objects that are objects for consciousness will be compared against concepts according to criteria provided by consciousness itself. The phenomenological project rules out any criteria that are external to consciousness. The phenomenologist must refrain from helping consciousness along; its function is limited to observation: ". . . all that is left for us to do is imply look on" (p. 54).[13] It is not evident that Hegel fully sustains this stated project, as the voice of the phenomenologist and consciousness become intertwined and at various points difficult to distinguish. The intention to restrict the project in this way is novel, apart from whether Hegel fulfills his goal.

Cognition is, of course, a concept that deserves treatment as a topic in its own right.[14] What is crucial for our purposes is that cognition necessitates a revision of epistemology, as it is traditionally understood, to feature what I have termed the psychology of knowledge. Epistemology falsifies experience when it is construed in terms of a relation between knowledge and an object. Instead, Hegel offers a threefold relation involving a knower, knowledge, and an object. Hegel clearly links cognition to the self in the chapter on Reason: "Cognition [Erkennen] thus makes it clear that it is just as essentially concerned with [zu tun ist] its own self as with things." (p. 149) Cognition must be understood as a double relation: the self to itself and the self to objects. These two distinct components come together under the banner of self-knowledge, the main theme of PhS.

Hegel revises the epistemological project by describing cognition as knowledge that coincides with satisfaction. Pointing out that satisfaction [Befriedigung] ought not be identified with any of the particular stages in consciousness's journey (p. 51), Hegel claims that consciousness must accept the challenge that it alone can provide a standard for itself, and that it ought not rest content with a "limited satisfaction" (p. 51). It is vanity, he argues, that impedes consciousness:

This conceit [Eitelkeit] which understands how to belittle every truth, in order to turn back into itself and gloat over its own understanding, which knows how to dissolve every thought and always find the same barren Ego instead of any content—this is a satisfaction [Befriedigung] which we must leave to itself, for it flees the universal, and seeks only to be for itself. (p. 52)

This passage illuminates Hegel's concern about how narcissism can interfere with satisfaction. Hegel anticipates precisely what will be enacted in the self-consciousness chapter: that pure being-for-itself is not the path to genuine satisfaction. By implicitly noting a contrast between satisfaction that is worth having and satisfaction that we can dispense with, though, Hegel raises issues that he does not squarely address. Those issues deserve further consideration.

Although the concept of satisfaction is used widely throughout his corpus (surprisingly so once one becomes aware of it), Hegel does not linger over its meaning. It is evident that Hegel means to stipulate a state of well-being. By itself this is not very informative. One might wonder, for example, whether satisfaction is meant to have connotations of producing an affective state. If so, one would have to consider how this could be reconciled with Hegel's description of the objectivity of cognition in the introduction. It might be argued that satisfaction accompanies valid cognition (analogous to the positive feeling that accompanies solving a problem or seeing something that one did not at first see), but this seems speculative at best.

Perhaps it makes sense to hypothesize that satisfaction incorporates both cognition and affect. For example, in PM #445 Hegel proposes that "true satisfaction [Die wahre Befriedigung] . . . is only afforded by an intuition permeated by intellect and mind." In affirming genuine satisfaction as based on cognition, he seems to reject the option of construing satisfaction in terms of an affective response to a cognitive experience. He observes that satisfaction is a manifestation of "the achievement of ends of absolute worth" [in der Ausführung an und für sich geltender Zwecke] (PR #124)—that is, satisfaction ought not be reduced to an affective afterglow; it must be understood as an expression of subjective freedom: "the right of the subject to find his satisfaction [Befriedigung] in the action" (PR #121). The pursuit of satisfaction, thus, is at the heart of what it means to be a human agent.

Satisfaction is both more desired and more difficult to attain in modern culture, according to Hegel. In PR #124 he writes: "The right of the subject's particularity, his right to be satisfied [sich befriedigt zu finden], or in other words the right of subjective freedom, is the pivot and centre of the difference between antiquity and modern times." The unstated premise here is not that satisfaction eluded the Greeks but that what satisfied the Greeks no longer satisfies us. The preface to PhS helps to contextualize the introduction on this point: in the modern world, 'Geist' has lost its former sense of *satisfaction* [Befriedigung], and we need to repair this by seeking the "production [Herstellung] through its agency of that lost sense of solid and substantial being." The preface and the introduction are consistent in claiming that philosophy, carried out as science, provides a genuine form of satisfaction, but the former accentuates that cognition is not removed from culture. The legendary difficulty of PhS as a text—as both the experience of consciousness and a phenomenology of Geist—is mitigated once we see that the aims of culture and philosophy (cognition) dovetail with satisfaction.

It is important to appreciate that Hegel takes dissatisfaction just as seriously as satisfaction. Indeed, the parameters of consciousness's experience are satisfaction and dissatisfaction. Consciousness gains the motivation to move forward by facing up to dissatisfaction and then reorienting itself to pursue satisfaction. Nevertheless, as we know, Hegel believes that in the modern world consciousness has failed to produce an enduring kind of satisfaction. Although satisfaction is revealed to be illusory and fleeting, this should not be taken to mean that Hegel denies the possibility of attaining genuine satisfaction in the world.[15] In PhS he directs us to see that satisfaction must be linked to our relation to others, and he reiterates this point in PR #199. Dissatisfaction, in contrast, is linked to a rejection of others wherein their equality is disrespected or violated.

The concept of experience [Erfahrung], which is related to both cognition and satisfaction, is worth considering in this connection. Hegel defines experience as the "dialectical movement which consciousness exercises on itself and which affects both its knowledge and its object" (PhS, p. 55). It entails comparisons of the meanings of propositions, and thus it is grounded in language.[16] Experience is negative in the sense that it undermines stages of cognition. "We learn," Hegel explains (p. 39), "that we meant something other than we meant to mean; and this correction of our meaning compels our knowing to go back to the proposition; and understand it in some other way." Yet experience also has an implicitly positive side: it aids consciousness to move forward and to improve its knowledge and its satisfaction. Experience unmasks some forms of satisfaction as false;

in the short term this leads to dissatisfaction, but ultimately it is the basis for hope about greater satisfaction in the future. Dissatisfaction means false or incomplete satisfaction; it need not imply an absence of satisfaction. According to Hegel, there is no way to avoid self-deception; it belongs to the nature of agency.

Hegel's claim that cognition bestows satisfaction occurs prior to the claim, which has garnered more attention, that desire is connected to satisfaction. Insofar as satisfaction is discussed, it is often simply assumed that it pertains exclusively to desire. Hegel introduces Desire in the Self-Consciousness chapter, just before the section on recognition; he depicts consciousness as having a devouring relation to objects. In Desire, consciousness seeks what is outside itself—life. This search proves to be unstable and self-defeating. Thus, the failure of desire to achieve a more genuine kind of satisfaction becomes a lesson: ". . . this satisfaction is itself only a fleeting one" (p. 118). Desire provides a self-certain kind of satisfaction that is inferior to the satisfaction achieved through recognition, although satisfaction still eludes consciousness at the stage of self-consciousness.

Desire represents the dawning of an active consciousness—one that seeks rather than receives stimuli (as in the first chapter of PhS, Consciousness). As the first stage of self-consciousness, Desire reveals the unfolding development of the self. As Kojève points out (1969, p. 37), "desire is always revealed as my desire, and to reveal desire, one must use the word 'I'." Hegel's attempt to insist on a demarcation between animals and humans based on desire is problematic in that he regards desire as a state that reveals how much of our experience is dependent on the natural experience of our bodies.[17] In both the *Philosophy of Mind* (#428) and the *Philosophy of Right* (#235), Hegel connects desire to the satisfaction of natural needs. As Butler argues (1987, p. 70), Kojève distorts Hegel in asserting "a radical disjunction between the sensuous between human consciousness and the natural world which deprives human reality of a natural or sensuous expression." Butler (ibid., p. 25) makes this insightful point in the context of arguing that "desire is intentional in that it is always desire of or for an other." In this interpretation, desire anticipates the move to recognition and is not at odds with the movement toward self-knowledge in PhS.

Recognition can be plausibly conceived as a refined form of desire. The difference between these two concepts can be located in the quality of their respective relations to others. It is mistaken to distinguish between desire and recognition as a non-relation to an other vs. a relation to an other. Borrowing from the language of object relations theory in psychoanalysis, one can say that desire entails a relation to a "part object" whereas recognition is a relation to a "whole object." In object relations theory, a distinction is drawn between an early stage of development in which a child responds omnipotently and selectively to the primary caregiver and a later stage in which the primary caregiver can be tolerated as separate and as genuinely other. In desire, the other is a threat insofar as he or she is experienced as an actual other; in recognition, this is no longer the case (although in false forms of recognition, this is precisely what occurs). In the psychoanalytic reading of Hegel that I develop in chapter 9, I will maintain that desire cannot fully be supplanted by recognition, even though humans are not doomed to remain in desire without recognition.

Having acknowledged that satisfaction is produced both by cognition and by desire, I will now reintroduce Taylor's terms from chapter 5. Cognition entails self-objectivation, since Hegel emphasizes the reflexivity that underlies such knowledge. Desire propels self-exploration, since it fosters an active consciousness in pursuit of stimulation from the environment. Notice, however, that neither self-objectivation nor self-exploration explicitly accounts for the notion of recognition, wherein self-knowledge depends on the crucial insight that the recognition of others spurs self-recognition. Neither self-objectivation nor self-exploration reflects the importance that Hegel attaches to being-for-another. Although the expressivist ideal of self-exploration includes the wish for union with others, this does not necessarily affirm how formative others are for an individual's sense of identity.

Hegel wishes to integrate the diverse aims of self-objectivation and self-exploration. Yet the manner in which he seeks to do so is more radical than was apparent in chapter 5. Hegel believes that self-knowledge must be understood contextually: to be a satisfied agent, one must define oneself in relation to culture. Although it is confusing that Hegel conceives of satisfaction so loosely—as having high (cognitive) and low (appetitive) aspects—the concept allows the distinctiveness of his philosophy to be seen in a new light. The project of self-fathoming, as was discussed in chapter 2, encompasses these diverse aspects of satisfaction. It is mistaken to equate self-fathoming with rational justification. Self-fathoming, as I understand it, is proof that Hegel sought to distinguish himself from the Kantian tradition.

I have covered a great deal quickly in this chapter. In the next two chapters, at a slower pace, I will provide a more in-depth reading of PhS. As we turn to the specific embodiments in which the recognition of others contributes to self-recognition, Hegel's theory of agency will emerge more clearly.

7

Recognition in the *Phenomenology of Spirit* (I)

The single individual is incomplete Spirit, a concrete shape in whose whole existence one determinateness predominates, the others being present only in blurred outline.

—Hegel, *Phenomenology of Spirit*

In chapter 6, I introduced Hegel's concept of recognition as a way to determine how he thinks about agency. I drew particular attention to the claim that the recognition of others is a spur to self-recognition. Agency, thus, is linked to our relation to others, and Hegel's ideal of self-fathoming is designed to reflect this. Yet a long journey awaits consciousness before it arrives at this self-understanding. Moreover, as I noted in chapter 6, Hegel believes that no progress can be made without failure and dissatisfaction.

In this chapter, I shall follow out the concept of recognition in PhS, beginning with its introduction in the Self-Consciousness chapter (where recognition fails) and ending with the Geist chapter (where recognition in ancient Greek culture is presented as natural and ethical). In chapter 8, I shall complete this story, entertaining the failure of mutual recognition in the modern world as well as Hegel's hope for mutual recognition (described in the chapters on Morality and Religion). Roughly speaking, my chapters 7 and 8 overlap, respectively, with my chapters 3 and 4. Although the main focus of my chapters 7 and 8 is on PhS, I also pay some attention to the development of the concept of recognition in Hegel's earlier works, especially those from the Jena period. Because I will be covering well trodden ground, it will be important to clarify my views in relation to other commentators.

7.1 True and False Recognition

Recognition is first at issue in the Self-Consciousness chapter when consciousness encounters a new object (viz., another consciousness like itself). The new object is accompanied, as we should expect, by a change in consciousness itself. Consciousness has departed from limiting itself to abstract experience and has entered into the realm of life. Consciousness thereby becomes self-consciousness (that is, consciousness that is aware of itself as knowing). The new object here is no mere object; it is another subject. As was discussed in chapter 6, recognition is a form of cognition and thus involves both a relation between a self and an object (another subject) and a relation between the self and itself. Besides this double relation (internal to the self), there is a relation between two different selves.

Thus, there are two senses of recognition to be distinguished at the Self-Consciousness stage: the interpersonal (a relation between selves) and self-knowledge (two sets of relations within the self). Hegel explains the concept of recognition here as follows: ". . . each is for the other what the other is for it" (p. 113). Two conditions are specified in order for "recognition proper" to exist: mutuality and equality. In Hegel's words (p. 112): "They recognize themselves as mutually recognizing one another." [Sie anerkennen sich, als gegenseitig sich anerkennend.] This is a moment of connection in which each consciousness perceives the other as like itself. The rich display of interpersonal dynamics, which follows directly in the Master/Slave section, has garnered so much attention that the sense of recognition as self-knowledge has not been given its due.

As the Master/Slave section unfolds, consciousness becomes aware of itself as a subject, although not as a self per se. In confronting another consciousness, consciousness becomes aware of itself as an object for the other consciousness, just as the other consciousness is an object for the first consciousness. This forces consciousness to reevaluate its sense of itself—to reflect on what it is. Insofar as the subject resolves that it is different from the other, it begins to form a notion of itself as a self. However, the discovery of oneself as an object for the other also creates discomfort for the subject, as it forces the subject to face the reality that it is not the center of the universe. The subject's resistance to being an object for the other subject leads to a resoluteness in its desire to be a pure subject; the life-and-death struggle thus breaks out, wherein both consciousness's are prepared to die rather than to yield and acknowledge the subjectivity of the other. At the moment that "one individual is confronted by another individual" (p. 113), others are perceived as threats to one's being-for-itself.

There is an irony here in that, in order to protect its identity as a subject, consciousness places itself at risk and is willing to chance death. There is something inherently contradictory about the struggle: to succeed and kill the other would preclude the possibility of being recognized. The dawning of this reality, thus, leads one consciousness to give in and abandon its identity as a subject, embracing pure objecthood. The victorious consciousness bathes in the glory of being pure subjectivity. In Hegel's language, the slave is pure being-for-another and the master is pure being-for-itself (p. 115). From what was said about the danger of one-sided identification with either being-for-itself or being-for-another in chapter 6, it is evident that this development is problematic for both agents. The master-slave relationship entails a kind of splitting in which each prospective agent embraces one aspect of itself at the expense of the other. In particular, the master exhibits the same conceit that we have already seen with desire, and its satisfaction will be revealed to be just as fleeting.[1]

Before considering the outcome of the master-slave struggle, let us ponder its motivation. No clear motive is suggested as to why the life-and-death struggle is inevitable. Commentators' speculations about its origins range from Kojève's suggestion (1969, p. 44) that Hegel was responding to the nearly contemporaneous Battle of Jena to Bonsiepen's metaphorical interpretation (1977, p. 90–91), which stresses that by the time of PhS Hegel had moved away conceiving of "struggle," and especially the threat of death, as literal. Siep (1974, p. 195) emphasizes that PhS does not offer any motivation for the struggle—in contrast to the early Jena writings—although he notes that it does not seem to be otherwise motivated. It is significant that there is not yet a social dimension in the account, but the struggle remains, as it was in the Jena writings, a struggle for honor.

Still, the struggle depicted in PhS has some distinctive features. In PhS, Hegel envisions the outcome neither as the negative extreme of death nor as the positive extreme of mutual recognition. In *System der Sittlichkeit*, death was clearly countenanced as a possible outcome of the struggle. In *First Philosophy of Spirit*, recognition is achieved directly as a result of the struggle; it occurs without a master/slave phase. Siep (1974, p. 71) makes the helpful proposal that the contrast between the positive outcomes in the early Jena writings and PhS reflects the twofold levels of recognition in PhS—between two I's at this juncture and between the I and the We later.

Like Siep, Kelly has stressed the interpersonal and not merely the social aspect of the experience in the Self-Consciousness chapter. Kelly's view is primarily directed against Kojève's reading, which he sees as guilty of smuggling a social reading in at this early stage. Yet Kelly's reading (1976, p. 197), unlike Siep's, rules out a premature social meaning to the struggle without specifying how and when it comes into play. In PhS, the social aspect appears implicitly in Reason chapter and explicitly in the Geist chapter. This is in contrast to the early Jena writings, where the social aspect belongs to the struggle itself. Ottmann (1981, p. 23) confirms that the distinctiveness of the treatment in PhS lies in that the struggle is not a transition to the people and the state, as in the early works.[2] Pippin (1989, p. 155) also cautions against reading the social aspect into this stage of PhS.[3]

It is important to realize that at the stage of self-consciousness the master-slave relationship does not occur between the I and the We. Evidence exists, though, that might make us question whether Hegel's intention was to exclude the social aspect. In the Phenomenology section of the *Philosophical Propaedeutic*, Hegel illustrates his discussion by invoking Pisistratus's relation to the Athenian people—a case of a master dominating a social environment. It is possible that Hegel changed his mind sometime after PhS and before PP. It is just as plausible, however, to acknowledge that, although in PhS the interpersonal interaction is featured and the social implications are not specified, Hegel's might not have had the explicit intention to rule out the social realm.[4]

Both Kelly and Pippin direct us to appreciate the phenomenological aspect of Hegel's project, where recognition involves an individual's relation to himself or herself, as well as the interpersonal and social realms. On the other hand, Siep fails to distinguish the aspect of phenomenology from the interpersonal and social realms. If the phenomenological aspect of recognition is not preserved, the connection between recognition and self-knowledge is more difficult to sustain. Moreover, the crucial matter of the agent's satisfaction can easily become obscured.[5] Indeed, it is through the phenomenological realm that we can glimpse Hegel's deft merger of epistemology and psychology. Consciousness's interactions are characterized by oscillations between being-for-itself and being-for-another, portrayed here with an emphasis on independence and dependence. Hegel's commitment to the psychology of knowledge means that he is not just concerned with justified belief or the sort of problems one associates with "other minds."

In Self-Consciousness, Hegel sees recognition as false: there is a disparity between the concept of recognition as stated and the unequal and one-sided result of the initial encounter between consciousnesses. As pure being-for-itself, the master treats the slave as a thing. As pure being-for-another, the slave subordinates itself to the master in fear and service. Fear and service, however, transform the slave, opening anew the path to satisfaction. It is illuminating to interpret fear and service in light of the diverse philosophical alternatives that emerge directly from Hegel in Kierkegaard and Marx.[6]

The anticipation of Marx is as familiar as it is evident: the slave reexperiences its own subjectivity through the salutary activity of laboring on "the thing," a third term that mediates between the two consciousnesses. The slave learns to value its work as its own and also to differentiate itself from the thing on which it has worked. Hegel draws attention to the contrast between desire (which sought to consume objects) and work (which nurtures them). Yet desire and work are not simply opposites. According to Hegel, work is "desire held in check" (p. 118). Although work is understood as critical to the slave's freedom, it is featured even more prominently in earlier Jena writings, such as *Philosophy of Spirit I and II*.

A foreshadowing of Kierkegaard's notion of Angst is also evident in Hegel. Hegel presents Angst as preceding the activity of labor, and he emphasizes the depths of this experience—that the slave's "whole being" must be affected. Twice observing the extent to which the slave trembles, Hegel's language is itself emotional. One can interpret this experience with two different emphases: that the slave's affect is generated by having faced its own death, which it risked in the struggle, and that the slave's affect is a product of its having been "traumatized" by its encounter with the master. According to the existentialist line of interpretation, it is the facticity of death that haunts the slave. Yet the alternative account would emphasize instead the slave's overwhelming experience of finding itself utterly alone and devastated by the awareness of the master's lack of regard. These emphases are not necessarily opposed to one another: the slave's victimization coincides with the encounter with death.[7] Indeed, one could read the fear of death as representing a kind of tyrannical master.[8]

Through the combination of fear and service, the slave reconnects with itself as a self: it acquires "a mind of its own" [Eigensinn] (p. 119).[9] The subjugation of the subject is contradicted as a result of its own active experience. The slave realizes, ironically enough, that it is for-itself, despite itself. Its apparent renunciation of narcissism is reversed at this point. The story continues to unfold with the master turning into an unessential consciousness, insofar as it is dependent on the slave to work for it. The slave becomes the essential consciousness as it frees itself from the master. In one sense, this essential consciousness becomes like consciousness before the struggle in its immersion in being-for-itself without genuine independence. In a deeper sense, this consciousness has become different, for it has been shocked by the encounter with the other and has retreated into itself. Hegel preserves both the emancipatory power generated from the slave's experience and its traumatic impact.

Hegel's narrative continues by following the self-enmeshment of consciousness. This has opposing forms: from initial postures of disdain for the other in the Stoicism and Skepticism section to the subsequent despair within oneself and longing for the other in the Unhappy Consciousness section. Hegel observes that Stoicism "could only appear on the scene in a time of universal fear and bondage, but also a time of universal culture [Bildung] which had raised itself to the level of thought" (p. 121). Confusion and chaos in the external world fuel the ambition to find satisfaction through the inner world of thought.[10]

The master-slave interaction results in the stage of unhappy consciousness, and the former experience can be discerned in the latter. states: ". . . the duplication which formerly was divided between two individuals, the master and the slave, is now lodged in one" (p. 126). The failure of recognition in self-consciousness is revealed not only in the split between individuals but also in the ensuing split within the individual. The self-division of the Hellenic era signifies the beginning of the end of the (satisfied) ancient world. The heightened attention to the self must be understood as a reaction to the corresponding devaluation of meaning in the external world. Although the unhappy consciousness is preoccupied with itself, the other is reintroduced from within as "the unattainable beyond," which Hegel describes in the dialectic between the changeable and the unchangeable. The need to fathom oneself as both finite and infinite transmogrifies into religious longing for the absolute other (that is, the divine). In the Stoicism and Skepticism section, Hegel contrasts this longing for the other in unhappy consciousness (which he sees as a positive acknowledgement of dependence) to the denial of such longing (which he sees as a hyperbolic commitment to independence).

Significantly, this new other in unhappy consciousness is a universal, not an individual. From this point on, recognition will involve not only a relation within the self (described in terms of being-for-itself and being-for-another) or a relation between individuals (described in terms of two I's) but also a relation between the individual and the universal (described in terms of the language of the I and the We). The interpersonal interaction that aided the discovery of oneself as an object, at first so threatening, ultimately leads to a deeper sense of self-identity. One uncovers one's own being-for-another; in addition, one's capacity for self-observation is enhanced by taking oneself in from the outside (through the perspective of the other, who is actually outside of oneself). Insofar as one accepts oneself as an object, one is tacitly accepting the other as a subject. For Hegel this becomes the basis of mutual recognition in the interpersonal and social senses.

7.2 Internal Recognition

Reason is, Hegel maintains, "the middle term between universal Geist and its individuality" (p. 178). Accordingly, the chapter on Reason belongs to both parts of PhS: that devoted to the single individual and that devoted to the universal individual or Geist. Reason completes the development of the human as a single individual in that consciousness reexamines itself, mending its inner division. At the same time, consciousness's withdrawal from the other becomes more pronounced: ". . . here consciousness is a relation purely of itself to itself: relation to an other, which would be a limitation of it has been eliminated [aufgehoben]" (p. 238).

Reason represents an attempt to mend the gulf in unhappy consciousness between the individual and the universal. Unity with the universal is attained when the individual identifies itself as the universal: ". . . the superseded [aufgehobene] single individual is the universal" (p. 139). In this context, the individual fully experiences the power of thought to determine itself actively. The middle section of this chapter, which is itself at the middle of the work, is titled The Actualization of Rational Self-Consciousness Through Its Own Activity. The Reason chapter gets underway, however, with a review of the experience of self-consciousness. Hegel notes that self-consciousness "is certain that this independent object for it is not something alien [Fremdes], and thus it knows that it is in principle [an sich], and in its inner certainty has to enter consciousness and becomes explicit for it [für es]" (p. 211).

While consciousness gropes after a one-sided, non-mutual, and at best implicit form of recognition in Self-Consciousness, it is more aware of itself, and it seeks an explicit form of recognition in Reason. Yet Hegel illustrates that the movement within self-consciousness is mirrored within reason: "Reason (will) run through the double movement of self-consciousness, and pass over [übergehen] from independence in its freedom" (p. 211).

In an important new development beyond the Self-Consciousness chapter, the universal begins to take on a social meaning in Reason. The self begins to grasp its social constitution: "in this notion there is disclosed the realm of ethical life [Sittlichkeit]. . . .The single individual consciousness . . . is aware of the universal consciousness in its individuality as its own being, since what it does and is, is the universal custom [Sitte]." (p. 212)

Recognition, therefore, no longer pertains to the relation between two individuals; it now pertains to the relation between the individual and the universal—which is, of course, a relation within the individual. The change is clearly demonstrated if one juxtaposes the description of recognition in this context ("I regard them as myself and myself as them," p. 214) with the description in the Master/Slave section (". . . each is for the other what the other is for it," p. 113). Insofar as reason construes the universal socially, as the individuals who are bound by custom, the human as universal individual [Geist] is presupposed—specifically, in the first section of the Geist chapter, Sittlichkeit.

Close attention to the experience of recognition in Reason is called for at this point. Consciousness, as universal reason, still remains an individual consciousness, "aware of the universal consciousness in its individuality as its own being" (p. 212). The individual recognizes universal consciousness, and it is aware of itself as being-for-itself. Although this also marks the dawning of a fuller acknowledgement of one's own being-for-another, universal consciousness exists only within individual consciousness. Therefore, this recognition is mainly internal. Real, live others are forsaken. The significance of Hegel's point here should not be missed: he is questioning the tradition of modern philosophy, which has fostered first-person experience at the expense of heeding our relation to others.

The contradictory nature of internal recognition dramatically unfolds in the middle subsection of the middle section of this middle chapter. Here consciousness posits itself as universal law: ". . . it knows that it has the universal of law immediately within itself, and because the law is immediately present in the being-for-self [Fürsichsein] of consciousness, it is called The Law of the Heart." (p. 221) This consciousness equates its own pleasure with the universal pleasure of all. It takes for itself the task of "promoting the welfare of mankind" (p. 222). Yet this merger of its particular origins to universal law fails to hold together:

The individual who wants to recognize [erkennen] universality only in the form of his immediate being-for-self [Fürsichseins] does not therefore recognize [erkennen] himself in this free universality, while at the same time he belongs to it, for it is his own doing. This doing, therefore, has the reverse [verkehrte] significance;

it contradicts the universal ordinance. For the individual's act is supposed to be the act of his particular heart, not a free universal reality; and at same time he has in fact recognized [anerkannt] the latter, for his action has the significance of positing his essential being as a free reality, i.e., of acknowledging [anzuerkennen] the real world to be his own essential being. (p. 233)[11]

Consciousness experiences its own particularity as jeopardized by merging itself to universal law and by having concealed its own tacit recognition of the latter. This dialectic parallels the experience in Self-Consciousness, where consciousness, threatened by its wish for union with the other, tries to subordinate the other to itself. At first there is aggression (the life-and-death struggle), which then yields to an unequal relation (the master-slave relationship). The dialectic exposes consciousness's distorted but real need for the other (recognition). The difference is that what happens in Self-Consciousness happens between two individuals in the world, whereas what happens in Reason happens in the mind.

In the Reason chapter, inevitably, consciousness runs up against reality: "The consciousness which sets up the law of the heart therefore meets [erfährt] resistance [Widerstand] from others, because it contradicts the equally individual law of their hearts." (p. 227) The attempt to find self-satisfaction through the law of the heart must fail because its price, the denial of others, is too high. This consciousness is presented at the exact middle of PhS because, in spite of consciousness's progress in the project of self-knowledge, it faces the absolute peril of dissociation from reality here. Consciousness's self-enforced isolation from others places it in complete opposition to the goal of mutual recognition, where the self knows itself as Geist, feels a bond to others, and is at home in the world.

Hegel demonstrates that reality is recalcitrant in the face of the law of the heart. The result is another variation of unhappy consciousness: deranged consciousness [Verrücktheit].[12] Deranged consciousness, like unhappy consciousness, is split not only from others but also within itself. It differs from unhappy consciousness in the way that recognition in Self-Consciousness differs from recognition in Reason. Deranged consciousness is aware of itself; not only does it feel the division within it, but it cries out in "the ravings of an insane self-conceit [des verrückten Eigendünkels]," and it "speaks of the universal order as a perversion [Verkehrung] of the law of the heart and of happiness, a perversion invented by fanatical priests, gluttonous despots and their minions" (p. 226). Although this consciousness is a resentful response to the real world, one might well juxtapose the positive element of self-expression here against the silent brooding of unhappy consciousness's initial turn away from the real world.

A parallel between unhappy consciousness and deranged consciousness can be sustained, nonetheless, in terms of the movement from an internally divided state to a state wherein universality is embraced at the expense of individuality. Unhappy consciousness is mended through universal reason, where the single individual is superseded. Consciousness preoccupies itself with "observing the laws of thought." Deranged consciousness is mended through the next stage, virtue, where "law is the essential moment, and individuality the one to be nullified [Aufzuhebende]" (p. 228). Virtue requires the sacrifice of individuality; eventually, it must face "the way of the world," the reality-bound consciousness rooted in the principle of individuality. The latter wins out: consciousness realizes that it must come to grips with its own individuality.

The Reason chapter culminates in a section titled The Individual as Real in and for Itself. The individual now knows itself as a unity. Hegel specifies that "whatever it is that the individual does, and whatever happens [widerfährt] to him, that he has done himself, and he is that himself" (p. 242). Recognition might seem irrelevant here, insofar as a relation between self and other is remote. But consciousness does begin to confront the world again in the form of what Hegel terms "die Sache selbst" (p. 214).[13] Through work, the common cause is realized as Sittlichkeit, where the individual's sense of belonging is expressed initially as knowing "immediately what is right and good" (p. 253).

Here we have already implicitly crossed over from Reason to Geist. Recognition in Reason fails just as recognition in Self-Consciousness failed. Yet recognition in Reason can be considered an improvement over recognition in Self-Consciousness in the sense that its concept bears a connection to the sittliche world (the universal), despite remaining bound to its individuality. In the Reason chapter, consciousness is withdrawn from the real world as a result of its initial, painful encounter with the other. Recognition is "internal," since what is foremost is consciousness's relation to itself. This "night-like void" passes, and we awake in the "daylight" of Geist's presence in actual history (p. 111).

It is only in the chapter on Geist that the various manifestations of a socially constituted self and the social sense of recognition are featured in PhS. Recognition becomes true in two senses: its treatment is explicitly rooted in actual history, and it contains Hegel's normative hope for mutual recognition in the future. Recognition in Geist represents a change in the discussion of recognition from the abstract to the concrete, and also a change from the theoretical to the practical. Instead of "shapes merely of consciousness," Hegel tells us, we will be dealing with "shapes of a world" (p. 265).

Although recognition in Geist represents a new dimension of recognition, we can recall that the concept of Geist was introduced in the Self-Consciousness chapter (p. 110): "'I' that is 'We' and 'We' that is 'I.'" The notion of Geist is realized in the living ethical world [Sittlichkeit], where "the self has completely lost the meaning of a being-for-self separated from the world" (p. 265). True recognition is mutual: the self is bound to the human world, understanding itself both as being-for-another and as being-for-itself and seeing the other (the universal, the We) as itself (the individual, the I). The treatment of recognition in Geist in terms of the individual and the universal— the I and the We—is reminiscent of the early Jena writings. Yet PhS broadens and deepens the treatment of recognition. The chapter on Geist constitutes approximately one-third of the entire work. Thus, it is somewhat misleading to see the chapter on Geist as the middle of the second half of the work, paralleling the chapter on Self-Consciousness as the middle of the first half of the work and Reason as the middle of the entire work. (See the appendix for more details.)

The chapter on Geist ranges over a great expanse of history, from the ancient world to Hegel's own world. Hegel's examples are rather selective; a "phenomenology of Geist" differs from a mere historical inquiry in highlighting and dramatizing certain key moments as exemplifications. Let us now follow Hegel's presentation of the historical forms of recognition. In the next two chapters, we will reencounter material that has already been covered. Although this will entail some repetition, it will also elucidate where these parts of PhS fit within the whole. Hegel's narrative leads us to face the absence of mutual recognition in the modern world; at the same time, it paves the way for a solution.

7.3 Natural and Ethical Recognition

The placement of Greek culture at the beginning of the chapter on Geist reveals Hegel's respect for its achievement. It also registers his revised stance after the Frankfurt era that this world had forever passed. Hegel's model for recognition can no longer follow from the mediating influence of Theseus, as Hegel portrayed it in *Philosophy of Spirit I*. Yet the Greek world is honored for its emphasis on the individual's abiding relation to the universal (the polis). Although the relation between the individual and the universal in Greek culture does not adequately deal with the individual's need for freedom in modern culture, the various stages of recognition that follow all reverberate from this initial stage. As I noted in chapters 3 and 4, for Hegel and Nietzsche there is a dialectic between ancient and modern culture, and modern culture must be measured against the backdrop of Greek culture. Greek tragedy provides a crucial link in openly presenting transgression against the social order.

An analogy can be made between the reverberation of the initial presentation of recognition in Self-Consciousness (both the concept and experience) through all the subsequent stages of recognition in PhS and the reverberation of the Greeks through all the subsequent stages of recognition in Geist. In fact, the movement in PhS from Self-Consciousness to Reason to Geist is repeated in the movement within Geist from the Greek world to the Roman world to the modern world. Recognition in the Greek world begins with individual family members, reflecting recognition in self-consciousness between individual self-consciousnesses.

Recognition between family members is the basis of Sittlichkeit because it involves, in part, individuals who are previously unrelated coming together in a bond. However, the bonding is one of love, a relation which is "natural" and not ethical. It is not ethical because the unity implied by love threatens individuality by failing to ensure autonomy. Recognition between family members eventually confronts the fact that recognition between citizens is different: ". . . the individual, so far as he is not a citizen but belongs to the family, is only an unreal impotent shadow" (p. 270). This struggle is portrayed through Greek tragedy—primarily through Hegel's favorite example, *Antigone*.

The struggle portrayed in tragedy is a life-and-death struggle at a higher level. One is reminded of the account in *System der Sittlichkeit*, which begins with recognition between family members and then evolves into a struggle. The difference is that in *System der Sittlichkeit* (and also in *Philosophy of Spirit II*) the struggle emerges from some transgression where honor is at stake, particularly concerning the exchange of property. PhS is restricted at this level to ancient Greek tragedy, in which property is not overtly at issue.

The movement of recognition in Geist is portrayed subtly and in great detail in PhS. In one sense, the struggle in tragedy repeats the earlier struggle in Self-Consciousness, passing over into the realm of master/slave: the Greek world is replaced by the Roman world. In another sense, the struggle in tragedy, according to Hegel, is a dead end: the protagonist is destroyed. This is a controversial interpretation of tragedy, and, revealingly, one Hegel chose to revise in the *Lectures on Aesthetics*.[14] Indeed, if the protagonist is destroyed, the reconciliation through suffering must exclude the protagonist.

Within the description of recognition between family members, Hegel further discriminates recognition between husband and wife and between brother and sister. Another distinction is also mentioned, which provides the transition between the first two: recognition between parents and children. Recognition between husband and wife is a natural kind of recognition in that the bond is mixed with feeling (erotic love) and is dependent for its grounding on something outside itself (the child). The child-parent relation is understood to interfere with the husband-wife relation as the child moves from dependence to independence. Here Hegel seems to be following the account in *Philosophy of Spirit I*, although he is even more explicit in dealing with family relations in that earlier work (PhilS I, pp. 233–235).

Recognition between child and parent, like that between husband and wife, is tinged with feeling. Recognition between brother and sister, however, occurs at a higher level: "They are free individualities in regard to each other." (p. 274) What Hegel means is that the "recognition [Anerkennung] of herself (the sister) in him (the brother) is pure and unmixed with any natural desire" (p. 275). The recognition is seen as ethical, which pertains to its purity but also to the sister's devotion to the universal. As Hegel tells us, clearly with Antigone in mind, "the loss of the brother is therefore irreparable to the sister and her duty toward him is the highest" (p. 275). Recognition between husband and wife lacks the sense of devotion that the blood bond entails, according to Hegel.

That recognition based on a blood bond is regarded as higher than recognition based on the contract of marriage is surprising—all the more so in view of the fact that Hegel's discussion is modeled on Greek tragedy. Conflict in tragedy arises from the difference between blood relations and marriage relations, the latter being closely associated with the state. If recognition between citizens surpasses recognition between family members, one might expect the husband-wife relation to be regarded as higher than the brother-sister relation. It seems that what Hegel values about the latter is the aspect of being-for-another and the implicit relation to the universal it contains. It is evident that for Hegel the brother-sister relation in tragedy foreshadows recognition as an agapaic vision of love.

Hegel's claim that the brother-sister relation is removed from natural desire, which he repeats twice (pp. 274–275), sounds dubious to post-Freudian ears.[15] Ironically, though, his explanation as to why devotion is lacking between husband and wife has a contemporary resonance, revealing what might be taken as a proto-feminist impulse.[16] Hegel says that the husband's devotion is split between being a citizen and husband, and that thus the wife's particularity is "a matter of indifference" to him (p. 275). As a result, "the wife is without the moment of knowing herself as this particular self in the partner" (p. 275). The point is that under the terms of the relation the recognition between husband and wife is not really mutual. Though Hegel does not make the point explicitly, if the husband is a kind of master then the wife is a kind of slave.[17] An implication that one might draw, based on the master/slave dialectic, is that freedom lies on the side of the wife's experience. (Though this interpretation is consistent with the psychology of Hegel's analysis, I do not mean to imply that it reflects Hegel's actual view.)

Recognition between family members is limited, according to Hegel, because it is between single individuals. But since Geist is dwelling in the Greek world, the individual defines himself (literally himself) not only as a family member but also as a citizen. The change from family member to citizen replays the change from natural to ethical Sittlichkeit. It also replays the change from self-consciousness to reason. More specifically, the self changes from seeing itself as merely a particular self to being a universal self too. This description can be misleading: not all family members, of course, turn into citizens; only the husbands are citizens. Hegel submits this dual identity as a problem: at the center of Greek tragedy is the struggle between the divine law (protecting the family) and human law (protecting the state). Greek tragedy thus follows earlier examples in PhS, where consciousness is not only divided from others, but is divided within itself. The protagonist is, like unhappy consciousness and deranged consciousness, a split consciousness.

Greek tragedy presents the individual cut off from society; it solves this problem, as Hegel sees it, by offering a kind of recognition that occurs at the price of the destruction of the individual. In burying her brother, Antigone is obeying divine law and transgressing human law. She upholds her relation to her brother (an individual) but severs her relation to society (the universal). Hegel claims that a solution to the problem is contingent on whether the acting individual, "like Antigone, knowingly commits the crime" (p. 284). In order to remain ethical, the individual must "acknowledge [anerkennen] its opposite as its own actuality, must acknowledge [anerkennen] its guilt" (p. 284). Hegel's interpretation is questionable, since it is far from clear that Antigone ever acknowledges guilt. Regardless, the use of *anerkennen* from Antigone's speech exemplifies Hegel's appropriation of the Greek sense of anagnorisis.[18]

Hegel sums up his view of tragedy by claiming that "the ethical individual is directly [unmittelbar] and intrinsically [an sich] one with his universal aspect, exists in it alone, and is capable of surviving the destruction of this ethical power by its opposite" (p. 284). From the division between divine and human law, the individual's flight into universality evolves. This is a replay of Self-Consciousness's flight from unhappy consciousness to Reason and of Reason's flight from deranged consciousness to virtue. The difference is that in those two experiences the split and healing occur within consciousness alone, whereas in tragedy the split individual becomes whole only by being restored to the community. For Hegel, "tragic" recognition ought to be designated as ethical. It presents the individual as necessarily subordinate to the universal, which according to Hegel was the cornerstone of the Greek world. The sacrifice of the individual to the universal signals the transition from Greece to Rome, from the polis to the imperium, and from ethical recognition to legal recognition.

8

Recognition in *The Phenomenology of Spirit* (II)

I make myself within a history that has always already made me.
—Cornelius Castoriadis, "Power, Politics, Autonomy"

In the preceding chapter, I covered the introduction of the concept of recognition, the failed attempt to realize it, and the natural and ethical recognition of ancient Greek culture. My narrative about recognition in PhS continues in this chapter. In the background is the dialectical movement between ancient and modern culture that was described in chapters 3 and 4. Yet there is a difference in spite of the appearance of repetition: Hegel introduces Roman culture as mediating between ancient Greece and modern culture.

Roman culture is responsible for the emergence of a new notion of recognition: legal recognition. Legal recognition may be considered true recognition in the sense that it codifies what remained merely implicit in ethical recognition. More specifically, in highlighting the concept of personhood, Roman culture constitutes a move in the direction of respecting individual freedom. As I argued in chapter 5, however, it is important to keep in mind that persons are not necessarily agents. Hegel sees personhood as an advance in the conceptualization of recognition, but he also emphasizes its limitations. Indeed, the limitations of personhood lead Hegel to posit a richer way to conceive of self-knowledge and to move in the direction of the notion of agency.

8.1 Legal Recognition

The Roman world is portrayed at the end of the first section of Geist, titled The Ethical Order. Its place within the structure of PhS is noteworthy: at the midpoint between the ancient world and the modern world. From one vantage point, the Roman world completes the development of the ancient world; from another vantage point, it anticipates the modern world. This dual role recalls the role of Reason as the completion of the human as individual and the anticipation of the human as universal individual [Geist]. Although Hegel spends just a few pages on Roman culture, the discussion makes a major contribution to the development of the recognition theme.

Recognition in the Roman world grows out of and is a response to Stoicism's and Skepticism's flight from the other. As Hegel understands them, Stoicism and Skepticism are negative reactions to the Greek expectation that the individual ought to sacrifice himself to the universal. Recognition in the Roman world, thus, must be understood as a contrast to the first form of recognition in Self-Consciousness. It is no longer false, since mutual recognition can be discerned. Recognition occurs between persons: ". . . the universal being thus split up into a mere multiplicity of individuals, this lifeless Spirit is an equality, in which all count as the same, i.e. as persons" (PhS, p. 390). Recognition between persons restores universality to individuals, but at a cost. The universality is "the sheer empty unit" (p. 291), and so recognition between the individual and the universal is jeopardized. What one recognizes in others is their legal rights, foremost of which is his property. This kind of recognition is familiar from the Jena writings, particularly the accounts in *System der Sittlichkeit* (p. 121) and *Philosophy of Spirit II* (p. 227).

There is a pro forma quality to the recognition that occurs at this stage: it is characterized "as something whose validity [Gelten] is recognized [anerkanntes]" (p. 292). Recognition concerns the external aspect of the individual.[1] Each person is an abstract universality whose "content is this rigid unyielding self, not the self that is dissolved in the substance" (p. 290). Legal recognition leads to a split between the private and public self, excluding the former from the scope of recognition. As a result, what it means to belong to a community shrinks in comparison to Greek culture.

Legal recognition ultimately repeats the pattern whereby the individual recoils from the universal. In allowing the private self to be exempt from recognition, legal recognition is reminiscent of earlier stages of self-immersion. The influence of Hellenistic Stoicism leaves its mark and is extended in the Roman world. Moreover, "identity in difference" can be discerned in the self-immersion that occurs between purely *internal* recognition, which occurs at the midpoint of the whole (in Reason), and purely *external* recognition, which occurs at the midpoint of the second half of PhS, the human as Geist (the Roman world).

In legal recognition, the single individual is glorified. This represents a fundamental change from classical Greek philosophy, which already had begun to manifest itself in Hellenistic and Roman philosophy. The change emerges in the imperium, which is presided over by the emperor. Hegel refers to the emperor as "the lord and master of the world" and sees him as "the absolute person" (p. 292). He claims that the (average) person and the absolute person do not mutually recognize each other: "For his (the absolute person) power is not the union and harmony of Spirit [Geist] in which persons would recognize [erkennen] their own self-consciousness." (p. 293)

Although I have suggested that Hegel regards legal recognition as true recognition, what Hegel means by this is that it is new truth—which is necessarily immediate and abstract. Hence, when Hegel invokes the emperor as a master, one becomes aware that legal recognition constitutes a repetition of the one-sided kind of recognition that occurs in the master-slave relationship. Historically, legal recognition belongs to and is the culmination of the ancient world. Yet it also provides passage to the modern world in establishing the basis of Hegel's distinction between civil society (which equates the individual with personhood) and the state (which absorbs but does not destroy individuality). The Roman world turns into the modern world by unmooring a part of the individual from society. This fosters a freedom that is not necessarily easy to assimilate. Hegel suggests that "the consciousness that is driven back into itself [in sich zurückgetrieben] from this actuality ponders [denkt] this its inessential nature" (p. 293). It lives, then, in a reality in which "it does not recognize [erkennt] itself" (p. 294).

The Roman world represents an advance over the Greek world; at the same time, there is a loss: ". . . the single individual as such is true only as a universal multiplicity of single individuals. Cut off [abgetrennt] from this multiplicity, the solitary self is, in fact, an unreal impotent self." (p. 292) Hegel's point is that when being-for-itself is relegated to the private sphere, being-for-another is altered and becomes artificial. Hegel believes that the problem detected here deepens in the modern world. The rest of PhS is devoted to a detailed description of this situation and to Hegel's meditations on how to overcome it.

8.2 Alienation at Home

The middle section of Geist, which is itself a middle chapter, is titled "Self-Alienated Spirit. Culture." We find ourselves in the modern world, specifically, pre-revolutionary France. Here Geist is both yearning and impoverished: not only is the self at odds with others, it is also at odds with itself. The specter of history recedes for consciousness even more than in Roman culture; it is faced with itself and its own world. Just as the shapes of consciousness are abstract in relation to the shapes of the world presented in Geist, the shapes of the world presented in Greek and Roman culture so far are abstract in relation to the concreteness of the modern world. The journey is leading back home—for consciousness, for the subject who has undertaken the labor, and for the readers (who inhabit the world Hegel is describing, or who at least can identify with it to some extent).

As we saw in chapter 4, consciousness in the modern world knows itself to be self-alienated; it knows that what it lacks is the satisfaction of recognition. Following the development of consciousness so far, we know that Hegel requires a form of recognition that will honor its authentic individuality, which was neglected in legal recognition. For Hegel, "it is therefore through culture [Bildung] that the individual acquires standing and actuality" (p. 298). Through self-cultivation, individuality is reclaimed; viz., Geist undergoes a process of "externalizing [entäussert] its own self and thus establishing itself as substance that has objective existence" (p. 299). The individual, in positing itself as one with "the universal objective existence," becomes cultured.

Hegel suggests that the self becomes actual through self-transcendence. Self-transcendence means, on the one hand, that progress is attained as the individual successfully molds himself or herself to culture; on the other hand, it means that something is displaced: ". . . its actuality consists solely in the setting aside [Aufheben] of its natural self" (p. 299). The stage of culture amends the complete absorption of the individual that characterized ethical recognition; it also amends the partial absorption of the individual that was manifest in legal recognition. Yet in the long run it too will prove unsatisfactory. Following Rousseau, and anticipating Nietzsche and Freud, Hegel regards the demand to reject our natural endowment as oppressive.

The failure of satisfaction in modern culture is first revealed in the dialectic of the noble and the base, the two forms of cultured consciousness that vie for power over the state. With this dialectic Hegel shows a dawning appreciation of the impact of the capitalism on society. Noble consciousness identifies itself with the authority of the state and serves it dutifully, sacrificing "possession and enjoyment" (p. 306). Base consciousness unabashedly seeks wealth and "sees in the sovereign power a fetter and suppression of its own being-for-itself" (p. 305). Hegel claims that, despite its virtue, noble consciousness has only apparently "removed its own pure self" (p. 307). Base consciousness is, in truth, more honest in presenting itself as being-for-itself. Each of these two consciousnesses turns out to be the opposite of what it appears to be. The inversion recalls the slave's overturning of the domination of the master. The awareness of this inversion leads to the next stage: disrupted [zerissene] consciousness.

Disrupted consciousness, like deranged consciousness, tries to articulate its outrage at its alienation. (These states occur at the midpoints of the Geist and Reason chapters, respectively.) Deranged consciousness, like unhappy consciousness, feels the lack of connection to the universal. Disrupted consciousness, however, is a response to the inversion of noble and base consciousness. It constitutes a higher level of awareness because it knows that it is implicated in the division and "derides its own self" (p. 319).

Unhappy consciousness, in Self-Consciousness, feels divided. Deranged consciousness, in Reason, is aware of being divided. Disrupted consciousness, in Geist, knows that being divided is a result of its own doing. Perhaps disrupted consciousness is the most anguished. All three cases portray consciousness as alienated from the universal and as dissatisfied. All three cases result in consciousness's taking flight back into universality. (The subordination of the individual to the polis in *Antigone* is another example). Unhappy consciousness results in Reason. Deranged consciousness results in virtue. Disrupted consciousness results in Faith.

At this point the focus of chapter 4 is immanent. Faith features a relation between the individual and the universal in a religious sense. Hegel reminds us of the stage of unhappy consciousness and then explains that Faith, through belief, is an attempt to overcome such division. Faith lifts itself up as "a mortal perishable self" into a beyond of its own construction (p. 326). This flight from the world occurs within consciousness itself. Insight is a response to the flight; it is an appeal to consciousness to return to this world from beyond: ". . . be for yourselves what you all are in yourselves—reasonable [vernüftig]" (p. 328). Yet this call to reason also represents a further rejection of the natural self. Insight is, of course, embodied in the historical movement known as the Enlightenment.

We are now in a better position to understand why the Enlightenment marks a crucial step in the development of Geist. Insight, the essence of the Enlightenment, opposes the abandonment of the self in the universal, either through culture (or noble consciousness) or through Faith. Insight is the reverse movement in which self-consciousness "knows essence, not as essence, but as absolute self" (p. 326). The reversal consists of moving the universal to the individual, rather than the other way around. Now the universal is embodied within the individual. This reversal is thus an internalizing of the external. Recognition occurs as being-for-itself finds itself in its being-for-another. This movement is mediated by a third term, the useful, just as "the thing" mediated between master and slave.

The middle subsection on the Enlightenment (II) occurs at the middle section, Culture (B), of this middle chapter, Geist (BB) (see appendix). Hegel underscores the self-confidence of insight as consciousness. He declares that "pure insight is thereby an actual consciousness satisfied [befriedigtes] within itself" (p. 355). This sense of confidence is extended to the world: ". . . the world is for it simply its own will" (pp.

356–357). The self identifies its own will with the general will. As in *Philosophy of Spirit II* , the general will—"the will of all individuals as such"(p. 357)—exists within the single individual.

The story now will be entirely familiar from the discussion in chapter 4. Insight opposes the individual's yielding himself to the universal in faith. Faith and Insight, therefore, are opposed to each other. Each, by itself, is one-sided. Insight unmasks the dissembling of Faith, although Hegel makes clear that Insight is no less an imaginary union. Insight and Faith converge in relying on hope, which inspires the French Revolution. In the section on The Terror, hope is smashed when the universal individual first confronts reality. Siep (1979, p. 110) points out that this discussion follows from *Philosophy of Spirit II*, not only in regard to the general will's residing in the single will but also in regard to how the example of the revolution and its aftermath correspond to the stage of Verbrechen und Strafe in *Philosophy of Spirit II*. Moreover, as in tragedy, the experience of destruction has a positive side. In this instance, Insight's achievement of infusing the individual with the universal is preserved and developed in Morality, the next section in PhS.

8.3 Toward Mutual Recognition

With the section on Morality, an important transition in PhS takes place: from 'is' to 'ought'—from actual history to the realm of ideas. This transition is evident from the titles of the sections: we have The Ethical World (Greece and Rome), then The World of Self-Alienated Spirit (France), but then The Moral View of the World (Kant).[2] The opposition between Faith and Insight dissolves into moral consciousness, just as the opposition between noble and base consciousness dissolved into disrupted consciousness. But moral consciousness, as opposed to the alienation of disrupted consciousness, is a self-certain state of consciousness. The positive outcome betokens our proximity to the telos of Hegel's goal—mutual recognition. This is a critical moment in the development of Geist, for consciousness's knowledge of itself finally coincides with "our" knowledge of it:

Here, then, knowledge appears at last to have become completely identical with its truth; for its truth is this very knowledge and any antithesis between the two sides

has vanished, not only *for us* or in itself (an sich), but for self-consciousness itself.
. . . Now, however the object is for consciousness itself the certainty of itself, viz.
knowledge. . . . [It] is pure knowledge. (p. 364)

Hegel emphasizes that this moment is not accomplished by a leap but
follows from "the strenuous effort" of consciousness through all the
previous stages of the work (p. 35):

It is absolute mediation, like the consciousness which cultivates itself [sich
bildende], and the consciousness which believes, for it is essentially the movement of the self to set aside [aufzuheben] the abstraction of immediate existence,
and to become conscious of itself as a universal. (p. 364)

The essence of moral consciousness, then, is mediation. Mediation
occurs between the self and the universal and also within the self. This
is accomplished through what Hegel terms "duty" [Pflicht]. Moral
consciousness, he explains, "is bound only by duty, and this substance
is its own pure consciousness, for which duty cannot receive the form
of something alien" (p. 365). It is evident that Hegel is thinking of
Kant's moral philosophy.

Hegel observes that moral consciousness depends on an absolute
antithesis between morality and nature. Nature is consciousness as
sensuousness, which "in the shape of volitions, as instincts and inclinations possesses a specific essentiality of its own, or has its own individual purposes, and thus is opposed to the pure will and its pure
purpose" (p. 367). Moral consciousness attempts to unite the antithesis in a familiar way: it tries to elevate sensuousness to reason in the
same way that the individual tries to raise himself (rejecting his natural being) to the universal in culture. This is a doomed venture, and
morality is faced with the impossibility of shaking the demands of
nature. Its self-certainty is thereby undermined. In becoming actualized, it goes through a stage of dissemblance or duplicity
[Verstellung]—a minor but new variety of split consciousness—
before it passes into the next stage, Conscience. The actualization of
morality leads consciousness to confront itself as aspiring to perfec-
tion, just as it must acknowledge its own imperfection.

Let me reiterate at this point that Hegel's project in PhS is delimited
by the satisfaction of consciousness and is not simply fueled by the
abstract ideal of rationality. This emerges unambiguously in the section

on moral consciousness when Hegel notes that it "is not, therefore, in earnest [Ernst] with the elimination [Aufheben] of inclinations and impulses, for it is just these that are the self-realizing self-consciousness" (p. 377). The experience of the self-realizing self-consciousness is grounded by the criterion of satisfaction. As we have seen, satisfaction embraces a range of experience (bodily and cognitive). It is apparent that Hegel's own phenomenological language, however arcane sounding, allows him to depart from assuming rationality as the exclusive criterion of agency.[3] There is a legitimacy to being-for-itself that an agent must acknowledge in order to be satisfied.

The failure of moral consciousness is exposed through the disparity of its denial of natural needs and the recurring presence of those needs. The awareness of the disparity leads to the concern that "there are no moral, perfect, actual self-consciousnesses" (p. 373). Morality is posited as existing only in "a holy moral lawgiver." In coming to see itself as unable to be perfectly moral, moral consciousness loses its sense of certainty and founders in the gap between 'ought' and 'is'. It is interesting that Hegel focuses his attack on the hypocrisy of this "moral view of the view." He shows that, in discounting happiness, the moral view of the world cloaks itself in a higher value and obscures its own "envy" of others (p. 379). Adorno (1993, p. 47) observes that in this passage Hegel anticipates Nietzsche's attack on morality as hypocritical, and that thus we ought to be wary of dismissing Hegel as a bourgeois philosopher.

Moral consciousness finds itself as it "retreats into itself" [geht . . . in sich zurück] (p. 384). We arrive at the next stage, Conscience, which results from moral consciousness's becoming actualized. Conscience provides the previously empty content of duty with a new meaning. Duty no longer "oppresses" the self with its demands. Hegel states succinctly that "it is now the law that exists for the sake of the self, not the self that exists for the sake of the law" (p. 387). Actual duty differs from pure duty in that the former is embedded in the realm of action. In acting dutifully, one is conscious of an other (p. 386). Actual duty, then, entails that the self knows itself as being-for-another and also being-for-itself. Being-for-another becomes "an essential moment" for consciousness, thus overcoming the antithesis of being-for-itself and being-for-another.

Although this achievement is precarious, conscience manages to attain a unity of self-identity. Moreover, this internal unity is equal to the unity that occurs in the realm of action between self and other. For Hegel, conscience is "the common element of the two self-consciousnesses," and "this element is the substance in which the deed has an enduring reality, the moment of being recognized and acknowledged [Anerkanntwerdens] by others" (p. 388). The deed attains enduring reality because of "the conviction" behind it. Conscience does not consist in the perfunctory exercise of what one is supposed to do. Rather, it requires "knowing one's purpose," which is connected to awareness of being a universal self-consciousness and also to "universal recognition" [allgemeine Anerkennen]. Universal recognition—that is, the flourishing of mutual recognition—is achieved in conscience.

Conscience at once signifies the deepening of our inner natures and the convergence of philosophy and religion. In Conscience, "for the first time a *subject* has made explicit all the moments of consciousness within it" (p. 389). Indeed, Hegel emphasizes that conscience is the culmination of all that went before: ". . . it knows the moments of consciousness as moments" (p. 389). More specifically, conscience is "the third self," emerging from and mediating the demands for absolute freedom of the cultural (second) self and the sacrifice of the (first) self as a legal person (p. 384). The claim that conscience represents the third and final development of the self in Geist indicates that Hegel is concerned with agency throughout the chapter on Geist. In keeping with the notion that Conscience [Gewissen] embodies and preserves the experience of consciousness, Hegel emphasizes that Con-science, as Knowing-with, is both a new form of knowing [Wissen] and a new form of certainty [Gewissheit]. The connection between recognition and knowledge is once again apparent. At this point, the disparity between claims about knowledge and truth, tested by consciousness for confirmation (experience), has been overcome.

Universal recognition completes the development of recognition. The notion of recognition as mutual recognition is finally attained. In universal recognition, consciousness knows itself. Knowing oneself means seeing oneself in the other, i.e., recognizing oneself as being-for-another and being-for-oneself. Hegel describes this process of interaction between two universal individuals. Yet, as we might expect, the fragile success in conscience will be tested and undermined in what follows.

For one thing, the interaction between two universal individuals is mediated by language, which "emerges as the middle term, mediating between independent and acknowledged [anerkannter] self-consciousness" (PhS, p. 396). Conscience seeks to express itself in language. It allows the self to remain within itself and to participate in universality. This follows the view of the early Jena writings, where language is at issue in earlier stages of development.[4] We now arrive at the true significance of conscience, wherein "this distinction between the universal consciousness and the individual self is just what has been superseded [aufgehoben], and the supersession [Aufheben] of it is conscience" (p. 397). Universality is incorporated within individuality. In the actual meeting of individuals, the reality of this experience is articulated and linked to the presence of the divine:

> The reconciling *Yea*, in which the two 'I's' let go their antithetical existence, is the existence of the 'I' which has expanded into a duality, and therein remains identical with itself, and, in its complete externalization and opposite, possesses the certainty of itself: it is God manifested in the midst of those who know themselves in the form of pure knowledge. (p. 409)

At this level, the interpersonal sense of recognition is preserved. The social sense is at least implicit; the religious sense has been reintroduced. In contrast to the early Jena writings and the *Philosophy of Right*, however, a role for the state is not emphasized.[5]

The journey of consciousness is still not quite complete. The harmony of universal recognition is disturbed by questions about the relation between word and deeds.[6] Duty degenerates to "a matter of words," and, once more, the individual withdraws to see itself as being-for-itself (p. 400). The absolute self-reliance of conscience means that recognition cannot be sustained. The name for consciousness that makes such a retreat is "the beautiful soul." It is aware of the loss of connection to others, yet, in its sadness, it denies this and maintains that it will follow only its own conscience. Hegel contrasts this with another variety of conscience: one that does not remove itself from action, but which is assessed as "evil" by universal consciousness.

It is difficult to follow Hegel's argument here, as he temporarily displaces the beautiful soul in order to focus on the dialectic between the consciousness (which is regarded as evil) and the consciousness (which judges the first as such). It is not clear what constitutes the evil of the first consciousness; it appears that the evil is due to the basis of its action "in opposition to the acknowledged [anerkannten] universal, according to its *own* inner law and conscience" (p. 402). Citing Hegel's reflections on conscience in the *Philosophy of Right*, Hyppolite (1974, p. 498) claims that what Hegel means by conscience in PhS is "good conscience," and that the "evil" that is subsequently introduced ought to be seen as a contrast to the first consciousness.[7] This would mean that evil denotes bad conscience rather than harmful actions. As this dialectic unfolds, Hegel registers empathy for the evil consciousness in relation to the harsh and arrogant judging consciousness. One consciousness confronts another and "judges" it as evil. The first consciousness is thus guilty of transgression in verbally criticizing the second and in placing itself above the realm of action. Hegel reveals that the mentality of judging is self-satisfied. The dictum "No man is a hero to his valet" is applied to the judging consciousness for aspiring to play the role of being a "moral valet." The situation mirrors the dialectic that we now have witnessed several times, particularly in the opposition between noble and base consciousness and, of course, in the master-slave relationship. Hegel discerns an aspect of truth in evil/base consciousness, however immoral it might seem. Moreover, Hegel reveals that judging/noble consciousness is disingenuous in denying its being-for-itself. Judging consciousness is unmasked as "base" and as exemplifying "hypocrisy" (p. 405). The subordination of the judged consciousness (the slave) to the judging consciousness (the master) is overturned through former's desire for recognition. What is different here is that recognition, in the form of confession, means that both the judging consciousness (as the other) transgresses and the judged consciousness (as the self) act transgressively.

Throughout PhS, the master-slave interaction reverberates as a threat to mutual recognition. At the same time, one must pay careful attention to the nuances of any of these interactions. Here not only does the slave (the judged consciousness) discover its being-for-another; the master (the judging consciousness) does as well. The latter renounces its hard-heartedness and sees its judging as a transgression.[8] Through the act of forgiveness, the transgresssion is overcome and reconciliation ensues. Mutual recognition is established through the reciprocal movements of the master and the slave toward each other.

The religious language of confession, reconciliation [Versöhnung], and forgiveness [Verzeihung] points us beyond Geist to Religion. This language also distinguishes the account of recognition in PhS from that in the early Jena writings.[9] Recognition is applied to the relation between the self and the Christian God, who appeared in human form and is "beheld as a self" (p. 459)). The relation between the self and the eternal being is called "loving recognition" [Anerkennen der Liebe] (p. 466). This apex of recognition presupposes community: God is recognized as presiding within a community in which people recognize one another. In this final development, the origins of the concept of recognition in the concept of love shine through.[10] It becomes apparent that Hegel's concept of recognition is consistent with and dependent on a Christian world view. The language of the final chapter (Absolute Spirit) makes this abundantly clear. The somewhat downbeat description of modern culture in the Culture section has now been supplanted by an upbeat prescription, which began in the section on Morality (the last section of the Geist chapter). The Absolute Spirit chapter is, of course, dizzying in its optimism.

8.4 Summarizing Recognition in the PhS

Recognition in PhS grows in complexity as it evolves. It is at issue throughout PhS. In Self-Consciousness, the bare concept is matched against the emerging self-awareness of individual self-consciousness and is at the greatest distance from realization. This recognition is false because of the disparity between concept and reality that ensues in the master-slave relationship. The danger of such unequal and one-sided bonding haunts the experience of recognition throughout PhS.

This crucial point is ignored by Williams and by other commentators who overreact to Kojève's influential reading of recognition.[11]

The even more extreme danger of a split (unhappy) consciousness longing for the universal, not bound to others, and alienated from itself also haunts the experience of recognition throughout PhS. Yet these threats of self-division are healed through self-identity. The recurrent incidents in which being-for-itself usurps the sphere of being-for-another yield in the face of the stubborn reality of the latter. Attempts to ignore and deny one's being-for-another impede self-knowledge and, furthermore, preclude the possibility of living a satisfied life. Insofar as one resolves to remove oneself from interaction with others, one's life is impoverished.

In Reason, the concept of recognition is modified so that recognition is described in terms of the individual and the universal (although these terms are first introduced in the unhappy consciousness section), thereby bringing recognition closer to realization. However, because recognition exists only within the individual, it is internal; thus, it is problematic to read the movement in terms of straightforward progress. Indeed, recognition is faced with the utter contradiction of requiring the other and, at the same time, dismissing the other's actuality. This is where the disparity between concept and reality is most glaring. The experience of recognition in Self-Consciousness and Reason will be played out again in the Geist chapter, where the gap between concept and reality is significantly smaller. All the various forms of recognition in Geist are at least attempts at mutual recognition. However, expectations of straightforward progress are marred here too by the replay in development which recognition undergoes—beginning with natural recognition between individual family members. The universal is (re)introduced in ethical recognition, just as recognition in reason amended recognition in self-consciousness. Recognition in the Greek world (natural and ethical) is seen as a kind of false recognition on a higher level in which the universal subsumes the individual.

With recognition in the Roman world, the movement from recognition in self-consciousness to recognition in reason is repeated once again. Legal recognition is between persons (that is, universal selves bonded to each other externally). Insofar as legal recognition portrays universality as residing within the individual, Hegel's solution to the individual/universal problem is implicit. However, in another sense, legal recognition augurs a more pernicious result than ethical recognition. The Roman world leaves out the inner aspect of the individual, thus constituting recognition in a way that does not reflect one's full individuality. Hegel rejects the solution of locating being-for-itself in the private domain and being-for-another in the public domain. Legal recognition has an external form; it represents the inverse of the internal recognition in reason.

Recognition in the modern world stands in relation to recognition in the Greek and Roman worlds as recognition in Geist stands in relation to recognition in Self-Consciousness and Reason. The disparity between concept and reality is overcome through consciousness's successful attempt to mediate the concept. In Culture, the individual seeks to bond himself to universality. This is a crucial new development, but it will turn out to be another overzealous attempt to achieve mutual recognition at the expense of individuality. In the Enlightenment, universality is shown to reside within the individual in the form of the general will. The bonding of the individual to the universal is ensured at the same time that the individual is protected from disappearing within the universal. The actualization of this occurs in conscience, which is linked to forgiveness and, more generally, to Christianity.

In the section on Conscience, Hegel reflects on the progress of the self through three stages: the legal, the cultured, and the moral self. His point is that each of these selves entails a relation between individuality and universality and between being-for-itself and being-for-another. The metaphor Hegel uses to explicate whether these selves attain satisfaction is fullness vs. emptiness. He suggests that for the legal self (which represents the culmination of recognition in the ancient world) the universal is full but the individual is empty, that for the cultured self (which represents the aftermath of the French Revolution) the universal is empty but the individual is full, and that for the moral self (which represents the Kantian revolution in philosophy) the universal and the individual are full. In this connection, recall that in the preface Hegel describes the ideal of culture as "the seriousness of fulfilled life" [dem Ernste des erfüllten Leben] and then contrasts it to the current reality of Geist's sense of emptiness and loss. PhS is a journey that, at the end, returns to its own beginning as Hegel reviews history and formulates the solution of mutual recognition.

Mutual recognition, in its final form, pertains to the relation between universal individuals (and within a universal individual). A social domain is presupposed, so that recognition involves a relation between the self and community (and its various institutions). Recognition here is interpersonal and thereby harks back to the initial interaction in self-consciousness, wherein "two individuals confront each other" in what Hegel labels in *System der Sittlichkeit* a Zweikampf. Finally, there is the dimension of self-recognition, in which the self knows itself both as for-itself and for-another.

Hegel's concept of recognition provides a model whereby the achievement of self-knowledge (self-recognition) leads to the restoration of social integration (mutual recognition). Mutual recognition occurs between consciousnesses who regard each other as free and equal. This provides a path for the individual to belong to society, where a strong bond is affirmed yet individuality is not obliterated. Through recognition, it becomes possible to break free from the domination and destruction of the master/slave paradigm. PhS leads philosophy, as part of culture, to play an indispensable role in the formation of a new cultural ideal, and, perhaps, in real social change. Although there is something wrong with modern culture, Hegel does not despair; his reading of the future is palpably optimistic.

Recognition is achieved in PhS insofar as the reader interacts with consciousness and with the phenomenologist, and insofar as all arrive at complementary conclusions. The reader sets this process in motion; thus, as I emphasized in the excursus at the end of chapter 3, PhS must be enacted as much as read. The engagement of the reader in the experience of consciousness and in the performance that takes place distinguishes Hegel's project from other philosophical works—including any of Hegel's other works. The inexorable need to interact with others, which Hegel attributes to the nature of consciousness, disturbs the isolation and withdrawal of the Cartesian subject.

It is, of course, hard to say to what extent Hegel really expected to transform and liberate the reader of PhS. And one must also wonder what it means to encounter the work almost 200 years after it was written. PhS is a unique philosophical work. In its attention to the reader, it harks back, as I noted in chapter 3, to Greek tragedy. Again and again, Hegel enacts dramas that reveal why defining agency in terms of being-for-itself to the exclusion of being-for-another is doomed to be self-contradictory and unsatisfying.

9

Hegelian Agency

Sometimes what is required is to think with Hegel against Hegel.
—Richard Bernstein, *The New Constellation*

Chapters 7 and 8 demonstrate that recognition is at issue throughout Hegel's PhS. Introduced in the Self-Consciousness chapter, it is not realized completely until late in the work, when all the connotations of recognition—interpersonal, social, and religious—are conjoined with self-knowledge. The theme of agency can be discerned in the concept of recognition, particularly in the Master/Slave section and, indeed, up through the chapter on Reason. Yet the theme of agency is not displaced in the chapter on Geist or beyond.

Hegel's intention to preserve the theme of agency throughout PhS is evident in the section on Conscience. In a passage I mentioned in my eighth chapter, Hegel reviews the developments in Geist and posits the existence of three varieties of selves. Hegel is not simply pausing to review the progress that has been made.[1] As I see it, Hegel recapitulates these stages of the journey in order to remind us about the theme of agency; this is necessary because, beginning in the Geist chapter, one might assume that socio-cultural concerns have replaced his concern with agency.

Hegel's elaboration of the three varieties of selves demonstrates the steadfastness of his interest in agency. He sees these selves as developing through history and as entailing variations in the relation between the individual and the universal, being-for-itself and being-for-another.[2]

The first self, which culminates with "the legal person" of the Roman era, is part of the truth of the "ethical world," which has its inception with the Greeks. The first moment of the dialectic is the natural Sittlichkeit of Greek culture; the second moment, which undermines this complacency, occurs in Greek tragedy. The conflict between the individual and the universal is then healed in Roman culture, but at a cost to individual identity. In the ancient world, according to Hegel, agency means that a universal identity has primacy over individual identity. A universal identity cannot support meaning for the individual; it requires sacrifice of being-for-itself. As Hegel puts it, the self is not "filled by itself" (p. 384).

The second self is the cultured self. As with the first self, Hegel begins with the culminating state in "absolute freedom," where "Geist has recovered [wiedergegebne] itself from its dividedness" (p. 384). The first moment of the dialectic is the self-division of culture; the second moment, the French Revolution, undermines but also refreshes the self. The self-division of culture is healed through the universal's regaining meaning. Yet the universal exists only in the will and knowledge of the individual. Hegel declares that "it does not have the form of an existence free from the self; in this self, therefore, it obtains no filling and no positive content, no world" (p. 384). The individual faces a challenge to raise himself up and to embody the general will within himself. But, unlike in the ancient world, the universal, in actuality, is unstable and even violent; thus, the universal no longer provides assurance.

The third self is the moral self, the culminating moment of the Conscience section. That narrative begins with moral self-consciousness, which does not try to reclaim objective meaning in the universal but which instead provides meaning for itself in terms of duty (i.e., respect for the law). Since duty brings about a conflict between being moral and satisfying natural needs, the first moment is superseded in the second moment, when this self acts in the world. The third self is reached when pure duty—an "empty criterion"—is abandoned in favor of autonomy and self-actualization. The third moment of the third self concludes the dialectic: the individual defines himself or herself as both universal and individual. Conscience is, therefore, the "absolute self": the universal lives within and guides the individual;

the individual is open to being-for-another, yet this is not at the expense of being-for-itself (pp. 386–387). Indeed, it is with the third self that "truth" is finally grasped not only as substance but also as subject.

Hegel's recollection of these three selves is a performance that has the aim of integration. Integration refers to a unified relation to oneself and the social world. Hegel does not conceptualize integration to the social world in PhS in much detail. He mainly emphasizes that self-division can be transformed into self-identity through the individual's relation to others. His argument presumes that self-recognition is the prelude to mutual recognition. In the *Philosophy of Right* Hegel is more descriptive, highlighting the diverse roles an individual has in the family, in civil society, and in the state. Thus, Hegel comes to have a deeper appreciation of how modern culture requires us to adopt a number of distinct identities. However, his later account is not as forceful as his critique of modern culture. In PhS, self-alienation and alienation from others impede satisfaction.[3]

Hegel's theory of agency specifies integration as a matter of harmonizing self-concern and attachment to others. In addition to a need for connection to individual others, we have an abiding need to be at home in society and in the universe. Psychoanalytic language is illuminating here: narcissism and individuation can be associated with being-for-itself, and relatedness with being-for-another. Yet, in contrast to psychoanalysis, Hegel appears to have in mind a sense of integration in which all existing conflicts can be mended. He seems to imagine self-fathoming as producing a final incarnation of self-transparency. This way of thinking about integration places an enormous and untenable burden on his concept of agency.

At this point I will widen my focus considerably. Going beyond Hegel's theory of agency, I will introduce interpretations of recognition that are Hegelian in a loose sense. This will help me to begin to sort out what remains relevant in Hegel, a process that will continue through my examination of Nietzschean agency. I shall begin the first section of this chapter with Kojève's influential interpretation of Hegel's concept of recognition. This interpretation deserves attention because of the extent of its influence and because it has lately become an object of criticism for a number of Hegel commentators.

9.1 A Reintroduction to the Reading of Hegel: Kojève

As is well known, Alexandre Kojève's lectures on Hegel, which feature the concept of recognition, influenced a generation of French philosophers,[4] including Marxists, Existentialists, Phenomenologists, Critical Theorists, and some who sought to combine two or more of those schools of thought. Indeed, Kojève's lectures affected virtually all Continental philosophers.

Although Kojève's interpretation of Hegel is often idiosyncratic and controversial, it forged deep connections between Hegel and Marx, and it reinvigorated Left Hegelianism. It also deserves credit for attempting to address Hegel's relation to the phenomenological movement. Moreover, in dramatizing the desire for recognition through risking one's life in a struggle for "pure prestige," and in invoking a Nietzschean discourse of "great politics," Kojève pursues one avenue of affirming the connection between Hegel's and Nietzsche's philosophy. However, it is more in line with how I see the relationship between Hegel and Nietzsche to value Kojève's attention to the theme of agency as underlying the need for philosophy to respond to culture.

The primacy of Kojève's commitment to understanding his own culture has the infelicitous consequence that he feels no compunction about picking and choosing various aspects of Hegel's philosophy. For example, his textual analysis of PhS spotlights the socio-political function of recognition and minimizes the epistemological function. Psychology informs Kojève's account of recognition in that he emphasizes satisfaction, although he does not pay much attention to the subjective experience of recognition. Furthermore, Kojève gives so much attention to the Master/Slave section of the Self-Consciousness chapter of PhS that he slights the subsequent chapters.[5] In fact, as I demonstrated in chapters 7 and 8, recognition runs throughout PhS. Kojève's reading of Hegel ought to be appreciated for what it is: an original appropriation, rather than a commentary.

In recent secondary work on Hegel, Kojève is held responsible for having spread misreadings of Hegel. For example, Paul Redding (1996, pp. 119–120) argues that Kojève contradicts himself on whether the life-and-death struggle is motivated by the desire for recognition or whether the desire for recognition ensues from it. This criticism points to a flaw in the logic of the argument without adequately noting that Kojève's strategy intentionally tracks the development of an implicit and deficient self-understanding to an explicit and better self-understanding. Redding tells us that his argument has its source in an interpretation originally made by Stanley Rosen, yet he bypasses Rosen's helpful assessment of the motivating impulse in Kojève's philosophy: a "revolutionary act, an act of propaganda" (Rosen 1987, p. 104).[6] Kojève is adamant about not aspiring to be an academic philosopher, and we should refrain from judging him according to standards that he does not care to uphold.[7]

Williams also wages an offensive against Kojève. In his response to Ludwig Siep's proposal that recognition is derived from a synthesis of love and struggle, Williams argues that Kojève dwells on struggle at the expense of love. Williams does not agree with Siep's insight; he sees love as more crucial than struggle. Thus, Kojève represents one end of the continuum in valorizing struggle to the exclusion of love, while Williams opts for the other end in emphasizing love to the exclusion of struggle. Williams's strongly Levinasian reading of Hegel does not correct Kojève's reading as much as it effaces it.

Kojève's emphasis on struggle coincides with his strongly sociopolitical approach to recognition. He hypothesizes the existence of a universal, homogeneous state—to be attained as the end of history—wherein recognition prevails in a community assembled by a forceful leader.[8] Kojève's understanding of recognition in terms of the wish to be recognized is very much consistent with his characterization of recognition in terms of "pure prestige" (Kojève 1969, p. 7). Featuring what we might call the "receiving" end of recognition, Kojève thereby discounts the "giving" end. This reading of Hegel overlooks the prospect of equality and reciprocity in the way it conceives of the relation between self and other.

Kojève has been justly criticized for failing to distinguish between the social and interpersonal levels of recognition in his approach to the relation between self and other (Kelly 1976, p. 197; Siep 1979, pp. 6–7).[9] Siep has argued that the distinction between interpersonal and social is fundamental; this distinction serves as a way to organize PhS into two stages of development. G. A. Kelly maintains that Kojève neglects not only the interpersonal level but also the phenomenolog-ical level of self-knowledge, wherein Hegel depicts the subjective experience of recognition.[10] That self-knowledge is at stake in recog-nition helps to direct our attention to the theme of agency. Kelly's crit-icism of Kojève has some plausibility, but his failure to address the issue of satisfaction means that he does not quite give Kojève his due.[11]

The satisfaction of agents is central to Kojève's interpretation of recognition. Kojève does not defend the socio-political function of recognition to the exclusion of psychology, though he does think about satisfaction primarily in terms of the individual's experience. Kojève's reflections in a letter to Leo Strauss are germane on this point. After beginning with an initial apology for the quality of his book, he avers: "But it contains some interesting things. Above all, about wisdom, fulfillment, and happiness (I follow Hegel in saying: satisfaction)."[12] Kojève's concern with individuality is evident in his lectures, where he asserts that "only the individual can be 'satisfied'" in the context of contrasting the ancient (Pagan) world, which does not value individuality, to the modern state, which does value it" (Kojève 1969, p. 59).[13]

Kojève's acknowledgement of the satisfaction of the individual does not negate Kelly's criticism of his failure to contend adequately with self-knowledge and the subjective experience of recognition. Kojève maintains that to be satisfied is to be "unique au monde et [néan-moins] universellement valable." This implies that the individual's sat-isfaction must occur within a larger framework; Kojève specifies, in fact, that only "le Chef de l'État" is truly satisfied, and that the lesser satisfaction of the rest of the citizenry is contingent on the satisfaction of the leader. There is something elusive in Kojève's portrait of satis-faction. Pippin (1997, p. 256) highlights this in showing that the attainment of satisfaction is supposed to be ensured by the end of his-tory, although Kojève wavers and ends up claiming that satisfaction is merely a possibility.[14]

As I mentioned in chapter 6, Kojève maintains that satisfaction demarcates animals from humans and thus ought to be regarded as a distinctively human achievement. This is a rather surprising claim, as satisfaction is most often linked to Hegel's discussion of Desire (that is, the consciousness that is immersed in the activity of consumption). As my investigation into Hegel's view of satisfaction emphasized, the concept of satisfaction cannot be restricted to appetite or bodily experience. For Kojève, satisfaction is grounded in the human choice to risk death, that is, to claim meaning for ourselves that is over and beyond mere survival. Kojève construes recognition in a way—contra Hegel—that oddly legitimizes the master's attachment to his own superiority.

Ultimately, Kojève's mirror yields a distorted image of Hegel. His introduction to Hegel is actually more of a self-reflection. For some commentators, including Williams and Pippin, Kojève's philosophical anthropology simply fails to do justice to Hegel.[15] In labeling Kojève's reading of Hegel "thumotic, Greek and non-Christian," Pippin also establishes his wariness of this point of view. Although Pippin urges us to realize that Kojève was "a child of his time," he is referring to the philosophical atmosphere in which neo-Kantian and Bergsonian positions were on the wane, thus obscuring Hegel's Kantian roots. He and other recent critics of Kojève do not linger to consider the specific social and cultural context outside of academic philosophy.

It is of enormous importance that Kojève's lectures were delivered in the period 1933–1939, between the Nazis' rise to power and the fall of France. (They were published in 1946.) This was, by any standards, an extraordinary time, and Kojève's ambitions must be judged in the context of a chaotic, brutal, polarized world. When Pippin complains about Kojève's apparent indifference to liberal democracy, for instance, it is without taking note of how dim the prospects were for liberal democracy at that time throughout Europe. If Kojève now seems dangerously apocalyptic, perhaps our reaction ought to be tempered by the particular circumstances under which he was writing. Indeed, one could argue that it is our own positionality in history that makes us uncomfortable with Kojève, and that the trend toward less Marxist readings of recognition is, in part, a measure of how remote social change appears.

I mean to offer neither an apology for Kojève nor a plea for the restoration of his influence on postwar Continental philosophy. Nevertheless, Kojève's interpretation of Hegel makes an enduring contribution in the spirit of Hegel's attempt to come to terms with his own culture, even though some of his views are anathema and are not well grounded in Hegel's work. As will be seen in the next section, it is possible to formulate a sophisticated contemporary version of the anthropological reading of the concept of recognition.

Kojève remains valuable because he puts the issue of Hegelian agency on the map. He highlights Hegel's interest in human activity, stressing that we are "not only . . . passive and positive contemplation, but also . . . active and negating desire" (Kojève 1969, p. 38). Indeed, Kojève directs us to appreciate Hegel's commitment to the notion of historical agency, despite how he simplifies the constitution of individual agency by dwelling on the wish for prestige. Kojève's engagement with his own world makes for problems in his interpretation of Hegel; however, as I see it, contextualizing Kojève's contribution is distinct from dismissing it.

9.2 New Readings of Recognition: Honneth and Benjamin

Two theorists of the "generation of 1968," Axel Honneth and Jessica Benjamin, develop Hegel's concept of recognition in a fruitful direction. Both Honneth and Benjamin are influenced by Kojève insofar as they utilize the concept of recognition as the basis of a philosophical anthropology. Yet Honneth and Benjamin overcome some of the limitations of Kojève's interpretation of Hegel. In particular, both resist Kojève's hyperbolic vision while preserving the socio-political ramifications of recognition.

Benjamin's reading of recognition is firmly rooted in psychoanalysis; Honneth's borrows from psychoanalysis. Both theorists appreciate that recognition has an affective side. For example, Honneth (1992b, p. 212; 1992a, p. 208f.) proposes that recognition denotes an "affective-rational relation of solidarity of a unique subject,"[16] and Benjamin (1987) connects Hegel's use of recognition to psychoanalytic theories of development, which highlight the affective quality in the relationship between an infant and its primary caregiver. The recognition of others, as Honneth and Benjamin see it, fosters emotional well-being and promotes the unfolding of a sense of agency.[17]

Psychoanalytic readings of recognition have an older origins: they can be linked directly from Kojève to Hyppolite and especially Lacan.[18] In fact, it is difficult to imagine how any psychoanalytic interpretation of Hegel can avoid grappling with Lacan. In view of Lacan's ambivalence about agency, however, it makes more sense to consider his perspective in connection with Nietzschean agency, which I will do in chapter 13. At this point in the book, I want to examine contemporary perspectives on recognition more closely.

Honneth's complex and insightful theory of recognition, based in Hegel, falls within the domain of critical theory and is strongly influenced by Habermas. However, Honneth's work offers a new direction for critical theory, embracing the theory of communicative rationality without abandoning the commitment to concrete social analysis—including the examination of irrational and destructive social forces—that characterized the first generation of critical theory. Honneth is an important influence on my thinking about recognition, so my discussion of his view will serve as a prelude to my elucidation of my own position.

Honneth delineates three elements of recognition: love [Liebe] (which occurs in primary relations [Primärbeziehungen]), rights [Rechte] (which occur in legal relations [Rechtsverhältnisse]), and solidarity [Solidarität] (which occurs in a community of values [Wertgemeinschaft]). These three elements correspond roughly to the family, civil society, and the state—the three divisions in Hegel's later social philosophy.[19] Honneth's interpretation emphasizes the interpersonal (the family) and the social (civil society and the state) senses of recognition, although a concern for self-recognition pervades his work.

Love, Honneth explains (1992a, p. 154), designates any strong emotional attachment, including that between husbands and wives and that between parents and children. It is a reciprocal relationship in which there exists an enduring tension between symbiotic self-sacrifice and individual self-assertion. This relationship is the basis for self-confidence [Selbstvertrauen]; thus, it is evident that Honneth does regard recognition as in some sense constitutive of agency. However, from a Hegelian point of view it is controversial to link love and recognition. Hegel adopts recognition as he departs from his early interest in love, as Siep argues. Whereas love is a relationship of unity, recognition is designed to preserve individuality.[20]

Honneth's second element of recognition, rights, is legal and embraces the autonomy of all members of the community of citizens.

Honneth emphasizes that this form of recognition is not affective, but relies on "a purely cognitive capacity of understanding" (1992a, p. 178). Legal recognition is not merely an abstract capacity to adhere to norms; at the same time, it stops short of according dignity to others (which falls more into the third category, solidarity). Self-respect [Selbstachtung], the aim of legal recognition, parallels self-confidence [Selbstvertrauen], the aim of love (ibid., p. 192).

Honneth's third element of recognition, solidarity, occurs within a community of values. It pertains to the mutual sympathy that one extends to another. Honneth emphasizes "not only passive tolerance but felt concern for the individual particularity of the other person" (1992a, p. 210). Such a community of values fosters self-dignity [Selbstschätzung]. Honneth, following Habermas, has as his primary interest presenting a social theory that utilizes Hegel's discovery of "original intersubjectivity" to uphold the ideal of mutual recognition. Indeed, Honneth's view of recognition operates on a much deeper level than Williams's. Williams is captivated by recognition without struggle.[21] As I showed in chapters 6–8, Hegel sees genuine recognition as achieved only as a result of failed attempts. Honneth conceptualizes struggle in terms of three forms of misrecognition that correspond to the three elements of recognition: violation of physical integrity (e.g., torture or rape), violation of moral self-respect (e.g., denying an individual's rights), and harming of social value (e.g., denigration of an individual's way of life through insult).[22] Honneth's attention to forms of misrecognition suggests that he is willing to take a critical look at problems in contemporary culture. His concern seems motivated by empathy for victims, whereas Kojève flirts with endorsing power politics.[23] Honneth is obliged to face the issue of how to reconcile pluralism with a community of values. Nevertheless, he has taken an important step in preserving the Hegelian insight that recognition is difficult to attain and is born from struggle.

Although Honneth's approach to recognition is attuned to its implications for individual agency, he informs us that this is not his main interest. In an important footnote, Honneth (1992a, p. 110) remarks that he, like Siep, is interested in Hegelian recognition "as a theoretical outline regarding the moral development of societies," whereas Wildt sees recognition "as the germ [Keimform] of a theory of moral development of the self [moralischen Bildung]."[24] Honneth's account affirms that recognition fosters autonomy and well-being; it also affirms the corollary that the failure of recognition produces various kinds of aggression. My own view is that in PhS Hegel attempts to link the moral development of societies and that of the self by positing the model of self-fathoming as leading to social integration. Where Honneth sees an either/or and chooses a side by following Siep and opposing Wildt, I believe that we are encountering a both/and and are obliged to preserve both sides.

Benjamin's work concurs with and in some respects anticipates Honneth's in claiming that recognition promotes individual agency.[25] Like Honneth, Benjamin borrows heavily from D. W. Winnicott's psychoanalytic account of how the primary caregiver abets the growth of the infant's sense of self. Benjamin also seems to agree with Honneth that aggression is elicited by the failure of recognition, although her view on this point has shifted from her first book to her most recent one. Overall, Benjamin offers a more extensive exploration than Honneth of the implications of recognition for individual agency. Nevertheless, the nature of individual agency is not Benjamin's exclusive concern. She is interested in the theme of mutuality in the caregiver-infant relation, and she is especially attentive to gender in regard to development. Moreover, she brings out a dimension of the socio-political function of recognition that does not figure as prominently in Honneth's account: domination/submission.[26] Ultimately, Benjamin argues that feminism is a vehicle for rethinking gender relations in terms of mutual recognition (1987, p. 224).

As Benjamin acknowledges (ibid., p. 16), her understanding of mutual recognition comes from research on "emotional attunement, mutual influence, affective mutuality, [and] sharing states of mind" in the caregiver-infant relationship. According to this research, the infant's sense of self is abetted by the caregiver's responsiveness to the infant. Such responsiveness requires an artful combination of being absorbed and involved with what the infant is experiencing and allowing the infant "space" for its own experience. Through recognition one receives confirmation from the other, Benjamin emphasizes, but one also discovers oneself in the process. Recognition fosters connection to the other; it also leads one to have a deeper sense of self.

A person, Benjamin observes (ibid., p. 21), comes to feel that "I am the doer who does, I am the author of my acts." Generalizing from this theme, Benjamin claims that recognition occurs insofar as each participant regards the other as a sovereign equal. Domination and submission arise from "a breakdown of the necessary tension between self-assertion and mutual recognition" (ibid., p. 12). Like Honneth, Benjamin sees domination and submission as produced by failure of recognition. Benjamin's "self-assertion" is not a psychoanalytic concept, and she does not fully explain what she means by it. Because her theory has its source in early, pre-linguistic development, her "self-assertion" must mean something more than "what we say about ourselves." Her proposal that a tension exists between self-assertion and mutual recognition suggests that the self has a motivation that is distinct from the capacity to be related to others. This is a crucial issue, particularly since Benjamin criticizes both Hegel and Freud for highlighting the wish for omnipotence at the expense of the desire to be connected to others.

According to Benjamin (ibid., p. 32), Hegel stresses that mutuality inevitably breaks down in the process of seeking recognition.[27] The reason for this, Benjamin maintains, lies in Hegel's insistence that the self begins in a state of omnipotence—a point that, Benjamin avers (ibid., p. 33), Freud also adopts. In Benjamin's reading, Hegel sees the self as resisting recognition: not wanting to recognize the other, it assents to recognition almost as a last resort.

Benjamin's perspective on Hegel may be translated as meaning that being-for-itself is overvalued because being-for-another is undervalued. There is a valid question to be raised about the implications of Hegel's beginning his discussion of self-consciousness with "Desire," a consciousness that is characterized by the aggressive stance it takes toward its objects. But is it fair to imply that Hegel intends for us to think that being-for-itself has primacy over being-for-another? My reading of Hegel over the last three chapters provides grounds for resisting such a conclusion.

Recall that, at the stage of Self-Consciousness, consciousness's self-understanding is undeveloped and proves to be flawed. Consciousness's experience will lead to the self-understanding of Geist, where Hegel tells us there is an identity between I and We. According to

Hegel, then, it can be argued that being-for-another is as essential for the human agent as being-for-itself. Like Kojève, Benjamin seems to base her interpretation rather heavily on the Master/Slave section. She ignores the numerous moments in which Hegel reveals that disregarding being-for-another dooms consciousness to dissatisfaction. Finally, although Hegel would concede that mutual recognition has eluded the modern world, there can be no doubt that he has a strong commitment to the possibility of realizing it.

Benjamin tends to view Hegel through the lens of her critique of the so-called classical model in psychoanalysis. *The Bonds of Love* was written just as the so-called relational position, which protested against the failure of the classical model to address intersubjectivity, was being articulated.[28] In that book, Benjamin constructs Hegel as a thinker who is captivated by omnipotence and fails to sustain and realize the importance of intersubjectivity. Although it makes sense to imagine that omnipotence is fueled by the failure of recognition, Hegel's notion of being-for-itself should not be reduced to omnipotence. As I argued in chapter 6, being-for-itself has the connotation of healthy narcissism and is linked to individuation.

In Benjamin's second book, *Like Subjects, Love Objects*, she addresses Hegel's juxtaposition of the self's wish for independence with the self's need for recognition (1995, p. 36). She goes on to associate the wish for independence with narcissism and also with omnipotence.[29] As a concept, narcissism is notoriously hard to pin down. Although it is fair to say that it overlaps with omnipotence, this is not so informative. Moreover, Benjamin's hypothesis that unmet narcissistic needs produce omnipotence seems uncontroversial. It is important, however, to distinguish between the healthy and the unhealthy aspects of both narcissism and omnipotence.[30] Benjamin misses some of Hegel's complexity because she overlooks the healthy aspect of being-for-itself and his affirmation of a reciprocal influence between being-for-itself and being-for-another.

Benjamin's position shifts in a subtle but important way in the course of *Like Subjects, Love Objects*.[31] Although her presentation of Hegel's view remains largely the same, her perspective on recognition changes to acknowledge the inevitability of breakdowns in relationships. Citing infant research, Benjamin concedes that no

relationship enjoys continuous harmony, and, thus, that relationships are better understood in terms of continuous disruption and
repair (1995, p. 47).[32] She concludes that intersubjectivity ought to
be conceived of in a richer and more varied way. She also recommends that the relational model of psychoanalysis ought to reorient
itself accordingly. In particular, she suggests that intrapsychic phenomena such as creativity and aggression should not be minimized.
A change can be detected from the vague notion in *The Bonds of Love*
of how "self-assertion" is in tension with recognition to the acknowledgement in *Like Subjects, Love Objects* of aggression as a necessary
feature of life (which is closer to the psychoanalytic model of conflict). This is also apparent in Benjamin's most recent book, *The
Shadow of the Other*, which reaffirms the point about inevitable breakdowns in all relationships and unambiguously states that omnipotence "is and always has been a central problem for the self" (1998,
p. 85).

Benjamin's work has evolved to dovetail with Hegel's view as I have
presented it. She makes space for a concept similar to Hegel's notion
of being-for-itself. Her solution is probably less optimistic than
Hegel's in urging us to accept the abiding tension between being-for-
itself and being-for-another, but it is in the same spirit of accommo-
dating these different aspects of human agency.

9.3 Reading Hegel Psychoanalytically

Hegel's concept of recognition undergoes a transformation in the
work of Honneth and Benjamin. In refining and developing the
Hegelian insight that the recognition of others spurs self-recognition,
they lend support to Stanley Cavell's declaration that psychoanalysis
renders German Idealism concrete and empirical (1987, p. 391). The
alternative to the Cartesian myth emerges clearly here: the subject
knows itself in a deeper way through interaction with others than
through introspection. In this last section of this chapter, I want to
continue to reflect on the ramifications of Honneth and Benjamin's
conception of recognition, and I will offer my own perspective on
recognition and its relation to Hegelian agency.

Honneth and Benjamin illustrate that recognition pertains to a variety of relationships, and both theorists contribute to what Hegel means by "being-for-another." Honneth and Benjamin demarcate relationships that have an affective valence and are based on attachment—e.g., relationships between husbands and wives, relationships between parents and children, relationships between friends. Honneth assimilates relationships of attachment under "love." Benjamin notes the inevitable difference in equality in the relationship between parents and children. It is appropriate in this connection to raise questions about how the body contributes to recognition, and also to ponder whether sexual relationships ought to be distinguished from other kinds of relationships.

Honneth's suggestion that there is a difference between relationships circumscribed by "love" and those circumscribed by "rights" forces us to realize that recognition is possible on a level that is distinct from intimate relationships, and that therefore the latter are not necessarily a model of the former. Our expectation in the case of rights is that that kind of recognition is less integral to one's sense of self. Consider the Israelis and the Palestinians, or the Protestants and the Catholics in Northern Ireland: it might be sufficient to hope that they recognize each other in the sense of adhering to the choice to refrain from killing one another, as opposed to aspiring to a higher standard of caring for one another. It is tempting, perhaps, to construe the contrast between love and rights in terms of a relation based on closeness and similarity vs. one based on distance and difference. Even relationships based on love, though, involve acceptance of distance and difference.

The addition of a third kind of relation, solidarity, constitutes a turn to the realm of a normative ideal. Honneth imagines that the relation between self and other is bounded by dignity. It can be said that here the self sees the other as being enough like the self to be accorded a status that the self cares to have; at the same time, the perception of difference is not understood as threatening. Solidarity brings together a measure of the affective bond found in love with the formal aspect of legal recognition. Taylor has argued that this should be especially applicable where differences are strong; in fact, he claims that it is not enough to accord respect to others, and that we must strive to be open to acknowledging their worth.[33]

There is something appealingly Hegelian about trying to preserve the sense of connection that Hegel discerned and valued about community without minimizing the inviolacy of individual rights. Two problems must be addressed here, however. First, it is easier to imagine such a notion of a community being attained in a homogeneous society than in a present-day multicultural society. Second, it would be necessary to grapple with the economic and psychological forces that effectively interfere with the possibility of such community. In regard to the second point, it is worth acknowledging that what Nancy Fraser calls "redistribution" (i.e., the redressing of economic injustice) might not overlap entirely with recognition.[34]

Recognition is not a monolithic category; it encompasses a range of human relationships. Contrary to Williams's supposition, I would conclude that not all relationships ought to be modeled on love. Indeed, though it might be the case that love relationships depend on recognition, it is simply not true that recognition in relationships must rely on love. Restricting recognition in this way, presupposing an agapaic vision as Williams does, renders the concept less interesting. As Benjamin shows, recognition is best conceived as partly in tension with individual agency. Yet Honneth nor Benjamin explores recognition without pondering the other side of this tension.

Hegelian agency has the merit of rooting itself both in being-for-itself and in being-for-another. Both Honneth and Benjamin dwell on how dissatisfaction distorts and harms the self. This, however, evades the question of how to understand being-for-itself apart from when it is impinged on. To what extent can one argue that being-for-itself overlaps with Nietzschean ideas about the will to power? Can one formulate an idea of being-for-itself that expresses a benign wish for mastery? One might also wonder whether it is being-for-itself that is responsible for struggle in the process of socialization. These questions point us in a Nietzschean direction and will soon be addressed.

Being-for-itself and being-for-another are equally fundamental for Hegelian agency. It takes no sides between the two; in fact, Hegelian agency urges us to appreciate how they are able to mediate one another. Surely, absolute knowledge connotes the possibility of perfect integration.[35] Yet Hegel is quite attuned to how difficult it is to attain such integration. As Bernstein has emphasized (1992, p. 299), Hegel's philosophy is as much about "rupture" as it is about "reconciliation." Hegel's hope that recognition might solve the problems of modernity places a huge burden on the concept. There are good reasons to strike a more modest stance. In particular, being-for-itself does not necessarily affirm recognition. Recognition is not a perpetual state for human agents; it is achieved and lost through the ongoing struggle and negotiation that defines relationships. The power of Hegelian agency rises insofar as the scope of recognition is narrowed. In the end, recognition is desirable, but it is hard to imagine that it can resolve the problems of culture as Hegel wished. To value recognition properly, we must neither overestimate nor underestimate its meaning for human agency. Recognition is a treasured human capacity, but it must be conceived for what it is: fragile and never subject to closure.

10
Nietzsche's Ambivalence toward Agency

I have to live rather than continue to know.

—Georges Bataille, *On Nietzsche*

There is a danger of philosophical conceit in ascribing a theory of agency to Nietzsche. No single work addresses itself to the issue of agency, and it is notoriously easy to find passages in Nietzsche's corpus that lend support to contradictory views. One can readily identify with Kurt Tucholsky's exasperated wit: "Tell me what you need and I will supply you with a Nietzsche citation . . . for Germany and against Germany; for peace and against peace; for literature and against literature—whatever you want." ("Fräulein Nietzsche," in Tucholsky 1960; also quoted on p. 274 of Aschheim 1992). The topic of agency is no exception: there is evidence both for and against a cogent Nietzschean theory of agency.

On the basis of my discussion of self-fathoming, it is plausible to attribute to Nietzsche at least a serious interest in agency. Nietzsche is clearly attracted to a dynamic sense of agency grounded in the pursuit of health and well-being. He sees this as the antidote to the threat of nihilism in modernity. Nevertheless, at the beginning of part II, in trying to pinpoint Nietzsche's engagement with self-exploration, self-objectivation, and self-control, I aimed to mark off an area of investigation without attempting to go further.

It is evident that Nietzsche appreciates self-exploration and is skeptical toward self-objectivation. His stance on self-control is less clear.

Sometimes he valorizes the capacity for self-control; other times he is enthusiastic about the value of relinquishing control. He articulates his perspective with phrases like "becoming who one is" and "self-overcoming" that are as vague as they are evocative. We will have to try to understand their meaning better, keeping in mind the running comparison between Nietzsche and Hegel.

Hegel's theory of agency has two components, being-for-itself and being-for-another, which can be harmonized to yield an integrated and unified sense of agency. Nietzsche's theory of agency has multiple and disparate components. Like Hegel, he regards conflict as a persistent feature of agency; however, he denies the possibility of any conventional notion of unified agency. Still, Nietzsche defends what legitimately can be termed a sense of integrated agency, wherein the self can achieve coherence and determination, although not transparency. In defending integrated agency, Nietzsche most obviously differs from Hegel in not presuming that integration produces social reconciliation. He also departs from Hegel's commitment to founding agency on self-knowledge—especially with its connotations of enclosure and absoluteness.

Recall Nietzsche's commitment to the project of self-fathoming, which includes understanding oneself in relation to one's own culture. The need for self-fathoming is acute. Modern European culture has produced a crisis of disharmony between the inner and the outer sense of self. The threat of nihilism requires a new model of agency, and this generates a project that, for Nietzsche, is strongly elitist. Nietzsche is uncomfortable with the idea of a universal model of agency; at most, he believes that what he has to say is relevant only for the few.[1]

10.1 Multiplicity and Agency

Nietzsche's description of human agency emphasizes that it is composed of multiple parts. Like Hegel, Nietzsche does not use 'agency' in the sense in which it is outlined in this book,[2] although there are reasons to think that he, like Hegel, might be sympathetic to it. Multiplicity is invoked as a way to capture what it is like to have a "soul," and Nietzsche understands being a "subject" as constituted through the attempt to pull together and organize the disparate experience of the soul. Two points are intended: that being a subject depends on eclipsing the nature of a soul (i.e., fabricating something as a replacement) and that the alternative conception we ought to entertain has to do with multiplicity. Nietzsche derides what he sees as a fantasy of "the subject," which simply assumes concordance and obscures that it must be created. In *The Will to Power* (#481, entry dated 1883–1888) he writes:

> The "subject" is not something given, it is something added and invented and projected behind what there is. Finally, is it necessary to posit an interpreter behind the interpretation? Even this is invention, hypothesis.

Though this passage underscores the first point, it does not explicitly make the second point.

The second point is clearly introduced in the following passage (WP #490, entry dated 1885):

> The assumption of one single subject is perhaps unnecessary; perhaps it is just as permissible to assume a multiplicity of subjects, whose interaction and struggle is the basis of our thought and our consciousness in general? A kind of aristocracy of 'cells' in which dominion resides? To be sure, an aristocracy of equals, used to ruling jointly and understanding how to command? *My hypotheses:* The subject as multiplicity.

Here Nietzsche raises questions and asks us to consider them, but he promises no more than a new and illuminating perspective that might dispense with the assumption of the "single subject" in favor of a notion of agency that acknowledges conflicting elements.[3] He seems to take it for granted that there can be a consensus among these elements, although how this is achieved is left unspecified. The metaphor of social class is used to explicate how certain elements prevail over others. This metaphor seems designed to accentuate that the mind is not exempt from the socio-cultural realm.

Nietzsche also describes the multiplicity of the soul in *Beyond Good and Evil*. In the context of reflecting on "soul atomism" (a view he links to Christianity), Nietzsche again urges us to entertain new, alternative hypotheses: ". . . such conceptions as 'mortal soul', and 'soul as subjective multiplicity', and 'soul as social structure of the drives and affects', want henceforth to have citizens' rights [Bürgerrecht] in science" (BGE #12). The idea of the soul as multiplicity is proposed as one hypothesis among others, yet for Nietzsche the main contrast is between the soul as a single unit and the soul as many.[4] Notice also the repetition of the category of the social: Nietzsche refers to the soul as "social structure of the drives and affects" and then presses the analogy with the idea of "citizens' rights."

It is worth pausing here to consider whether there is a link among the hypotheses of the soul as mortal, as multiplicity, and as structured socially by drives and affects. All convey Nietzsche's commitment to the affirmation of life. The mortality of the soul appeals to Nietzsche as an affirmation of life; it serves as a contrast to the immortality of the soul, which requires us to devalue life by postulating a world beyond this world. The hypotheses of the soul as multiplicity and as structured socially by drives and affects both affirm life and are interconnected in a way that at first glance may not be obvious. It is possible to explicate multiplicity by the distinction between consciousness and the unconscious.

Nietzsche sees consciousness as a developmental modification that arises out of exigency, and as our "weakest and most fallible organ" (GM II #16). He anticipates Freud's notion that consciousness is like the tip of an iceberg. Moreover, like Freud, Nietzsche points out that the unconscious, the repository of the id and the instincts, has been ignored as a factor in mental life. "For the longest time," he proclaims, "conscious thought was considered thought itself. Only now does truth dawn on us that by far the greatest part of our spirit's activity remains unconscious and unfelt." (GS #333) Although it would be a mistake to reduce the meaning of multiplicity to consciousness and the unconscious, this division is an important one because it places a limiting condition on our self-understanding. According to Nietzsche, self-transparency is an illusory goal that we ought to forsake.

Multiplicity has many components, not just two. In his discussion of multiplicity, Graham Parkes (1994, p. 253) points out that Nietzsche was influenced by early Greek ideas about the soul, which do not presume unity. Parkes (p. 70) also notes the relevance to Nietzsche of Dionysus, the god who presides over dismemberment into multiplicity and then reconstitution into an original unity. Parkes's work is also helpful in articulating the broader implications of Nietzsche's interest in multiplicity: how it alters religious and philosophical approaches to the soul.[5] Still, it is not obvious how we ought to think about agency in light of Dionysian experience. Multiplicity raises deep questions about what it could mean to be an agent, yet we need not to assume that it simply represents a threat to agency. Nietzsche construes multiplicity as presenting a challenge for us to have a higher standard of truthfulness about ourselves.

Let us consider some passages in which Nietzsche moves beyond his critique of religion and philosophy in its presentation of multiplicity. In "Losing Oneself" (HAH II 2 #306) he highlights the desirability of multiple identity:

Once one has found oneself one must understand how from time to time to *lose* oneself—and then how to find oneself again: supposing, that is, that one is a thinker. For the thinker it is disadvantageous to be tied to one person all the time.

Nietzsche sees this kind of identity as a challenge, not just an automatic fact attributable to the unconscious. His proposal here about the advantage of having a number of relations to the self is consistent with his perspectivism. There is clearly a reluctance to endorse self-knowledge as an ideal of tranquil self-possession; genuine self-knowledge requires that one be brave enough to experiment with oneself, including experimentation with self-abandonment, as is consistent with Dionysian experience. This passage also reminds us of Nietzsche's attraction to dissimilation, expressed in his claim that "every profound spirit needs a mask" (BGE #40). Finally, the passage conveys Nietzsche's mixed assessment of how the self is constituted as much by forgetting as by remembering.

The dialectic of forgetting and remembering is crucial for Nietzsche. In a famous aphorism (BGE #68), he declares: "'I have done that,' says my memory. 'I cannot have done that,' says my pride, and remains inexorable. Eventually—memory yields." Though this passage pits two components of agency against each other and makes the possibility of a unified sense of agency seem dubious, caution forbids us to assume that Nietzsche regards conflict as impossible to mediate. The aphorism "We Incomprehensible Ones" (GS #371) is helpful in clarifying this:

. . . we shed our old bark, we shed our skins every spring, we keep becoming younger, fuller of future, taller, stronger, we push our roots ever more powerfully into the depths—into evil—while at the same time we embrace the heavens ever more lovingly, more broadly, imbibing their light ever more thirstily with all our twigs and leaves. Like trees we grow—this is hard to understand, as is all of life— not in one place only but everywhere, not in one direction but equally upward and outward and inward and downward; our energy is at work simultaneously in the trunk, branches, and roots; we are no longer free to do only one particular thing, to *be* only one particular thing.

Here multiplicity is characterized affirmatively; it is even celebrated for its connection to growth and development. Multiplicity is also linked with self-acceptance (that is, with what Nietzsche in other contexts calls amor fati—the love of one's life for what it is, without regrets). Multiplicity entails a rejection of a static sense of identity. The possibility of attaining integration extends from the ongoing process of becoming.

Nietzsche's defense of multiplicity might seem to imply that he abandons the conceptual apparatus that often accompanies the description of the soul. Yet this is not actually the case. He does not reject the idea of the "ego," but he regards it as one component among others.

In *Thus Spoke Zarathustra* Nietzsche defends the value of the ego: "Indeed, this ego and the ego's contradiction and confusion still speak more honestly of its being—this creating, willing, valuing ego, which is the measure and value of things." (Z I, "On the After-worldly"). However, in *Twilight of the Idols* ("The Four Great Errors," #3) he presents the ego as a fiction, just as the subject was. And elsewhere in Z I ("On the Despisers of the Body") he uses 'self' to mean a more encompassing sense of identity; in particular, he stresses that the self must be tied to the body.[6] At no point does he use 'self' in a disavowal of multiplicity. There is fluctuation, though, in Nietzsche's use of the 'self' and related words, and it is simply impossible to draw sharp distinctions about the soul, the subject, and the self—not to mention agency. It is clear that Nietzsche wants to claim that all these terms denote entities that have multiple parts. But under what conditions and toward what end can integration of multiplicity occur? When we address these questions, we will see that the concept of agency serves a useful and distinctive purpose.

10.2 Integrated Agency

Whether one believes that Nietzsche defends integrated agency depends greatly on what one means by integration. As I shall argue, integrated agency, according to Nietzsche, presents a challenge: it can be achieved, but it is not always desirable, and it has limitations related to the self's incapacity to overcome internal conflict. At the minimum, Nietzsche believes that the self can establish a relation to itself whereby it distinguishes between what is desirable for it and what is alien for it. Nietzsche focuses on the capacity for judgment, although he does not want to deny or exclude false judgment. In BGE #4 he explains: "The question is to what extent it [judgment] is life-promoting, life-preserving, species-preserving, perhaps even species-cultivating." Being an integrated agent means that one is able to sort out what is life and species-promoting and what is not. But this claim takes us only so far.

In GS #15 Nietzsche maintains that self-knowledge eludes those who can only look at themselves from a distance. He goes on to affirm the value of self-evaluation: "But we, we others who thirst after reason [Vernunft-Durstigen], are determined to scrutinize our experiences as severely as a scientific experiment [wollen unseren Erlebnissen so streng in's Auge sehen, wie einem wissenschaftlichen Versuche]— hour after hour, day after day. We ourselves wish to be our experiments and guinea pigs [Experimente und Versuchs-Thiere]." (GS #319) The latter passage is proof of how one-sided it is to identify Nietzsche with self-invention without acknowledging his discussions of self-observation and self-reflection.

Of course, Nietzsche does express reservations about self-observation and self-reflection. As we saw in section 10.1, Nietzsche affirms the value of losing and forgetting oneself, and he clearly does not want to locate the self in the ego—especially if it is conceived as having a central, executive function. Indeed, though Nietzsche endorses the integration of the self, he is even more concerned with how the self can fulfill itself through action. This tilt toward action supports the use of 'agency' in connection with integration.

"How To Become What One Is," which Nietzsche adopted from Pindar and used as the subtitle of *Ecce Homo*, serves as a grounding point for his idea of integrated agency.[7] In EH, "Why I Am So Clever," #9, Nietzsche writes: "To become what one is, one must not have the faintest notion *what* one is." [Dass man wird, was man ist, setzt voraus, dass man nicht im Entferntesten ahnt, was man ist.] When he refers to not having the faintest notion of what one is, Nietzsche reminds us of the importance of mistakes, wrong turns, and false judgments. Knowing oneself is predicated on ridding oneself of expectations, especially the fantasy of reaching a fixed and final state of rest.[8]

In one illuminating passage (HAH II 2 #266), Nietzsche highlights self-mastery as the key for integrated agency. He begins by musing that what is most important for a youth to learn and know is himself. He contrasts the impatience of youth, in which we strive to be "master of our own workshop," with the higher status of becoming "master of our own art of living." This contrast helps us to understand Nietzsche's approach to integrated agency. Indeed, the ideal of such self-mastery opposes the interpretation of multiple agency as perpetual, unresolved conflict and absence of organized inner structure. Elsewhere, Nietzsche highlights the creative aspect of self-mastery. In GS #290 he formulates the challenge of bestowing "style to character." Style is not merely a matter of aesthetic novelty; it requires that we learn to craft ourselves according to values consistent with what is life-affirming. Although Nietzsche wants to grant us the liberty of self-invention, this must be reconciled with his appreciation for self-evaluation. There are moments when Nietzsche seems to provide license for a radical mode of self-invention, lawless and unbound by truthfulness. Yet Nietzsche has a serious commitment to gaining access to parts of the self that are blocked or difficult to grasp. There is ample attention to and respect for the value of fathoming oneself through active experience. Being an integrated agent is clearly preferable to being an unintegrated agent.

10.3 Four Factors of Integrated Agency

Let me now describe the components that determine integrated agency for Nietzsche. In moving in this direction, I am aware of gravitating to a controversial interpretation of Nietzsche. For some philosophers who see Nietzsche exclusively in terms of heralding postmodernism, it might seem that integration can be invoked only at the price of minimizing Nietzsche's anticipation of decentered agency. For reasons that will emerge in chapter 13 and in the epilogue, I do not agree that integration and decentering are necessarily opposed.

In this section I will restrict myself to delineating the four factors of integrated agency: acceptance of self-interest as the source of our motivation, acknowledgement of the demands of the body (specifically, the importance of satisfying one's instincts—which does not necessarily mean acting freely upon them), having access to and making use of one's affects (expressing them and maintaining them under control), and understanding oneself in relation to the past (which refers to cultural context as much as to one's own past). Integration means something more than having a coherent identity and something less than is implied by having a unified identity.[9]

The first factor can be discerned in Nietzsche's belief that morality falsifies nature, coercing us to be altruistic and blinding us to the egoistic motivation for our actions. In *On The Genealogy of Morals*, master morality is presented as unabashedly selfish and is contrasted with the hypocrisy of slave morality, which is swayed by the pretense to altruism and which thereby displaces egoism—or at least tries to do so. The point of Nietzsche's parable about birds of prey (master morality) and lambs (slave morality) is that the birds of prey do what comes naturally and enjoy the lambs as tasty; they are perfectly content to pursue their self-interest. The lambs, no less self-interested, form a philosophy that self-servingly condemns the birds of prey (GM I #13). Egoism has a way of reasserting itself in the face of its denial. "Even in your folly and contempt," Zarathustra observes in Z I #4, "you despisers of the body, you serve your self."

Though it is possible to read Nietzsche as claiming that all altruism is hypocritical or impossible, it is not clear that he intends to make a declaration against altruism per se.[10] A cautious reading of Nietzsche's perspective would be that we ought to be suspicious of any standpoint that needs to deny egoism. It would be perspicuous, then, to argue that Nietzsche's critique of morality challenges the very opposition between altruism and egoism. In particular, he wants to dispute the easy categorization of altruism as inherently good and egotism as inherently evil.

Nietzsche construes the principle of self-interest in psychological terms: as a function of our fundamental narcissism. This is confirmed in Zarathustra's assertion that "for the first time . . . *selfishness* [Selbstsucht] [is] blessed, the wholesome, healthy selfishness that wells from a powerful soul . . . around which everything becomes a mirror" (Z III, "On the Three Evils"). *Selbstsucht* is a concept that expresses the primacy of our self-concern—our absorption in "ego ipissimus," as Nietzsche says in the preface to HAH II. It remains uncertain to what extent this is intended to mean that we are selfish, that is, concerned about ourselves to the point of not being genuinely concerned for others. 'Selbstsucht' is introduced in the context of celebrating the lust to rule [Herrensucht]. Nietzsche demands that we take account of narcissism, not that we endorse it. Yet clearly he is attracted to the healthy aspect of narcissism (the investment in self-gratification), and he does not have much to say about the unhealthy aspect (that others are reduced to mirrored reflections of the self).[11]

The second factor concerning integrated agency pertains to the body and our relation to our own instincts. For Nietzsche, humans are animals who are endowed with powerful instincts and thus are bound to suffer if the gratification of those instincts is denied. Nietzsche celebrates release through the body as life-affirming. In general, he sees instinctual expression as healthy and its repression (as encouraged by Christianity) as sick. Yet Nietzsche does not espouse instinctual expression in a blanket sense. He recognizes the value of spiritualizing the senses (that is, directing their energy into other activities—sublimation).[12] Furthermore, he does not hesitate to be critical of an undifferentiated kind of instinctual gratification: "All unspirituality, all vulgar commonness, depend on the inability to resist a stimulus: one *must* react, one follows every impulse." (TI, "What the Germans Lack," #6) This view is anticipated in a passage in GS #76 that deserves special recognition: "The greatest danger that always hovered over humanity and still hovers over it is the eruption of madness—which means the eruption of arbitrariness in feeling, seeing, and hearing, the enjoyment of the mind's lack of discipline, the joy in human unreason."

According to Nietzsche, acknowledging the body does not mean using it exclusively as a vehicle of pleasure; it means that (in contrast with religion and philosophy, which commonly grant priority to the soul) we discipline the body, learn from it, and refuse to diminish what it has to offer. In Z I #3, Nietzsche declares that earthly meaning must be created through our bodies:

Listen rather, my brothers, to the voice of the healthy body: that is a more honest and purer voice. More honestly and purely speaks the healthy body that is perfect and perpendicular: it speaks of the meaning of the Earth.

Though it is possible to deny the importance of the body, it is absurd to think that we could rid ourselves of our instincts. Instincts thus lie at the basis of integrated agency: a necessary, but insufficient condition of such agency. Without an instinctual basis, agency lacks a coherent direction.

Affects constitute the third factor which defines integrated agency. They are closely related to the body, although Nietzsche does not specify this interconnection. Nietzsche's comments about affects are dispersed throughout his work; just as with instincts, he believes that repression has bad health effects and that harnessing affects in an appropriate way has good health effects. In WP #933 Nietzsche declares:

In summa: domination of the passions, not their weakening or extirpation!—The greater the dominating power of a will, the more freedom may the passions be allowed. The "great man" is great owing to the free play and scope of his desires and to the yet greater power that knows how to press these magnificent monsters into service.

Nietzsche contrasts the "good man" (who lives moderately and combines "the harmless" and "the useful") with the "great man" (who has access to his affects, is adept at their expression, and refuses to stifle them). Yet, in referring to affects as "magnificent monsters," Nietzsche acknowledges that affects are powerful and potentially dangerous.

WP #778 contains an astonishing description of affects. Here Nietzsche observes that a weak individual, feeling unable to restrain the senses, the desires, and the passions, will fear them. He proceeds to suggest that the excess associated with passions is not a threat to the strong. He hypothesizes that passions have acquired a bad name precisely because they overwhelm those who are weak. Here Nietzsche again acknowledges that passions can be akin to sickness, but he tells us that they should not be avoided. As he describes it, they provide a shock that is ultimately beneficial. He then sketches a threefold distinction having to do with affects and agency:

1. the dominating passion, which even brings with it the supremest form of health; here the co-ordination of the inner systems and their operation in the service of one end is best achieved—but this is almost the definition of health.

2. the antagonism of the passions; two, three, a multiplicity of "souls in one breast": very unhealthy, inner ruin, disintegration, betraying, and increasing and inner conflict and anarchism— unless one passion at last becomes master. Return to health—

3. juxtaposition without antagonism or collaboration: often periodic, and then, as soon as an order has been established, also healthy. The most interesting men, the chameleons, belong here; they are not in contradiction with themselves, they are happy and secure, but they do not develop—their differing states lie juxtaposed, even if they are separated sevenfold. They change, they do not become.

In the first of these points, Nietzsche enthusiastically highlights the connection between being guided by a strong affect and a sense of agency in which the inner systems are coordinated. He leaves no doubt that he regards such integration as supremely healthy, and in the second point he suggests that an absence of integration can be unhealthy. Indeed, it becomes apparent that Nietzsche shows concern about the potential for multiplicity to pull us in different directions and to interfere with integration. Yet he also indicates in the third point that it is not necessarily the case that multiplicity bodes ill for agency: those who are unruffled by diverse affects do not suffer. This does not preclude that such people can change, although apparently the way they change can be differentiated from development.

Nietzsche's thinking is convoluted here. There is no question that he regards strong affects as influencing the sense of agency and as contributing to health, yet he stresses the importance of keeping affects under control as opposed to allowing strong affects to dominate (WP #928). He recommends that we place our affects under "a protracted tyranny" so they will "they love us as good servants and go voluntarily wherever our best interests lie" (WP #384). The severity of such self-tyranny is consistent with Nietzsche's defense of discipline and with his understanding of moderation as analogous to the pleasure of riding "a fiery steed" (WP #884).[13] In his approach to affects, Nietzsche wants to make room both for their expression and for their regulation.

The fourth factor which defines integrated agency concerns one's relation to the past. Nietzsche's abiding interest in the past is often overlooked. This may be due to the prominence in Nietzsche's thinking of the Dionysian impulse, which beckons us to revel in forgetfulness. In UDHL #1 and in GM II #1, Nietzsche unambiguously suggests that forgetting is salutary. Yet his glorification of forgetting must be read against what he has to say in other contexts. For example, in HAH II 1 #223 he proclaims: "Direct self-observation is not nearly sufficient for us to know ourselves: we require history, for the past continues to flow within us in a hundred waves; we ourselves are, indeed, nothing but that which at every moment we experience of this continuing flow." Indeed, this passage from Nietzsche's middle period concludes on a Hegelian-sounding note: ". . . self-knowledge will become universal knowledge with regard to all that is past: just as, merely to allude to another chain of reflections, self-determination and self-education could, in the freest and most far-sighted spirits, one day become universal determination with regard to all future humanity."

It would be misleading to base an interpretation of Nietzsche entirely on his so-called positivist stage. In UM #1, Nietzsche's focus is on how too much concern with history is "harmful and ultimately fatal to the living thing, whether this living thing be a man or a people or a culture." Nietzsche continues, however, by offering a qualification:

To determine this degree, and therewith the boundary at which the past has to be forgotten if it is not to become the gravedigger of the present, one would have to know exactly how great the *plastic power* [die plastische Kraft] of a man, a people, a culture is: I mean by plastic power the capacity to develop out of oneself in one's own way, to transform and incorporate [umzubilden und einzuverleiben] into oneself what is past and foreign, to heal wounds, to replace what has been lost, to recreate broken moulds. . . . And this is a universal law: a living thing can be healthy, strong and fruitful only when bounded by a horizon; if it is incapable of drawing a horizon around itself, and at the same time too self-centred to enclose its own view within that of another, it will pine away slowly or hasten to its timely end. Cheerfulness, the good conscience, the joyful deed, confidence in the future—all of them depend, in the case of the individual as of a nation, on the existence of a line dividing the bright and discernible from the illuminable and dark; on one's being just as able to forget at the right time as to remember at the right time; on the possession of a powerful instinct for sensing when it is necessary to feel historically and when unhistorically.

This brilliant passage establishes that, while Nietzsche is wary of enshrining the past, he does not advocate a sweeping rejection of it. The notion of "plastic power" reminds us of Nietzsche's commitment to a dynamic view of agency. When he invokes "transformation" and "incorporation," he is describing the task of working through the past. The key point here, as I see it, has to do with the notion of boundaries. Nietzsche sees the creation of boundaries as enabling the individual to differentiate between inside and outside, and between self and other. He encourages us to erect boundaries that are neither too permeable nor too rigid.

The task of creating boundaries sustains a dialectical approach to forgetting and remembering. Nietzsche does not simply assert the desirability of forgetting over remembering; rather, he contrasts the kind of remembering that makes use of the past with the kind that is imprisoned by the past, in addition to contrasting the kind of forgetting that moves beyond the past with the kind that escapes or denies it. Despite the change in Nietzsche's position that occurs in *Human, All Too Human*, he still preserves a measure of ambivalence—ambivalence in the sense of maintaining two sides, rather than in the sense of being unable to decide. On the one hand, he claims that the past has an ongoing and surreptitious effect. The most persuasive statement of this occurs in a passage I cited in chapter 2: "The best in us has perhaps been inherited from the sensibilities of earlier ages to which we hardly any longer have access by direct paths; the sun has already set, but the sky of our life still glows with its light, even though we no longer see it." (HAH I #223) On the other hand, Nietzsche has not given up his skepticism about memory. In "Good Memory" (HAH II 1 #122) he declares: "Many a man fails to become a thinker only because his memory is too good."

Although Nietzsche values the past, he is skeptical about allowing the wish for knowledge to become too important. Parkes (1994, pp.

91–93) argues that Nietzsche encourages the use of fantasy, and that he regards the drive for knowledge as unhealthy unless it is regulated. This suggests that integrated agency is not understood as a matter of knowledge. Indeed, Nietzsche is content to see integration as a looser and more tentative construct. Although he is hard to pin down, it is clear that he does not turn to integration as a way to override multiplicity.[14]

The four factors—narcissism, the body, affects and the past—are the underpinnings of what Nietzsche means by integrated agency. It hardly needs to be said, however, that Nietzsche does not conceive of integrated agency as a mechanical checklist. It requires an audacious willingness to undergo struggle and discipline. One cannot assume that integration is a normative part of development. Only members of an elite—nobles, or free spirits—seek to undertake this challenge. It is important to reiterate that the capacity to integrate the multiple and diverse parts of the self does not imply that one can or should strive to do this in a complete sense. Paradoxically, Nietzsche's concept of agency insists that room be made for contingency and even for the abandonment of agency. Letting go, or self-abandonment, disrupts but does not necessarily negate agency.

10.4 Anti-Agency

No reading of Nietzsche can afford to neglect his comments that are skeptical about and even hostile to the possibility of human agency. In turning to address this side of Nietzsche, one cannot simply flip the page and begin anew. Indeed, it is crucial to come to terms with how the theme of Nietzsche's "anti-agency" alters and contradicts what he suggests about integrated agency. More specifically, I would like to investigate whether the apparent contradiction between integrated agency and anti-agency can be explained as a reflection of the nature of agency itself. In this section, I present evidence concerning Nietzsche's rejection of agency and then reflect on it in relation to what was said earlier in the chapter.

Nietzsche was infatuated with the philosophy of Dionysus. Dionysian experience does not heed the bounds of agency: it celebrates the joy of relinquishing self-control, and it revels in oblivion and merger. The gratification that Nietzsche detects in self-abandonment has no counterpart in Hegel's thinking. Although self-identity is lost and gained again and again in Hegel's narrative in PhS, agency is never voluntarily forsaken. For Nietzsche, though, we are drawn to alleviate the burdens of being an agent.[15] Nietzsche values freedom from agency, whereas for Hegel freedom must be attained through agency.

However, Nietzsche seems most attracted to disburdening that occurs in temporary, emancipatory moments. This is evident in a passage I mentioned in section 10.1: "Once one has found oneself one must understand how from time to time to *lose* oneself—and then how to find oneself again." (HAH II 2 #306) "Self-Control" (GS #305) does not feature the return to oneself, but it does acknowledge the transcient and heuristic value of self-abandonment: ". . . one must be able to lose oneself occasionally if one wants to learn something from things different from oneself." Though Nietzsche urges us to be less attached to our own agency, he does not mean that we ought to dispense with agency entirely. Rather, as in BGE #292, he argues that the philosopher often runs away from himself (out of fear) but is "too inquisitive not to 'come to' again—always back to himself."

From another perspective, Nietzsche's anti-agency can be located, not simply in his infatuation with Dionysian moments, but in the illusory quality of agency itself. At times, Nietzsche portrays agency as a fantasy and not as something real. Agency amounts to being a kind of wish that serves as a bulwark against fatalism. Nietzsche protests against both the theocentrism of religious belief and the anthropocentrism of Kant. In GM I #13, he exclaims: "There is no being behind doing . . . 'the doer' is merely a fiction added to the deed." Nietzsche is suspicious about any underlying assumptions concerning agency.

As I have already discussed, Nietzsche rejects the idea that the soul is determined by our conscious awareness. His commitment to the unconscious conditions the possibility of agency. As I understand Nietzsche, he does not want us to infer that agency is impossible, but he demands that we acknowledge its limitations. In this connection, it is also important to consider Nietzsche's belief that self-deception is inescapable. Like Hegel, he thinks that knowing falsely is a part of knowledge. Self-fathoming, by definition, entails self-thwarting. Nietzsche asks us to view agency as a construct, yet we cannot assume that he thinks that we can or should live without it. As we will see, the value of agency is found in the experience of satisfaction as well as in the exercise of power.

This brings us to a crucial consideration regarding anti-agency. Nietzsche's interest in agency originates from his sense that modern culture fails to provide satisfaction. Indeed, the point of defining integrated agency in terms of narcissism, the body, affects, and the past is that it promises a more genuine kind of satisfaction. A problem arises, however, in considering how Nietzsche's anti-agency leads him to scoff at the pursuit of happiness. Let us turn to some of Nietzsche's reservations about the pursuit of happiness and then return to address the relation between happiness and satisfaction.

In *Thus Spoke Zarathustra*, Nietzsche questions the ideal of being happy. For example, in "The Honey Sacrifice" Zarathustra says to one of his animals: "What matters happiness?. . . I have long ceased to be concerned with happiness; I am concerned with my work." Of course Zarathustra is not recommending the workaholic lifestyle. Nietzsche's concern is with the pursuit of worthy goals. This is apparent in "On the Spirit of Gravity" #2, where Zarathustra ridicules the "omnisatisfied" [Allgenügsamen] as tasting everything but having no taste.

Zarathustra's resistance to the pursuit of happiness can be readily discerned in the description of the "last men," who are concerned with small things. Regarding all humans as the same, they are concerned with living long rather than living well. Unable to despise themselves, they are preoccupied with comfort and ease. Perhaps most noteworthy, they claim to have invented happiness (Z 1 #5). As Nietzsche represents them, the last men are in search of a kind of happiness that is not worth having.

In BGE #200 Nietzsche describes the kind of happiness that emerges in late cultures as an attempt to eradicate all conflict. This is a happiness "of resting, of not being disturbed, of satiety, of finally attained unity." Saint Augustine is named as an example. An unlikely group of people are introduced as counterexamples: Alcibiades,

Caesar, Frederick II, and Leonardo da Vinci. Operating out of the same cultural conditions, the latter embrace conflict and attain self-control. Nietzsche stresses that they refuse complacency, but presumably this does not doom them to unhappiness.

A distinction can be upheld between a ready-made, easy-to-attain version of happiness (which Nietzsche disdains, but which he claims is what most people want) and the vital challenge of satisfaction (which he generally welcomes, but which he regards as rare). Nietzsche is not necessarily arguing that satisfaction must be arduous to achieve, since he wants to ground satisfaction in bodily experience. Along with the intensity of Dionysian pleasures, he celebrates cheerfulness—a simple and natural state of mind that he also associates with the Greeks. Above all, Nietzsche rejects the idea that knowledge provides a path to satisfied agency. As he expresses it in *Daybreak* #116, the idea that right knowledge leads to right action is the "most fateful of prejudices, that profoundest of error." As was discussed in chapter 1, Nietzsche parts company with Hegel on the ultimate value of knowledge. Not surprisingly, then, Nietzsche distances himself from making knowledge the basis of agency.

What can we conclude about Nietzsche's defense of integrated agency and anti-agency? They seem to be unreconcilable discourses, carrying equal authority. Nietzsche might well embrace the contradiction as in line with the spirit of his perspectivism without feeling the obligation to have more to say. Yet we should not assume that integrated agency and anti-agency cannot be reconciled or that they are incompatible. Nietzsche accepts the prospect of coherent agency, which is guided by an inner organization. He is open to the challenge of working toward a sense of integrated agency. As he sees it, though, integration is necessarily incomplete.

Of course, Nietzsche does not view integration as tantamount to unified agency. In one voice, he upholds the option of realizing a fulfilled, satisfied life. In another voice, he is scathing about making life into a project and urges us to pursue our lives more recklessly. Self-overcoming in Nietzsche connotes both becoming a better self and a willingness to be less attached to the self. It is impossible to come to terms with what Nietzsche means by self-overcoming without introducing the will to power, which he describes as "the unexhausted procreative will of life" [der unerschöpfte zeugende Lebens-Wille] (Z II, "On Self-Overcoming"). Indeed, the will to power has remained in the background in this chapter, and we will have to examine it further in order to determine in what sense Nietzsche believes in a satisfied life. Although it would be unrealistic to expect the will to power to resolve all the questions that have emerged here, it will allow us to bring Nietzsche's ambivalence about agency into greater focus.

11

The Will to Power and Agency in Nietzsche

I contradict as has never been contradicted before and am nevertheless the opposite of a No-saying spirit.
—Nietzsche, *Ecce Homo*

The will to power underlies and undergirds Nietzsche's understanding of what it means to be an agent. This is not to ignore that some regard the will to power as having a broader significance—as a principle that explains life itself, and/or as the key to Nietzsche's entire philosophy.[1] My perspective on the will to power will be restricted, and I shall not attempt to grapple with the sense in which the will to power is offered as a cosmological principle. I will follow out Nietzsche's suggestion that psychology offers the deepest interpretation of human beings and can be identified with "the doctrine of the development [Entwicklungslehre] of the will to power" (BGE #23).

Although Nietzsche refers to the will to power as a "doctrine," it is not clear how to interpret this. For example, in BGE #36 Nietzsche identifies the will to power as "my proposition" he goes on to equate it with a total explanation of "all organic functions" and as a way to "determine *all* efficient force univocally." But this aphorism begins with a conditional ("supposing [Setzt] that nothing is real except our drives (such as our desires and passions)"), and Nietzsche uses 'Setzt' two more times in the same aphorism. He also labels his perspective an experiment [Versuch]. Although there is no question that he believes he is offering a worthy hypothesis, he does not want to enshrine the will to power as a metaphysical truth.

In pursuing the idea of the will to power, I want to avoid either reifying it into being a static doctrine or reducing it to a flight of fantasy. Alexander Nehamas and Mark Warren have rightfully stressed the heuristic element in their interpretations of the will to power.[2] Maudemarie Clark (1989, p. 227) has emphasized that the will to power is a "construction of the world from the viewpoint of his [Nietzsche's] moral values." I would agree that Nietzsche offers the will to power as both a heuristic device and a self-conscious construction, and that he surely would be prepared to acknowledge that it reflects his own values. Yet my emphasis will be on the will to power as a psychological notion, signifying Nietzsche's intention to add a new discourse to the discourses of morality and philosophy.

Nietzsche is certainly not bashful about his own originality as a psychologist. Indeed, in EH, "Why I Am a Destiny," #6, he proclaims: "There was no psychology at all before me." In particular, when psychology was limited to the study of consciousness Nietzsche believes that it relied on a naive conception of the will. In contrast, Nietzsche opts for a psychology that ventures to explore the entirety of the human being. Yet, as I discussed in chapter 1, there is a certain ambiguity to how Nietzsche construes the relationship between psychology and philosophy. At times, Nietzsche sounds as if psychology might replace philosophy; other times, he seems to be imploring us to reimagine philosophy as inclusive of psychology. Nietzsche is not always clear about differentiating between psychology as it has been practiced and understood and the psychology he credits himself with inventing. This ambiguity emerges fully in Nietzsche's convoluted reflections on the will.

11.1 Will

To understand the will to power psychologically, we must begin with Nietzsche's concept of the will. As is often the case with Nietzsche, it is easier to see what he is opposed to than to see what he embraces. In numerous passages he thunders against traditional notions of the will, and he even argues that there really is no such thing as the will.[3] He especially objects to philosophers' and psychologists' propensity to appeal to the will as an absolute and irreducible entity that may be used to explain all human action. From *Daybreak* (#124) to *Twilight of the Idols* ("The Four Great Errors," #1–#5), he suggests that it is absurd to believe that the will is a cause for effects that happen in the world. Lurking behind the idea of a free will, as he sees it, is religious prejudice. Nietzsche reviles free will as "the foulest of theologians' artifices," suggesting that the idea was invented for the sake of punishment and guilt (TI, "The Four Great Errors," #7). One might be tempted to conclude from this that Nietzsche expects us to give up the concept of the will as unnecessary and counterproductive. However, by no means does Nietzsche abandon the will.

Indeed, Nietzsche makes frequent, affirmative comments about the will. In Z IV, "The Welcome," one of the kings declares: "Nothing more delightful grows on Earth, O Zarathustra, than a lofty, strong will: that is the earth's most beautiful plant."[4] Zarathustra himself lauds the will as liberatory.[5] In GS #347, Nietzsche, in his own voice, associates the will with "the affect of command," which he calls "the decisive sign of sovereignty and strength." Thus, the contrast between strong wills (which Nietzsche celebrates) and weak wills (which he reviles) amounts to a crucial distinction.[6] Yet Nietzsche is not specific about how to discriminate between strong and weak wills.

Nietzsche's account of the ingredients that form the will is helpful in this regard. In GS #127 he disavows the idea that "willing is something simple, a brute datum, underivable, and intelligible by itself." Nietzsche also criticizes philosophers en masse for positing "magically effective forces" in their use of the will (ibid.), and in BGE #19 he condemns their "inadequate caution." In WP #692, as in BGE #19, he singles out Schopenhauer for making us complacent about our knowledge about the will and for failing to carry out "an analysis of the will."

For Nietzsche, willing is "something complicated" and must be regarded as "a manifold thing" (BGE #19). In this crucial aphorism, Nietzsche undertakes a dissection of the will that is worth examining in detail. The notion of a will, he writes, is based on a plurality of sensations (elaborated by reference to two alternative reactions, "away from which" and "towards which"), on thinking ("in every act of the will there is a ruling thought" [einen commandirenden Gedanken]), and on affect ("the affect of command" [Affekt des Commandos].

This affect, rooted in inner certainty, aims at superiority over others, but it also aims at getting one to obey "within oneself." The aphorism culminates with the claim that "freedom of the will" is a product of the "complex state of delight" [Lust-Zustand] that comes from exercising the will in a way that reduplicates the hierarchy of social structure onto the body.

Nietzsche traces the constitution of the will from the rather primitive and passive experience of sensations, which directs us either to move toward or to move away. Nietzsche elaborates in another context (GS #127 that "the will to come into being an idea of pleasure [Lust] and displeasure [Unlust] is needed." In describing the genesis of the will in these terms, Nietzsche anticipates the psychoanalytic notion of "primary process."[7] Primary process is the mental functioning that is guided by the avoidance of displeasure (which in Freud's first formulation[8] has satisfaction as its aim) and ultimately by what Freud terms the "pleasure principle" [Lustprinzip].[9]

The second component of the will, thinking, reveals that Nietzsche does not see volition and cognition as separate and independent categories. He does not say much about thinking in BGE #19, but in BGE #3 and #36 he stresses that thinking is itself an instinctual activity. Rendering thinking as part of the will highlights Nietzsche's interest in challenging the customary disjunction between affects and cognition. Indeed, Nietzsche's choice to include thinking as part of the will seems to imply that the will to power utilizes, rather than dispenses with, knowledge. It also clarifies that Nietzsche does not intend to exclude rationality from his thinking about agency. As we will see, the thinking component of the will reinforces Nietzsche's perspective that "interpretation itself is a form of the will to power" (WP #556).[10] In describing the emergence of a "ruling thought" in the above passage, Nietzsche also takes the first step toward positing an active element to the will—in contrast to the reactive response of moving toward a sensation.

The third component of the will, the affect to command, picks up the motivation to have pleasure from the first component and the need to assert oneself from the second. Nietzsche presents the ingredients of the will in terms that correspond to a progressively greater sense of agency. He interprets freedom of the will as the name of the affect of "superiority," which attends the experience of commanding another to obey.[11] His reading of freedom of the will here is that it is an effect, manifested through the pleasure of discharging one's volition, rather than (as philosophers liked to claim) a cause. Here he does not discountenance freedom of the will, as he does later.[12]

As Nietzsche sees it, it is a mistake to inflate the will in order to exaggerate what we know. This does not mean, however, that the will lacks value or that it cannot be fruitfully cultivated. Nietzsche is wary of reifying the will to be "an unjustified generalization" (WP #692), and he urges us not to confuse flawed understandings of the will with the will to power. Interpretive caution is warranted here, however, as Nietzsche does not maintain a strict separation between the will and the will to power. Indeed, there is evidence that Nietzsche regards the will and the will to power as integrally connected. For instance, in BGE #36 he calls the will to power "*one* basic form of the will" and characterizes this as "*my* proposition." Once Nietzsche links his conception of the will to the affect of command, the concept of power is implicit.

11.2 Power

Numerous scholars have focused on power as the way to come to terms with Nietzsche's idea of the will to power. Nietzsche invokes the notion of power to account for the collision of any forces—which, of course, would include the collision of wills. A fundamental question that arises for all interpretations of power is: How should 'power' be construed? Does it mean something closer to mastery, or something closer to domination? A related question is this: Is power about the pleasure of exercising it, or is it about the desire to have more power? A third question is: To what extent Nietzsche is concerned with power over ourselves, and to what extent is he concerned with power over others?

According to the view that power means mastery, which Kaufmann championed and which Clark, Warren, and Ansell-Pearson endorse, power is a benign notion that principally denotes self-mastery. Power and agency coincide in this view, which can be contrasted with the idea that power accepts and even encourages domination (especially

over others). Kaufmann's project of disentangling Nietzsche's repu-
tation from the Nazis leads him to see power as self-empowerment:
". . . there can be no question but that Nietzsche agreed with that
ancient tradition which we can trace through continents and centuries to Laotze: that the man who conquers himself shows greater
power than he who conquers others" (Kaufmann 1968, p. 252). Clark
(1989, p. 211) offers a more sober reflection, suggesting that power
has "nothing essential to do with power over others, but is a sense of
one's effectiveness in the world." Both of these views make the
assumption, which is not obvious, that a disjunction exists between
power over oneself and power over others. Ansell-Pearson (1994, p.
46) turns to etymology to address the notion of power:

It is worth noting that in German the word Nietzsche uses for 'power' in the com-
pound formulation 'will to power', *Macht,* is derived from the verb *mögen,* meaning to want or desire, and the word *möglich,* meaning potential (it is also related
to *machen,* meaning to make or create). For Nietzsche, 'power' exists as potentiality, so that in the term 'will to power' the word 'power' denotes not simply a
fixed and unchangeable entity like force or strength, but an 'accomplishment' of
the will overcoming or overpowering itself.

Ultimately, Ansell-Pearson supports Kaufmann and Clark's interpretations of power as self-mastery. Nietzsche's use of power is at once
creative and pragmatic. Yet from these thinkers' perspective it seems
as if power—to invoke an ancient saying—"has nothing to do with
Dionysus."

Warren's view is related but distinct. He claims that Nietzsche "characterizes power in terms of the attributes of self-conscious, self-inter-
preting creatures that have 'one more condition' of existence than
other kinds of creatures" (1987, p. 136).[13] Moreover, Warren argues
that "the universal motive identified by the concept of will to power is
not domination but self-constitution" (ibid., p. 232). Warren's emphasis
shifts away from power over ourselves to the hypothesis of a uniquely
human capacity. Kaufmann, Clark, Ansell-Pearson, and Warren all
concur that power does not centrally refer to domination. These
views can be sustained only at the price of minimizing how important
pleasure is for Nietzsche as a fundamental human motivation. In particular, Nietzsche demands that we face up to the reality that activities
of cruelty, hostility, and exploitation can be pleasurable.[14] One must

also reckon with the association in *Thus Spoke Zarathustra* between creativity and destruction. "Whoever must be a creator always annihilates [Immer vernichtet, wer ein Schöpfer sein muss]," Nietzsche writes in Z I #15. Nice and naughty pleasures, according to Nietzsche, may not be clearly separable.

French Nietzscheans have been more attuned to power as domination and to what one might even call the malignant side to Nietzsche's notion of power.[15] Bataille (1992, p. xxvi) asserts that Nietzsche is a "philosopher of evil" for whom, "the attraction and *value* of evil . . . gave significance to what he intended when he spoke of power." In a diary entry from June or July of 1944, Bataille describes the will to power as "the will to evil, amounting to the will to *expenditure* or risk" (ibid., p. 151). Although the notion of expenditure properly belongs to Bataille's own philosophy of excess, there is evidence for finding such a view in Nietzsche. In HAH II 1 #365 Nietzsche asserts that "the employment of excess as cure is one of the more refined artifices in the art of living." In GS #349 he comments that power seeks its own expansion, and he unambiguously distinguishes power from self-preservation, concluding that nature is governed by "overflow and squandering, even to the point of absurdity."[16]

Deleuze explicates power in terms of the contestation of active and reactive forces and argues that Nietzsche, while acknowledging and criticizing the triumph of reactive forces, advocates the superiority of active forces (Deleuze 1983, p. 60). It is crucial, as Deleuze sees it, to set Nietzsche's affirmation of affirmation against the negativity of Hegelian dialectic. Deleuze's gloss on power emphasizes its creative and giving aspect; it is, as he paraphrases Nietzsche, "the bestowing virtue" (ibid., p. 85).[17] It is revealing that Deleuze construes Nietzsche's notion of the "pathos of distance" in terms of difference and play, as this seems to soften the connection between power and domination. Clearly, Deleuze distances himself from the emancipatory edge of Bataille's interpretation.

Foucault's interpretation of power as domination is appropriated from Nietzsche via Deleuze and used for his own purposes.[18] Identifying Nietzsche as "the philosopher of power," Foucault (1980, p. 53) states that Nietzsche was "a philosopher who managed to think of power without having to confine himself within a political theory in order to do so." Power conveys the inevitability of struggle among humans and thus reveals the impossibility of escaping from the master/slave paradigm. Foucault is especially influenced by Nietzsche's rejection of "the longing for a form of power innocent of all coercion, discipline and normalization" (ibid., p. 117). In contrast to Nietzsche's identification with nobility, however, Foucault has sympathy for those who are victimized by power. Foucault claims, in fact, that his general project is to reveal domination and to "expose both its latent nature and its brutality" (ibid., p. 95).[19]

Deleuze's reading of Foucault highlights their mutual interest in power[20]: "Power has no essence; it is simply operational. It is not an attribute but a relation: the power-relation is the set of possible relations between forces, which passes through the dominated forces no less than through the dominating, as both these forces constitute unique elements." (Deleuze 1988, p. 27) In one sense, this seems like a good interpretation of Foucault, who calls power "a machine in which everyone is caught" (Foucault 1980, p. 156). In another sense, Foucault is more wary than Deleuze of using power as a monolithic category; instead, his "microphysics of power" offers detailed analyses of power in everyday life, "where it becomes capillary, that is, in its more regional and local forms and institutions" (ibid., p. 96). It is not my intention, of course, to try to do justice to Foucault's own complex notion of power in this context. The key point is Foucault's belief that domination is a fact of life. Although there is in Foucault a certain acceptance of aggression, and perhaps even a subliminal fascination with it, he also affirms the desire to find pleasure in release. Concerned about exploitation, he does not share Bataille's malignant interpretation of power. This does not mean that he accepts the benign interpretation of power as mastery.

My own perspective is that there is genuine tension and undecidability between the interpretation of power as mastery and that of power as domination. Although the two interpretations seem antithetical, I do not think they are mutually exclusive. It is possible to argue that they can coexist—a view indirectly suggested by Nehamas (1985, p. 80) in connection with his interpretation of the will to power: "The will to power is an activity that consists in expanding a particular sphere of influence, physical or mental, as far as it can possibly go. As such, it ranges from the crudest to the most sophisticated, from mere physical resistance and brute subjugation to rational persuasion." This view has the merit of not whitewashing Nietzsche's self-consciously dangerous interpretation of power, yet it does not concur with the French Nietzscheans. As I see it, there is no compelling reason to have to conceive of self-mastery as wholly defined by a struggle to dominate or be dominated. In other words, there is something mistaken in supposing that Nietzsche intends to use power only in the malignant sense. However, in emphasizing self-mastery, one can overlook Nietzsche's opposition to "self-control" and his fascination with letting go.[21] My stance is not a perfunctory matter of splitting the difference to make sure to validate both sides to the same degree. It seems to me that Nietzsche sees power mainly in terms of mastery, but that he also is attracted to domination—not in a blanket sense, but in a sense that allows for the cultivation of strength in those he regards as deserving to prevail.[22]

Let me refine this position. It is apparent that those who conceive of power in terms of mastery are partial to viewing power as an enabling factor for oneself, rather than having to do with one's relation to others. Hence, mastery indicates self-mastery and self-empowerment; presumably it helps an individual to flourish in the world. There is a tendency on the part of those who advocate mastery to misrepresent the opposing position by dwelling on the occasional statements that justify aggression in one's relation to others.

As I have demonstrated, however, it is important not to ignore that French Nietzscheans see power in terms of a relation to the self. Although they attend to the malignant aspect of power, which includes hostility and aggression to others, they are primarily concerned with the self's experience of overflowing and indulging in excess. This is, indeed, an important theme for Nietzsche: he values self-empowerment more because of the actual gratification it provides than because it marks self-efficacy. Pleasure is a manifestation of power, but not necessarily its sole aim.[23] Perhaps we could surmise that pleasure is a major reason why power is desirable, yet this would leave room for occasions when the demands of power lead us to endure pain. Consider a passage in which Nietzsche muses on the importance of cruelty:

> . . . we must . . . chase away the clumsy psychology of bygone times which had nothing to teach about cruelty except that it came into being at the sight of the suffering of *others*. There is also an abundant, overabundant enjoyment at one's own suffering, at making oneself suffer. (BGE #229)

In view of Nietzsche's claim that there is gratification even in one's own suffering, his picture of pleasure and pain is more complicated. Any attempt to capture what Nietzsche thinks of cruelty is obliged not to go too far in the direction of construing it only as cruelty to others, since he never restricts cruelty in this way.

Nietzsche seems to me to be concerned predominantly with mastery over the self, although he does not rule out the need to dominate others. At the very least, there is nothing in itself inconsistent with domination in Nietzsche's understanding of mastery. In chapters 12 and 13 I will consider the implications of this. My conclusion so far is that neither the representatives of mastery nor the representatives of domination have shown sufficient appreciation of the breadth of Nietzsche's view. For Nietzsche, the self as agent features both self-regulation and self-abandonment. The exponents of mastery tend to emphasize self-regulation over self-abandonment; the exponents of domination tend to emphasize self-abandonment over self-regulation.[24]

The parameters of self-regulation and self-abandonment are admittedly wide. Both must be joined with Nietzsche's commitment to the ideal of self-acceptance—expressed by his notions of amor fati and eternal recurrence. The importance of self-acceptance helps to establish that Nietzsche regards power more in terms of what it actually bestows on us, rather than as a relentless pursuit of more power. The position that the will to power means "the will to more power" (Lingis 1977, p. 43) is thus unwarranted. Nietzsche uses 'life' [Leben] to convey an eternally flowing, Heraclitean state of flux, and occasionally he links this to the will to power. Yet there is no way to support this interpretation of the will to power without seriously diminishing Nietzsche's interest in agency. It is true that power enjoys its own enhancement, but this does not mean that we can infer that power cannot and does not exist in a form that coincides with agency.

11.3 Agency Infused with Will to Power

Let us now reconsider my argument about multiplicity, integration, and anti-agency in chapter 10. There I maintained that multiplicity and integration were not inconsistent as long as integration means that the multiplicity yields coherence rather than unity. I also claimed that Nietzsche does not try to mediate between integration and his anti-agency. In this section, I want to reassess both of these points in light of what has been said about the will to power.

The will to power helps us to grasp the motivation of integrated agency. An integrated agent is more powerful than one who is not integrated in the sense of possessing more options and having a greater awareness of the choices he or she possesses; moreover, an integrated agent will be able to act on the basis of combining and connecting the multiple components of the self. It is especially important to reflect on how the will to power influences the four factors that determine integration: narcissism, instincts, affects, and relation to the past.

It is not difficult to link the will to power with narcissism. As Zarathustra says in praising selfishness [Selbstsucht], it is the "wholesome, healthy selfishness that wells up from a powerful soul—from a powerful soul to which belongs the high body, beautiful, triumphant, refreshing, around which everything becomes a mirror" (Z III #2). In BGE #265 Nietzsche stresses that the noble soul "accepts this fact of its egoism without any question mark."

The will to power also has connections to our instinctual endowment; it is a kind of synthesis of libido and aggression. As Nietzsche claims in the context of contrasting "adaptation" to the will to power, the latter gives priority to "spontaneous, aggressive, expansive, form-giving forces that give new interpretations and directions" (BGE #12). As we glimpsed in the preceding section, power can mean domination. Yet, when Nietzsche invokes aggression, it points to the creation of new ways of thinking as much as to violent action. The will to power is not distorted in appearing in sublimated form.

The connection between the will to power and affects is affirmed through interpretation. Nietzsche tells us in WP #556 that interpretation is a form of will to power and also that it is affective. Recall from chapter 1 that in WP #556 Nietzsche specifically links his perspectivism with affective interpretations. Indeed, as Nietzsche declares in SW 12 (p. 190): "Who interprets? our affects." Insofar as the will to power includes making interpretations, then, it must make use of our affects.

Ultimately, the best way to describe the will to power is as "the strongest, most life-affirming drive" (GM III #18). Still, it is questionable whether the will to power ought to be assimilated to the status of a biological drive. As we saw earlier, in his discussion of the third component of the will Nietzsche is really addressing himself to a dimension that concerns how we feel about and understand ourselves. Nietzsche is quite specific in claiming that knowledge can function as an expression of the will to power, and that the will to power contributes to our making interpretations of the world (WP #480, #556, #643). Indeed, he is careful to distinguish the will to power from the mere desire for self-preservation—that is, between what we might see as the aim of thriving and mere surviving (BGE #12, #13).[25]

It is less evident that the will to power has a connection to our relation to the past. There is no reason why the will to power would have to entail a rejection of our relation to the past. Yet the will to power is in search of gratification in the present and of its own flourishing in the future. Moreover, Nietzsche tends to associate attachment to the past with an unwillingness to change, whereas he sees the will to power as a dynamic force promoting growth, strength, and health. The will to power bestows satisfaction on us—as long as we do not confuse satisfaction with the kind of happiness that seeks to be at rest.

In suggesting that the will to power helps to sustain integrated agency and that it bestows satisfaction, we must come up against and entertain the opposite conclusion: that the will to power can be at odds with agency and represents a standard that is independent of satisfaction. Though it is true that the will to power extends agency, Nietzsche also believes that it can limit and undermine agency. In Nietzschean terms, the will to power coerces and dominates us at the same time as it is used to make us into who we are. As Butler has expressed it (1997a, p. 13), "power *acts on* a subject but . . . *enacts* the subject into being." I will take up Butler's argument, which borrows from the Nietzschean idea that there is no doer behind the deed, in chapter 13. For the moment, it is sufficient to register her interpretation that "subjection" belongs to the very nature of being a subject.

Here we seem to have returned to the dilemma of reconciling Nietzsche's commitment with both integrated agency and anti-agency. Although in my opinion this is not necessarily contradictory, Nietzsche never addresses whether he thinks it is, or if it is not, what the implications of that might be. He regards the will to power as serving agency and as contributing to satisfaction; yet he also introduces the perspective that power complicates and limits agency, which intimates that there is a standard that supersedes satisfaction. In thinking about the will to power as a force that precedes and is larger than the individual agent, the prospect of autonomy would have to be diminished.[26]

Nietzsche does not show much interest in defending autonomy. Although there are certainly passages in which he celebrates sovereignty of the will and even independence, a kind of fatalism emerges in his later writings that is difficult to reconcile with freedom of the will.[27] It does not seem to be the case that Nietzsche is signaling an intention to abandon his appreciation of freedom by adopting the will to power. Rather, Nietzsche's discourse allows the will to power and freedom to remain side by side. At the risk of irony, one might say that it is the fate of the Nietzschean free spirit to embrace amor fati willingly.[28]

Nietzsche's idea of the will to power is meant to be a rebuke to the emphasis on freedom that one finds in the tradition of German Idealism. Without displacing freedom entirely, it challenges the aim of human agency as freedom. In an important sense, the will to power ought to be understood as a reaction to and an expansion of Hegel's notion of being-for-itself. If Nietzsche were seeking simply to replace freedom with the will to power, his philosophy could be pigeonholed more easily. As he would see it, the ambiguities that we have detected in his philosophy reflect life itself. Nietzsche resists placing too much faith in agency, on the ground that we should not underestimate the forces that oppose it. However, Nietzsche clearly believes that there would be less hope for human beings if they lacked the capacity for agency.

There is one missing piece in the puzzle of understanding Nietzsche's view of agency: our relations to others. To what extent must we rely on others in order to achieve an integrated sense of agency? And what are the implications of the will to power for our relation to others? Does Nietzsche believe that it is possible to achieve satisfaction without others? For Nietzsche, in contrast with Hegel, it is not obvious that others are integral for one's own sense of agency.

In this chapter and in chapter 10 I have not said much about Nietzsche's view of our relations to others. In the next chapter, however, I will argue that it is important not to neglect this topic in Nietzsche. Although his discussion is not formalized, and although it is scattered throughout his writings, Nietzsche gives a surprising amount of attention to issues concerning our relations to others.

Self and Other in Nietzsche

We must give up trying to know those to whom we are linked by something essential; by this I mean we must greet them in the relation with the unknown in which they greet us as well, in our estrangement.

—Maurice Blanchot, *Friendship*

In chapter 11 we encountered different positions as to whether to construe power in terms of mastery or in terms of domination. That issue forms a backdrop for my investigation of Nietzsche's understanding of the relation between self and other in this chapter. In particular, I want to consider the difficult question of what role others play in the way Nietzsche conceives of agency. Of course, raising the question of the role of others evinces the shadow of Hegel.

As we saw earlier in the book, others are constitutive of agency for Hegel in a double sense. Others help us know ourselves in a way that is simply not possible without them; they are necessary for the project of self-knowledge and self-fathoming. Moreover, according to Hegel, self-knowledge entails coming to terms with the fact that one is both being-for-itself and being-for-another. Agency involves struggle and interaction; yet, as Hegel sees it, nothing precludes the possibility of realizing it in a complete sense—that is, of fully integrating individual self-knowledge and mutual recognition on the interpersonal, social, and religious planes.

Competing tendencies mark Nietzsche's attitude toward others. On the one hand, he seems to countenance cruelty and exploitation (even if he does not glorify them), and he repeatedly stresses the theme of solitude. On the other hand, he conceptualizes human relationships broadly and with a subtlety and a psychological astuteness that should not be overlooked. In this chapter, I shall first focus on Nietzsche's conception of our need for others and examine his numerous comments about exchange (especially the relationship between creditor and debtor), gratitude (which serves as the opposite of resentment), respect (which members of the elite extend to one another), and mercy (which serves as the opposite of pity).

12.1 Self-Enclosed Gardens with Hospitable Gates

For Nietzsche, a degree of cruelty and exploitation in human relationships is inevitable. Although he offers no blanket justification for violence against others, neither does he feel compelled to specify how and when it is legitimate. In analogizing noble morality to birds of prey and slave morality to lambs (GM I #13), he seems to understand the aggression of birds of prey as simply a matter of their nature. It is not the case that he glamorizes aggression, as some vulgar Nietzsche enthusiasts might have it. Nevertheless, one is hard pressed to find much empathy for victims in Nietzsche. Indeed, concern for victims tends to be read as weakness or in terms of the emotion of pity, which Nietzsche opposes and even despises. There is no reason to whitewash Nietzsche's views. My aim will be to try to give expression to the full range of perspectives on human relationships that one finds in his work.

Nietzsche embraces and even relishes the ideal of a solitary life.[1] Aloneness is a condition of life, he tells us, and this is particularly true for the thinker. Occasionally, Nietzsche is quite despairing about the possibility of establishing lasting connections to others. However, he seems to regard a solitary life as a matter of choice as much as it is an unavoidable fact. A solitary life requires strength, and "the strong are as naturally inclined to *separate* as the weak are to *congregate*" (GM III #18). It is not that the strong are unable to unite, but that they do so only "with the aim of aggressive collection action [Gesammt Aktion] and collective satisfaction [Gesammt Befriedigung] of their will to power." It is evident that Nietzsche is not tempted, as Hegel was, by the hope of social integration.

Nietzsche's commitment to solitude can easily occlude his affirmation of the human need for others. In HAH I #589 he rather cheerfully recommends that "the best way of beginning each day well is to think on awakening whether one cannot this day give pleasure to at any rate *one* person." More substantively, Nietzsche claims that consciousness itself evolved as a result of the need that humans have to communicate with one another:

Consciousness is really only a net of communication between human beings; it is only as such that it had to develop; a solitary human being who lived like a beast of prey would not have needed it. . . . It was only as a social animal that man acquired self-consciousness—which he is still in the process of doing, more and more. (GS #354)

This strong statement implies that humans have an inherent desire to be connected, and that this can be used to explain why society develops. In HAH I #216, Nietzsche suggests that the gestures between mother and infant are a form of communication that precedes the capacity for verbal communication.

In HAH I #98, Nietzsche draws attention to the overall importance of human relationships, claiming that relatedness is more satisfactory than solitude:

To feel sensations of pleasure on the basis of human relations on the whole makes men better; joy, pleasure, is enhanced when it is enjoyed together with others, it gives the individual security, makes him good-natured, banishes distrust and envy: for one feels a sense of well-being [wohl] and sees that others are likewise feeling a sense of well-being. *Similar expressions of pleasure* awaken the fantasy of empathy [Mitempfindung], the feeling of being like something else: the same effect is produced by common suffering, by experiencing bad weather, dangers, enemies in common. . . . And thus the social instinct [der sociale Instinct] grows out of the feeling of pleasure.

The attention to empathy reveals a side of Nietzsche that is easy to overlook, though he does grapple with it in other places.[2]

In a more personal vein, Nietzsche reflects on his own need for others in the preface to *Human, All Too Human.* Having described his own feeling of isolation, he remarks:

What I again and again needed most for my cure and self-restoration, however, was the belief that I was *not* thus isolated, not alone in *seeing* as I did—an enchanted surmising of relatedness [Verwandtschaft] and identity in eye and desires, a reposing trust of friendship, a blindness in concert with another without suspicion or question-marks. . . .

The wish for "relatedness," and in particular for friendship, is expressed dramatically.

In GM II #8 and #9, Nietzsche avers that early humans were preoccupied with "exchange"—with establishing and maintaining value in relation to one another. He treats exchange, therefore, as a kind of organizing principle in society. In particular, Nietzsche tells us, exchange governed the interaction between creditors and debtors. He emphasizes that creditors unabashedly asserted their right to enact pain on the body of those who could not repay their debts. Indeed, the gratification that is part of such cruelty is the only way debtors could remedy such situations. The interaction between creditors and debtors, like most of the relationships that capture Nietzsche's attention, resembles the dynamics of the master-slave relationship.[3]

Nietzsche's recounting of master morality and slave morality locates a contrast between the "gratitude" exhibited by the masters and the "resentment" manifested in the slaves.[4] Gratitude informs the masters' beliefs as well as how they treat each other. Nietzsche also contrasts ancient Greek religion, which he sees as permeated with gratitude, to Christianity, which he diagnoses as rampant with fear (BGE #49). "Respect" is also mentioned in connection with gratitude. The masters do value others whom they see as being like themselves, even if they are primarily interested in their own narcissistic gratification. The respect they extend to each other is an alternative to the "pathos of distance" that characterizes their relation to everyone else in society. Nietzsche seems nostalgic about the exuberant, life-affirming spirit of the masters; however, he is not tempted to envision the return of such types.

It might seem that Nietzsche's attraction to master morality would leave little room for warmth and compassion in human relationships. As I have mentioned, Nietzsche consistently attacks the emotion of pity as fit only for the weak. Yet one ought not ignore Nietzsche's comments on "mercy," which help to fill out his view of human relationships. For him, mercy represents the self-overcoming of justice: the more powerful one becomes, the less one will hang onto the desire to punish others. Nietzsche is supposing here that healthy self-regard will make one more generous. The lure of cruelty, which at first commands Nietzsche's attention, yields to a higher kind of gratification. Mercy, unlike pity, is freely given as a result of supreme self-confidence.

In *Daybreak* Nietzsche adopts a delightful metaphor that synthesizes what I have attributed to Nietzsche about human relationships. Expressing wariness toward altruistic moralities that are built around "sympathetic affections," he contrasts them with other kinds of moralities that give us the freedom to create ourselves—a source of pleasure to ourselves but also to others. Nietzsche proposes that such moralities may be analogized to "a beautiful, restful, self-enclosed garden [in sich abgeschlossenen Garten] . . . with high walls against storms and the storm of the roadway but also a hospitable gate [eine gastfreundliche Pforte]" (D #174). He is urging us to cherish the solitude provided by the garden's self-enclosed walls, but to do so in a way that welcomes rather than excludes others who wish to enter through the gate.

12.2 Friendship

It is difficult and ultimately inconclusive to generalize from Nietzsche's sporadic comments on exchange, gratitude, respect, and mercy. In this section, I want to add to our understanding of the relationship between self and other in Nietzsche by focusing on his view of friendship. Although Nietzsche returns to this theme again and again, it has not claimed the attention of many Nietzsche scholars.[5]

For the most part, Nietzsche values friendship highly. He emphasizes, in particular, how important friendship was in the ancient world. In "In Honor of Friendship" (GS #61) he notes that "in antiquity the feeling of friendship was considered the highest feeling, even higher than the most celebrated pride of the self-sufficient sage—somehow as the sole and still more sacred sibling of this pride."[6] Yet there are also many passages in which Nietzsche seems much less confident about the overall value of friendship. In "Of friends" (HAH I #376), he asserts:

Only reflect to yourself how various are the feelings, how divided the opinions, even among your closest acquaintances, how even the same opinions are of a quite different rank or intensity in the heads of your friends than they are in yours; how manifold are the occasions for misunderstanding, for hostility and rupture [zum feindseligen Auseinanderfliehen]. After reflecting on all this you must tell yourself: how uncertain is the ground upon which all our alliances and friendships rest, how close at hand are icy downpours in stormy weather, how isolated each man is!

It is the frailty and instability of friendship that captures Nietzsche's attention here. One could argue that Nietzsche is not contradicting himself, as his praise of friendship is not inconsistent with his intention to claim that modern culture has rendered friendship precarious. It is not clear, however, that this is the focus of Nietzsche's concern.

Consider Nietzsche's perspective in "A Good Friendship" (HAH II 1 #241):

A good friendship originates when one party has a great respect for the other, more indeed than for himself, when one party likewise loves the other, though not so much as he does himself, and when, finally, one party knows how to facilitate the association by adding to it a delicate tinge of intimacy while at the same time prudently withholding actual and genuine intimacy and the confounding of I and Thou.

Friendship is presented as reciprocal, but unequal and non-mutual.[7] One might even wonder if the insistence on asymmetry in the relationship entails a muted version of the master/slave paradigm. Nietzsche builds a measure of distance into the bond between friends, apparently because of the assumption that "actual and genuine intimacy" threatens the relationship and endangers the integrity of separate identity.[8] To some extent, Nietzsche is simply drawing attention to the importance of boundaries between friends.

A tendency toward cynicism is manifest in "Trust and Intimacy" (HAH I #304): "He who deliberately seeks to establish an intimacy with another person is usually in doubt as to whether he possesses his trust. He who is sure he is trusted sets little value on intimacy." The juxtaposition of trust and intimacy is peculiar; it seems to contradict the side of Nietzsche that prizes human connection. There is a mixture of attitudes toward friendship in Nietzsche, ranging from prudent, ardent affirmation to defensive, wary skepticism. It does not seem as if he is simply marking a boundary of appropriate distance here.

Nietzsche invokes an even sharper edge to friendship at times. In HAH II 1 #263 he points out that "many people mistreat even their friends out of vanity when there are witnesses present to whom they want to demonstrate their superiority." In the preface to *Ecce Homo*, Nietzsche quotes from Z I #3 a passage that has a flamboyant twist: "The man of knowledge must not only love his enemies, he must also be able to hate his friends." Friends and enemies are again taken up in the following passage (HAH I #491):

Man is very well defended against himself, against being reconnoitred and besieged by himself, he is usually able to perceive of himself only his outer walls [Aussenwerke]. The actual fortress is inaccessible, even invisible to him, unless his friends and enemies play the traitor and conduct him in by a secret path.

This is a difficult passage to interpret. The main point concerns the limits of self-knowledge through self-observation. (The title of the aphorism is "Self-Observation" [Selbstbeobachtung].) Nietzsche proceeds to maintain that others can offer us something that, by ourselves, we lack. However, unlike for Hegel, this experience has a negative valence. Whereas it makes sense to imagine that our enemies would betray us, Nietzsche surprises us by attributing the same thing to friends.

The mixed assessment of friendship directs us back to Nietzsche's preoccupation with solitude. The desire to depend on others must come up against Nietzsche's strong belief in self-reliance.[9] In the context of affirming "self-education" [Selbst-Erziehung] as a way to avoid conformity, Nietzsche recommends that one turn to others only after "one discovers oneself [entdeckt man sich selber] . . . as one who has educated himself and who thus knows how it is done [als einen Selbst-Erzogenen, der Erfahrung hat]" (HAH II 2 #267). Even more emphatic is this claim:

To satisfy one's necessary requirements as completely as possible oneself [selber befriedigen], even if imperfectly, is the road to freedom of spirit and person. To let others satisfy many of one's requirements [sich befriedigen lassen], even superfluous ones, and as perfectly as possible—is a training in unfreedom. (HAH II 2 #318)

The ambivalence in Nietzsche's attitude toward friendship shows an important difference between Hegel and Nietzsche. At the risk of leaning too much in a Hegelian direction, one could say that Nietzsche depicts satisfaction as a product of being-for-itself, rather than as a product of being-for-another.

Nietzsche exhibits a clear preference for being-for-itself; at the same time, he does not disavow being-for-another as much as he simply fails to account for it. Nietzsche finds human connection appealing, but often he manages to smuggle in an expectation of malevolence or at least an anticipation of breakdown in empathy. A good example of this occurs in a passage in *Human, All Too Human* titled "Deceptive and Yet Tenable." Nietzsche maintains that, especially in youth, we seek out others to rely upon—as a "railing." He goes on to state: "It is true that, if we were really in great danger, they would not help us if we sought to rely on them." (HAH I #600) There is something jarring and counterintuitive here—the more we need help, the less we can expect it. How can we understand this? Is Nietzsche supposing that the experience of looking to a mentor necessarily leads to disappointment? Or does he intend to make a larger point?

Insofar as Nietzsche intends to make a larger point, it would concern the issue of empathy or the lack of it in human relationships. Indeed, there are passages in which failed empathy seems to be a concern for Nietzsche. An excellent example is the following: "Our personal and profoundest suffering is incomprehensible and inaccessible to almost everyone; here we remain hidden from our neighbor, even if we eat from one pot. But whenever people *notice* that we suffer, they interpret our suffering superficially." (GS #338) Another example: "He has experienced a misfortune, and now the 'compassionate' come along and depict his misfortune for him in detail—at length they go away content and elevated: they have gloated over the unfortunate man's distress and over their own and passed a pleasant afternoon." (D #224) Although the compassionate "empathize" with the unfortunate in sharing distress, there is a curious absence of feeling for the other as an other. How are we to assess such pleasant afternoon gratification? Nietzsche is not quite prepared to claim that we are moved by the suffering of others; in fact, he seems to be captivated by the secret Schadenfreude in this encounter, which he presents not merely as a possibility but as the norm.

There is, then, an anguished side to Nietzsche's representation of human relationships. There are passages, such as the following, in which he seems to be upholding something like compulsory misrecognition:

> They were friends but have ceased to be, and they both severed their friendship at the same time: the one because he thought himself too much misunderstood, the other because he thought himself understood too well—and both were deceiving themselves!—for neither understood himself well enough. (D #287)

Again we must wonder what Nietzsche expects us to infer. The most pessimistic conclusion would be that mutuality and self-deception go hand in hand. A slightly more optimistic conclusion would be that it is difficult, perhaps even impossible, to find the middle ground that friendship requires between failing to be understood and being completely understood.

Nietzsche was deeply impressed by the precariousness and impermanence of friendship. In HAH II 1 #242 he notes that, as we change, friends become like ghosts to us. In a crucial passage in "Star Friendship" (GS #279), he describes friends who have become estranged, conjecturing that "perhaps" they will never meet again or that if they do meet they will "fail to recognize each other" [erkennen uns nicht wieder]. He seems to be urging us to accept the larger, stellar forces that might produce this, which make friendship "more sacred." Yet Nietzsche is not simply offering a paean to friendship itself. The passage culminates with the request that we appreciate "star friendship" in spite of the transformation into being "Earth enemies." It is revealing that Nietzsche portrays former friends as current enemies, as this fosters an either/or perspective in which there are no degrees, in which there is no possibility of renewing relationships.

Friendship, Nietzsche seems to be suggesting, obeys a law that exceeds our understanding. He salutes friendship, even as he doubts both its reliability and durability. The urge to appreciate friendship competes with his tacit belief that it brings disappointment. This rather bleak view of friendship is hard to reconcile with Nietzsche's vaunted ideal of life-affirming values. To want friends but not really believe in them is agonizing. Nietzsche is brutally honest about friendship's appeal and about the suffering that it entails. Although friendship alleviates some of the burden of being alone, it comes with limits, and it exposes us to a new set of problems.

12.3 Too Much Solitude?

It is natural to suspect that Nietzsche's perspective on friendship reflects his own life experience. Of course, pondering this does not free us of the obligation to come to a theoretical understanding of the limits that Nietzsche attributes to friendship.

Though Nietzsche obviously values friendship highly, he persistently shows it to be spoiled. One has to wonder why transience and failure figure so prominently in his discussion of friendship. By Nietzsche's own standard of judgment (GS #381), clues to this might be found in his own life experience. In particular, one might wonder how his friendship with Richard Wagner influenced his view of friendship. As is well known, this friendship continued to preoccupy Nietzsche after its unhappy end. Löwith (1997, p. 22) has gone so far as to maintain that this friendship was a decisive event in Nietzsche's life, and that he never recovered from its ending. In the introduction to *Nietzsche: The Birth of Tragedy and Other Writings*, Raymond Geuss concurs with Löwith on the importance of the friendship and stresses its love-hate quality: "The love was there virtually from the beginning, as was the hate; both lasted to the very end."

In interpreting his ideas through his life, one must take Nietzsche's self-understanding into account. I do not think Nietzsche would have trouble acknowledging that he suffered on account of his friendship with Wagner. (See HAH II, preface and #3.) Yet, as he sees it (ibid., #4), he was able to move beyond the friendship. This is not to say that Nietzsche did not continue to see himself as suffering from solitude. He clearly did. In mid-December 1882, in a letter to Lou Andreas Salome and Paul Rée, Nietzsche poignantly referred to himself as "a headache-plagued, half-lunatic, crazed by too much solitude."[10] And, if anything, his solitude dramatically increased after this point.

However illuminating it is to take account of such aspects of Nietzsche's life, it is desirable to avoid being reductionistic about how his personal experience made him despairing about human relationships in his philosophy. As we saw in chapter 11, Nietzsche emphasizes narcissism, instincts, affects, and the past in his conception of agency—precisely the terrain of what Hegel calls "being-for-itself." Nietzsche probes being-for-itself in a new and profound way. Yet he portrays being-for-another awkwardly and uncertainly, which correspondingly renders it far more difficult to assess. There is something unresolved in Nietzsche's attitude toward the other.

In the crucial aphorism "Of Friends" (HAH I #376), Nietzsche reflects on the gulf that necessarily exists between individuals: "How manifold are the occasions for misunderstanding, for hostility, and rupture [wie hundertfältig der Anlass kommt zum Missverstehen, zum feindseligen Auseinanderfliehen]." The sense of the precariousness of friendship is present, and in this connection Nietzsche mentions the bitterness of the sage who is ready to declare "Friends, there are no friends." In order for friendship to exist, we must learn "how to keep silent." There remains the danger of friendship's falling apart if friends truly share what they know about each other. Nietzsche urges us to "despise ourself a little," as there is even less reason to think well of ourselves than to think well of others. The passage culminates as follows:

And so, since we can endure [aushalten] ourself, let us also endure other people; and perhaps to each of us there will come the more joyful hour when we exclaim: 'Friends, there are no friends!' thus said the dying sage; 'Foes, there are no foes' say I, the living fool.

Nietzsche hopes that we will give up our illusions about friendship, and, as we have seen before, that we will remain aware of the potential for friendship to be undermined. Yet he refuses to conclude pessimistically. He directs us to affirm friendship for what it is, and he mocks the wisdom of the dying sage by introducing the fool's celebration of life. Nietzsche imagines that he is offering a playful, life-affirming response here, but much remains unclear. In substituting "no foes" for "no friends," what has been accomplished? Does the mentality of having no foes really affirm friendship?

The aphorism quoted above is crucial in Derrida's *Politics of Friendship* (1997), which begins with an interpretation of "O my Friends, there is no friend," a variation of the citation that Nietzsche adopts (for which there is a long tradition of attributing to Aristotle—for example by Montaigne).[11] What is most relevant here is Derrida's claim that Nietzsche introduces an alternative conception of friendship. Rather than see friendship in terms of a relation of the self to an other who is like the self and with whom the self has all things in common, Nietzsche establishes distance as part of how he understands friendship.[12] Derrida emphasizes the desirability of silence. He also accentuates the fact that Nietzsche regards "disproportion" as essential to friendship—that friendship requires the rupture of reciprocity or equality (ibid., p. 62).

As Derrida reads Nietzsche, friendship entails the demand that we face up to the otherness of the other. The transposition of "friends" into "foes" in the above-quoted passage is construed by Derrida as signaling an intention to question the philosophical tradition. As Derrida puts it (ibid., p. 76), Nietzsche "does not yet have a friend." This is meant as a statement of Nietzsche's profound solitude, but it also registers a future hope for friendship. Derrida stresses what he sees as the political implications of Nietzsche's concept of friendship. Although it is hard to pin down Derrida exactly, it is evident that he sees Nietzsche as articulating the voice of the "community of solitary friends"—that is, in the language of Bataille, the "community of those without community" (ibid., p. 37). Without ever stating it explicitly, Derrida takes Nietzsche as an emblematic figure.

Derrida's reading of Nietzsche is provocative. Not only does he suggest that it is a mistake to view Nietzsche as an opponent of democracy; he also defends the complexity of Nietzsche's view of women, even in the face of trying to reckon with some of Nietzsche's bizarre notions, such as that women are incapable of friendship.[13] Along with Sarah Kofman, Derrida is largely responsible for inspiring the extensive secondary literature on the topic of Nietzsche and women,[14] which urges us not to be dissuaded by Nietzsche's more overtly sexist comments and to remain open to how his views are germane to feminism and to the critique of patriarchy.

Let us linger on the crucial issue of alterity. Derrida is right that Nietzsche's rejection of the notion that the other (friend) is like the self leads him to be sensitive about the otherness of the other. However, Derrida downplays problems in the way that Nietzsche characterizes the relationship between self and other. As I see it, Nietzsche ranges across extremes; he accomplishes an inversion, which moves from identity to difference, from the overestimation of what friends share to an underestimation of it, without acknowledging that anything could lie between. Early in *The Politics of Friendship*, Derrida points out that Aristotle believed that "loving" was better than "being loved"; however, he does not grapple with the implications of the possibility that Nietzsche concurs with rather than protests against this aspect of friendship. One consequence of Nietzsche's decided preference for activity over passivity is that he is averse to the reception of love from the other. This is due to his conventional association of masculinity with activity and femininity with passivity. A second consequence is that mutuality is overlooked or devalued as a matter of reciprocal exchange.

It is important to realize that, though mutuality can denote two parties doing the same time to each other and having the same experience, it also can denote something looser and closer to empathy. In this second sense of mutuality, one party responds to the other without the premise that they are having the same experience. Nietzsche is not completely indifferent to the theme of mutuality. In "Friend" (HAH I #499), he observes that "fellow rejoicing [Mitfreude], not fellow suffering [Mitleiden], makes the friend." Yet this insight pertains to mutuality in the first sense—two parties feeling the same thing at the same time. Nietzsche's main concern seems to be to invert the commonplace and suspiciously slavish ideal of adversity's breeding closeness in favor of a more positive ideal. It is not clear, however, why Nietzsche assumes that these choices must cancel each other. The one-sided choices here reverberate from the one-sided choices Nietzsche offers between identity and difference in friendship.

In connection with the second sense of mutuality, recall that Nietzsche does refer to mercy in a positive light. At the same, he typically derides concern for others as hypocritical.[15] His repeated condemnation of pity offers tacit justification for discounting the feelings for others. In her haunting address to Nietzsche, Irigaray (1991, p. 19) picks up on this point and contrasts her love of sharing with Nietzsche's wish "to keep everything for yourself." Nietzsche fails to value empathy adequately, and this muddies his thinking about the relationship between self and other. Empathy becomes entangled with Nietzsche's commitment to celebrating strength over weakness.[16] The notion that empathy could be produced by strength is not easy for Nietzsche to accommodate philosophically. There is little textual evidence to support the interpretive stretch that Derrida ventures: that by speaking in the name of the strongest, Nietzsche is also speaking in the name of the weakest (Derrida 1994, pp. 31–32).

Nietzsche's concern with self-gratification—with such things as narcissism, instinctual satisfaction, and the will to power—interferes with the way he characterizes the relationship between self and others. It is significant, for example, that in Z I, "On the Friend," Nietzsche presents the hermit as engaged in a dialogue between "I and me," which seems to suggest that a friend represents an intrusion of a third party. Nietzsche's theory of agency goes deeper than Hegel in fathoming being-for-itself, but he leaves the issue of our relation to others unresolved. Nietzsche himself acknowledges the social constitution of agency, yet he opts not to pursue this and not to concentrate fully on coming to terms with the experience of being-for-another.

In the end, there is something deficient in Nietzsche's description of relationships to others because he wavers in presenting positive, gratifying aspects. My point is not that he is obliged to present the positive aspects to the exclusion of negative ones; indeed, Hegel's affirmation of the positive aspects of human relationships hardly ignores the reality of negative aspects. That it is worthwhile to focus on frustration, disappointment, alienation, and sadness in relationships does not justify Nietzsche's vagueness in explicating the potential for pleasure with others.

It is instructive in thinking about Nietzsche not to lose sight of the distinction between his fantasies about himself and the reality. In one sense the former threatens to obscure the latter, and perhaps we can understand the former as a defense for or a denial of the latter. In another sense, it is a credit to Nietzsche that he was able to forge an image of himself that conjures power and authority. As Chamberlain (1996, p. 196) comments, "out of his incapacity to live he created a formidable life."

Nietzsche's self-invention as a character in his own work is now widely appreciated.[17] There is no doubt that Nietzsche reinvents himself as a character; he does so, however, in a way that does not fully disguise his suffering and solitude. The tension between who Nietzsche was and who he might like to be is present on every page of his work. What makes Nietzsche so contemporary is precisely the degree to which he reveals himself, intentionally and unintentionally . His sense of being painfully alone never led to resignation, and his hope for friendship staved off bitterness. Yet an unmistakable sadness leaks through his manic wish for joyous affirmation of life.

13

Nietzschean Agency

One might say that the purposes of power are not always the purposes of agency.

—Judith Butler, *The Psychic Life of Power*

Nietzsche never aspired to have a theory of agency, yet agency is a pervasive theme throughout his work. Although he avoids a definition of what it means to be an agent, he explores the question many times and from many angles.

As we have seen over the last few chapters, a number of obstacles stand in the way of making sense of "Nietzschean agency." First, Nietzsche's ambivalence toward agency means that he defends the possibility of integrated agency while staking out a position of anti-agency. Second, there is tension and indecision as to whether the will to power denotes mastery or domination. Third, Nietzsche wavers in his portrayal of the relationship between self and others, valuing others but also traumatized by them and determined to defend solitude.

One might conclude that no conclusions about Nietzschean agency are valid. I think this would be mistaken. Borrowing from psychoanalytic language (as I did in chapter 9), one could say that Nietzschean agency is more concerned with narcissism than with relatedness. It is not the case that Nietzsche rejects the category of relatedness, but his account of it is more confusing and ultimately less satisfying than his examination of the cluster of issues around narcissism. Nietzsche strongly defends the desirability and the legitimacy of self-concern.

He expresses skepticism toward altruistic moralities, and he promotes the acceptance of egotism. In Z I, "On the Afterworldly," he writes: "Indeed, this ego and the ego's contradiction and confusion still speak more honestly of its being—this creating, willing, valuing ego, which is the measure and value of things."

Let us also recall Nietzsche's enthusiasm for Selbstsucht, a concept that closely resembles narcissism. In "On the Three Evils" (Z III #2) he proclaims: ". . . it happened for the first time—that his word pronounced selfishness [selbstsucht] blessed, the wholesome, healthy selfishness that wells from a powerful soul—from a powerful soul to which belongs the high body, beautiful, triumphant, refreshing, around which everything becomes a mirror. . . ." This passage draws attention to narcissism as healthy. It also shows the close connection between the body and the mirroring effect of narcissism, and it reminds us of Nietzsche's belief that narcissism and the will to power mutually reinforce each other.

Resorting to psychoanalytic language is much less of a leap with Nietzsche than with Hegel. Nietzsche relished his intellectual identity as a psychologist, and his affirmation of psychology has informed my reading throughout this book. From one perspective, Nietzsche looks to psychology as a way to escape from the limits of the philosophical tradition. From another perspective, however, he is seeking to enlarge the domain of philosophy to be open to and inclusive of psychology.

Nietzsche anticipates Freud in demanding that we heed our instincts in order to be satisfied and in worrying about the price of forgoing satisfaction. Although Nietzsche, like Freud, develops a notion of sublimation in which instincts are transmuted for the sake of a higher purpose, sublimation does not have the same importance for Nietzsche that it does for Freud. In honoring our instincts, Nietzsche is less sanguine than Freud about accommodation.[1]

13.1 Nietzschean Variations

As is well known, Nietzsche's work was not widely recognized during his lifetime. It became better known around the time he drifted into insanity, and it won greater acclaim after he died. Although Nietzsche held the conviction that he was ahead of his time, it is undeniable that he suffered a great deal because his work failed to generate the response he thought it deserved.[2] What a difference a century makes! Anyone writing about Nietzsche now can commiserate about keeping up with the proliferation of scholarship about his work. One would be hard pressed, though, to argue that there is a single issue or set of issues that is at the source of such compelling interest. Indeed, there are marked differences between the Anglo-American literature, which prefers to locate Nietzsche within the philosophical tradition, and the French, which honors his resistance to that tradition.

The Anglo-American literature shows a predilection for Nietzsche's views on truth, values, and art. Though Nietzsche is readily identified as a proponent of self-overcoming, his anti-agency is not well represented. Consistent with this, the will to power is more often construed as mastery than as domination. Anglo-American commentators have been less interested than French commentators in Nietzsche's anticipation of psychoanalysis. According to Schrift (1995, p. xiv), the Anglo-American attitude toward Nietzsche has wavered from hostility to silence. I would qualify this by acknowledging commentary that, though polemical, is not guilty of either simply attacking or ignoring the French literature.

Two further points are worth stressing. First, French Nietzscheans do not primarily see themselves as commentators. Bataille, Deleuze, Derrida, and Foucault are original thinkers who are inspired by Nietzsche but who seek to offer interpretations in the spirit of Nietzsche. Second, questions might be raised about the meaningfulness of the term "French Nietzscheans." The closer one looks, the less obvious it seems that a unanimity of opinion exists among these thinkers. For example, Bataille is interested in rethinking the relationship between Hegel and Nietzsche; Derrida, Deleuze, and Foucault, however, accept that a fundamental rift underlies that relationship. One might also contrast Bataille's consuming interest in Nietzsche's ideas about how to live with Derrida's focus on Nietzsche's writing. Or one might confront the rivalry and opposition between Derrida and Foucault on the theme of madness.

In this section, I shall contend selectively with aspects of the legacy of the French Nietzscheans. No attempt will be made to be comprehensive, and I would acknowledge happily that my choices are somewhat arbitrary; other choices are clearly possible. Nothing can really justify, for example, the decision not to inquire further into the views of Deleuze and Foucault. The choice to overlook Deleuze is lamentable in view of the fact that his book on Nietzsche was the opening salvo of poststructuralism. Yet, as I see it, Deleuze's interpretation has proved to be more timely than untimely, ignoring crucial aspects of Nietzsche's thought such as the critique of modernity and his notion of agency. The choice not to grapple with Foucault's relation to Nietzsche is mitigated only by its familiarity. Also, I will have the occasion to refer to Foucault's interpretation of Nietzsche in the context of exploring Butler's thinking.

13.2 Derrida: Renewing Nietzsche

Derrida has written extensively about Nietzsche's work and has incorporated Nietzschean elements in the practice of deconstruction. His 1985 book *The Ear of the Other*[3] widens the scope of Heidegger's Nietzsche interpretation by shifting the focus from the doctrine of the will to power and the question of whether Nietzsche overcomes the metaphysical tradition to what he calls the "borderline" between Nietzsche's work and life.[4] Derrida (ibid., p. 6) stresses that Nietzsche chooses to address us "with his name and in his name," and that thus there is a link between Kierkegaard and Freud and him. In particular, Nietzsche undertakes new risks in revealing himself in *Ecce Homo*. This does not necessarily mean that Nietzsche communicates directly, and Derrida appreciates Nietzsche's use of masks to disguise himself. Derrida's point is that Nietzsche opts not to conceal or deny the inevitable blend of the personal and the theoretical that informs all writing.

In restricting himself to the theoretical realm of Nietzsche's ideas, Heidegger ignores this Nietzschean insight; thus, one could say that Derrida uses Nietzsche to turn Heidegger against himself. By doing so, Derrida is able to create distance between Heidegger and himself.[5] In a more positive vein, one could say that Derrida's attraction to Nietzsche is a vehicle for him to nurture his own philosophy. Derrida has a serious interest in psychoanalysis, which, he points out, has no counterpart in Heidegger.[6] Outside of the phenomenological tradition, Nietzsche and Freud are the two main thinkers who presage deconstruction. Those two thinkers are, in fact, often conjoined in Derrida's work. "Freud and the Scene of Writing" (Derrida 1978, p. 201) contains a pointed comment about Freud's early thinking: "We . . . already know that psychic life is neither the transparency of meaning nor the opacity of force, but the difference within the exertion of forces. As Nietzsche had already said." So Nietzsche is credited with rejecting mental transparency and with endorsing the play of forces.

Consider, too, the extended engagement with Freud in *The Post Card* (Derrida 1987). In this context, Derrida argues that, for Freud, "binding" underlies the pleasure principle. As Derrida reads Freud, binding is "the most ancient, most primitive, quasi-congenital, and therefore essential functions" of the mind (ibid., p. 393). Derrida proceeds to establish a connection between binding and "the motif of power." It turns out that for Derrida (ibid., p. 405) what lies "beyond the pleasure principle" is precisely the Nietzschean notion of will to power. By invoking Nietzsche against Freud in this way, Derrida enacts a kind of return of the repressed. Earlier in the same work, Derrida dwells on Freud's aversion to Nietzsche (and, in fact, to all philosophical speculation); he goes on to reveal Freud's debt to Nietzsche and Freud's failure to restrain himself from indulging in speculation. Thus, like Heidegger, Derrida uses Nietzsche to turn Freud against himself.

Insofar as deconstruction is a method of doing philosophy, it can be grasped through Derrida's readings of philosophers. He immerses himself in texts, offering first a dominant reading and then a reading that subverts it. The point is to leave us, quite deliberately, with undecidable interpretations. The expectation that Derrida will sort out various interpretations in order to make it clear where he stands is sure to meet with disappointment. It is as unlikely that a theory of agency will be uncovered in Derrida as it was with Nietzsche. Still, Derrida has claimed to be invested in rethinking the subject, and it is evident that he is partial to decentered agency; in particular, he emphasizes that the unconscious interferes with and limits self-fathoming.[7] "Nietzschean affirmation" is itself affirmed by Derrida (1978, p. 292) because it "determines the noncenter otherwise than as loss of center." Although Derrida identifies himself with Nietzsche's forceful affirmation of life, he does not focus much attention on affects or on our instinctual endowment.

A crucial aspect of Derrida's rethinking of agency concerns the role of others. Derrida is strongly influenced by Levinas's ideas about alterity and empathy for victims, and increasingly he has portrayed deconstruction in terms of justice, responsibility, and ethics.[8] Derrida focuses on Levinas's attempt to distance himself from the philosophical tradition because of our primordial experience of Others. As Derrida emphasizes (1978, p. 90), Levinas's description of the encounter with "the face of the Other" precedes solidarity, companionship, and even the Heideggerian idea of Mitsein. Although traditional metaphysics has tried to ignore the importance of the face of the Other, the very attempt to renounce the Other presupposes a certain kind of relation to the Other. According to Levinas, philosophy has demanded that we define ourselves as enclosed within solitude. To oppose this, Levinas offers a new ontology—or, as he ultimately claims, ethics rather than ontology.

Derrida's reading of Levinas is particularly attentive to both its contrast and its similarity to Hegel. On the one hand, Derrida suggests that no philosopher was more sensitive than Hegel to the profound impact of the Other, and he notes Levinas's affinity to Hegel.[9] On the other hand, Derrida stresses the difference in their respective notions of desire. Whereas for Hegel desire is unhappy and is determined to overcome the otherness of the Other, Levinas construes desire as opening and freedom, as allowing the (irreducible) otherness of the Other to remain. For Levinas, Hegel is a representative of the tradition in which the relation between the Same and the Other is reduced to the relation between the Same and the Same.

As I suggested in chapter 9, Hegel himself does not respect the Otherness of the Other, although this does not mean that it is impossible to imagine Hegelian agency in a way that is compatible with doing so. Still, Derrida is right to confirm this difference between Hegel and Levinas. It is a crucial aspect of Levinas's philosophy to beckon us to have "a non-allergic relation with alterity" (Levinas 1969, p. 47)—in contrast with Hegel, who documents the vicissitudes of our possible relation to others. There is a primacy to our responsiveness to others—especially to those who are victims; indeed, Levinas explicitly claims that being-for-another precedes being-for-itself ("Dialogue on Thinking-of-the-Other," in Levinas 1998, p. 202). Using psychoanalytic language, one might observe that Levinas is critical of the philosophical tradition for defending narcissism at the expense of relatedness. A qualification is necessary, however, as Levinas does not assume that our responsiveness to others is equivalent to emotional closeness. Our responsiveness to others does not negate experiences of distance and separation from others.

In "At this very moment in this work here I am" (reprinted in Bernasconi and Critchley 1991), Derrida underscores his deep kinship with Levinas. Derrida's criticisms of Levinas in that essay are more pointed and less mediated by Levinas's relationship to Husserl, Heidegger, and other thinkers than those in the earlier essay "Violence and Metaphysics" (in *Writing and Difference*). In "At this very moment in this work here I am" Derrida asserts that "ingratitude" is required in order to respond to Levinas in a way that avoids reducing the Other to the Same. In the course of the essay, Derrida illustrates this by showing the inadequacy of Levinas's portrayal of sexual difference.[10] Yet Derrida engages Levinas's work with obvious respect. Indeed, toward the conclusion of the essay Derrida exclaims: "I no longer hear your voice, I have difficulty distinguishing it from mine, from any other, your fault suddenly becomes illegible to me. Interrupt me!" It is not clear what to make of this outburst, which unabashedly acknowledges the experience of merger and the wish for the Other to respond to the Other's response. In an uncanny way, it anticipates Derrida's moving eulogy for Levinas, in which Derrida "straightforwardly" (a Levinasian term) addresses his "gratitude" (Derrida 1996b, pp. 1–10, especially p. 7).

It is plausible to wonder if the influence of Levinas's ideas about alterity and ethics might be taken to imply an intention on Derrida's part to distance himself from Nietzsche. Yet this is not the case. As I discussed in chapter 12, Derrida appears to believe that Nietzsche is empathic to others who are victims. This is quite speculative on Derrida's part, and he supplies no evidence in support of the claim. It is hard to square his position with Nietzsche's wish to endorse being-for-itself over being-for-another, narcissism over relatedness. Nietzsche would argue that it falsifies reality to imagine that we are responsive to others in the way that Levinas claims. Nietzsche might see it, in fact, as unhealthy. It is strange that Derrida chooses to overlook and not to confront Nietzsche's and Levinas's opposing views about the Other.[11]

There is also something revealing in Derrida's failure to address this issue. To chalk it up to undecidability strikes me as an evasion. Derrida is strongly influenced by Nietzsche, and his readings of Nietzsche are astute and always interesting. There is no doubt that deconstruction follows in the trajectory of Nietzschean agency. However, it is important to notice that Derrida does not concern himself with modernity, and that he has not made good on his ostensive commitment to rethink agency.[12] There are indications that Derrida affirms narcissism; for example, he suggests that a healthy kind of narcissism contributes to, rather than undermines, respect for the Other. However, as far as I am aware, this theme is not sustained in his work.[13] Indeed, one might note a rather striking contrast between Derrida and Lacan, the latter of whom pays much less attention to Nietzsche but augments our understanding of Nietzschean agency by relying on psychoanalytic theory. In turning now to describe the extension of Nietzschean agency in Lacan, I will pass over worthy questions about the influence of Lacanian psychoanalysis on deconstruction, and I will not dwell in detail on the complex relationship between Derrida and Lacan.[14]

One brief point will have to suffice as a bridge between these two thinkers, who are well aware of each other's work and who have written on the same topics (e.g., Poe's "Purloined Letter" and Freud's *Beyond the Pleasure Principle*): In Derrida's essay "For the Love of Lacan," Lacan is richly praised for his contribution to philosophical culture.[15] Derrida proceeds to recall a comment that Lacan apparently made about him to René Girard after hearing Derrida speak in Baltimore, where Lacan and Derrida met for the first time in 1966: "Yes, yes, it's good, but the difference between him and me is that he does not deal with people who are suffering." (Derrida 1998, p. 67) Derrida, huffily and a bit defensively, labels Lacan's remark "very careless." He asserts that Lacan could not have really meant suffering (as he, too, deals with suffering—appealing to the audience as sufferers); nor could he have meant to be referring to transference (as such "love"—and here we should recall the title of Derrida's piece—is not limited to the domain of analysis). Although Derrida's response to the ad hominem quality of Lacan's provocation is understandable, it quickly degenerates into a counteroffensive.

In *Resistances of Psychoanalysis*, Derrida dredges up another past wound: Lacan's "compulsive blunder" of publicly claiming that Derrida was in psychoanalysis. Derrida points out that he had already discussed the question of his psychoanalysis in *The Post Card*; he also refers us to Elisabeth Roudinesco's book *La bataille de cent ans: Historie de la psychoanalyse en France* for supplementary documentation.[16] He then assures us: "The fact that I have never been in analysis, in the institutional sense of the analytic situation, does not mean that I am not, here and there, in a way that cannot be easily toted up, analysand and analyst in my own time and in my own way." Derrida's personal revelation exemplifies undecidability: he was never in analysis, but this does not mean that he has not been analyzed. Yet a latent message can be surmised here, which might be translated to mean "No analyst is worthy of me (even Lacan), and I am capable of analyzing myself (like Freud himself)."

The tenor of this "interaction" does no honor to either thinker. Although Lacan's comment is clearly self-serving, Derrida's response, which refuses to acknowledge that the work of a clinician brings one into contact with human lives in a way that differs from other kinds of theoretical interventions, is equally dismaying. One can interpret Lacan's intention as exposing a delicate nerve in Derrida's philosophy: how un-Nietzschean it is to be preoccupied with textuality in lieu of the pursuit of how to live. Let us now turn to consider Lacan, keeping in mind his investment in thinking of himself as a clinician and not just as a theorist.[17]

13.3 Lacan: Big Other

Lacan rarely discusses Nietzsche and is less overtly influenced by him than by the group of philosophers who fall under the heading of French Nietzscheans. Not only is Nietzsche infrequently mentioned in Lacan's oeuvre, but his references to Nietzsche do not suggest great familiarity with his work.[18] This has been used by theorists as different as Žižek (1989, p. 198) and Dews (1995, p. 238) to identify Lacan as an important alternative to Nietzschean-influenced poststructuralist thinking. To be fair to them, neither Žižek nor Dews seek to grapple with Nietzsche in his own right. They are concerned with how his influence promoted a rejectionist stance against the subject—that is, with the side of Nietzsche that overlaps with his "anti-agency." This interpretation of Nietzsche's reception is potentially misleading, however, as it obscures the full complexity of Nietzsche's view about agency. Lacan's foremost predecessors are indisputably Hegel and Freud, and thus there is reason to be cautious about linking Nietzsche and Lacan directly. Nevertheless, Nietzsche offers an early version of the notion of decentered agency that ought not be reduced to signify an attack on agency. As I shall argue here, Lacan develops Nietzschean agency in a way that is innovative yet broadly consistent.[19]

The question of the subject is fundamental for Lacan. As he sees it (1981, p. 77), the aim of psychoanalysis "is historically defined by the elaboration of the notion of the subject. It poses this notion in a new way, by leading the subject back to his signifying dependence." Lacan stresses that psychoanalysis is neither a Weltanschauung nor a philosophy that strives to offer a complete explanation of the universe. It is the "notion of the subject" and its "signifying dependence" that ought to be paramount. Here Lacan is directing our attention to the unconscious (which he comprehends linguistically in terms of being the signifier), and thus away from the dominant psychoanalytic paradigm of the time: ego psychology (which celebrated the ego for its autonomy, that is, its non-dependence).

Lacan's well-known formulation that the unconscious is structured as a language draws from both Saussure's linguistics and Lévi-Strauss's notion of the symbolic order. For Lacan, nature provides "signifiers" for the unconscious, which organize human relationships. The relation between signifiers and signified is arbitrary, however, and thus cannot be apprehended (Lacan 1981, p. 20). Lacan's slogan of going "back to Freud" is intended to dramatize the limits of knowledge and to protest against what he sees as the unfortunate tendency in ego psychology to render psychoanalysis a normalizing doctrine. Lacan's version of psychoanalysis resists cultural assimilation, the consequence of which is that Freud is brought into closer proximity to Nietzsche as a thinker. Lacan affirms Freud's belief that there can be no easy access to the unconscious; indeed, he pushes this point further.

In Lacanian terms, the unconscious is "the discourse of the Other" (Lacan 1977, p. 172). This use of the term 'the Other', which has its source in phenomenology, can be distinguished from Levinas's use of the term. For Lacan, the Other has implications for our relation to ourselves, not just for our relation to others. For Levinas, the Other has a value that is precious; for Lacan, the Other represents something more disturbing and discomforting. Another difference is that for Levinas the face of the Other is crucial, whereas for Lacan our relation to the Other must be mediated by language. Yet there are similarities between Lacan and Levinas: Both mark the distinction between the Other and others. Both also play on how "what is Other" can be understood in terms of "what is not like/or the same as us," but also in terms of "what is enticing to us." This latter point is more apparent in Levinas, but it can be found in Lacan as well. Consider Lacan's interpretation of Freud's "Wo es war, soll ich werden." Opposing the conventional notion that Freud intends to recommend the replacement of the id by the ego, Lacan (ibid., pp. 33, 44) proposes his own translation: "Whatever it is, I must go there." For Lacan, the unconscious is opaque, but it possesses a power to draw us to it.

When Lacan attends to our actual relation to others, he emphasizes how fantasy complicates and interferes with the self-other relationship. He affirms intersubjectivity in the sense that language mediates all relationships. Yet in his descriptions of our relation to others there is often a specter of malevolence, which is reminiscent of Nietzsche. For example, Lacan's discussion of the biblical injunction "Love thy neighbor" highlights its impossibility in Freud's eyes and in his own. He goes on to make an interesting association about the injunction: the neighbor's jouissance is "harmful" and "malignant," and it "poses a problem for my love" (Lacan 1992, p. 187). One is hard pressed to find passages in which Lacan endorses mutual gratification in human relationships.

The most important ramification of thinking about the unconscious as an Other is that the subject is and must remain "decentered." Lacan stresses that being whole is, at best, an ideal, and a rather questionable ideal at that. He observes: "I'm not whole. Neither are you." (Lacan 1992, p. 243) Like Nietzsche, Lacan believes that conflict necessarily defines our psyches. Although Lacan offers a more elaborate account of the unconscious, both thinkers would concur that self-transparent self-knowledge eludes us. In place of the autonomous ego, Lacan insists on "radical heteronomy," just as Nietzsche emphasized the theme of multiplicity.

Lacan follows Nietzsche, too, in his suspiciousness about the ego. Like Nietzsche, Lacan suggests that the ego is a "mirage" that perpetuates "misrecognition." Yet, whereas Nietzsche makes some room for the healthy ego, Lacan sees the ego as by nature fraudulent and inflated. Although Lacan fails to present the ego in a full light, this is not necessarily proof of his rejection of the subject.[20] Lacan is dismissive of attempts to elevate and overestimate the importance of the ego—especially, for example, psychoanalytic ideas about the analysand's building his or her ego by means of the analyst's ego. Lacan is committed to a kind of psychoanalysis that is at once bolder and more humble: the hope for the analysand to "speak truly" while accepting the impossibility of attaining a unified psyche.

I will return shortly to add to Lacan's perspective about the clinical side of psychoanalysis. Let us keep in mind, too, the important question of whether Lacan would rule out the possibility of integrated agency in the sense that I have attributed to Nietzsche. In order to be able to assess this, it will be necessary first to introduce the key Lacanian concept of desire. The term sounds suspiciously Hegelian, and indeed, Lacan uses it to mean the desire for recognition. Desire expresses the sense of lack and frustration that characterizes human agency. Its nature is to be "radically torn" (Lacan 1988, p. 166). The reason for this is that, according to Lacan, desire is a doomed effort to attain jouissance—that is, libidinal merger with the mother's body.

During Lacan's "mirror stage," the infant is engaged in seeking to refind or recover itself, an effort that is fraught with narcissism. In the "symbolic stage," which follows, there is triangulation: along with love for the mother, there is the prohibition of the "law of the father." So desire must negotiate the abiding wish to be reunited with the mother together with awareness of the father's prohibition. In Hegel, desire is superseded by recognition. Lacan offers no hope for such reconciliation. Lacan's reading of Freud stresses that narcissism is inescapable, and that it pervades all object relations (Lacan 1988, p. 167). Lacan's pessimism about reconciliation is solidified in his later work with the introduction of the terms "the real" and "the object petit a." These terms indicate that there is a realm beyond signification to which access is impossible.

Lacanian desire is a reading of Hegelian desire through the lens of Kojève. Desire is always desire for the Other but is never satisfied. Indeed, Lacan (1977, pp. 286–287) makes a crucial distinction concerning the nature of desire: between "need" as a biological drive and "demand," which entails love and recognition. Need can be tied to Nietzschean agency but is less of a factor in Hegelian agency; demand can be tied to Hegelian agency but is not well conceived in Nietzschean agency. Thus, Lacanian psychoanalysis can be construed as constituting a pathway that might be wide enough to accommodate both Hegel and Nietzsche. As I read Lacan, the emphasis on the impossibility of reconciliation ultimately places him more in the Nietzschean camp. The elusiveness of jouissance in Lacan, however, may be contrasted with Nietzsche's commitment to Dionysian praxis.

As an analyst, Lacan aspires to listen to the unconscious despite the interference from conscious awareness. Although psychoanalytic treatment is designed to help the patient gain access to the unconscious, this must occur within the interstices of language. Lacan's notion of "true speaking" must be read in this light. It cannot mean that we gain access to "the Truth"; it is more a matter of become able to speak in an authentic way. Lacan tells us: "The subject begins analysis by speaking about himself without speaking to you or by speaking to you without speaking about himself. When he can speak to you about himself, the analysis will be over."[21] This dialectical formulation is both insightful and nebulous. The paradigm of the analysand speaking and the analyst listening, standard for its time, fails to take account of mutuality in the relationship.

In the 1950s, Lacan did not hesitate to use the language of authenticity to explicate psychoanalysis. Indeed, he went so far as to suggest that the subject "re-integrates his disjointed limbs, and recognizes, reaggregates his experience" (Lacan 1988, p. 247). At this early stage of his thinking, Lacan's understanding of analysis seems consistent with Nietzsche's understanding of integrated agency. Neither imagines that such integration bestows self-transparency, but both appreciate the possibility of an agent's self-coherence. For Lacan, this is an experience that happens with the Other in language. Nietzsche does not specify the Other as essential; he places higher value on the body and on affects. It is important to clarify, however, that, as Lacan makes room for the "real" (i.e., that which is beyond signification), he moves away from the possibility of integrated agency. Still, let us not ignore that for Lacan decentered agency is a premise as much as it is a conclusion.

13.4 Butler: Back to the Psyche

Butler, like Lacan, does not fit squarely into the category of French Nietzschean. Her first book, *Subjects of Desire*, centered around various French receptions of Hegel, yet the affinity to poststructuralism that emerges at the end of that book suggests an indirect connection to Nietzsche. More specifically, Butler's interest in Nietzsche follows from her interest in Foucault, and so there is justification for affirming her connection to the French Nietzscheans. Lacan does not play a major part in Butler's book, although her interest in Lacan develops over the course of her next few books. Indeed, a deepening investment in psychoanalytic thinking can be discerned in Butler's work. This does not mean that Foucault is displaced. The subtitle of one of Butler's recent essays helps to situate her position: "between Freud and Foucault." Butler is an original, psychologically minded thinker, though, who is not merely engaged in interpreting the views of other philosophers. Her work on gender and on rethinking the subject has an allegiance to poststructuralist thought, but it offers a distinctive point of view that merits careful consideration.

Butler is indebted to Lacan's notion of decentered agency. She accepts the opacity of the unconscious, and her account of the subject highlights "foreclosure" (which means that the subject can never be self-identical). In a related formulation, Butler (1993, p. 3) proposes that the subject "is constituted through the force of exclusion and abjection." 'Exclusion' and 'abjection' refer to what is cast out from sociality (ibid., p. 243, note 2). Butler's reaction to the Lacanian hypothesis that the subject is founded upon the primary repression of merger with the maternal body, though, is mixed. On the one hand, Butler appreciates the force of the prohibitive "law of the father"; on the other hand, she expresses concern about granting this notion an inviolate status. In particular, Butler criticizes Lacan's conception of the law as rigid and thus as rendering resistance impossible. Although Lacan's emphasis on the phallus as the signifier is not intended to confirm the status of women as inferior, neither does it, according to Butler, contribute to imagining an alternative perspective. Furthermore, Butler raises some questions about Lacan's adulation of the body part, and she is overtly critical of his claim that homosexuality is a response to disappointment.[22]

It is desirable, Butler argues (1990, p. 27), to substitute Foucault's notion of "regulatory practices" for Lacan's notion of "the law of the father."[23] The advantage of the former is that it is less speculative as well as less dependent on language. Even more important, it permits us to envision modification and transformation. Butler regards the subject as formed through subordination but not necessarily by the Lacanian notion of primary repression. The crucial implication of either of these perspectives is that agency never can be free of ambivalence. "Painful, dynamic and promising," writes Butler (1997a, p. 18), "this vacillation between the already-there and the yet-to-come is a crossroads that rejoins every step by which it is traversed, a reiterated ambivalence at the heart of agency." It is doubtful that Butler would imagine that solace for such ambivalence could be found in psychoanalytic treatment.

Interestingly enough, Butler turns to Nietzsche to confirm her frustration with Lacan's structuralism. She suggests that Lacanian theory might be considered as a kind of slave morality, insofar as it posits the symbolic as inaccessible by the will to power, which thus only serves to establish and reinforce powerlessness.[24] Butler implies that, ironically put, "original jouissance" comes a bit too close to being the flip side of original sin. As Butler moves on to establish her own point of view on gender, the Nietzschean-Foucaultian notion of power, a kind of floating signifier, acquires greater significance.

Butler's work has garnered considerable attention for its espousal of the notion that gender is constituted by performance. This idea was read as sounding the final death knell of cultural feminism and thereby ushering in a kind of paradigm shift for feminist philosophy. In Butler's own words (1990, p. 33): ". . . gender is a repeated stylization of the body, a set of repeated acts within a highly rigid regulatory frame that congeals over time to produce an appearance of substance, of a natural sort of being." She proceeds to contest the "compulsive heterosexuality" of our culture, which she sees as distorting the experience of heterosexuals as well as oppressing homosexuals. Butler's concern here with the construction of identity and with the violent imposition of culture on the body reveal the influence of Foucault and his Nietzsche interpretation.

In *Gender Trouble*, Butler describes her project as a "feminist genealogy of the category of women." Seeking to denaturalize "women," she regards the instability of the concept as affirming the importance of thinking in terms of gender. Butler's project challenges theories of agency that purport to be universal. It is impossible, as Butler sees it, to tease apart "identity" and gender. She wants us to confront how deeply ingrained the forces are that deny women and gays a sense of agency. But she also wishes to deconstruct the very notion of identity as arbitrary and incoherent. Butler combines a serious playfulness with an adamant refusal to compromise that is inspired by Nietzsche. However, her politics of subversion and resistance differs from Nietzsche (or Lacan), although it might be seen as a part of the venerable tradition of left Nietzscheanism.

A tension exists in Butler between the implied voluntarism of gender as performance and her emphasis on the extent to which subjects are formed through regulation and coercion. In *Bodies that Matter*, Butler acknowledges the constraints that limit the possibilities for self-invention. In particular, she maintains that performance is "reiterative and citational," not self-determining. In *The Psychic Life of Power*, Butler continues to engage this issue by dwelling on the relation between power and agency. Power does not merely act on us, since it enacts us into being. Power and agency are bidirectional; they can function in alliance, although this is not necessarily the case. Whereas in *Gender Trouble* Butler interrogates the concept of identity and asks us to consider it as a matter of practice, in *The Psychic Life of Power* she takes up the terms 'agency' and 'psyche' with renewed interest.[25]

Butler's choice to study the impact of power on the psyche signals some dissatisfaction with Foucault, as she notes that this issue was all but ignored by him.[26] Butler tentatively acknowledges her own "intellectual relation" to psychoanalysis, yet it is evident that she remains wary of it in some respects, such as its conception of gender and its indifference to the category of the social (Butler 1997a, p. 138). She does not wish to take sides between "the theory of power" (which derives from Foucault) and "the theory of the psyche" (which derives from Freud and Lacan). She traces the intersecting themes of power and the psyche back to Hegel, but Nietzsche emerges as the crucial figure with links to both the lineage of Foucault and that of psychoanalysis. Butler traces a trajectory from Hegel to Nietzsche to Freud that features the subject turning on itself and turning against itself. Thus, she is not beholden to the usual antinomy between Hegel and Nietzsche. She maintains that the subject is formed by the reproach of conscience, which in Hegelian terms means that the slave rids itself of domination of the master only to subjugate itself to itself. The capacity for self-thwarting is critical in her reading of Nietzsche as well as in Freud and in Foucault. Being a subject, Butler argues, is precisely to be subjected.

In connection with this historical perspective, Butler pursues the question of how the human subject comes into existence. She stresses that the I is formed in dependence. The very distinction between inner and outer, she asserts, is produced through social norms. Butler interprets Freud as claiming that the ego is created as a result of the melancholic response to loss. The influence of Lacan's suspiciousness of the ego can be discerned in this account. Yet Butler offers an original account of self-beratement in melancholy, claiming that it disguises anger which is first aimed at the (lost) object. Implicitly at least, this seems to be an acknowledgement of the strength of the need for connection to the object. Butler's theory passes over closeness and connection in its exclusive focus on the experience of the loss of the object. It is no slight to the experience of loss to wonder why there is no acknowledgement of attunement and rapprochement. Although Butler does not aspire to make a contribution to developmental psychology, it would be interesting for her to confront the post-Freudian psychoanalytic literature on this subject.[27]

Butler links melancholy to "negative narcissism" (that is, lowered self-esteem). In observing that negative narcissism is at the center of Freud's interpretation of narcissism, she seems to want to imply that positive narcissism has been neglected by psychoanalysis. Yet Butler never opts to elaborate on positive narcissism. Indeed, there is something confusing about her deployment of the terms 'negative narcissism' and 'positive narcissism'. On the one hand, the distinction concerns the opposite poles of what the psychoanalyst Sheldon Bach has labeled 'deflated narcissism' and 'inflated narcissism'.[28] On the other hand, the distinction approximates one between unhealthy and healthy narcissism. The problem is then that neither self-deflation nor self-inflation coincides with healthy narcissism. Butler probably would be uncomfortable using the term 'healthy narcissism'. Her preference, it seems, is to follow the "irreducible equivocation" between narcissism and sociality that she detects in Lacan (Butler 1993, p. 76).

Butler affirms the Lacanian notion that narcissism prevails even in object love. She does not declare her agreement explicitly, but Lacan is clearly in the background of her thinking about the relation between self and other. In particular, she is strongly influenced by Louis Althusser's reading of Lacan, which features the concept of "interpellation." Interpellation, according to Althusser, is the address of the Other to us that is manifested in the experience of being called by the police. Butler suggests that interpellation has the quality of being "exemplary and allegorical." This suggests that, just as in Nietzsche and Lacan, the Other has connotations that are persecutory. Although Butler refers to our "passionate attachment" to others, the scope of intersubjectivity that she contemplates is rather narrow.

The Hegelian notion of mutual recognition is as anathema for Butler, as it is for Lacan. Yet Butler's commitment to political engagement may be contrasted to Nietzsche and Lacan. It is revealing, for instance, that her response to Kristeva's semiotic theory is to worry that, in the end, it is merely aesthetic and ultimately elitist. In contrast with Derrida, Butler is not content to analyze textuality; nor would she be willing, as Lacan is, to place much stock in the clinical practice of psychoanalysis. She embraces subversion, although her "postliberatory" perspective remains steadfastly anti-utopian.

13.5 Nietzsche and His Discontents

Derrida, Lacan, and Butler extend Nietzschean agency in a psychoanalytic direction. Under the influence of Levinas, Derrida highlights our relation to others, which is clearly a problematic area in Nietzsche's own thinking. Derrida's focus on textuality, however, as Lacan implicitly suggests, evades Nietzschean questions about how to live. Furthermore, although Derrida affirms the ethical commitment of deconstruction, he pays little attention to modernity (or to postmodernity as an epoch). In spite of Derrida's good intentions, deconstruction has yet to contribute much to the rethinking of agency. Derrida is sympathetic to decentered agency and to psychoanalysis, which he construes as consistent with his emphasis on undecidability. Insofar as undecidability refers to the limits of knowledge and the contingency of life, it has validity. Insofar as undecidability might leave us without any incentive to strive to face ourselves, Derrida departs from Nietzschean and psychoanalytic agency. Derrida has not tried to address the distinction between what is undecidable and what is not, nor has he investigated what it means to decide in light of undecidability (although he does make some preliminary comment in the context of his discussion of Schmidt in *Politics of Friendship*).

Lacan offers a significant description of decentered agency. His return to Freud, which reiterates the power and the mystery of the unconscious, makes a salutary contribution to psychoanalysis. However, his insistence that the unconscious is a language is problematic, at least in the sense that, by definition, it appears to exclude pre-linguistic (and especially affective) experience. Also, Lacan's defense of the unconscious leads to an impoverished conception of the function of the ego. Conjuring the ego as defined by misrecognition overlooks the possibility that the ego learns from its failures. Moreover, Lacan's suspiciousness of the ego in no way justifies his apparent disinterest in being-for-another and in human connection.

In view of the strong affirmation of narcissism in Lacanian theory, it is especially pressing to have a better account of relatedness.

Butler offers a new and distinctive perspective on decentered agency. In bringing together Foucaultian themes of the body and power with the intrapsychic domain of psychoanalysis, she has undertaken a valuable step toward specifying the meaning of decentered agency. Butler's emphasis on gender, particularly its malleability, reminds us of the contingency that determines agency while not forsaking hope for socio-political change. There are competing tendencies in Butler: her "post-liberatory" politics concedes the limits of what can be done, but her political activism refuses compliance. Following Lacan, Butler sees decentered agency as a hedge against models of agency that rely on self-reflection. Her assessment of self-reflection as basically a matter of self-recrimination allows her to avoid direct discussion of other perspectives on self-reflection. It is one-sided, albeit self-consciously so.

Derrida, Lacan, and Butler understand decentered agency as a refutation of German Idealist assumptions about self-reflexivity, especially concerning the production of self-transparency. But is it necessary to think of decentered agency as being at odds with self-fathoming and self-reflexivity? If, as we see with Nietzsche, self-fathoming does not necessarily presuppose self-transparency, perhaps we do not have to construe decentered agency as incompatible with self-reflexivity. There is no reason to take for granted that self-fathoming must culminate with the finality that Hegel imagines.

The issue of self-reflexivity is complex and contentious. Butler explicates it with the notions of turning back and turning on oneself. On this account, self-reflexivity operates to constrain and contain us—precisely the opposite of the intuition that one finds in philosophers such as Charles Taylor (see chapter 5 above) and in psychoanalytic developmental theorists such as Peter Fonagy. Indeed, in view of Butler's interest in the question of how agency is formed, it is worth considering recent psychoanalytic research. Fonagy and Target (1996a,b) trace the emergence of self-reflexivity in 2–5 year olds as a function of the attachment between the primary caregiver and the infant.[29] Their work relies, in part, on Gergely and Watson's hypothesis (1996) that before 6–9 months infants lack the intentional stance and that the sense of agency begins to emerge through "affective mir-roring," whereby the caregiver imitates the affects of the infant in an approximate way that spurs the infant to identify and to modulate its internal states as well as creating representations of such experiences. Butler's foray into developmental theory does not portray the extent to which self-reflexivity depends on affectively charged interaction.

Decentered agency does not absolve us from reckoning with inter-subjectivity. Proponents of decentered agency tend to downplay intersubjectivity, and proponents of intersubjectivity too often disre-gard decentered agency. Of Derrida, Lacan, and Butler, Derrida is the least prone to characterizing decentered agency as antithetical to intersubjectivity. However, decentered agency has not been a focus of his work. Lacan and Butler follow Nietzsche in being skeptical about intersubjectivity, associating it with coercion and conformism. There is in Lacan and Butler a failure to acknowledge mutuality. It should be emphasized that appreciating the value of mutual experience does not presume the fixed and abiding connotations of Hegelian recognition.

As self-reflexivity is conceived psychoanalytically, it bestows more rather than less flexibility. Although the psychoanalytic literature tends not to engage the social directly, it offers a potentially rich and differentiated account of self-reflexivity: it does not exclude turning against oneself, but it countenances more turning—turning back to oneself, turning beyond oneself. Why fixate, as Butler does, on the moment of turning against oneself? Self-reflexivity promotes fluidity as much as it oppresses us. It can be argued, too, that self-reflexivity serves to develop individuation. Clearly, individuation is a concept fraught with cultural baggage, and a full elaboration will not be attempted in this context. What I mean is a sense of being unique, an appreciation of the combination of intentionality and contingency that have formed one as a human being. This does not suppose a sin-gle narrative, and it presumes no permanent unity. Individuation does not, in my account, override decentered agency.

Individuation, thus conceived, coincides with and furthers Nietzschean agency. As I conceive it, individuation also has political ramifications. It redraws the ideal of personal autonomy, in some ways limiting it (given the affirmation of decentered agency) and in some ways expanding it (given a higher standard of psychological self-inquiry). Let me go a step further. Individuation necessarily has connotations of self-indulgence and self-involvement—that is, of providing fuel for atomization. Yet this is where appealing to Hegel and to psychoanalysis is helpful: not only is self-fathoming abetted by input from others, but others reside within us. The consequence is that individuation avows one's own sense of being-for-others, one's own relatedness. Paradoxically, one could argue that individuation serves to moderate narcissism, making us less attached to our own individuality. It is perfectly consistent with this description of individuation to imagine that it enhances our engagement in the world.

Recently, Jonathan Lear (1998, p. 31) has argued that the emphasis on individuation in psychoanalysis coincides with the values of democracy. In a Butlerian vein, I would add the qualification that individuation must be distinguished from normal socialization; it ought to resist the non-democratic tendencies that exist in present-day democracies. By itself, individuation does not solve social and political problems. Yet it is a hedge against subtle and overt forms of coercion.

Hegel and Nietzsche are important forbears of the psychoanalytic notion of individuation. Hegel stresses how fundamental others are for this process; but his commitment to rationality leads him to excise contingency and to insist on an absolute telos. Nietzsche forces us to acknowledge contingency and the unexpungeability of the irrational in human life. Indeed, the centrality of affects in Nietzschean agency—a point not well conceived in the writings of Derrida, Lacan, or Butler—should not be overlooked.[30] Nietzsche associates affects with interpretation itself. Moreover, affects are a necessary component in how Nietzsche imagines integrated agency.

Epilogue

The familiar [Das Bekannte], precisely because it is familiar, is unknown [nicht erkannt].

—Hegel, *Phenomenology of Spirit*

What is familiar [Das Bekannte] is what we are used to [das Gewohnte]; and what we are used to is most difficult to "know" [erkennen]—that is, to see as a problem; that is, to see as strange, as distant, as "outside us."

—Nietzsche, *The Gay Science*[1]

It is not at all inadvertent that both Hegel and Nietzsche assert that the familiar is unknown. We have witnessed their commitment to reevaluating philosophical distinctions and assumptions, and, in particular, to working through what are ostensibly opposing concepts. In this study, I have aspired to exemplify this same commitment by engaging in a reevaluation of the opposing "concepts" of Hegel and Nietzsche. The point has not been to argue that they agree with each other; rather, in challenging the juxtaposition of Hegel and Nietzsche as opposites, I have sought to present a more complex and differentiated sense of their relationship.

I have argued that Hegel and Nietzsche share a commitment to the integral relationship between philosophy and culture, and that both look to the psychology of knowledge in order to overcome the Cartesian myth. Both are drawn to self-fathoming and to the formulation of a notion of agency designed to overcome the dissatisfaction of modern culture. Both use ancient Greek culture, especially tragedy, as a backdrop for an understanding of modern culture. Both assert that modern culture has brought about a division in self-identity, and that an empty subjectivity has ensued from this.

Hegel remains more of a philosopher than Nietzsche. Although he wants to distance himself from the Cartesian myth, the foundational myth of modern philosophy, Hegel does not reject it entirely. Indeed, he values knowledge in a way that Nietzsche does not, even in his middle period. Still, Nietzsche's view that knowledge matters insofar as it helps us to live well is not far removed from Hegel's persistent concern with satisfaction. Hegel never abandons his investment in psychological thinking; however, psychology remains implicit and somewhat buried in his philosophy. Nietzsche fully embraces psychology as a revolutionary way to free ourselves from the constraints of the philosophical tradition.

The new understanding of culture that Hegel and Nietzsche introduce for modern culture is best characterized as self-fathoming. Self-fathoming modifies the subjective emphasis of Bildung without returning to the objective emphasis of customs. It allows us to appreciate what the psychology of knowledge implies: that we must seek well-being through contextual self-understanding. Still, this does not mean that Hegel and Nietzsche see self-fathoming in exactly the same light. For Hegel, it is hard to separate the activity that self-fathoming involves from its telos in a state of absolute certainty; for Nietzsche, self-fathoming has no such goal. Self-fathoming offers a loose framework in which to highlight what Hegel and Nietzsche share; for further clarification, we must turn to their respective notions of agency.

At the core of this study is the claim that agency is a crucial concept for both Hegel and Nietzsche. Agency represents the path beyond the dissatisfaction of modern culture. Hegel and Nietzsche concur that modern culture has failed us, and they dramatize this by reference to ancient Greek culture. Coming to terms with our dissatisfaction means that we must assume the burden of specifying what satisfaction means. Of course, Hegel is more optimistic about the prospect of modern culture's altering its direction; indeed, in his later work his concern about dissatisfaction recedes into the background. Nietzsche stands more adamantly against modern culture, branding its institutions and its denizens pathological. The despair that Nietzsche expresses by the nineteenth century's end can be traced back to the alienation Hegel describes in the early part of the century. Nietzsche was never really captivated by the hope of social reconciliation on a broad scale. It is enough for him to conjure a better fate for elite individuals. Nietzsche did flirt with the notion of a "great politics," which today has frighteningly bad associations and little relevance.

Hegel's concept of recognition is intended as a solution for the problems of modern culture. It also contains a model of the kind of agency that is necessary for us to be genuinely satisfied. Hegel seems to believe that the right self-knowledge might produce or at least contribute to the creation of social reconciliation. He envisions a seamless web of recognition, involving self-recognition, the recognition of others, and social recognition. The continuing relevance of recognition thus depends on scaling back our expectations of its promise. The hope that Hegel had for social reconciliation is no longer realistic in complex, multicultural societies. Perhaps it is possible, though, to reinterpret recognition without overestimating its importance (as Hegel does) or underestimating it (as Nietzsche does).

Recognition is best conceived as a necessary but not sufficient condition for moral and social agency. It promises something unreplaceable for human beings; yet, in itself, it cannot undo economic hardship and suffering. Given that recognition represents a high standard for human beings, we should not be surprised by having to come to terms with its failure. Indeed, as Honneth demonstrates, the value of recognition must be tied to the varieties of misrecognition that exist. The lack in Nietzsche of a concept comparable to recognition means that he has no standpoint by which to analyze, much less protest, misrecognition. On the one hand, Nietzsche might not feel a need to have such a standpoint—we might think of his disdain for pity in this connection. On the other hand, he does acknowledge injustice, and he is sensitive to the need that humans have for others.

Hegel's appreciation of how constitutive others are for our own sense of identity is a superb insight that has become well documented in developmental psychology and psychoanalysis. This point of view helps us to realize that recognition is not merely a desirable option but a fundamental need that no human willingly abdicates. Here it is worth emphasizing that it is not just a matter of possessing the desire to be recognized by others; it is a matter of partaking in a mutual process. Nietzsche appreciates our need for others, but he has little to say about mutuality. Although it is hard to imagine how recognition could be mutual on an abstract, universal level, especially in mass society, mutual recognition permeates our everyday interactions. Perhaps only trauma can make a human being indifferent to its power.

Despite the problems in Nietzsche's account of human relatedness, in his approach to agency he focuses on motivation more extensively than Hegel does. Nietzsche's interest in "depth psychology" leads him to heed how much of human behavior is governed by elemental and primitive sources. His affirmation of irrationality does not indicate hostility to reason. Irrationality must grasped in its own right; it must not be construed simply as a failure of rationality. Nietzsche anticipates Freud in arguing that facing up to irrationality and giving up fantasies about its elimination produces a more honest human self-assessment than is found in philosophy. Nietzsche accepts the limits of agency. At times he seems to be infatuated with and to give license to extreme forms of conduct, but he is inconsistent on this issue. As I have argued, the fact that Nietzsche countenances "letting go" does not mean that he does not approve of self-control and an integrated notion of agency.

Hegel's approach to agency has the merit of valuing both narcissism and relatedness. His argument that they can be reconciled is hard to accept, at least in the idealized form that Hegel suggests. Perhaps Hegel's interest in narcissism has not been widely discussed because of the weight of his commitment to relatedness. Nietzsche's approach to agency tilts toward narcissism; in fact, his notion of the will to power highlights that human motivation is guided by instinctual and affective forces that cannot be eradicated. Thus, in my estimation, Nietzsche gives us a deeper and more complex picture of human motivation.

In the remainder of the epilogue, I want to draw out the implications of my study of Hegel and Nietzsche using contemporary language. Let me begin with the supposition that Hegel is a forerunner of intersubjective basis of agency, while Nietzsche is a forerunner of decentered agency. Intersubjectivity and decentering are often assumed to represent opposing perspectives on agency. Yet, as I shall argue, this depends on some of the underlying premises of each perspective. Indeed, I shall claim that intersubjectivity and decentered agency are not necessarily contradictory and are potentially even complementary.

Proponents of intersubjectivity stress that intersubjective interaction contributes to the development of subjectivity. It is not clear, however, how to understand the nature of this subjectivity. Is subjectivity is really just a product of intersubjective interaction, or must we account for its existence before intersubjective interaction? As a preliminary response, I would observe that it is perfectly coherent to maintain that, whereas the trajectory of subjectivity is altered by intersubjectivity, subjectivity has an independent existence—one that is not solely dependent on intersubjectivity. Most forms of the intersubjective model of agency have a difficult time, for example, accounting for aggression, especially if we do not conceive of it as deriving entirely from environmental frustration. A related issue is whether intersubjectivity cultivates a unified and transparent kind of self-knowledge. Should we suppose that others offer us an objective self-reflection that completes our understanding of ourselves? Is it possible to construe the role of others as contributing to our self-knowledge—without further assumptions about unity and transparency?

Proponents of decentered agency reject the possibility of a unified and transparent kind of self-knowledge. Insofar as our minds have multiple components (especially if we include the unconscious as one of these components), it will always be impossible to attain perfect self-knowledge. Decentered agency leads us to acknowledge the limits of agency, and the force of contingency, without necessarily negating the intelligibility of agency. It is possible to distinguish two distinct tendencies in the way decentered agency is portrayed.

The first way of conceiving of decentered agency emphasizes its self-defeating implications. 'Decentering', in this sense, means that there is a sheer impossibility in our efforts to know ourselves. The wish for something like integration results in a vicious circle. According to this perspective, we misunderstand ourselves in a compulsory way. In the powerful words of Julia Kristeva (1991, p. 1), the foreigner "lives within us." In thinking about this sense of decentering, we find ourselves at the bounds of agency as an intelligible concept.

There is another sense of decentering from which quite different conclusions can be drawn. Decentering might entail that we elude ourselves, but it does not have to mean that we are locked into a repetitive cycle of trying and failing. In light of the impossibility of unity and self-transparency, we have to devise new ways to imagine integration. The underlying intuition here, in comparison to the first sense of decentering, is that we can adjust and create better ways to cope with our limitations. Misunderstanding need not breed more misunderstanding; we can learn from it. A stronger libidinal attachment to life is evident in the second sense. Despite some flirtation with the first sense, Nietzsche is an advocate of the second sense, especially because it is life-affirming and open to the "superfluity" of life.

An inherent problem for all proponents of decentered agency is how to regard socialization. Is it coercive and violent, or is it a mixed blessing that makes life difficult but also has some advantages? All proponents of decentered agency will be at least somewhat wary of how socialization is imposed. Thus, there will be an attraction to the liminal realm as a space not determined by extrinsic values. Proponents of intersubjective agency, on the other hand, are less likely to associate socialization with either coercion or violence. Thus, the issue of socialization stands at the crux of what separates proponents of decentered agency from proponents of intersubjective agency.

If one regards self-knowledge as self-defeating and socialization as coercive and violent, mediating between intersubjectivity and decentering will not be a serious option. The possibility of mediation hinges on thinking about decentering and intersubjectivity in terms of the kind of agency that no longer strives for unity and self-transparency. It also depends on understanding socialization as a mixed blessing, and perhaps as something beneficial. As I suggested toward the end of chapter 13, we can look to psychoanalysis to find a model in which intersubjectivity and decentered agency are not doomed to be conflictual.

Recall in this connection my psychoanalysis-influenced account of recognition in chapter 9, which emphasized an affective aspect of this relation. Recall also, from chapters 12 and 13, Butler's account of self-reflexivity as a turning against oneself—a kind of self-reproach. Butler construes self-reflexivity as a product of the wish to look at oneself from outside oneself in a rational and objective way. I would like to suggest that things look differently if we see affects and affect regulation as integrally related to the sense of agency. Affects are consistent with decentering in that they occur without our choice and in that they have a basis in biological responses. Yet it is certainly possible to be aware of one's affects and to regulate them to be in accordance with one's desires. Indeed, affects do not occur only in unmediated forms; they are strongly influenced by social and cultural values. Indeed, affects play an important role in negotiating our relationship with others. More often than not, affective experience has an intersubjective dimension.

In bringing affective experience to bear on agency, a debt to Nietzsche is obvious. As I emphasized in discussing integrated agency, Nietzsche values affects as an indispensable component. It is less clear that Hegel would be sympathetic to this perspective; however, we should not overlook his opposition to the Kantian demand to distance ourselves from our affects. Hegel can be read as defending an expanded idea of rational agency that is meant to be inclusive of affects. Although Nietzsche would not find Hegel's view appealing, he might be prepared to recognize it as a step in the right direction. Hegel anticipates Nietzsche, even though Nietzsche embarks on a new direction that is not entirely new.

Appendix

The importance of the theme of recognition seems to be confirmed by its place in the structure of the *Philosophy of Spirit*, which is as follows:

A	Consciousness	1
		2
		3
B	Self-Consciousness	4
C/AA	Reason	5
BB	Geist	6
CC	Religion	7
DD	Absolute Knowing	8

(The double letters are not Hegel's own but are generally accepted as the ordering for the second half. The divisions follow Hegel's own in the *Encyclopedia*. It is not clear why Hegel gave letters to the first half and numbers to the whole work.)

The first significant discussion of recognition is in the fourth chapter, "Self-Consciousness," which (if one considers the last chapter a summary of the first seven) is the midpoint of the book. However, the fourth chapter can also be seen as the midpoint of the first half of the work, since it falls between A and C. The latter perspective is better in that the discussion of recognition concerns the human as (single) individual.

The midpoint of the work as a whole, on the basis of the letter divisions, is Reason (C/AA). This makes sense in that Reason represents the transition from the human as (single) individual to the human as Geist (universal individual). The discusssion of recognition takes place, in fact, in the middle subsection (b) of the middle section (B).

The final and most extensive discussion of recognition occurs at the midpoint of the second half of the work: in Geist (BB), between AA and CC. It can be argued that this chapter forms the midpoint of the entire work. Using the divisions of Hegel's later system, Lukàcs (1976) breaks down the PhS into Subjective Geist (1–5), Objective Geist (6), and Absolute Geist (7–8). Lukàcs (ibid., p. 263) calls the middle subsection (II) of the middle section (B) in Geist "the most important chapter in the *Phenomenology*."

To summarize: Recognition is discussed at the midpoint of the PhS from three separate perspectives:

in Self-Consciousness: 1   2   3   ④   5   6   7   (8)

in Reason: A   B   C/AA   BB   CC   (DD)
                       B
                       b

in Geist: 1   2   3   4   5   6   7   8
                                     B
                                     II

It is also plausible to regard these three midpoints as the midpoints, respectively, of the first half, the work as a whole, and the second half:

in Self-Consciousness: A   ⓑ   C/AA   BB   CC   (DD)

in Reason: A   B   (C/AA)   BB   CC   (DD)

in Geist: A   B   CC/AA   (BB)   CC   (DD)

Regardless of which perspective one adopts, the significant discussions of recognition lie at the very heart of the work:

A (B   C/AA   BB)   CC   (DD)

1   2   3   (4   5   6)   7   (8)

Discussion of recognition occurs throughout the work and at crucial junctures. Caution must be used, though, in interpreting the work by examining its structure.

Notes

Introduction

1. One could strengthen this intuition by supplementing it with a Hegel/Marx axis and a Nietzsche/Heidegger axis, as do Ferry and Renault (1990). The distinction then would be especially apt as a description of the generational politics of French philosophy. Foucault, Derrida, and Deleuze, all of whom were influenced by Nietzsche, rebelled against the Kojève-influenced generation of philosophers (especially Jean Hyppolite, their teacher), who were deeply influenced by Hegel. Yet numerous questions would still abound. What about the importance of Husserl? And what about Hegel's influence on Derrida, not to mention his influence on Heidegger?

2. The distinction between a Hegel/Marx axis and a Nietzsche/Heidegger axis would have to address the influence of Nietzsche and Heidegger on the Frankfurt School. Even Habermas went through a phase of being influenced by Heidegger. (For a discussion of the Frankfurt School's responses to Heidegger, see McCarthy 1991, pp. 83–96.)

3. A voluminous literature concerning the legacy of the Enlightenment has grown out of the work of Habermas and his students and colleagues. See, e.g., Honneth et al. 1992a and 1992b. Nietzsche is too often read as exclusively a figure of the counter-Enlightenment. One must assess Nietzsche's view in light of a passage like the following (from a section of *Daybreak* titled "German Hostility to the Enlightenment"): "The Enlightenment we must now carry further forward [weiterzuführen]: let us not worry about the 'great revolution' and the 'great reaction' against it which have taken place—they are no more than the sporting of waves in comparison with the truly great flood which bears us along!" (D #197). Danto (1993, p. 136) has argued that Nietzsche is a part of the Enlightenment project, "agreeing in large measure with its logic, but dismissing the complacency of regarding homo sapiens europanesis as the apex."

4. The translation here amends Miller's "the strenuous effort of the Notion" (die Anstrengung des Begriffs).

5. Löwith (1967, p. vi) speaks of Hegel's "consummation" and Nietzsche's "new beginning."

6. Kaufmann (1968) finds a parallel between Hegel and Nietzsche in their "dialectical monism." Breazeale (1975), in a much more complex assessment, compares Hegel and Nietzsche in the framework of "the crisis of modern thought," ultimately viewing them as "allies in the struggle against metaphysical, moral and epistemological dualism" (pp. 147, 162). Breazeale's article thoroughly explores Nietzsche's references to Hegel; it also contains the best historical survey of writing on the topic of the relationship between Hegel and Nietzsche. Houlgate (1986) focuses on Hegel's and Nietzsche's critiques of metaphysics and argues that the key to understanding the relationship between the two thinkers is to be found in their discussions of Greek tragedy. In some ways, Houlgate's view comes closest to my own; in his conclusion, he asserts that "Hegel and Nietzsche are actually allies against metaphysical abstraction and against the fragmented weakness and 'decadence' of the modern age" (p. 220).

7. For a good discussion of Hegel's and Nietzsche's influence on Bataille's thinking, see Stoekl 1992, pp. 261–301.

8. Butler (1997a, pp. 24, 32) draws attention to some parallels between Hegel and Nietzsche concerning the self-thwarting of "unhappy unconsciousness" and "slave morality" and also concerning how the subject is defined by turning inward and turning against itself. Butler emphasizes the theme of self-thwarting to the exclusion of what I term "self-fathoming." Other scholars have made scattered comments about the relationship between Hegel and Nietzsche that are deserving of notice here. Rosen (1989, p. 204) declares that "those who insist upon a sharp juxtaposition between Hegel and Nietzsche have understood neither one nor the other." White (1987, p. 40) argues that "the conflict between Nietzsche and Hegel has never, I believe, been adequately analyzed, much less resolved." Rorty (1989, p. 79) observes in passing that Hegel transforms philosophy into a literary genre by offering ironic redescriptions of the past, and that Nietzsche then fulfills that ideal: "Nietzsche may have been the first philosopher to do consciously what Hegel had done unconsciously." (ibid., p. 103)

Chapter 1

1. My proposal about the Cartesian myth is offered protreptically; it is a difficult claim to substantiate. All philosophers have imbibed the ideal, whether they agree with it or whether they dismiss it. As Taylor (1995, p. viii) points out, "loud denunciations of Descartes are not of themselves a sign of a writer's having escaped Descartes." In invoking the idea of a myth, my intention is not to debunk philosophy or to be cynical about valid argument as a worthy standard in philosophy. The infamous charge against philosophy as "logocentric" obscures how mythos and logos have coexisted in the history of philosophy. The idea of a myth does suggest that there are interesting narrative features that govern our understanding of the tradition; it is also conveys the larger-than-life quality of Cartesian philosophy. Nevertheless, one ought to remain vigilant about tensions between Descartes's actual views and how they have come to be represented.

2. Feminist philosophers have debated whether there is something essentially male about Cartesianism. Bordo (1987) has argued that the glorification of reason and the alienation from the body is typical of men. Lloyd (1993) offers a more cautious thesis that Cartesianism has reinforced a sexist distinction between male/reason vs. female/emotions, even if this was not part of Descartes's intention. Atherton (1993) challenges Bordo and Lloyd by emphasizing that Cartesianism served to establish a universal standard in the seventeenth century, which, in fact, was a favorable thing for women philosophers. Though the allegedly progressive, historical outcome of

Cartesian philosophy is important to appreciate, it does not replace the question of whether the "culture of philosophy" led by the Cartesian myth affirms and resonates more for men than for women.

3. In volume 3 of LHP, Hegel refers to Descartes as "a bold spirit" [ein Heros] whose influence on "the culture of philosophy [die Bildung der Philosophie] cannot be sufficiently expressed" (p. 221). Hegel's own identification with Descartes (and the Cartesian myth) is revealed in the image of an epic journey: "Here, we may say, we are at home, and like the mariner after a long voyage in a tempestuous sea, we may now hail the sight of land." (p. 217) Derrida (1989, p. 26) makes an interesting inference about this passage: "Did not Hegel hail Descartes as the Christopher Columbus of philosophical modernity?" I shall say more about Hegel's response to the Cartesian myth later in the chapter.

4. In some respects, analytic philosophy has been quite critical of the Cartesian myth (e.g., the linguistic turn in Wittgenstein; ordinary-language philosophy). It is revealing, though, that even when analytic philosophy turned to study ordinary language, thus in a sense embracing the social realm, it did not reflect on its own particularity.

5. For an investigation into the history of analytic philosophy, see Hylton 1990. For an excellent discussion of this and related issues, see pp. 59–76 of Dews 1995.

6. For a discussion of this issue, see Jurist 1992.

7. Dasenbrock (1989, p. 4 and note 5) traces the recent prominence of Hegel and Nietzsche in the United States back to the influence of deconstruction in literary theory. This is only partly accurate. As I see it, the influence of Deconstructionism has diminished the importance of Hegel, serious interest in whom had been developing since the 1960s in connection with Marx and the Frankfurt School. It ought to be acknowledged, though, that Derrida (1981b, pp. 77–78) has stressed the importance of continuing to read Hegel: "We will never be finished with the reading or rereading of Hegel, and, in a certain way, I do nothing other than attempt to explain myself on this point." In an interview (Ross 1988, p. 275), Cornel West has observed that the "rise" of Nietzsche and the "fall" of Hegel is unfortunate precisely because the American context does not have a background in Marxist culture, whereas the French context does.

8. Appiah (1992–93) makes an interesting point in this connection: that it is false to suppose that claims about the relationship between philosophy and culture would have to mean, for example, that one ought somehow to be able to discern the influence of the Kennedy years on W. V. O. Quine's *Word and Object* (published in 1962). The point is not that there are no underlying cultural commitments in Quine's work; rather, it is that specifying the influence of culture in every work may not be worthwhile. As I see it, raising this issue may be desirable, as it may allow the emergence of genuine philosophical concerns that ought not be relegated to sociology or metaphilosophy.

9. This is my translation. In the Miller translation of PhS, it is "the earnestness of life in its concrete richness."

10. Forster (1989, p. 103) emphasizes that Hegel's reluctance to define epistemology in terms of first-person experience is, in part, a reflection of his sympathy with ancient skepticism, which is not mainly concerned with knowledge of the external world and which, in general, has a more positive bent than modern skepticism.

11. This offers quite a contrast to Hegel's earliest perspective (e.g., in "The Oldest Program Towards a System in German Idealism"), where the philosopher is depicted as a poet who should render ideas in aesthetic and mythological form in order to communicate effectively and thereby stimulate cultural change.

12. Lukàcs (1976, p. 262) aptly notes that "for Hegel philosophy was always connected intimately with the general, socio-political and cultural problems of the present."

13. Among the last words Hegel put to paper were these, from Cicero's *Tusculan Disputations* (book II, chapter I), which he meant to add to the revised version of the *Logic*: "Est enim philosophia paucis contenta judicibus, multitudem consulto ipsa fugiens, eique suspecta et invisa." [For philosophy is content with few judges. With fixed purpose it avoids, for its part, the multitude, which in turn views it as an object of suspicion and dislike.] (*Hegel: The Letters*, p. 551). Although Hegel's view of philosophy eventually became more elitist, in 1809 he responded to a student's complaint about the lack of interest in German philosophy in Holland that "nowhere does [philosophy] have such value for more than a few" (ibid., p. 588).

14. The letter to Zellman was written on January 23, 1807. Hegel delivered part of the manuscript of PhS in September 1806, part in October 1806, and the preface in January 1807. The English translation is mine; the letter appears in a slightly different form on p. 122 of *Hegel: The Letters*.

15. Several of Hegel's letters also express his sense that philosophy requires solitary pursuit. For example, in a letter from 1829, Hegel observed: "However much someone who has been long occupied by himself with his thinking may have found satisfaction [Befriedigung] for himself in its course, to encounter assent in the minds of others is just as delightful a confirmation and support." (*Hegel: The Letters*, p. 542).

16. The emphasis here is on Hegel's philosophy as featuring becoming and development, rather than being. In WP #253, Nietzsche suggests that Hegel's philosophy is one of strength because it presents "the self-revealing and self-realizing ideal."

17. See *Selected Letters of Friedrich Nietzsche*, #9: "Of the more recent philosophers, I have studied Kant and Schopenhauer with especial predilection." Although this letter dates from 1871, I would question the validity of Deleuze's assumption (1983, p. 162) that "we have every reason to suppose that Nietzsche had a profound knowledge of the Hegelian movement, from Hegel to Stirner." Indeed, it is even possible to question how seriously Nietzsche read Kant. As Hamacher (1990, pp. 29–30) points out, "it is uncertain how far Nietzsche's knowledge of Kant extended beyond the distortions of Schopenhauer and Kuno Fischer or beyond his study of the second part of the *Critique of Judgement*, which he subjected to a precise analysis in 1868, in connection with a planned dissertation to be titled *Teleology Since Kant*." Pippin (1991a, p. 82 and note 3) cites this passage from Hamacher and concurs with it.

18. For example, in CW #10 Nietzsche observes that Hegel is not a German taste but a European one. He credits Hegel's cosmopolitan sensibility in D #193, linking it to the French notion of esprit. In the same passage, however, Nietzsche criticizes Hegel's bad style.

19. In UM #7, Nietzsche lauds Schopenhauer, projecting his fame as exceeding Hegel's. In GM (III #7), Nietzsche refers to Hegel as one of Schopenhauer's enemies (along with women, sensuality, the whole will to existence, and persistence) in the con-

text of elaborating on the latter's commitment to the ascetic ideal. In BGE #204, Nietzsche is openly critical of Schopenhauer, noting "his unintelligent wrath against Hegel." In BGE #252, Nietzsche offers the assessment of Hegel and Schopenhauer as "two hostile brothers geniuses who strove apart toward opposite poles of the German spirit and in the process wronged each other as only brothers wrong each other." Although it is significant that Nietzsche acknowledges Hegel as being wronged by Schopenhauer as well as that he was a genius, we can also see the extent to which Nietzsche's concern with Hegel is a side effect of his attitude toward Schopenhauer. Nietzsche begins WP #382 being critical of Schopenhauer, then brushes Kant aside as "absolutely antihistorical. . . and a moral fanatic" and cryptically asserts: "I need a critique of the *saint*—Hegel's value. 'Passion.'" It is difficult to say what Nietzsche has in mind here. Unfortunately, the rest of the passage does not make Nietzsche's point intelligible. He moves on immediately to criticize the "shopkeeper's philosophy of Mr. Spencer" and then to complain about the pervasiveness of morality in philosophy. He seems to include Hegel in the latter complaint, despite his apparent recognition of Hegel's "value."

20. See, e.g., TI, "What the Germans Lack," #4.

21. When Nietzsche proclaims in the preface to GM that "we are unknown to ourselves, we men of knowledge" and then concludes "we are not 'men of knowledge' with respect to ourselves," he is holding out the option to conjoin our ideas and our lives.

22. See also SW 1, p. 731.

23. As late as the preface to the second edition of GS, Nietzsche speaks of the "philosopher physician." I accept the standard division of Nietzsche's writing into three periods, the first beginning with BT, the second with HAH, and the third period with Z. It is clear, for example, that in the middle period Nietzsche is open to philosophy in a way that he was not in BT. I find it difficult to take a position on the controversy about the use of the *Nachlass*. Obviously, some caution must be exercised in its use. The reason why I shall not take a firm position on its use is that, though the *Nachlass* contains some ideas that Nietzsche later published, it also contains some ideas that he contemplated and rejected. As with interpreting Nietzsche in general, it is wrong to place too much weight on single statements; often other statements will contradict and/or add texture to the first one.

24. In HAH I, Nietzsche proclaims that the free spirit "hates all habituation and rules, everything enduring and definitive" (#427), associates the free spirit with moderation (#464), and claims that "justice as the only goddess we [i.e., free spirits] recognize [anerkennen] over us" (#637).

25. In BGE #211, Nietzsche contrasts the creation of one's own values to philosophers (e.g. Hegel) who are obsessive about the past.

26. In this connection, see WP #421 (where Nietzsche emphasizes that the philosopher must have more than learning) and BGE #39 (where he emphasizes that the philosopher does not just write books).

27. See also SW 1, p. 743.

28. In BGE #211, Nietzsche refers to the "noble model of Kant and Hegel" as "philosophical laborers" in the context of urging philosophers to be more creative.

Nietzsche identifies with philosophers of the future, but he is not dismissive about these predecessors, observing that they have carried out "preliminary labor." In a less flattering light, Nietzsche refers to German philosophers as "'unconscious' counter-feiters," adding that "Fichte, Schelling, Schopenhauer, Hegel, and Schleiermacher deserve this epithet as well as Kant and Leibniz" (EH, on CW, #3). For praise of play, see BGE #94 and EH, "Why I Am So Clever," #10.

29. Nietzsche repeatedly describes himself as a hermit in his letters. See *Selected Letters*, nos. 62, 84, 99, 107, 145, and 153.

30. Pippin (1997) makes a similar point and then offers an insightful comparison of Nietzsche's use of 'we' to Hegel's.

31. Although Foucault mentions Vico, he distinguishes Kant's interest in the present from Vico's future-oriented concern with the subject as immersed in history and culture. Foucault's comments on Vico are found in "What Is Enlightenment?" (Foucault 1997, p. 305). For an in-depth discussion of Vico's criticism of Descartes, see Berlin 1976. Berlin (ibid., p. 87) maintains that Vico challenges Descartes for "leaving out the richest and most important part of human experience—everything that is not in the realm of natural science—daily life, history, human laws and institutions, the modes of human self-expression."

32. This view has been argued recently by DeSousa (1987) and by Stocker (1996).

33. Earlier (BGE #2), Nietzsche had discussed the many unquestioned assumptions that philosophers make, citing the instance of failing to doubt—despite having vowed "*de omnibus dubitandum.*" In an unpublished notebook entry from 1885, Nietzsche ironically muses: "Supposing God is still a deceiver, in spite of Descartes?" (SW 11, p. 442). In WP #436 (1885–86), Nietzsche stresses that acknowledging the veracity of God as the guarantor of our knowledge enables Descartes to smuggle a moral preju-dice into his defense of rationality. Thus, Nietzsche challenges both Descartes's retreat from life and his allegiance to morality and religion.

34. Parkes (1994) points to an interesting passage from the *Nachlass* (SW 9, p. 466) in which Nietzsche asserts that the impersonal is simply a weakened version of the per-sonal but then moves on to acknowledge that an impersonal view might be desirable in cases in which passion clouds our vision (ibid., p. 303). Although this implies that it is not impossible to attain an impersonal view, it falls short of being a genuine appreciation of the impersonal.

35. Pinkard (1994, p. 282) argues that Hegel values both the impersonal and the per-sonal, distinguishing between the rights of the "person" in social space from the self-reflection of the "subject." His argument suggests that Hegel defends the personal as an unspecified domain, not that he rejects its value altogether. Thus, we must be cau-tious not to assume that Hegel sees philosophy as concerned with the impersonal to the exclusion of the personal.

36. Hegel values the ideal of "disengagement"—a term Taylor (1989) has used to describe the emphasis on self-objectivation, whereby one uses a first-person perspec-tive to overcome its relation to one's own body and the world. Disengagement is a means to the end of re-engagement in Hegel; in Descartes it comes closer to being an end in itself.

37. Nietzsche's acceptance of subjectivity is at the center of Heidegger's presentation of Nietzsche's relation to Descartes and the metaphysical tradition (*Nietzsche*, volume 4, pp. 123–138). Heidegger rightly claims that Nietzsche invokes psychology in the form of the will to power against Descartes. In my opinion, however, Heidegger underestimates the extent to which the postulation of a link between philosophy and culture allows Nietzsche to distance himself from the Cartesian myth.

38. Nietzsche declares that psychology ought to be appreciated as "the queen of the sciences, for whose service and preparation the other sciences exist" and emphasizes that "psychology is now again the path to fundamental problems" (BGE #23). This might suggest that, according to Nietzsche, psychology supplants philosophy. However, in other contexts he proposes that psychologists are captivated by the question of the relationship between "health and philosophy" (GS, preface to second edition and #2). In other words, psychology might alter how we think about philosophy, rather than replacing it.

39. For Hegel, psychology is defined by its subjective stance; it is limited, and hence inferior to philosophy, in forsaking the objective realm. According to the organization of PM, Hegel delineates three parts to the "Subjective Mind": anthropology, phenomenology, and psychology. Psychology thus represents the last and most developed moment of the subjective mind. In PM #440, Hegel offers the definition of psychology as "the faculties or general modes of mental activity *qua* mental." For a discussion of what Hegel means by 'psychology', see Christensen 1968 and Leary 1980. Leary's article documents the relatively unknown history of psychologists who were influenced by Hegel. For a more recent exploration of related issues, see Berthold-Bond 1995.

Chapter 2

1. For an excellent discussion of Nietzsche's interest in culture, see Blondel 1991. Blondel claims that "the problem of culture in Nietzsche has been underestimated, and yet it forms the origin and centre of his thought" (p. 51). He also points to parallels between Hegel and Nietzsche (pp. 46; 61) but does not develop this theme. Bataille (1992, p. 171) notes that "in Nietzsche's mind everything is subordinated to culture."

2. Of course, conceiving of culture in terms of internal coherence has come under criticism in contemporary anthropology. For a discussion of changes in the use of the concept by anthropologists, see W. Sewell, "The Concept(s) of Culture," in Bonnell and Hunt 1999. For a helpful review of how the concept of culture has been used in general, see Eagleton 2000.

3. That Hegel replaces the concept of culture with Geist is emphasized in Kroeber and Kluckhohn 1952 (pp. 42–43) and in Kopp 1974 (p. 110).

4. The anthropological sense is commonly traced back to Edward Tylor. Kroeber and Kluckhohn (1952) suggest that Tylor's perspective has its origins in the work of Gustav Klemm. Kroeber and Kluckhohn suggest wrongly, I think, that Nietzsche was in the tradition of the anthropological sense of culture. As will become evident, Nietzsche is hardly reluctant to conceive of culture evaluatively.

5. The word 'culture' is derived from the Latin 'coloere' (meaning plowing) and 'cultura' (agriculture) and derives from the Greek 'boukólos' (herdsman). See Brunkhorst

1992, pp. 145–146. Culture is thus specifically tied to the overcoming of nature. Gadamer suggests that this represents a contrast to 'paidea', the Greek word for culture (Brunkhorst 1992, p. 175). Kopp (1974, p. 3) argues that the Latin 'cultura' has multiple meanings, including connotations of "Pflege, Aufzucht, and Fürsorge."

6. See, e.g., PM #485.

7. See also LPH, p. 267.

8. PR #151, Zusatz: "Custom is what right and morality have not reached, namely spirit."

9. See also D #544.

10. Nietzsche makes a similar point in UDHL #10, where culture is presented as "new and improved physis," and also in SE #1, where culture as described as "the perfecting of nature." In SE #3, he also articulates the longing for a genuine culture in terms of a "transformed physis."

11. An interesting parallel can be made between Nietzsche and Callicles in Plato's *Gorgias* (483): that nomos (custom) exists to protect the weak, whereas physis is the law of the strong.

12. On Rousseau see WP #99. On the Stoics see BGE #9.

13. In PR (#153 Zusatz), Hegel anticipates Nietzsche in criticizing the naiveté of a return to nature as Rousseau imagined it.

14. Pöggeler (1980) offers a helpful discussion of Hegel's long-standing interest in secondary education as well as in university education.

15. For comparisons of PhS to Bildungsroman, see Royce 1919 (p. 147ff.) and Kaufmann 1966 (p. 143). Abrams (1971) comments on Royce and proposes "Bildungsbiographie" as a description of PhS. As I will try to demonstrate, there are problems with this assumption: PhS is better conceived as Geist's autobiography—ghost-written by Hegel.

16. Kelly (1969, p. 343) argues that the "main problem of the *Phenomenology* is not history, but Bildung." Kelly also maintains that Hegel's interest in Bildung constitutes an interest in psychology, since the work presents "a series of attitudes or postures related to the process of education." It is one of the aims of this chapter to develop why Bildung and psychology are linked.

17. It is interesting to ponder what to make of Hegel's association of Bildung with eighteenth-century French culture—it seems at once to highlight a culture in its particularity (perhaps with an implicit contrast to his own culture in mind) and to claim this era as illustrative of a larger mentality. For a discussion on this point that comes down on the side of the latter view—that Hegel was using eighteenth-century France merely as an example, see van Dooren 1973.

18. Pöggeler (1980) points out that, whereas alienation has a negative connotation in the Frankfurt-Schriften, it becomes integral to Bildung in PhS.

19. There is a good discussion of this point in Smith 1988. Smith offers an extensive review of Hegel's views of Bildung, and I learned a great deal from reading his book.

Although I do not fully agree with Smith's emphasis on the influence of rhetoric on Hegel's thinking, his attention to the shifting views of Hegel's use of 'Bildung' and his suggestion that Hegel's own Bildung is embodied in his views of the concept are illuminating. Though Hegel exhibits tolerance toward Jews, he is not above making vulgar comments—e.g., in a letter to a friend dated December 22, 1810, he writes: "But to show that I am not of Jewish blood I am sending you a few gingerbreads, and wish you happy holidays as well" (*Hegel: The Letters*, p. 231). For an extensive discussion of Hegel's and Nietzsche's attitudes toward the Jews, see Yovel 1998.

20. In PM #395 (Zusatz), Hegel specifically describes Bildung in terms of the reshaping of the soul in a way that expunges the personal and contingent.

21. Hegel does not abandon the idea of practical Bildung in PR #197, but he construes it differently—in terms of work rather than health.

22. See also RH, p. 63.

23. See also Lauer 1993, pp. 213–223. In the context of arguing for the close connection between Bildung and religion, Lauer rightly suggests that Bildung is the key concept for understanding the movement of Geist.

24. Here Nietzsche uses 'Erziehung' and 'Bildung' interchangeably.

25. In claiming that Schopenhauer is the last German he reveres, Nietzsche virtually contradicts himself.

26. In EH, "Why I Am So Clever," #3, Nietzsche declares "I believe only in French culture."

27. Hegel is quite critical of play in connection with child development (see PM #396 Zusatz). He emphasizes discipline, and, in particular, the necessity of opposing the self-will of the child.

28. See TI, "Skirmishes of an Untimely Man," #47; see also Blondel 1991, pp. 201–238.

29. See also GS #55.

30. As I noted in chapter 1, Nietzsche cherished the image of the philosopher as a hermit.

31. In GS #109 Nietzsche emphasizes that eternal chaos and disorder define the universe.

32. The passage is worth quoting at some length: "This romantic fiction is chivalry become serious again with a real subject-matter. The contingency of external existence has been transformed into a firm and secure order of civil society and the state, so that police, law-courts, the army, political government replace the chimerical ends which the knights errant set before themselves. Thereby the knight-errantry of the heroes as they act in more modern romances is also altered. As individuals with their subjective ends of love, honour, and ambition, or with their ideals of world-reform, they stand opposed to this substantial order and the prose of actuality which puts difficulties in their way on all sides. Therefore, in this opposition, subjective wishes and demands are screwed up to immeasurable heights; for each man finds before him and

enchanted and quite alien world which he must fight because it obstructs him and in its inflexible firmness does not give way to his passions but interposes as a hindrance the will of a father or an aunt and civil relationships, etc. Young people especially are these modern knights who must force their way through the course of the world which realizes itself instead of their ideals, and they regard it as a misfortune that there is any family, civil society, state, laws, professional business, etc., because these substantive relations of life with their barriers cruelly oppose the ideals and the infinite rights of the heart. Now the thing is to breach the order of things, to change the world, to improve it, or at least in spite of it to carve out of it a heaven upon Earth: to seek for the ideal girl, find her, win her away from her wicked relations or other discordant ties, and carry her off in defiance. But in the modern world these fights are nothing more than 'apprenticeship', the education [Erziehung] of the individual into the realities of the present, and thereby they acquire their true significance. For the end of such apprenticeship consists in this, that the subject sows his wild oats, builds himself with his wishes and opinions into harmony with subsisting relationships and their rationality, enters the concatenation of the world, and acquires for himself an appropriate attitude toward it. However much he may have quarreled with the world, or been pushed about in it, in most cases at last he gets his girl and some sort of position, marries her and becomes as good a Philistine as others." (*Hegel's Aesthetics*, volume I, pp. 592–593) This passage clearly must be taken into account in ascribing the genre of Bildungsroman to PhS. Regardless of Nietzsche's claim to originality because of his invention of the term 'Bildungsphilister', Hegel anticipates the notion.

33. McGinn (1975) emphasizes this point. In BT, Nietzsche combines the terms 'Bildung' and 'Geist'.

34. Warren emphasizes this point (1987, p. 262, note 1). However, it should be noted that Nietzsche's sense of breeding implies a more biologistic reading.

35. There are passages where Nietzsche unambiguously warns against valorizing the will—e.g., D #124: "We laugh at him who steps out of his room / at the moment when the sun steps out of its / room, and then says: 'I will that the sun / shall rise'; and at him who cannot stop a / wheel, and says 'I will that it shall not / roll'; and at him who is thrown down in / wrestling, and says: 'here I lie, but I will / lie here!' But, all laughter aside, are we / ourselves ever acting any differently whenever / we employ the expression: 'I will'?" Thus, I am not implying that Nietzsche is endorsing the Hegelian notion of the subject. I will explore Nietzsche's view of the will more thoroughly in chapter 11.

36. Heidegger (1979, p. 144) draws attention to the difference between the respective eras of Hegel and Nietzsche: "When Goethe or Hegel says the word 'education' [Bildung], and when an educated man of the 1890s says it, not only is the formal content of the utterance different, but the kind of world encapsulated in the saying is different, though not unrelated." Unfortunately, Heidegger fails to clarify what he means by "not unrelated." Heidegger's interpretation pushes Nietzsche into proximity to Hegel; indeed, Heidegger declares rather sanctimoniously that "for the one decade of creative labor on his [Nietzsche's] major work did not grant him the time and tranquillity to linger in the vast halls of Hegel's and Schelling's works" (ibid., p. 63). It is pure fantasy, however, to imagine that Nietzsche would have cared to immerse himself deeper in German idealism. It is tempting to want to remind Heidegger that Nietzsche's exit from the academy, unlike his, was voluntary. Nietzsche resigned his university post in May 1879. Although plagued by illness, he enjoyed the liberty of being able to pursue his own thinking. In November 1880, while writing *Dawn*,

Nietzsche declared in a letter from Genoa (*Selected Letters* #85): "I want also to have no more to do with the aspirations of contemporary 'idealism,' least of all, German Idealism. Let us all do our work; posterity may decide, or may not decide, how we should be placed. . . ." Although Nietzsche's focus here is on contemporary forms of idealism (it appears that Nietzsche sent Eduard von Hartmann's *Phänomenologie des sittlichen Bewusstseins* along with this letter to Overbeck), Nietzsche reveled in his sun-filled Mediterranean life (see EH, "Dawn," #1). Finally, at best it is ambivalence that governs Nietzsche's reaction to German idealism. In "Daybreak (Dawn)" #190 he mentions Schelling, Hegel, and other philosophers and concludes that they are "insupportable . . . pitiable and moving." Nietzsche sees their work as overvalued, although he is not dismissive. Still, there is no basis for the notion that Nietzsche would have wanted to immerse himself further in their thinking.

37. Of course, my drawing attention to this shared perspective is in no way meant to override the fundamental differences between Hegel and Nietzsche that have been uncovered.

38. See also LPWH (p. 57), where Hegel emphasizes that "culture [Bildung] is the form of our thinking."

39. See also Warren 1997, pp. 159–160.

Chapter 3

1. In a famous metaphor, Hegel likens the Greeks to a young girl beckoning to us with a piece of fruit. For an interpretation of that passage, see Jurist 1993.

2. In TI, "The Problem of Socrates," Nietzsche offers more of a mixed assessment of the influence of Socrates. Socrates is seen as representing a shift from the past, but he is no longer blamed for the demise of Greek culture. He is portrayed ambivalently: as a buffoon and an erotic.

3. The theme of homelessness is also discussed in GS #377.

4. The theme of transgression can be traced from *Natural Law* (1802–03) to *System of Sittlichkeit* (1803–04) and *Realphilosophie* (or *Second Philosophy of Spirit* (1805–06). In these two works from the Jena period, Hegel continues to link transgression to recognition. In the latter work, in contrast to "tragedy in the realm of the ethical," the power of the state is longer seen as an infringement on on the freedom of the individual.

5. The second section is titled Culture and the third Morality.

6. The first section of that chapter, Natural Religion, concerns what Hegel regards as primitive religions; the third, Revealed Religion, concerns Christianity.

7. Hegel's reading of tragedy has too often been caricatured in terms of conceptual antinomies. For a recent exception, see Nussbaum 1986, p. 67ff. Hegel's view is at least in part inspired by Aristotle's subordination of character to plot in the *Poetics* (50a20f).

8. A. C. Bradley ("Hegel's Theory of Tragedy," reprinted in *Hegel on Tragedy*, ed. A. and H. Paolucci) interprets the collision in terms of "self-division" and "self-waste." Rosenstein (1970, p. 525) challenges Bradley's notion of self-waste.

9. For a comparison of Hegel's interpretation of *Antigone* with other interpretations, see Steiner 1984. In chapter 7 I discuss feminist responses to Hegel's interpretation in connection with "natural and ethical recognition."

10. For an exploration of the connection between Hegel's notion of recognition [Anerkennung] and Aristotle's notion of recognition [Anagnorisis], see Jurist 1987.

11. In *Aesthetics* (II, p. 1197), Hegel modifies the point about the protagonist being destroyed: "Therefore what is superseded in the tragic denouement is only the one-sided particular which had not been able to adapt itself to this harmony, and now (and this is the tragic thing in its action), unable to renounce itself and its intention, finds itself condemned to total destruction, or at the very least, forced to abandon, if it can, the accomplishment of its aim."

12. Dickey (1987, p. 183) suggests that Hegel's hope for recollectivization in the modern world, which incorporated the values of Protestant civil piety alongside the model of the polis, was given up as a result of his acceptance of the reality of "emergent, irreversible and centrifugal socioeconomic forces" after reading the Scottish economists.

13. See also Steiner 1961. "The Oldest Program Towards a System in German Idealism" (1797), which was probably written by Hegel, represents a perspective shared by Hölderlin, Schelling, and Hegel. Some highlights: "The supreme act of reason, because it embraces all ideas, is an aesthetic act." "The philosopher must possess as much aesthetic force as the poet. Those human beings who are devoid of aesthetic sense are our pedantic philosophers." "Poetry will thereby attain a higher dignity; in the end she will again become what she was in the beginning—the instructress of humanity." "Until we make the ideas aesthetic, i. e. mythological, they will have no interest for the people."

14. See Jamme 1986, p. 367.

15. For a good discussion of the four stages, see pp. 82–87 of McGinn 1975.

16. Sallis (1991, p. 56) argues that the two impulses ought not be misconstrued as a "binary opposition."

17. I do not read Nietzsche as attacking knowledge per se in this context. Rather, he opposes the overestimation of knowledge (that is, Socrates's elevation of it to be a "panacea" (BT #17)), and he worries that the embrace of knowledge can serve as a defense against difficult emotions. Nietzsche clearly detects Socrates's ongoing influence in philosophy; however, he also points to Kant and Schopenhauer as philosophers who accept limitations to knowledge (BT #20).

18. Houlgate (1986, p. 193) emphasizes that Nietzsche's more mature work features "the isolated heroic individual" who insists on his subjectivity rather than his dissolution.

19. Heidegger (1979, p. 103) suggests that Hölderlin anticpated Nietzsche's concepts of the Apollonian and the Dionysian. For discussions of Hölderlin's interpretation of the ancient Greeks, see Steiner 1984 and Henrich 1971.

20. Silk and Stern (1981, p. 325) hypothesize that the one-sidedness in both Hegel's and Nietzsche's treatment of tragedy is revealed in looking at examples from tragedy:

that Hegel's focus on conflicting principles means that he cannot account for a play like *Oedipus Tyrannus*, while Nietzsche's focus on transgression and the horror of life is hard to reconcile with the *Oresteia*. Their point captures something about the broadly different tendencies in Hegel and Nietzsche, but it does not do justice to either thinker. For one thing, it is certainly possible to see conflicting principles as existing within Oedipus himself. Oedipus's search for self-knowledge is reflected in the journey of consciousness that Hegel presents. Although reconciliation does not take place on stage, this does not mean that it ought not come from the spectator. I develop this theme in the excursus at the end of the present chapter. Finally, Oedipus does achieve reconciliation with the human community in *Oedipus at Colonus*. Similarly, I do not read Nietzsche as condemning reconciliation in tragedy. The ending of the *Oresteia* does not mitigate the horror of what has occurred. It is correct that Nietzsche wants to stress the fragility of reconciliation and that he warns against reducing tragedies to morality plays. Nietzsche does not feature reconciliation in a social sense, but this does not mean that he dismisses it as a factor. Indeed, in BT #17 Nietzsche praises the "reconciling tones" as "purest" in *Oedipus at Colonus*.

21. A promising direction in which to look would be psychoanalysis, wherein we find there is an interest in emotions and the limits of rationality as well as appreciation of the conflicts that necessarily attend to our sense of belonging to a social group.

22. 'Tyrannos' means *king*; the primary meaning of 'pharmakos' is *sacrifical animal* (usually a goat). See Segal 1982, p. 240; Vernant 1981, p. 100.

23. I will explore the multiple connotations of Hegel's term "being-for-itself" in chapter 6.

24. Kojève (1969, p. 10) interprets the first moment of Desire explicitly in terms of animal behavior: ". . . when the 'first' two men confront one another for the first time, the one sees in the other only an animal (and a hostile and dangerous one at that) that is to be destroyed." He makes a distinction between animal and human desire, the latter of which is created through risking one's life in the life-and-death struggle (p. 7). The consciousness who does not go through with risking his own life must be seen as still an animal (p. 16). He is a slave, who must serve a master as a beast of burden.

25. In many ways, the tragedy that the PhS most resembles is *Oedipus Tyrannos*, as several commentators have noted. See Lewis (unpublished), Sklar 1976, and Hyppolite 1971. The parallel between consciousness and Oedipus is particularly striking in the introduction to PhS, where Hegel lays out the structure of knowledge for consciousness along with its itinerary. Hegel claims that at the starting point consciousness's knowledge is illusory, even though it takes itself as having real knowledge. So there is a disparity between consciousness's image of itself and its actual state of ignorance. The path which consciousness takes has the result of: "the loss of its own self, for it does lose its truth on this path" (PhS, p. 49). The path then is a "way of despair" (ibid.). Hegel explains: ". . . consciousness suffers violence at its own hands: it spoils its own limited satisfaction. When consciousness feels this violence, its anxiety may well make its retreat from the truth, and strive to hold onto what it is in danger of losing. But it can find no peace." (PhS, p. 51) One resulting option is for consciousness to allow its "burning zeal for truth" to degenerate into a kind of "vanity," in which consciousness is for-itself only. More specifically, being clever is utilized by consciousness as compensation for its alienation from others. This self-division can be healed only through consciousness's self-examination, whereby its knowledge is reconciled with truth. Hegel is careful to stress that this process is as much a testing of what self-knowledge

is itself as it is a testing of what consciousness knows. In other terms, consciousness learns what self-knowledge is as part of the process of achieving self-knowledge. Consciousness must learn, in particular, that its object in knowledge is itself. The entire process in PhS—from the starting point, to the way of despair, to the culmination in self-knowledge—seems to emulate Oedipus. The story of Oedipus begins with his false sense of confidence, which is eroded at the same time that he hurdles along a path of destruction in which he is progressively cut off from others. He comes into self-knowledge by coming to terms with the painful truth of his past. His self-knowledge is an illustration of what self-knowledge is: as both the discoverer and the object of discovery.

26. The philosophical importance of narrative has been much at issue lately. For a defense of narrative as a legitimate form of knowledge itself, see Lyotard 1984. For another kind of defense of narrative, which upholds narrative fiction as addressing human emotion and choice, and therefore as being a form of philosophy itself, see Nussbaum 1988. Finally, for yet another defense of narrative, which links it to the challenge for philosophy to be responsive to its own cultural milieu, see MacIntyre 1984.

27. Heidegger (1975) takes a position on the we as in between being observers or participants. He argues that the we is present and interacts with consciousness; it is ahead of consciousness but has not necessarily attained absolute knowledge (p. 128).

28. Such an idea is proposed but not defended on pp. 115–117 of Gadamer 1975.

29. Else (1957, p. 433) questions the interpretation of *katharsis* in terms of emotions only: for "the tragic emotions. . . comport an element of judgment." He sees tragedy as "a pleasure springing from emotion, but an emotion authorized and released by our intellectually conditioned pleasure of action" (p. 449). See also Nussbaum 1986, pp. 388–391; Golden 1962, pp. 41–60. Hegel anticipates a cognitive interpretation of 'katharsis' in the *Aesthetics* (p. 1197), maintaining that what Aristotle meant by the concept was "not mere feelings but what corresponds with reason and spiritual truth."

30. In this sense, one can maintain that PhS contains two tragedies: the first one ends with the Reason chapter, where the individual's self-immersion and isolation reaches a peak; the second one ends with the Absolute Terror, where the universal individual is crushed by the universal order. The allegedly happy ending to PhS has led one scholar to conclude that PhS was a comedy—see Loewenberg 1965, p. 20.

31. See Vernant 1981 and Segal 1982. See also Vernant 1980; Segal 1986; Knox 1957.

32. Harris (1983, p. 542) paraphrases Hegel's view that would encourage this kind of interpretation as follows: "Creon and Antigone exhibit for us the inward conceptual necessity of what was beginning in the historic world at the very time that Sophocles's play was produced: the Peloponnesian War."

Chapter 4

1. Some philosophers maintain that Hegel defends customs. Solomon (1996, note 51, pp. 220–221) suggests that Hegel "openly rejects formal 'morality' in favor of a more situated 'custom-ethics' in both his *Phenomenology of Spirit* in 1807 and his *Philosophy of Right* in 1821." Kolb (1986, p. 36) claims that "Hegel says that the guides we need are customs, Sitten. We need customs that tell us what kind of person we

should be." As stated, these views are misleading: they fail to observe the contrast Hegel makes between the subordination of the individual to the community in the ancient world and the freedom of the individual to internalize the universal in the modern world.

2. Nietzsche, Blondel notes (1991, p. 56), reminds us that Bildung bears a relation to paideia.

3. Forster (1998, p. 474) cites and discusses this passage.

4. For an excerpt from *Fragment of a System*, see Forster 1998, pp. 581–582.

5. 'Recovery' is A. V. Miller's evocative but leading translation of 'Herstellung', which more commonly means 'establishment' or 'production'. J. B. Baillie's translation in the Harper & Row edition, 'restoration', goes further in implying a rear-guard maneuver for philosophy. Although it is hard to say exactly what Hegel intends, I do not think that Herstellung is meant to encourage a return to the past. On the contrary, Hegel wishes to redirect philosophy to move beyond epistemology to include the psychology of knowledge, that is, not only to be concerned with justification, but with actual human dissatisfaction.

6. Hegel comes close to describing narcissism, as it is used as a clinical and theoretical concept in psychoanalysis: an oscillating sense of self-esteem—in which there is a lack of integration of the self—precisely, as Hegel suggests, "not a single self." In addition, Hegel shows narcissism to be a self-enclosed world in which, in the language of H. Kohut, others are merely self-objects. The "certainty" that Hegel detects can be seen as corresponding to the grandiosity ascribed to narcissism.

7. I owe this reference to M. Hardimon (1994, p. 30).

8. Hardimon 1994 is an important and original assessment of Hegel's mature view of modern culture. A consequence of Hardimon's focus on reconciliation in a social sense in the later work, however, is that he does not pay attention to the concept's broader application in Hegel's philosophy. More specifically, Hardimon's emphasis on reconciliation as denoting being at home in the (social) world obscures the sense in which reconciliation contends with the finite and the infinite—precisely what Hegel depicts in the dialectic between Faith and Insight in PhS. Furthermore, Hardimon does not discuss the distinction between interpersonal and social relationships.

9. One can conclude that the more that one takes Hegel's systematic aspirations seriously, the more one will be sympathetic to his later works. Kolb (1986) offers an interesting argument for including the *Logic* in thinking about Hegel's view of modernity. Forster (1998) makes the original argument that PhS contains a coherent perspective that is not inconsistent with Hegel's ultimate system of philosophy. One strong piece of evidence that Hegel did not abandon interest in PhS is that he was revising it when he died.

10. Although my interpretation of Hegel relies more on PhS, I shall compare these two works where it is relevant. Traditionally, of course, interest in PhS versus PR was understood to be a function of being a left versus a right Hegelian. There is a parallel issue, too, between those who are drawn to Hegel as challenging the philosophical tradition and those who place greater emphasis on Hegel's connection to the tradition.

11. This Habermasian interpretation of Hegel, however much it is implicit in earlier left Hegelian thinkers such as Lukàcs, Adorno, and Marcuse, has recently become prominent in the work of Robert Pippin (1991a), who nonetheless distinguishes himself from a critical-theory perspective.

12. In one sense I would agree with Habermas that the *Dialectic of Enlightenment* is peculiar and badly organized, lacks rigorous argument, and can be infuriatingly obscure. In another sense, his criticism of it as "black" implies that Horkheimer and Adorno were being excessively negative, rather than that the social reality they were describing in 1943 was pretty bleak.

13. There are tensions *between* Horkheimer and Adorno to consider: Horkheimer was attracted to Schopenhauerean pessimism, whereas in Adorno we find statements like this (1998, p. 158): "Philosophy lives in symbiosis with science and cannot break from it without turning into dogmatism and ultimately relapsing into mythology."

14. Nietzsche is particularly critical of German culture; in fact, he often contrasts it with French culture, which he calls "a real and productive culture" (DS #1). See also EH, "Why I Am So Clever," #2. In HAH I #221, Nietzsche claims that French culture has more in common with Greek culture than with German culture.

15. Kolb (1986, p. 124) makes the interesting point that although the growth of science and technology was not a central concern of Hegel's, it did play "a very important, if subordinate role in characterizing modernity" and would not necessarily require him to change his general view.

16. See Kohut 1971, 1966; Kernberg 1985, 1970.

17. Clark presents a finely detailed argument that Nietzsche came to a neo-Kantian position on knowledge.

18. This metaphor might be seen as a commentary on Hegel's famous metaphor of organic development in the preface to PhS.

19. For Hegel's description of organic development, see the preface to PhS.

20. This theme is developed in Berman 1982 and in Frisby 1986.

21. Horkheimer and Adorno's sympathy to myth and their reservations about ratio are drawn directly from Nietzsche

22. In fairness to Megill, it ought to be said that his view of Nietzsche's aestheticism means, not the division of the world into aesthetic and non-aesthetic, but the aestheticizing of all human experience (Megill 1985, p. 2).

23. In WP #233 Nietzsche speaks of placing psychology on a physiological basis.

24. In "The Age of the World Picture," Heidegger (1977, p. 116) offers a summary account of modernity that names five defining phenomena: science, machine technology, art's moving into the purview of aesthetics, human activity's being conceived and consummated as culture, and the loss of the gods. This account overlaps with the one in *An Introduction to Metaphysics*, except for the elements of culture and art as aesthetics. The fourth point is alien to Nietzsche's philosophy.

25. One of the most insightful treatments of the merits and the limitations of Heidegger's view of technology is found in Richard Bernstein's essay "Heidegger's Silence? Éthos and Technology" (in Bernstein 1992).

26. This is surprising in the sense that Horkheimer and Adorno were Marxist, Jewish, and anti-fascist, whereas Heidegger was none of the above. Moreover, Adorno's *Jargon of Authenticity* (1973b) offers a severe indictment of Heidegger, linking his philosophy to fascism. Indeed, it is in this context that Adorno makes the devastatingly incisive point that Heidegger "condemns idle chatter, but not brutality" (ibid., p. 102). On the relationship between Adorno and Heidegger, see Mörchen 1980, Honneth 1991, and Safranski 1998.

27. In regard to Heidegger and Nietzsche on nihilism, see Smith 1996 and Vattimo 1988. Vattimo emphasizes the positive value of embracing nihilism; he downplays Nietzsche's claim (WP #13) that nihilism must be embraced in order to be overcome. For a compelling exploration of the theme of nihilism, see Critchley 1997.

28. Ferry and Renaut (1990a, p. 69) argue that Heidegger is an anti-modern. Kolb (1986, p. 182) correctly notes that Heidegger's offers few concrete suggestions for social change.

29. Derrida (1982, p. 136) observes in this connection that Heidegger fails to appreciate Nietzsche's call for an active forgetting of Being.

30. Heidegger's interest in affects is amply demonstrated in *Being and Time*. His concern with reconceptualizing the body is amply demonstrated in the dictum "We do not 'have' a body; rather, we 'are' bodily." (Heidegger 1979, p. 99) There is a tension, however, between volume 1 of Heidegger's *Nietzsche*, where he credits Nietzsche with breaking free from the metaphysics of the soul, and volume 4, where he insists that "the fact that Nietzsche posits the body in place of the soul and consciousness alters nothing in the fundamental metaphysical position which is determined by Descartes" (1987, p. 133). For a good discussion of the tension between Heidegger's first and fourth volumes, see T. Siegel, "Of Untergang and Übergang" (unpublished).

31. The liability of Heidegger's "quietism" is intensified by its combination with a portentous insistence on heteronomy. I am thinking of his famous remark about "only a God can save us" in the 1966 *Spiegel* interview, and also of a candid and revealing comment that, according to his son Hermann, Heidegger occasionally would make to him: "It thinks in me. I cannot resist it." (Safranski 1998, p. 315) No latent love for the metaphysics of subjectivity is implied by dismay at this aspect of Heidegger's thought.

32. In his later work, Hegel makes a firm distinction between myth and thought, exiling the former from philosophy. See LHP, p. 158.

33. Again, a contrast can be noted between PhS and PR. In the latter, Hegel is quite specific about politics, defending constitutional monarchy. Hegel's concept of mutual recognition will be explored in detail in chapters 6–9.

34. The source of this epithet is Georg Brandes's description of Nietzsche's philosophy—a description that Nietzsche endorsed.

35. Despite Nietzsche's identification with aristocracy, his philosophy apparently was never well received by the aristocratic class in Germany. See p. 118 of Aschheim 1992.

36. The passage to which Warren refers is from D #112, where Nietzsche refers to rights' being recognized [anerkannte]. Warren suggests that Nietzsche follows Hegel in the belief that the self needs recognition.

37. Warren (1987, p. 209) concludes his argument with the stimulating claim that there is an inconsistency between Nietzsche's postmodern philosophizing and his pre-modern politics.

38. Recent thinking in philosophy (see DeSousa 1987, Stocker 1996, Griffiths 1997) and in "affective science" (a new subfield created by psychologists and neuroscientists) supports Nietzsche's view of the unexpungeability of emotions. More specifically, the "basic emotions" position (represented by Silvan Tomkins, Paul Ekman, and others in psychology) and neuroscientific research by Antonio Damasio and Joseph LeDoux emphasize the primacy of affects as a human response system.

39. It is certainly not my intention to tarnish Habermas with a superficial charge of anti-Semitism. Not only has Habermas made a point of acknowledging the affinity of Jewish philsophers to German Idealism; he has spoken out repeatedly against anti-Semitism in contemporary Germany. He has also made pointed, dramatic statements about the Holocaust: "[At Auschwitz] something happened that up to now nobody considered as even possible. There one touched on something which represents the deep layer of solidarity among all that wears a human face; notwithstanding all the usual acts of beastliness of human history, the integrity of this common layer had been taken for granted." (from *Eine Art Schadensabwicklung*; quoted on p. 49 of Friedländer 1993) Habermas (1983a, p. 102) has commented sympathetically on Adorno's "exile and emigration in flight from anti-Semitism." In "Remarks on the Development of Horkheimer's Work" (in Benhabib et al. 1993), Habermas specifically acknowledges that the *Dialectic of Enlightenment* was composed in the context of fascism. Finally, in an interview with M. Haller that appears in *The Past as Future* (1994), Habermas mentions the appeal of Adorno's aesthetic thinking in *Dialectic of Enlightenment* to Foucault, but adds that Adorno "has something more to say to us." "It is," he continues, "a thinking that stands as the indeligible register of the experience of the emigrant, faced with the sheer accident of his own escape from the death camps." Habermas proceeds to offer a candid and personal reflection of his own experience of realizing at age 16 the mag-nitude of what had occurred, which left upon him an ongoing "anxiety of regression." All this notwithstanding, Habermas does not face the hypocrisy of the Enlightenment revealed in anti-Semitism—articulated from the time of Mendelssohn down to Horkeimer and Adorno—in his defense of the Enlightenment. *The Dialectic of Enlightenment* is a confusing book in many ways; however, there can be doubt that the theme of anti-Semitism is central to its purpose. It is problematic that Habermas ignores this; it is also problematic that Habermas restores a connection between the Reformation and the Enlightenment, as the anti-Semitism of Erasmus and Luther is even less incidental. (See Jurist 1991.) The theme of anti-Semitism is obscured and complicated in *the Dialectic of Enlightenment* by the theme of Odysseus as the embodi-ment of Enlightenment. Horkheimer and Adorno (1986, p. 61) draw attention to a parallel between Odysseus and the Jews, the latter having been mobile, economically enterprising, and hence disruptive of the feudal order. It is strange—even tortured—that Horkheimer and Adorno, in exile among the Lotus-Eaters (and, unlike Odysseus, having no home to return to), posited anti-Semitism as the underbelly of the Enlightenment and at the same time implicitly connected the Enlightenment with the cosmopolitanism of Jews. For a fair-minded assessment of the analysis of anti-Semitism in *The Dialectic of Enlightenment*, see D. Diner, "Reason and the 'Other': Horkheimer's Reflections on Anti-Semitism and Mass Annhilation," in Benhabib et al. 1993.

40. In view of the fact that Horkheimer (1947 pp. 114–115) notes a connection between mimesis and children, it is worth recalling Aristotle's view of mimesis as a natural extension from childhood pleasure and as a source of learning (*Poetics*, 1448a–b).

41. But not the Freudian unconscious. For a discussion of Habermas's neglect of it, see Whitebook 1985. For Habermas's candid description of the vicissitudes of his interest in Heidegger, see Habermas 1989. In "Anti-Semitism and Fascist Propaganda" (1994) Adorno offers what is tantamount to a rejoinder to Habermas's impulse to write off irrationality. Adorno makes the point that anti-Semitic propaganda is never simply irrational and then adds that "the term, irrationality, is much too vague to describe so complex a psychological phenomena" (ibid., p. 165).

42. Habermas's aversion to irrationality leads to problems in his handling of aesthetics, Adorno's aesthetics in particular. Bernstein (1989, p. 57) argues that to Adorno autonomous art is enigmatic—a point that Habermas obscures.

43. See also Frisby 1986, p. 72.

44. Pippin offers a number of probing comments on the relationship between Hegel and Nietzsche. The most relevant is that it is central for both thinkers to critique modern culture, and that Nietzsche is responding to Hegel's "promissory notes" (Pippin 1991a, p. 105). Pippin claims that, in part, Nietzsche is defending a complete and self-determining self-consciousness that is within the tradition of German Idealism (ibid., p. 82). In more recent work (1997, p. 22), Pippin observes that both Hegel and Nietzsche insist on viewing modernity as practical—as a way of life.

Chapter 5

1. This literature is too vast to summarize here. Locke set the agenda for a large portion of this literature. Recently, though, the domain of inquiry associated with personal identity has been challenged. Marya Schechtman (1996) begins with the observation that "the contemporary philosophical discussion of identity omits a great deal that seems central to the topic of personal identity" (p. ix) and goes on to argue that "the reidentification question" will never satisfy the demands of "the characterization question," the latter of which appeals to "an individual's inner life and her attitude toward her actions and experiences" (p. 95). The issues raised by the characterization question, according to Schechtman, rely on a "narrative self constitution" view (pp. 93–135). Carol Anne Rovane (1998) works within a more conventional neo-Lockean framework, but she arrives at the strange conclusion that "group persons" and multiple persons within one individual are conceivable. On the one hand, Schechtman's book seems more germane to the issues that are connected to Hegel's and Nietzsche's perspectives on agency than Rovane. However, in strong contrast to Hegel, Schechtman's view of narrative self-constitution is virtually silent about the role of others, whereas Rovane (pp. 162–165) explicitly acknowledges the theme of mutual recognition (though without mentioning the wealth of literature on the subject). Schectman's and Rovane's books are good examples of the widening scope of personal identity in the analytic literature.

2. Some philosophers emphasize that we ought to think of persons and agents as closely related. For example, Christine Korsgaard (1989) uses Kant's notion of agency, which is a practical standpoint that based on viewing ourselves as free and responsible, against Parfit. Kant's notion of agency is an important backdrop for both Hegel and Nietzsche.

3. It is not easy to reconcile the perspectives that Taylor offers about agency in "What is Human Agency?" (originally published in 1977) and in "The Concept of a Person" (originally given as a lecture in 1981 and published in 1983). These two pieces are republished in volume 1 of Taylor 1985.

4. The description of Taylor's work as genealogical makes sense in that he approaches the past in order to understand the present better. However, insofar as genealogy implies the impossibility of higher-order goods (in Taylor's language, "hyper goods"), it is misleading. Despite this warning, I think the description is warranted, since Taylor clearly sees our self-understanding to be at stake in investigating the past.

5. This is not one of Taylor's best-known articles, but it states his case strongly and concisely. Before offering his genealogy of agency, Taylor describes a distinction between theories of modernity, some of which aspire to an acultural standpoint and others of which identify themselves as cultural. Taylor sees the former as more familiar and dominant; he argues that the latter have a valuable contribution to make. In the first sentence of the article, Taylor states his modest goal: to "start a dialogue." My intention is to continue this dialogue by reflecting on the genealogy and continuing it in my argument about the cultural side of Hegel's and Nietzsche's theories of modernity.

6. Taylor's first extended discussion of expressivism is in *Hegel* (1975), where he proposes that this background is critical for understanding Hegel's philosophical project. In *Sources of the Self* (1989), Taylor develops his narrative to a greater extent through the nineteenth and twentieth centuries. In "Inwardness and the Culture of Modernity" (1992), Taylor does not contend with the theme of expressivism.

7. Individuation here owes something to the metaphysical connotation of distinguishing one thing from another, but its meaning is distinct.

8. In *Hegel and Modern Society*, Taylor discusses the premise of homogeneity that limits Hegel's applicability to our diverse world.

9. See also Taylor 1995, p. 16.

10. Alexander Nehamas (1985) specifies how self-exploration is played out in Nietzsche: the author invents himself as a character in his work.

11. Havas (1995) argues that, while Nietzsche distances from responsibility as it is understood by morality, he does value "responsiveness." Berkowitz (1995) stresses Nietzsche's appreciation of "intellectual conscience."

12. See also WP #384 (1885–86); WP #966 (1884).

13. The contrast between the Stoic and Aristotelian paradigms about affects is a central theme in Nussbaum 1994.

Chapter 6

1. A number of commentators have emphasized that Hegel's concept of recognition has its origins in Fichte's concept of recognition. Hegel amends Fichte's abstract deduction of recognition, replacing it with a concept that is rooted in the concrete experience of love and struggle. (See Siep 1979; Wildt 1982; Williams 1992; Honneth 1992a; Jurist 1994a,b.)

2. It is worth noting again that Hegel offers no clear definition of "satisfaction." Wood (1991) offers an interesting discussion of Hegel's view of happiness. Wood's conclusion is that for Hegel the final human good is freedom, not happiness (p. 77). Yet Wood acknowledges that "in contrast to Kant, Hegel sees happiness and freedom as intimately connected" (p. 70). Wood does not consider that Hegel's use of 'satisfaction' ought to be distinguished from empirical happiness. Hegel distinguishes between the aims of happiness and satisfaction in LPWH, where he argues that the world-historical individual does not aim for (mere) happiness (p. 79). In a letter to his wife before they were married, too, Hegel makes the distinction between happiness and satisfaction: the latter is blessed (that is, it is part of religion and morality), whereas as the former is fleeting and hence inferior. Hegel adds a sober reflection is this connection: that "in nonsuperficial natures every sensation of happiness is connected with a sensation of melancholy" (*Hegel: The Letters*, pp. 243–244). Perhaps we might think of satisfaction as an encompassing way for Hegel to affirm both happiness and freedom.

3. This previously untranslated sketch appears on p. 615 of Forster 1998.

4. Berthold-Bond (1995, p. 77) makes an interesting connection between narcissism and desire.

5. This interpretation is highlighted by Kojève, whose interpretation of Hegel will be developed in chapter 9.

6. I discussed this in chapter 2 in connection with the idea of self-fathoming. I also discussed it in chapter 5 in connection with Taylor's notion of expressivism, particularly the theme of self-exploration.

7. Forster (1998, pp. 252–253) associates being-for-another with "deference," which has the misleading connotation of submission. Not only is this too specific, but it overlooks mutuality.

8. Hegel uses various forms of the verb 'handeln' and the noun 'Tätigkeit' to refer to action. However, it is usually the case that where the English translation 'agent' occurs Hegel is using 'Subjekt'. See e.g. PM #505, #508, #509, #510.

9. See chapter 3 of Pinkard 1994.

10. For a brief but cogent review of matters relating to the composition of PhS, see Marx 1975, pp. ix–xiv. The main controversy concerns whether Hegel changed his mind about the scope of the original project. Pöggeler (1966) argues that Hegel departed from his original scheme of consciousness, self-consciousness, and reason to include spirit, religion, and absolute knowing. Fulda (1965) maintains that PhS was composed in one piece. See also Pinkard 1994; Pippin 1993; Forster 1998. See my appendix for an illustration of the place of recognition throughout PhS.

11. Such a division is made by Lukàcs (1976, p. 472f.) and by Dove (1971, p. 42). For a detailed presentation of recognition within the structure of PhS, see my appendix.

12. This distinction captures Hegel's critique of the Cartesian narrative; however, it obscures the important distinction between the interpersonal and the social dimension.

13. The issue of the "we" was discussed in the excursus at the end of chapter 3. For a variety of opinions on the issue of who is meant to be included in this "for us" designation, see Dove 1971, pp. 45–56.

14. For recent attempts, see Forster 1998, Rockmore 1997, and Pippin 1989.

15. The only condition that must be taken into account is that finite experience, by definition, indicates a limited kind of satisfaction. (See *Hegel's Aesthetics*, volume 1, p. 99.) For Hegel, true satisfaction requires a union of the finite and the infinite.

16. In *Hegel's Concept of Experience*, Heidegger plays up the element of language [Sprache] by transforming experience from "a dialectical movement" to "the movement of the dialogue [Gespräche] between natural and absolute knowledge" (1975, p. 148). Heidegger's dialogue with Hegel stresses the importance of the concept of experience for the task of phenomenology: ". . . the nature of experience is the nature of phenomenology" (ibid., p. 144). It is interesting that Heidegger ends his dialogue with Hegel with the opening lines of the Self-Consciousness chapter—my entry point to the concept of recognition in PhS. Is Heidegger suggesting that his starting point is where Hegel ends? Hegel's opening lines recap the movement up to self-consciousness, asserting that the abstract notion has now been superseded by a new, actual object. For Heidegger, Hegel's natural consciousness is an unnecessary abstraction from the already-thereness that defines the experience of Dasein.

17. Hegel is making a point that is consistent with and anticipates Freud: that our first sense of ego comes from the body. See "The Ego and the Id" (Freud, *Standard Edition*, volume 19, p. 26).

Chapter 7

1. A qualifying note must be added here, as Hegel implies that the master attains satisfaction whereas the desiring consciousness fails to do so (PhS, p. 116). Clearly, however, the satisfaction of the master is short-lived.

2. Ottmann 1981 is an excellent introduction to the history of interpretations of the master/slave relationship. It examines the master/slave relationship in the Jena writings as well as in the works after PhS.

3. Although Pippin is apparently interested in "satisfaction" enough to include it in his subtitle, he does not discuss it in any length.

4. Forster (1998, pp. 317–322) argues that the Master/Slave section of PhS is supposed to invoke the decline of fifth-century-B.C. Athens. This makes sense in that the Stoicism and Skepticism section clearly refer to the Hellenistic period. At the same time, the historical reference in the Master/Slave section is oblique, and we should keep in mind that the trajectory toward concrete history is not realized until the Geist chapter. Forster's commentary on the Master/Slave section (ibid., p. 248) is particularly helpful in drawing attention to a rare source that influenced Hegel's account: Johann Friedrich Reitenmeier's *Geschichte und Zustand der Sklaverei und Leibengenschaft in Griechenland* .

5. Both Wildt (1982) and Williams (1997) emphasize the importance of autonomy in relation to recognition. Wildt is interested in the dimension of moral and psychological development. Williams (p. 386) discounts psychological development and claims that recognition concerns "sociopolitical and cultural history."

6. On how Hegel anticipates both Marx and Kierkegaard, see Bernstein 1971.

7. Miller's translation of PhS obscures Hegel's use of the phrase "the fear of death" [die Furcht des Todes] here (p. 117).

8. Butler (1997a, p. 43) comes close to offering such a reading, emphasizing how the slave recoils from facing its own death.

9. Harris (1980, p. 239) contrasts this with PhilS. I, where Eigensinn is presupposed before the struggle take place.

10. In PR #138, Hegel makes this point in more general terms: "As one of the commoner features of history (e. g. in Socrates, the Stoics, and others), the tendency to look deeper into oneself and to know and determine from within oneself what is right and good appears in ages when what is recognized as right and good in contemporary manners cannot satisfy [befriedigen] the will of better men." The positing of universality in Stoicism is picked up in Hegel's discussion of legal recognition in the Roman world, which will be discussed in the next chapter.

11. This passage serves as an example of how closely—and sometimes imprecisely— Hegel uses 'erkennen' and 'anerkennen'. The same imprecision exists in the Miller translation of PhS, in particular, sometimes 'erkennen' is translated as 'recognize'.

12. Hyppolite (1974) emphasizes the persistence of unhappy consciousness even at higher levels of consciousness; on p. 190 he suggests that it is "the fundamental theme" of PhS.

13. "The common cause"—Taylor's (1980) rendering—stretches the original to be sure, but it provides intelligibility where Miller's "the matter at hand" fails.

14. See *Hegel's Aesthetics*, volume 2, p. 1197. This passage is cited in a note to chapter 3.

15. Derrida, in *Glas* (1986), dwells on how Hegel's interpretation of Antigone confines her to the role of sister, depriving her of other roles. Derrida subjects Hegel's interpretation of Antigone to a psychoanalytic reading about Hegel's relationship to his own sister. Hegel's sister had a history of mental problems and eventually committed suicide in 1832, a year after Hegel's death. Hegel was quite involved with his sister's treatment, urging upon her the new therapy of Pinel, which was based on empathy and winning the trust of the patient. Hegel saw his sister's problem as hysteria (what else!) and encouraged her to be moderate: "For once we have learned what passes as happiness in this life, and how those who are often called happy fare, what we learn to value most is having nonetheless been satisfied within ourselves and outwardly having been in a passable state—even if not satisfied with everything." (*Hegel: The Letters*, p. 419) Hegel's tone here is quite ambivalent concerning happiness; it is not clear whether to interpret this as evincing solidarity with his sister or as hinting at his own suffering.

16. Hegel has been accused of a male bias in ignoring the relationship between Antigone and Ismene (Diprose 1991). Irigaray's reading (1985) shows that Hegel is not open to questioning sexual difference and thus cannot account for Antigone's Otherness. Hegel's proto-feminism is implicit at best.

17. Benjamin (1987, p. 8) applies to the master/slave dialectic to male-female relations. Her views are discussed further in chapter 9.

18. In Jurist 1987 I explore the parallels between Hegel's concept of recognition and Aristotle's concept of anagnorisis from the *Poetics*.

Chapter 8

1. Hegel does not use the specific phrase "legal recognition." He does speak of the self as a "legal person," and recognition is clearly at issue here.

2. Lukàcs (1976, p. 487) highlights this change, remarking that the section on Morality represents "Hegel's utopian dream of a Germany under the domination of Napoleon."

3. Of course I do not mean to imply that Hegel is in any sense an anti-rationalist. His valorization of reason, however, should not be understood in narrow terms. In PhS he comes close to anticipating the criticism of his philosophy leveled by Ludwig Feuerbach. On this point, see Toews 1993, pp. 378–413.

4. On the overall importance of language in Philosophy of Spirit II, see Habermas 1973.

5. This does not mean that a role for the state does not exist; however, it is no longer the end of Geist's development. Siep (1979, p. 116) puts it this way: "Der absolute Geist—nicht der Staat—ist somit das Telos der Anerkennungsbewegung in der Phänomenologie."

6. One might understand Hegel's point here to be echoed in the psychoanalytic developmental theory of Daniel Stern, who shows in *The Interpersonal World of the Infant* (1985) how the growing reliance on language in the second year of life (the "verbal self") at once increases the possibility of connection to others and insulates us from others. According to Stern, language "makes some parts of our experience less share-able with others and ourselves" and "drives a wedge between two simultaneous forms of interpersonal experience: as it is lived and as it is verbally represented" (p. 162). I do not mean to suggest that this is precisely what Hegel wanted to maintain, as he seems to believe that all lived experience can be represented verbally. Nevertheless, there is something psychologically rich about Hegel's depiction of the delicate balance between self and other through language.

7. See also PR #137.

8. Hard-heartedness is especially linked to the beautiful soul; thus, there is an implicit connection between the beautiful soul and the judging consciousness. Adorno (1993, p. 47) offers an interesting reflection on hard-heartedness as anticipating what Nietzsche terms "ressentiment."

9. The incompleteness of the Jena manuscripts bears on the absence of a discussion of religion. For a discussion of the role of religion in relation to Sittlichkeit, see H. S. Harris's introduction to *Sittlichkeit* and *Philosophy of Spirit I*, especially pp. 81–85.

10. Against Siep's idea that recognition entails a synthesis of love and struggle, Robert Williams emphasizes love as the crucial factor in both of his books on recognition, *Recognition* and *Hegel's Ethics of Recognition*. In the next chapter, I shall argue that Williams underestimates the importance of the factor of struggle and that he does not adequately consider the tension between love and recognition.

11. In his first book, *Recognition*, Williams refers to the master-slave relation "as a particular determinate instance of recognition" (p. 143). He reiterates this in *Hegel's*

Ethics of Recognition, observing that the master-slave relation is "one such deficient realization of the concept of recognition" (p. 49). Williams is right that it is problematic to focus on the master-slave relation to the exclusion of what follows in PhS, as Kojève is guilty of doing; yet it is just as mistaken to overlook the numerous stages in which the trauma of the master-slave relation repeats itself. I shall take a closer look at Kojève in chapter 9.

Chapter 9

1. The significance of the passage transcends Hyppolite's suggestion (1974, p. 491) that, in view of the complexity of PhS, Hegel feels the need to "look back and summarize prior stages." Hyppolite (pp. 491–492) maintains that the three selves which Hegel describes correspond to: the abstract person, the revolutionary citizen and the moral will. He infers that "the Kantian system contains the apex of the idea of the self, of the autonomous spiritual subject," adding the qualification that, according to Hegel, this self is not actualized in Kant's moral view of the world.

2. Being-for-itself overlaps with individuality, although the autonomous, self-realizing, self-fathoming individual is produced over the course of history, whereas being-for-itself belongs to the nature of consciousness itself. Being-for-another overlaps with the universal, although the meaning of the universal shifts and is ambiguous, whereas being-for-another belongs to the nature of consciousness itself. The universal refers not only to the social realm and our need to find connection to others, but to a realm of meaning that is larger than the human realm. In other words, the universal denotes the social world, but also our identification with what is larger than human consciousness—God, the infinite, and the cosmos.

3. For a useful discussion of divorce, war, and poverty—forms of alienation that, according to Hegel, could but do not upset social reconciliation—see Hardimon 1994, pp. 228–250.

4. I will be quoting from Kojève 1947 (the original French edition) and from Kojève 1969 (a partial English translation). On Kojève's influence on French philosophy, see Descombes 1980.

5. This impression is, perhaps, artificially strengthened by the English translation of Kojève's lectures, which amounts to less than half of the French version, the latter of which includes commentary on sections of PhS after the Master/Slave section.

6. Redding refers to p. 120 of Rosen 1974a. My quotation is from p. 104 of Rosen 1987. In this context, Rosen (p. 106) candidly discusses a first-hand story about Kojève's wish to play God. Drury's (1994, p. 4) reading of Kojève contains this observation: "For him, interpreting Hegel was not just an academic matter; on the contrary, he considered it a work of 'political propaganda' intended to influence action ad determine the shape of the future." Kojève himself uses the phrase "political propaganda" in "Hegel, Marx et christianisme" (1946).

7. Kojève took pride in his career as a diplomat and in the fact that he was not a professor of philosophy. This attitude sometimes shaded into arrogance, as it did in a letter dated March 29, 1962: "It is really a matter of indifference to me what the philosophical gentlemen think or say about Hegel" (Strauss 1991, p. 307). (This was his response to an invitation from Gadamer to give a talk in Heidelberg.)

8. Kojève saw Napoleon as dividing history and thus as representing the last major turn in European history. Even more bizarre, Kojève was infatuated with Stalin as a latter-day Napoleon.

9. In this connection, Harris (1980, pp. 229–248) notes that recognition as a relation between self and other includes our relation to God. The religious sense is especially at issue in the later stages of PhS; however, as Harris points out, it is already in evidence in the Frankfurt "theological" writings.

10. A similar line of argument in Wildt 1982 focuses on the influence of Fichte on Hegel.

11. Forster (1998, p. 249) also stresses that Kojève neglects how recognition is constitutive of the individual mind and thus concludes that the psychological aspect of Hegel's view is neglected. However, there is a sense in which Kojève appreciates the psychological aspect of Hegel in featuring satisfaction.

12. This letter, written on June 22, 1946, appears on p. 234 of Strauss's On Tyranny, which includes correspondence between Kojève and Strauss.

13. Although Kojève adopts Hegel's view that modern culture's demand for the right of the individual is not adequately protected in the polis, he departs from Hegel in implying an absence of satisfaction in ancient Greek culture.

14. Pippin 1997, p. 257) offers an astute commentary on the Kojève-Strauss debate (which included Kojève's response to Strauss's On Tyranny, published along with Strauss's restatement), focusing attention on Strauss's criticism of Kojève that the end of history would seem to resemble Nietzsche's "last men," whose "satisfaction" is hardly enviable. Kojève fails to address this important concern, to which I shall return in chapter 10.

15. Williams is simply dismissive, whereas Pippin offers a detailed reflection on Kojève.

16. See also Cooke 1995, in which the role of affect in self-realization is highlighted.

17. It is revealing that Benjamin reads the failure of recognition in terms of omnipotence, as this unnecessarily pathologizes what I see as the problem of narcissism in Freud.

18. See Hyppolite 1971; Lacan 1977, 1988.

19. Hardimon's view of "reconciliation" in Hegel can be correlated to Honneth's view of recognition, although Hardimon does not cite Honneth.

20. Hegel amends his understanding of love from the theological writings in the Jena writings; for example, in PhilG. II, love is described as a cognitive relation.

21. Williams (1997) cites the example of Hegel's 1820 version of the Philosophy of Spirit as supporting the possibility of recognition without struggle. At most, this evidence shows that Hegel's later view entertained that prospect—not surprising, since his critique of modernity had softened in comparison to the time of PhS. Whether or not Hegel seriously envisioned recognition without struggle, Williams's one-sided defense of love as the basis of recognition is not justified.

22. In "The Politics of Recognition" (in Taylor 1995, p. 225), Taylor also emphasizes how misrecognition can be damaging to the "victim" if that person internalizes it.

23. Empathy for victims is also apparent in Taylor's work on recognition and misrecognition.

24. Siep's *Anerkennung als Prinzip der praktischen Philosophie* is praised in a footnote on p. 109 of Honneth 1992a. Despite the overall difference with Wildt, Honneth acknowledges his debt to Wildt's *Autonomie und Anerkennung*.

25. Benjamin's first book, *The Bonds of Love*, was written before Honneth's *Struggle for Recognition* and is cited frequently in it.

26. This is not to imply that Honneth is unresponsive to the link between gender and recognition. As I mentioned, Honneth reads Benjamin's work sympathetically.

27. Benjamin is not primarily interested in interpreting Hegel and certainly does not claim to be making a contribution to Hegel scholarship. My examination of her view of Hegel elucidates her position as a prelude to comparing it to my position.

28. Over the last 15 years or so, much has changed in the psychoanalytic world. The classical model has fewer adherents, and many Freudians have moved in the direction of appreciating intersubjectivity. The relational model, first articulated by S. Mitchell and J. Greenberg, has evolved and is now more open to rethinking old ideas rather than rejecting them. Benjamin's views exemplify the relational model at its best.

29. In an illuminating note on page 89 of *Like Subjects, Love Objects*, Benjamin suggests that omnipotence plays the role as primary narcissism does in the classical model.

30. One reason for the confusion is that, while Benjamin attributes a pathological version of omnipotence to Hegel and Freud, she considers a version of omnipotence derived from the work of the psychoanalyst Winnicott a normal and even necessary part of development.

31. My intention in noting this shift in Benjamin's position is not to expose inconsistency. I believe that her openness to modifying her views (especially in response to criticism) is a strength and deserves our admiration.

32. Benjamin relies heavily on infant research by Beatrice Beebe and Edward Tronick.

33. Taylor, "The Politics of Recognition" (in Taylor 1995), p. 250. In *The Inclusion of the Other* (p. 222), Habermas resists Taylor's conclusions, worrying about the implications of an obligation to perpetuate the values of a particular culture or ethnic group as "a kind of preservation of species by administrative means." For Habermas, recognition of special rights can interfere with what ought to be most cherished: equal rights.

34. Fraser (1997, p. 12) argues against an either/or conception of the (social) project of redistribution and the (cultural) project of recognition, claiming that both are crucial for analyzing injustice and fighting for justice. Thus, Fraser (ibid., p. 34, note 13) distinguishes her view from what she sees as Honneth's claim that recognition is the basis of redistribution.

35. Pinkard (1994, p. 267) makes a cogent argument concerning what Hegel meant absolute knowledge: "Absolute knowledge is the internal reflection on the social practices of a modern community that takes its authoritative standards to come only from within the structure of the practices it uses to legitimate and authenticate itself." Although I find this argument appealing, I am not sure I am convinced by it. It offers plausibility at the risk of taming the grandiosity of Hegel's fantasy.

Chapter 10

1. Nevertheless, there are passages in which Nietzsche does not distance himself from a universal model of agency. One such passage occurs in HAH II 1 #223, where Nietzsche argues that self-knowledge [Selbst-Erkenntnis] is universal when it is linked to the past and then declares that "self-determination and self-education [Selbst-bestimmung und Selbsterziehung] could, in the freest and most far-sighted spirits, one day become universal determination with regard to all future humanity."

2. Nietzsche does use 'Handelnde', meaning one who acts. See UDHL #1.

3. Ricoeur (1992, p. 16) observes that Nietzsche seems to be "trying out this idea" rather than dogmatically asserting it.

4. The German word for multiplicity is 'Vielheit'.

5. Parkes (1994, p. 320) comments: "If there are multiple knowers and agents in each person, the complexity of epistemological problems and questions of moral responsibility are intriguingly compounded."

6. Corngold (1986, p. 105) argues that Nietzsche's attack on the subject does not mean an attack on the ego and the self. He also points out that the self is given priority over the ego, although the terms 'ego' and 'self' do overlap and "ego" but not "the self" is occasionally criticized.

7. In a letter to Lou Salomé dated June 10, 1882, Nietzsche writes specifically: "Pindar sagt einmal, 'werde der, der du bist!'"

8. Nietzsche invokes the ideal of "becoming what one is" as early as HAH I #263, where he suggests that "becoming what one is" means "to discharge [talent] in works and actions." Later in HAH (II 1 #366), Nietzsche proclaims that "active, successful natures act, not according to the dictum 'know thyself,' but as there hovered before them the commandment: *will* a self and thou shalt *become* a self." The latter passage highlights agency as dynamic and self-constituting. It does not stipulate the value of self-ignorance as the passage from *Ecce Homo* does; moreover, it is conspicuously silent about self-evaluation. Yet I do not think that this means that "becoming what one is" stands opposed to the project of self-fathoming.

9. Alexander Nehamas has used the term 'integration' to depict identity as a coherent whole that does not imply completion; however, he regards integration as meaning unity. According to Nehamas (1985, pp. 185, 190), Nietzsche renders his life into being a character. Nehamas's project, as I see it, features playfulness at the expense of dangerousness.

10. In WP #389, Nietzsche sounds as if he wants to claim that altruism is impossible; he refers to "the psychological impossibility of a purely selfless action."

11. Corngold (1986, p. 113) suggests that "selige Selbstsucht" is appropriated from a poem in which Goethe speaks of "selige Sehnsucht." Corngold also makes the point that the medium of self-becoming is, for Nietzsche, another part of oneself; not an other, as for Goethe.

12. On the importance of the senses, including their spiritualization, see WP #820. Kaufmann (1968, p. 220) emphasizes the importance of sublimation in Nietzsche's work: "Nietzsche believed that a sexual impulse, for example could be channeled into a creative spiritual activity, instead of being fulfilled directly." This reading has merit, but it must be reconciled with Kaufmann's blatant intention to depict a gentler, kinder Nietzsche.

13. In this passage in an entry from 1884, Nietzsche argues that we must distinguish between moderation for the weak and moderation for the strong: the strong find pleasure in moderation.

14. In WP #966 Nietzsche describes the task of keeping contradictory instincts under control, which suggests that multiplicity does not disappear with integration.

15. This is implied, I think, in passages like the following (from GS #283): ". . . believe me: the secret for harvesting from existence the greatest fruitfulness and the greatest enjoyment is—to live dangerously!"

Chapter 11

1. As Bernd Magnus (1986, pp. 79–98) has argued, the evidence for the will to power as a cosmological principle primarily comes from the *Nachlass*, and Nietzsche seems to have abandoned the concept in this sense after 1888. Heidegger has been the main proponent of the view that Nietzsche's entire philosophy can be identified with the will to power: "We call Nietzsche's thought of will to power his *sole* thought." (Heidegger 1987, volume 3, p. 10). Löwith (1997) discusses the will to power as a cosmological principle while appreciating its other aspects.

2. See chapter 3 of Nehamas 1985 and chapter 4 of Warren 1987.

3. In WP #488, #671, #692, and #715, Nietzsche tells us that there is no such thing as the will.

4. The king continues: "A whole landscape is refreshed by one such tree. Whoever grows up high like you, O Zarathustra, I compare to the pine: long, hard, silent, alone, of the best and most resilient wood, magnificent—and in the end reaching out with strong green branches for his *own* dominion, questioning wind and weather and whatever else is at home on the heights with forceful questions, and answering yet more forcefully, a commander, triumphant: oh, who would not climb high mountains to see such plants? Your tree here, O Zarathustra, refreshes even the gloomy ones, the failures; your sight reassures and heals the heart even of the restless. (Z, IV, "The Welcome"). In comparing Zarathustra's strong will to a tree, Nietzsche adopts an organic metaphor that centers on majesty. Though solitude is a part of this description, Zarathustra also is shown to be inquiring and to have a healthy influence on others.

5. "Willing liberates," announces Zarathustra in Z II #2; "that is the true teaching of will and liberty."

6. Nietzsche starkly emphasizes this point in BGE #21: "... in real life it is only a matter of strong and weak wills."

7. Warren (1987, p. 144) has observed that Dionysian experience coincides with what Freud termed "primary process."

8. Freud, *The Interpretation of Dreams* (*Standard Edition*, volume 5).

9. Freud, *Beyond the Pleasure Principle* (*Standard Edition*, volume 18). Further modifications of psychoanalytic theory, including Melanie Klein's object relations theory, focus on primitive aspects of human experience. For Kleinians, primary process persists and periodically is manifest even in normal adult functioning. According to the Kleinian theory of development, the infant's early life is governed by a split world of experience, where things are all good or all bad, symbolized by the good breast, representing the satisfaction of being gratified by the primary caregiver, and the bad breast, representing the frustration and sense of persecution from the delay or absence of satisfaction. For a contemporary statement of Kleinian theory, see Ogden 1989.

10. See also WP #643.

11. This positive evaluation of freedom of will represents a problem for Nehamas's (1985, p. 186) summary judgment that Nietzsche is "a great enemy of the notion of the freedom of the will."

12. In TI, "The Four Great Errors," #7, freedom of the will is portrayed vitriolically as a hoax perpetrated by theologians.

13. The quotation of Nietzsche is from GS #1.

14. See e.g. GM II #5 and #6; BGE #259. Although Nietzsche never explicitly recommends violence for the sake of violence, he repeatedly comments on the gratification in retaliation and is fascinated by the prospect of evil. In TI, "What I Owe the Ancients," #5, he speaks of the joy in destruction.

15. I think it is legitimate to refer to French Nietzscheans without making the mistake of attributing unanimity to such a diverse array of philosophers. Three main sources of this perspective in English are Allison 1977; "Nietzsche's Return," *Semiotexte* 3 (1978), no. 1: 4–149; and Rickels 1990. The word 'malignant' is used here to denote that power legitimizes at least some forms of evil conduct and that it bears an uneasy relation to religious and social institutions. The word is limited by its inevitable association with pathology. Insofar as one attributes to Nietzsche a belief in power as domination, this is a positive thing: agents acting on such a basis would not see themselves as engaging in bad or undesirable conduct.

16. See also WP #650, BGE #13, and TI, "Skirmishes of an Untimely Man," #14.

17. The notion of power as the "bestowing virtue" is taken from Z III, "Of the Three Evil Things."

18. For an useful discussion of Foucault's Nietzschean-influenced use of power, see Hoy 1986.

19. This entails a problem for Foucault, as a number of commentators have pointed out. According to Jay (1984, p. 528), "Foucault was clearly outraged at certain forms of that domination, but it was never clear from what normative vantage point, aside from his own personal preferences." Fraser (1989, p. 29) adds: "Foucault calls in no uncertain terms for resistance to domination. But why? Why is struggle preferable to domination? Why ought domination be resisted?" Fraser is concerned about whether Foucault's desire to suspend the normative applies to any and all frameworks or simply the one supplied by liberal theory (the former is more problematic from her point of view). Regardless, Fraser concludes that "clearly what Foucault needs, and needs desperately, are normative criteria for distinguishing acceptable from unacceptable forms of power" (ibid., p. 33). Honneth (1991, p. 162) sharpens this critique of Foucault, claiming that Foucault's theory of power is guilty of "political decisionism" in that he makes the unwarranted assumption that while social struggle is ongoing, legal norms and moral attitudes are blanketly regarded as "historically variable superstructures."

20. Deleuze (1983, p. 85) also points out that the will to power "does not mean that the will wants more power" and "is essentially creative and giving."

21. For Nietzsche's criticism of self-control, see GS #305. See also D #109, where Nietzsche's comments on "self-mastery," emphasizing that it is constituted by various kinds of attempts to regulate drives. He concludes that self-mastery is, in the end, merely one drive set against another.

22. Nietzsche countenances misunderstanding, and he sees limits to our self-knowledge, but not to the same extent as Lacan or Bataille. Nietzsche shares Lacan's skepticism toward equating the ego with the self. I do not think that Nietzsche would have been attracted to the masochistic aspect of self-annihilation in Bataille, as it comes perilously close to a life-denying impulse. For a helpful discussion of related issues, see Dean 1992.

23. Two passages in WP, both from the period March–June 1888, bear on this issue. In WP #688, which attracted Heidegger's attention because it posits the will to power as an essential principle (the aphorism is titled "Unitary Conception of Psychology"), Nietzsche argues that pleasure is a "symptom. . . an accompaniment. . . not the motive" of power. In WP #1023, Nietzsche affirms a link between pleasure and power: ". . . pleasure appears where there is a feeling of power."

24. To some extent, it depends on what self-regulation means. In the second volume of his *History of Sexuality*, Foucault draws a contrast between the Greek ideal of self-regulation as revealed in 'enkrateia' (literally em-powered) and in 'sophrosyne', which he calls "heautocratic," and the Christian ideal, which he calls hostile to pleasure (p. 70).

25. See also WP #652.

26. Warren (1987, p. 129) argues that the will to power is consistent with the goal of autonomy and with unified agency.

27. One such passage in which Nietzsche praises independence is BGE #29.

28. Löwith (1997, p. 122) emphasizes that Nietzsche had taken up the themes of freedom and fate by the time he was 18 years old.

Chapter 12

1. A good example of this is found in BGE #44, where Nietzsche describes free spirits as we "born, sworn, jealous friends of solitude."

2. For example, D #142.

3. Nietzsche claims, for example, that the creditor "participates in a *right of the masters.*" (GM II #5).

4. In HAH I #43, Nietzsche suggests that gratitude represents a milder form of revenge as a way not to lose self-esteem in relation to their benefactors. In his later view, gratitude is not portrayed as reactive in this way.

5. The major exception is Derrida's *Politics of Friendship*, which I will discuss in section 12.3.

6. See also D #503.

7. Nietzsche does not always endorse reciprocity; in WP #926 he lambasts it as "vulgar" because it is a way to obscure our uniqueness.

8. Berkowitz (1995, p. 173) points out that Nietzsche fails to account for moments of intimacy and melting of barriers in friendships.

9. The last chapter of part I of HAH is titled "Man Alone with Himself." It is followed by an epilogue, titled "Among Friends." The two stanzas have the same refrain: "Shall we do this, friends, again? / Amen! and *auf Wiedersehn!*" Thus, the beginning (the preface on isolation and the hope for relatedness) and the end of the first part of HAH are dominated by the theme of human connection.

10. The letter is quoted on p. 17 of Stern 1979.

11. I will not try to do justice to Derrida's whole convoluted argument in this context. I will return to his Nietzsche interpretation in chapter 13.

12. Derrida (1979, pp. 47–49), too, features the theme of distance in his interpretation of Nietzsche on women.

13. See Derrida 1997, pp. 64 (on democracy) and 281 (on women). In an interview conducted by Richard Beardsworth, Derrida (1994) is quite specific in claiming that Nietzsche's critique of democracy is "made in the name of what I would call a 'democracy to come.'" He adds: "I don't consider Nietzsche to be an enemy of democracy in general." Derrida first explored Nietzsche's view of women in *Spurs* (1979).

14. See, e.g., Burgard 1994; Patton 1994; Oliver 1988, 1994; Shapiro 1991; Graybeal 1990; Krell 1986; Bergoffen 1989; Ormiston 1994.

15. For example, in GM II #10 Nietzsche describes mercy as the self-overcoming of justice and concludes that it "remains the privilege of the most powerful men."

16. Schrift (1995, p. 100) analyzes "the logic of the gift" and, borrowing from Helene Cixous, criticizes Nietzsche for associating reception with need and weakness.

17. See Nehamas 1985 and Chamberlain 1996.

Chapter 13

1. This is not the place to pursue a comparison between Nietzsche and Freud, although in the course of this chapter I will have occasion to explore the proto-psychoanalytic direction of Nietzsche's philosophy.

2. Schaberg (1995) documents Nietzsche's consuming interest in and frustration with the response to his work.

3. On the title page of Derrida's book, the letter 'a' in 'Ear' is backwards.

4. Derrida (1985, p. 5) points out that "we no longer consider the biography of a 'philosopher' as a corpus of empirical accidents that leaves both a name and a signature outside a system which itself be offered up to immanent philosophical reading—the only kind of reading held to be philosophically legitimate." In the context of his debate with Gadamer, Derrida notes that in Heidegger "biography, autobiography, the scene or the powers of the proper name, of proper names, signatures, and so on, are again accorded minority status, are again given the inessential place they have always occupied in the history of metaphysics" (Michelfelder and Palmer 1989, p. 59).

5. Behler (1991, p. vii) emphasizes that Derrida's relationship with Heidegger is bound with his interpretation of Nietzsche.

6. Derrida (1978, p. 198; 1987, pp. 191 and 357) discusses Heidegger and Freud as "a couple." On p. 179 of *The Ear of the Other*, Derrida specifically criticizes Heidegger for ignoring sexuality and sexual difference and for his apparent indifference to psychoanalysis. For an earlier statement of this same point, see Derrida 1979, p. 109. Derrida's commitment to psychoanalysis is persistent in his later work. On pp. 54 and 55 of *Archive Fever* (1996a), Derrida cautions against trying to discuss psychoanalysis or any other social or human science from an apsychoanalytic point of view.

7. In a 1983 interview with Catherine David (quoted on p. 127 of Derrida 1995b), Derrida declares: "Psychoanalysis should oblige one to rethink the whole axiomatics of law, of morality, of 'human rights,' the whole discourse constructed on the agency of the self and of conscious responsibility, the politician's rhetoric, the concept of torture, legal psychiatry and its whole system."

8. An astute account of Derrida's relationship to Levinas is found in Critchley 1992.

9. Here I am simplifying Derrida's argument, which focuses on the sense of sight and compares it to other senses in both Hegel and Levinas.

10. In brief, Derrida shows how Levinas's refusal of sexual difference affirms patriarchy. Several of the essays in Bernasconi and Critchley 1991 focus on Levinas's affirmation of patriarchy. For example, Irigaray argues (in parallel to her argument about Nietzsche, mentioned in chapter 12 above) that Levinas makes no room for shared pleasure.

11. My point here is that it is reasonable to expect Derrida to have more to say about this issue. It is possible to argue, for instance, that Nietzsche's and Levinas's view on

the Other are not as opposed as they seem—especially if one takes account of both philosophers' interests in affects. The "basic emotions" view in psychology, which has its source in Darwin but which was developed by Tomkins and Ekman, supports the notion that emotions are displayed facially and is echoed by Levinas.

12. In *The Ear of the Other* (1985), Derrida writes: ". . . I'm no fan of modernity. I have no simple belief in the irreducible specificity of 'modernity. ' I even wonder if I have ever used that word." The gulf between Derrida and Nietzsche is evident here.

13. See "There Is No One Narcissism," in Derrida 1995b.

14. For a comparison of Derrida's and Lacan's ideas, see Dews 1995 and Frank 1989. For Derrida's reflections on his relationship to Lacan, see Derrida 1998.

15. In a 1982 interview (quoted on p. 81 of Derrida 1995b), Derrida claims: "Psychoanalysis owes to Lacan some of its most original advances. It has been taken thereby to its limits, sometimes beyond itself, and it is especially in this way that it keeps fortunately that value of provocation also for what is most vital today in philosophy as well as in literature and the human sciences."

16. *Jacques Lacan & Co.* (Roudinesco 1990) is the English translation.

17. Felman (1987, p. 6) emphasizes that Lacan saw himself first and foremost as a clinician. See also Dor 1999.

18. At times, Lacan points out differences between Nietzsche and Freud. See, e.g., Lacan 1977, pp. 118–119.

19. Frank (1989, pp. 202–205) suggests some parallels between Nietzsche and Lacan in terms of the subject as the origin of misapprehension.

20. For an account of the limitations of Lacan's notion of the ego, see pp. 119–164 of Whitebook 1995.

21. This passage, translated from the French edition of *Écrits*, is quoted on p. 67 of Dews 1995.

22. Butler's position on the notion of the phallus is nuanced: she protests Lacan's valorization of the body part, but she opts not to reject the term by invoking the notion of the "lesbian phallus."

23. See also Butler 1997a, p. 22.

24. Butler makes this argument in *Gender Trouble* (pp. 56–57) and in *Bodies That Matter* (p. 14).

25. Butler (1997a, p. 206, note 5) contrasts the "psyche" (inclusive of the unconscious) with the "subject" (exclusive of the unconscious).

26. An impulse to defend psychoanalysis is arguably already present in *Gender Trouble*—for example, in Butler's response to Wittig's rejection of psychoanalysis as dependent on an economy of lack and negation (p. 118). Butler also raises questions Foucault's "repression hypothesis," which makes no attempt to imagine a psychoanalytic redescription of sex in *Bodies That Matter* (p. 22) and in *Excitable Speech* (p. 94).

27. Among the issues that Butler would encounter are the sense of agency that exists before the unfolding of conscience (the affect of "shame" does not develop until 14–16 months), the capacity to regulate affects (which has both a social and biological aspect), the interaction between the family (especially the primary caregiver) and the institution of social norms, and the quality of mutuality between primary caregiver and infant.

28. Bach (1994, p. 31) argues that self-deflation means being locked into objective awareness (wherein one feels like an object among other objects, a self among selves), and that self-inflation means being locked into subjective awareness (wherein one has the immediate experience of oneself as the center of thought, feelings, and action). Bach defends the importance of knowing how and when to remain in these modes of consciousness and how and when to shift between them. See also Bach 1985.

29. Another interesting consequence of Fonagy and Target's work is to demonstrate that there are pathological results of the failure of self-reflexivity.

30. Derrida (1995a, p. 16) discusses affects in the context of criticizing Kant, but he does not mention Nietzsche.

Epilogue

1. In a related point, Nietzsche also tells us that "to derive something unknown [Unbekanntes] from something familiar [Bekanntes] relieves, comforts, and satisfies [befriedigt], besides giving a feeling of power" (TI, "The Four Great Errors," #5).

Bibliography

Hegel in German

Gesammelte Werke (**GW**). In *Auftrag der Deutschen Forschungsgemeinschaft von der Rheinisch-Westfälischen Akademie der Wissenschaften.*

Band [volume] 1: *Frühe Schriften.* 1989.

Band 3: *Frühe Exzerpte.* 1991.

Band 4: *Jenaer Kritische Schriften.* 1968.

Band 5: *Schriften und Entwürfe.* 1998.

Band 6: *Jenaer Systementwürfe I.* 1975.

Band 7: *Jenaer Systementwürfe II.* 1971.

Band 8: *Jenaer Systementwürfe III.* 1976.

Band 9: *Phänomenologie des Geistes.* 1980.

Briefe von und an Hegel. volume 1: 1785–1812. Meiner, 1969.

Frühe Politische Systeme. Ullstein, 1974.

Der Geist des Christentums. Ullstein, 1978.

Mythologie der Vernunft. Suhrkamp, 1984.

Politische Schriften. Frankfurt, 1966.

Sämtliche Werke, Bände 1–20. Meiner, 1968.

Vorlesungen über die Geschichte der Philosophie, Bände 6–9.

Vorlesungen über die Philosophie der Weltgeschichte, Band 12.

Werke in 20 Bänden. Suhrkamp, 1969.

Hegel in English

Hegel's Aesthetics, volumes 1 and 2. Clarendon, 1975.

The Berlin Phenomenology. Reidel, 1981.

Difference between the Systems of Fichte and Schelling. State University of New York Press, 1976.

Early Theological Writings. University of Pennyslvania Press, 1971.

Elements of the Philosophy of Right. Cambridge University Pres, 1991.

Faith and Knowledge. State University of New York Press, 1977.

Hegel and the Human Spirit: Jena Lectures on the Philosophy of Spirit (1805–1806) (**PhilS II**). Wayne State University, 1983.

Hegel's Idea of History. Fordham University Press, 1971.

Hegel's Lectures on the History of Philosophy (**LHP**), volumes 1–3. Humanities Press, 1974 (reprint).

Lectures on the Philosophy of Religion, volumes 1–3. Humanities Press, 1974 (reprint).

Lectures on the Philosophy of World History (**LPWH**). Cambridge University Press, 1975.

Natural Law (**NL**). University of Pennsylvania Press, 1975.

The Oldest Program Towards a System in German Idealism (1797). *Owl of Minerva* 17 (1985), no. 1: 5–19.

The Phenomenology of Mind. Harper & Row, 1967.

Hegel's Phenomenology of Spirit (**PhS**). Clarendon, 1977.

The Philosophy of History. Dover, 1956.

Hegel's Philosophy of Mind (**PM**) (part III of *Encyclopedia of the Philosophical Sciences*). Clarendon, 1971.

Hegel's Philosophy of Right (**PR**). Oxford University Press, 1967.

Hegel's Political Writings. Clarendon, 1964.

The Philosophical Propaedeutic (**PP**). Blackwell, 1986.

Reason in History (**RH**). Bobbs-Merrill, 1953.

Bibliography

Hegel's Science of Logic. Humanities Press, 1969.

System of Ethical Life (**SS**) and *First Philosophy of Spirit* (**PhilS I**) (part III of *System of Speculative Philosophy*, 1803–04). State University of New York Press, 1979.

Hegel on Tragedy, ed. A. Paolucci and H. Paolucci. Doubleday, 1962.

Three Essays 1793–1795. University of Notre Dame Press, 1984.

The Tübingen Essay of 1793. In *Hegel's Development.* Clarendon, 1972.

Two Fragments of 1797 on Love. *Clio* 8 (1979), no. 2: 258–265.

Hegel: The Letters. Indiana University Press, 1984.

Nietzsche in German

Sämtliche Werke (**SW**). Walter de Gruyter, 1967.

Nietzsches Werke: Grossoktavausgabe, second edition. Alfred Kröner, 1901–1926.

Werke in drei Bänden. Carl Hanser, 1954–1956.

Nietzsche Briefwechsel: Kritische Gesamtausgabe. Walter deGruyter, 1975.

Nietzsche in English

The Antichrist (**A**). In *The Portable Nietzsche.* Viking, 1954.

Basic Writings of Nietzsche. Random House, 1968.

Beyond Good and Evil (**BGE**). In *Basic Writings of Nietzsche*, ed. W. Kaufmann. Random House, 1968.

Nietzsche: The Birth of Tragedy and Other Writings. Cambridge University Press, 1999.

The Birth of Tragedy (**BT**). In *Basic Writings of Nietzsche.* Random House, 1968.

The Complete Works of Friedrich Nietzsche. Gordon, 1909–1911.

The Portable Nietzsche, ed. W. Kaufmann. Viking, 1954.

The Case of Wagner (**CW**). Vintage, 1967.

Daybreak (**D**). Cambridge University Press, 1982.

Ecce Homo (**EH**). In *Basic Writings of Nietzsche.* Random House, 1968.

The Gay Science (**GS**). Vintage, 1974.

Human, All Too Human (**HAH**). Cambridge University Press, 1986.

On the Future of Our Educational Institutions (**FEI**). Volume 3 of *The Complete Works of Friedrich Nietzsche*. Macmillan, 1911.

On the Genealogy of Morals (**GM**). In *Basic Writings of Nietzsche*. Random House, 1968.

Philosophy in the Tragic Age of the Greeks (**PTG**). Regnery, 1962.

Selected Letters of Friedrich Nietzsche, ed. C. Middleton. University of Chicago Press, 1969.

Philosophy and Truth (**PT**). Humanities Press, 1979.

Twilight of the Idols (**TI**). In *The Portable Nietzsche*. Viking, 1954.

Untimely Meditations (**UM**). Cambridge University Press, 1983. Includes "David Strauss, the Confessor and the Writer" (**DS**), "On the Uses and Disadvantages of History for Life" (**UDHL**), "Schopenhauer as Educator" (**SE**), and "Richard Wagner in Bayreuth" (**RWB**)

The Will to Power (**WP**). Viking, 1968.

Thus Spoke Zarathustra (**Z**). In *The Portable Nietzsche*. Viking, 1954.

Other Works

Abrams, M. H. 1971. *Natural Supernaturalism*. Norton.

Adorno, T. 1973a. *Negative Dialectics*. Seabury.

Adorno, T. 1973b. *The Jargon of Authenticity*. Northwestern University Press.

Adorno, T. 1974. *Minima Moralia*. Verso.

Adorno, T. 1981. *Prisms*. MIT Press.

Adorno, T. 1993. *Hegel: Three Studies*. MIT Press.

Adorno, T. 1994. *The Stars Down to Earth*. Routledge.

Adorno, T. 1998. *Critical Models: Interventions and Catchwords*. Columbia University Press.

Adorno, T. 1994. Anti-Semitism and Fascist Propaganda. In *The Stars Down to Earth and Other Essays*, ed. S. Crook. Routledge.

Allison, D. B., ed. 1977. *The New Nietzsche*. Delta.

Althaus, H. 1992. *Hegel und die herioschen Jahre der Philosophie*. Hauser.

Ansell-Pearson, K. 1994. *An Introduction to Nietzsche as Political Thinker*. Cambridge University Press.

Bibliography

Appiah, A. 1992–93. African-American Philosophy. *Philosophical Forum* 24, no. 1–3: 11–34.

Aristotle. 1987. *Poetics.* Hackett.

Aschheim, S. 1992. *The Nietzsche Legacy in Germany, 1890–1990.* University of California Press.

Asveld, P. 1953. *La pensée e religieuse du jeune Hegel.* Publications universitaires de Louvain.

Atherton, M. 1993. Cartesian Reason and Gendered Reason. In *A Mind of One's Own,* ed. L. Anthony and C. Witt. Westview.

Avineri, S. 1972. *Hegel's Theory of the Modern State.* Cambridge University Press.

Bach, S. 1985. *Narcissistic States and the Therapeutic Process.* Aronson.

Bach, S. 1994. *The Language of Love and the Language of Perversion.* Aronson.

Bakhtin, M. 1986. *Speech Genres and Other Late Essays.* University of Texas Press.

Barnett, S., ed. 1998. *Hegel after Derrida.* Routledge.

Bataille, G. 1985. *Visions of Excess: Selected Writings 1927–1939.* University of Minnesota Press.

Bataille, G. 1992. *On Nietzsche.* Paragon House.

Baum, M., and Meist, K. 1977. Durch Philosophie Leben Lernen. Hegel's Konzeption der Philosophie nach den neu aufgefundenen Jenaer Manuscripten. *Hegel-Studien* 12: 43–81.

Beebe, B., and Lachmann, F. 1988. The Contribution of Mother-Infant Mutual Influence to the Origins of Self and Object Representations. *Psychoanalytic Psychology* 5: 305–337.

Beebe, B., Jaffe, J., and Lachmann, F. 1992. A Dyadic Systems View of Communication. In *Relational Perspectives in Psychoanalysis,* ed. N. Skolnick and S. Warshaw. Analytic Press.

Beerling, B. F. 1961. Hegel und Nietzsche. *Hegel-Studien* 1–2: 229–246.

Behler, E. 1991. *Confrontations: Derrida/Heidegger/Nietzsche.* Stanford University Press.

Beiser, F., ed. 1993. *The Cambridge Companion to Hegel.* Cambridge University Press.

Benhabib, S. 1986. *Critique, Norm and Utopia.* Columbia University Press.

Benhabib, S. 1992. *Situating the Self.* Routledge.

Benhabib, S., Bonss, W., and McCole, J., eds. 1993. *On Max Horkheimer.* MIT Press.

Benjamin, J. 1987. *The Bonds of Love*. Pantheon Books.

Benjamin, J. 1992. Recognition and Destruction: An Outline of Intersubjectivity. In *Relational Perspectives in Psychoanalysis*, ed. N. Skolnick and S. Warshaw. Analytic Press.

Benjamin, J. 1995. *Like Subjects, Love Objects*. Yale University Press.

Benjamin, J. 1998. *The Shadow of the Other*. Routledge.

Bergmann, P. 1987. *Nietzsche: The Last Unpolitical German*. University of Indiana Press.

Bergoffen, D. B. 1989. On the Advantage and Disadvantage of Nietzsche for Women. In *The Question of the Other*, ed. A. B. Dallery and C. E. Scott. State University of New York Press.

Berkowitz, P. 1995. *Nietzsche: The Ethics of an Immoralist*. Harvard University Press.

Berlin, I. 1976. *Vico and Herder*. Viking Press.

Berman, M. 1982. *All That Is Solid Melts in the Air*. Simon & Schuster.

Bernasconi, R., and Critchley, S., eds. 1991. *Rereading Levinas*. Indiana University Press.

Bernstein, J. 1989. Art against Enlightenment: Adorno's Critique of Habermas. In *The Problems of Modernity*, ed. A. Benjamin. Routledge.

Bernstein, R. 1971. *Praxis and Action*. University of Pennsylvania Press.

Bernstein, R. 1983. *Beyond Objectivism and Relativism*. University of Pennsylvania Press.

Bernstein, R., ed. 1985. *Habermas and Modernity*. MIT Press.

Bernstein, R. 1992. *The New Constellation: The Ethical-Political Horizons of Modernity/Postmodernity*. MIT Press.

Berthold-Bond, D. 1995. *Hegel's Theory of Madness*. State University of New York Press.

Blanchot, M. 1997. *Friendship*. Stanford University Press.

Blondel, E. 1991. *Nietzsche: The Body and Culture*. Stanford University Press.

Blumenberg, H. 1985. *The Legitimacy of the Modern Age*. MIT Press.

Bonnell, V., and Hunt, L., eds. 1999. *Beyond the Cultural Turn*. University of California Press.

Bonsiepen, W. 1977. Der Begriff der Negativität in Jenaer Schriften Hegels. *Hegel-Studien* Beiheft 16.

Bordo, S. 1987. *The Flight to Objectivity: Essays on Cartesianism and Culture*. State University of New York Press.

Bradley, A. C. 1962. Hegel's Theory of Tragedy. In *Hegel on Tragedy*, ed. A. and H. Paolucci. Doubleday.

Breazeale, D. 1975. The Hegel-Nietzsche Problem. *Nietzsche-Studien* 4: 146–164.

Brunkhorst, H. 1992. Culture and Bourgeois Society: The Unity of Reason in a Divided Society. In *Cultural-Political Interventions in the Unfinished Project of the Enlightenment*, ed. A. Honneth et al. MIT Press.

Burgard, P. J., ed. 1994. *Nietzsche and the Feminine*. University of Virginia Press.

Butler, J. 1987. *Subjects of Desire*. Columbia University Press.

Butler, J. 1990. *Gender Trouble*. Routledge.

Butler, J. 1993. *Bodies That Matter: On the Discursive Limits of Sex*. Routledge.

Butler, J. 1997a. *The Psychic Life of Power*. Stanford University Press.

Butler, J. 1997b. *Excitable Speech*. Routledge.

Cascardi, A. J. *The Subject of Modernity*. Cambridge University Press 1992.

Cavell, S. 1987. Freud and Philosophy. *Critical Inquiry* 13, no. 2: 386–393.

Chamberlain, L. 1996. *Nietzsche in Turin*. Picador.

Clark, M. 1989. *Nietzsche on Truth and Philosophy*. Cambridge University Press.

Cooke, M. 1994. Realizing the Post-Conventional Self. *Philosophy and Social Criticism* 20, no. 1/2: 87–101.

Cooke, M. 1995. Selfhood and Solidarity. *Constellations* 3, January: 337–357.

Corngold, S. 1986. *The Fate of the Self*. Columbia University Press.

Christensen, D. 1968. The Theory of Mental Derangement and the Role and Function of Subjectivity. *Personalist* 49: 433–452.

Critchley, S. 1992. *The Ethics of Deconstruction*. Blackwell.

Critchley, S. 1997. *Very Little, Almost Nothing*. Routledge.

Damasio, A. 1994. *Descartes' Error*. Putnam.

Danto, A. 1965. *Nietzsche as Philosopher*. Macmillan.

Danto, A. 1993. The Shape of Artistic Pasts. In *Philosophical Imagination and Cultural Memory*, ed. P. Cook. Duke University Press.

Dasenbrock, R. W., ed. 1989. *Redrawing the Line: Analytic Philosophy, Deconstruction and Literary Theory*. University of Minnesota Press.

Dean, C. 1992. *The Self and Its Pleasures: Bataille, Lacan and the History of the Decentered Subject.* Cornell University Press.

Deleuze, G. 1983. *Nietzsche and Philosophy.* Columbia University Press.

Deleuze, G. 1988. *Foucault.* University of Minnesota Press.

Deleuze, G., and Guattari, F. 1983. *Anti-Oedipus: Capitalism and Schizophrenia.* University of Minnesota Press.

Derrida, J. 1978. *Writing and Difference.* University of Chicago Press.

Derrida, J. 1979. *Spurs: Nietzsche's Styles.* University of Chicago Press.

Derrida, J. 1981a. *Disseminations.* University of Chicago Press.

Derrida, J. 1981b. *Positions.* University of Chicago Press.

Derrida, J. 1982 *Margins of Philosophy.* University of Chicago Press.

Derrida, J. 1985. *The Ear of the Other.* University of Nebraska Press.

Derrida, J. 1986. *Glas.* University of Nebraska Press.

Derrida, J. 1987. *The Post Card.* University of Chicago Press.

Derrida, J. 1989. *Of Spirit: Heidegger and the Question.* University of Chicago Press.

Derrida, J. 1994. Nietzsche and the Machine (interview with Derrida by R. Beardsworth). *Journal of Nietzsche Studies* 7, spring: 7–66.

Derrida, J. 1995a *On the Name.* Stanford University Press.

Derrida, J. 1995b. *Points: Interviews 1974–1994.* Stanford University Press.

Derrida, J. 1996a. *Archive Fever: A Freudian Impression.* University of Chicago Press.

Derrida, J. 1996b. Adieu. *Critical Inquiry* 23, no. 1: 1–10.

Derrida, J. 1997. *Politics of Friendship.* Verso.

Derrida, J. 1998. *Resistances of Psychoanalysis.* Stanford University Press.

Descartes, R. 1986. *Meditations on First Philosophy.* Cambridge University Press.

Descombes, V. 1980. *Modern French Philosophy.* Cambridge University Press.

DeSousa, R. 1987. *The Rationality of Emotion.* MIT Press.

Detwiler, B. 1990. *Nietzsche and the Politics of Aristocratic Radicalism.* University of Chicago Press.

DeVries, W. 1988. *Hegel's Theory of Mental Activity.* Cornell University Press.

Dews, P. 1987. *Logics of Disintegration.* Verso.

Dews, P. 1995. *The Limits of Disenchantment.* Verso.

d'Hondt, J., ed. 1974. *Hegel et la pensée grecque.* Presses universitaires de France.

Dickey, L. 1987. *Hegel: Religion, Economics and the Politics of the Spirit.* Cambridge University Press.

Dilthey, W. 1963. *Die Jugendgeschichte Hegels in Gessammelte Schriften,* volume 4. Teubner.

Diprose, R. 1991. In Excess: The Body and the Habit of Sexual Difference. *Hypatia* 6: 156–171.

Dodds, E. R. 1968. *The Greeks and the Irrational.* University of California Press.

Dor, J. 1999. *The Clinical Lacan.* Other Press.

Dove, K. 1971. Hegel's Phenomenological Method. In *New Studies in Hegel's Philosophy,* ed. W. Steinkraus. Holt, Rinehart and Winston.

Dreyfus, H., and Rabinow, P. 1983. *Michel Foucault: Beyond Structuralism and Hermeneutics.* University of Chicago Press.

Drury, S. 1994. *Alexandre Kojève: The Roots of Postmodern Politics.* St. Martin's Press.

Düsing, K. 1969. Spekulation und Reflexion. Zur Zusammenarbeit Schellings und Hegel in Jena. *Hegel-Studien* 5: 95–128.

Eagleton, T. 2000. *The Idea of Culture.* Blackwell.

Ekman, P. 1992. An Argument for Basic Emotions. *Cognition and Emotion* 6, no. 3/4: 169–200.

Else, G. 1957. *Aristotle's Poetics: The Argument.* Harvard University Press.

Emde, R. 1983. The Prerepresentational Self and Its Affective Core. *Psychoanalytic Study of the Child* 38: 165–192

Felman, S. 1987. *Jacques Lacan and the Adventure of Insight: Psychoanalysis in Contemporary Culture.* Harvard University Press.

Ferrara, A. 1998. *Reflective Modernity: Rethinking the Project of Modernity.* Routledge.

Ferry, L., and Renaut, A. 1990a. *Heidegger and Modernity.* Chicago University Press.

Ferry, L., and Renaut, A. 1990b. *French Philosophy of the Sixties.* University of Massachusetts Press.

Findlay, J. N. 1962. *Hegel: A Re-Examination.* Oxford University Press.

Flax, J. 1993. *Disputed Subjects: Essays on Psychoanalysis, Politics and Philosophy.* Routledge.

Fonagy, P., and Target, M. 1996a. Playing with Reality. I. Theory of Mind and the Normal Development of Psychic Reality. *International Journal of Psycho-Analysis* 77: 217–233.

Fonagy, P., and Target, M. 1996b. Playing with Reality. II. The Development of Psychic Reality from a Theoretical Perspective. *International Journal of Psycho-Analysis* 77: 459–479.

Forster, M. 1989. *Hegel and Skepticism.* Cambridge University Press.

Forster, M. 1998. *Hegel's Idea of a Phenomenology of Spirit.* University of Chicago Press.

Foucault, M. 1977. *Language, Counter-Memory, Practice: Selected Essays and Interviews,* ed. D. Bouchard. Cornell University Press.

Foucault, M. 1980. *Power/Knowledge: Selected Interviews and Other Writings 1972–1977.* Pantheon.

Foucault, M. 1985. *History of Sexuality, The Uses of Pleasure.* Random House.

Foucault, M. 1997. *Ethics: Subjectivity and Truth.* New Press.

Frank, M. 1989. *What Is Neostructuralism?* University of Minnesota Press.

Frankfurt, H. 1971. Freedom of the Will and the Concept of a Person. *Journal of Philosophy* 67, no. 1: 5–20.

Fraser, N. 1997. *Justice Interruptus: Critical Reflections on the Postsocialist Condition.* Routledge.

Fraser, N. 1989. *Unruly Practices: Power, Discourse and Gender in Contemporary Social Theory.* University of Minnesota Press.

Freud, S. 1953–. *The Standard Edition.* Hogarth.

Friedländer, S. 1993. *Memory, History and the Extermination of the Jews of Europe.* Indiana University Press.

Frisby, D. 1986. *Fragments of Modernity.* MIT Press.

Fulda, H. F. 1965. *Das Problem einer Einleitung in Hegels Wissenschaft der Logik.* Klosterman.

Fulda, H. F., and Henrich, D., eds. 1967. *Das Recht der Philosophie in Hegels Philosophie des Rechts.* Klosterman.

Fulda, H. F., and Henrich, D., eds. 1973. *Materialen zu Hegels Phänomenologie des Geistes.* Suhrkamp.

Gadamer, H. G. 1975. *Truth and Method.* Seabury.

Gadamer, H. G. 1976. *Hegel's Dialectic.* Yale University Press.

Gadamer, H. G. 1992. Culture and Media. In *Cultural-Political Interventions in the Unfinished Project of Enlightenment*, ed. A. Honneth et al. MIT Press.

Gauss, C. 1957. *The Papers of Christian Gauss*, ed. K. Jackson and H. Haydn. Random House.

Gergely, G., and Watson, J. 1996. The Social Biofeedback Theory of Parental Affect-Mirroring: The Development of Emotional Self-Awarenesss and Self-Control in Infancy. *International Journal of Psycho-Analysis* 77: 1181–1212.

Geuss, R. 1981. *The Idea of a Critical Theory*. Cambridge University Press.

Geuss, R. 1996. Kultur, Bildung, Geist. *History and Theory* 35, no. 2: 151–164.

Gilman, S. 1981. Hegel, Schopenhauer and Nietzsche See the Black. *Hegel-Studien* 16: 163–188.

Golden, L. 1962. Catharsis. *Transactions of the American Philological Association* 93: 57–60.

Gray, G. 1941. *Hegel's Hellenic Ideal*. Harper & Row.

Graybeal, J. 1990. *Language and the Feminine in Nietzsche and Heidegger*. Indiana University Press.

Greene, M. 1972. *Hegel on the Soul*. Martinus Nijhoff.

Griffiths, P. 1997. *What Emotions Really Are*. University of Chicago Press.

Habermas, J. 1971. *Knowledge and Human Interests*. Beacon.

Habermas, J. 1973. Labor and Interaction: Remarks on Hegel's Jena Philosophy of Mind. In *Theory and Practice*. Beacon.

Habermas, J. 1981. *The Theory of Communicative Action*, volume 1. Beacon.

Habermas, J. 1983a. *Philosophical-Political Profiles*. MIT Press.

Habermas, J. 1983b. Interpretive Social Science vs. Hermeneutics. In *Social Science as Moral Inquiry*, ed. R. Haan et al. Columbia University Press.

Habermas, J. 1987. *The Philosophical Discourse of Modernity*. MIT Press.

Habermas, J. 1989. Work and Weltanschauung: The Heidegger Controversy from a German Perspective. *Critical Inquiry* 15, no. 2: 431–456.

Habermas, J. 1994. *The Past as Future*. University of Nebraska Press.

Habermas, J. 1998. *The Inclusion of the Other*. MIT Press.

Hamacher, W. 1990. The Promise of Interpretation: Reflections on the Hermeneutical Imperative in Kant and Nietzsche. In *Looking after Nietzsche*, ed. L. Rickels. State University of New York Press.

Hardimon, M. 1994. *Hegel's Social Philosophy: The Project of Reconciliation.* Cambridge University Press.

Harris, H. S. 1972. *Hegel's Development: Towards the Sunlight (1770–1801).* Clarendon.

Harris, H. S. 1980. The Concept of Recognition in Hegel's Jena Manuscripts. *Hegel-Studien* 20: 229–248.

Harris, H. S. 1983. *Hegel's Development: Night Thoughts (Jena 1801–06).* Oxford University Press.

Hartmann, N. 1957. *"Aristoteles und Hegel" in Kleinere Schriften II.* Walter de Gruyter.

Havas, R. 1995. *Nietzsche's Genealogy: Nihilism and the Will to Knowledge.* Cornell University Press.

Heidegger, M. 1959. *An Introduction to Metaphysics.* Doubleday.

Heidegger, M. 1960. Hegel und die Griechen. In *Die Gegenwart der Griechen im neuren Denken: Festschrift fur H. G. Gadamer,* ed. D. Henrich et al. Mohr.

Heidegger, M. 1962. *Being and Time.* Harper & Row.

Heidegger, M. 1966. *Discourse on Thinking.* Harper & Row.

Heidegger, M. 1971. The Origin of the Work of Art. In *Poetry, Language, Thought.* Harper & Row.

Heidegger, M. 1975. *Hegel's Concept of Experience.* Harper & Row.

Heidegger, M. 1979. *Nietzsche,* volume 1. Harper & Row.

Heidegger, M. 1988. *Hegel's Phenomenology of Spirit.* Indiana University Press.

Heidegger, M. 1987. *Nietzsche,* volumes 3 and 4. Harper & Row.

Heidegger, M. 1977. The Age of the World Picture. In *The Question Concerning Technology and Other Essays.* Harper & Row.

Henrich, D. 1971. *Hegel im Kontext.* Suhrkamp.

Honneth, A. 1991. *The Critique of Power.* MIT Press.

Honneth, A. 1992a. *Kampf um Anerkennung.* Suhrkamp.

Honneth, A. 1992b. Moral Development and Social Struggle: Hegel's Early Social-Philosophical Doctrines. In *Cultural-Political Interventions in the Unfinished Project of Enlightenment,* ed. A. Honneth et al. MIT Press.

Honneth, A., McCarthy, T., Offe, C, and Wellmer, A., eds. 1992a. *Philosophical Interventions in the Unfinished Project of the Enlightenment.* MIT Press.

Honneth, A., McCarthy, T., Offe, C, and Wellmer, A., eds. 1992b. *Cultural-Political Interventions in the Unfinished Project of Enlightenment*. MIT Press.

Horkheimer, M. 1947. *Eclipse of Reason*. Seabury.

Horkheimer, M., and Adorno, T. 1986. *Dialectic of Enlightenment*. Continuum.

Horstmann, R. P. 1972. Probleme der Wandlung in Hegels Jenaer Systemkonzeption. *Philosophisches Rundschau* 9: 87–118.

Hösle, V. 1987. *Hegels System: Der Idealismus der Subjectivität und das Problem der Intersubjectivität*, volumes 1 and 2. Meiner.

Houlgate, S. 1986. *Hegel, Nietzsche and the Criticism of Metaphysics*. Cambridge University Press.

Hoy, D. 1986. Power, Repression, Progress: Foucault, Lukes and the Frankfurt School. In *Foucault: A Critical Reader*, ed. D. Hoy. Blackwell.

Hoy, D., and McCarthy, T. 1994. *Critical Theory*. Blackwell.

Hylton, P. 1990. *Russell, Idealism and the Origins of Analytical Philosophy*. Oxford University Press.

Hyppolite, J. 1969. *Studies on Marx and Hegel*. Basic Books.

Hyppolite, J. 1971. Hegel's Phenomenology and Psychoanalysis. In *New Studies in Hegel's Philosophy*, ed. W. Steinkraus. Holt, Rinehart and Winston.

Hyppolite, J. 1974. *Genesis and Structure of Hegel's Phenomenology of Spirit*. Northwestern University Press.

Irigaray, L. 1985. *Speculum of the Other Woman*. Cornell University Press.

Irigaray, L. 1991. *Marine Lover of Friedrich Nietzsche*. Columbia University Press.

Jaeger, W. 1965. *Paideia: The Ideals of Greek Culture*, volume 1. Oxford University Press.

Jaggar, A. M., and Bordo, S., eds. 1989. *Gender/Body/Knowledge*. Rutgers University Press.

Jamme, C. 1986. Hegel and Hölderlin. *Clio* 15, no. 4: 359–377.

Janicaud, D. 1975. *Hegel et le destin de la Grèce*. Vrin.

Jay, M. 1973. *The Dialectical Imagination*. Little, Brown.

Jay, M. 1984. *Marxism and Totality*. University of California Press.

Jay, M. 1986. *Permanent Exiles: Essays on the Intellectual Migration from Germany to America*. Columbia University Press.

Jurist, E. L. 1987. Hegel's Concept of Recognition. *Owl of Minerva* 19, no. 1: 5–22.

Jurist, E. L. 1991. Anti-Semitism and Erasmus. *Jewish Currents* 45, no. 3: 32–35.

Jurist, E. L. 1992. Recognizing the Past. *History and Theory* 31, no. 2: 163–181.

Jurist, E. L. 1993. Tragedy in/and/of Hegel. *Philosophical Forum* 25, no. 2: 151–172.

Jurist, E. L. 1994a. Review of Robert Williams, *Recognition: Fichte and Hegel on the Other.* *Owl of Minerva* 26, no. 1: 59–65.

Jurist, E. L. 1994b. Review of Axel Honneth, *Kampf um Anerkennung. Constellations* 1, no. 1: 171–180.

Kaufmann, W., ed. 1954. *The Portable Nietzsche.* Viking.

Kaufmann, W. 1966. *Hegel: A Reinterpretation.* Doubleday.

Kaufmann, W. 1968. *Nietzsche.* Vintage.

Kelly, G. A. 1969. *Idealism, Politics, and History: Sources of Hegelian Thought.* Cambridge University Press.

Kelly, G. A. 1976. Notes on Hegel's Lordship and Bondage. In *Hegel*, ed. A. MacIntyre. University of Notre Dame Press.

Kernberg, O. 1970. Factors in the Psychoanalytic Treatment of Narcissistic Personalities. In *Essential Papers on Narcissism*, ed. A. Morrison. New York University Press, 1986.

Kernberg, O. 1985. *Borderline Conditions and Pathological Narcissism.* Aronson.

Kierkegaard, S. 1983. *Fear and Trembling.* Princeton University Press.

Knox, B. 1957. *Oedipus at Thebes.* Norton.

Kofman, S. 1988. Baubo: Theological Perversion and Fetishism. In *Nietzsche's New Seas*, ed. M. Gillespie and T. Strong. University of Chicago Press.

Kohut, H. 1966. Forms and Transformations of Narcissism. In *Essential Papers on Narcissism*, ed. A. Morrison. New York University Press, 1986.

Kohut, H. 1971. *The Analysis of the Self.* International Universities Press.

Kojève, A. 1946. Hegel, Marx et christianisme. *Critique* 7, August-September: 339–366.

Kojève, A. 1947. *Introduction à la lecture de Hegel.* Gallimard.

Kojève, A. 1969. *Introduction to the Reading of Hegel.* Basic Books.

Kolb, D. 1986. *The Critique of Modernity: Hegel, Heidegger and After.* University of Chicago Press.

Kolb, C., ed. 1990. *Nietzsche as Postmodernist.* State University of New York Press.

Kopp, B. 1974. *Beiträge zur Kulturphilosophie der deutschen Klassik: Eine Untersuchung im Zusammenhang mit dem Bedeutungswandel des Wortes Kultur*. Haim.

Korsgaard, C. 1989. Personal Identity and the Unity of Agency: A Kantian Response to Parfit. *Philosophy and Public Affairs* 28, no. 2: 101–132.

Krell, D. F. 1986. *Postponements*. Indiana University Press.

Kristeva, J. 1991. *Strangers to Ourselves*. Columbia University Press.

Kroeber, A. L., and Kluckhohn, C. 1952. *Culture*. Vintage.

Kroner, R. 1921. *Von Kant bis Hegel*, volume 2. Mohr.

Kuhns, R. 1970. *Structures of Experience*. Basic Books.

Lacan, J. 1977. *Écrits*. Norton.

Lacan, J. 1981. *The Four Fundamental Concepts of Psycho-Analysis*. Norton.

Lacan, J. 1988. *The Seminar of Jacques Lacan*, book 2: *The Ego in Freud's Theory and in the Technique of Psychoanalysis 1954–55*, ed. J.-A. Miller. Norton.

Lacan, J. 1992. *The Seminar of Jacques Lacan*, book 7: *The Ethics of Psychoanalysis*, ed. J.-A. Miller. Norton.

Lauer, Q. 1983. Religion and Culture in Hegel. In *Hegel's Philosophy of Action*, ed. L. Stepelevich and D. Lamb. Humanities Press.

Lauer, Q. 1993. Religion and Culture. In *Selected Essays on G. W. F. Hegel*, ed. L. Stepelevich. Humanities Press.

Lear, J. 1998. *Open Minded: Working Out the Logic of the Soul*. Harvard University Press.

Leary, D. 1980. German Idealism and the Development of Psychology in the Nineteenth Century. *Journal of the History of Philosophy* 18: 299–317.

LeDoux, J. 1996. *The Emotional Brain*. Simon & Schuster.

Levinas, E. 1969. *Totality and Infinity*. Duquesne University Press.

Levinas, E. 1998. *Entre Nous*. Columbia University Press.

Lewis, C. Versions of Oedipus: The Problem of Tragedy in German Idealism. Unpublished.

Lingis, A. 1977. The Will to Power. In *The New Nietzsche*, ed. D. Allison. Delta.

Lloyd, G. 1993. *The Man of Reason: Male and Female in Western Philosophy*. University of Minnesota Press.

Loewenberg, J. 1965. *Hegel's Phenomenology: Dialogue on the Life of the Mind*. Open Court.

Longo, O. 1990. The Theater of Polis. In *Nothing to Do with Dionysos?* ed. J. Winkler and F. Zeitlin. Princeton University Press.

Löwith, K. 1967. *From Hegel to Nietzsche.* Doubleday.

Löwith, K. 1997. *Nietzsche's Philosophy of the Eternal Recurrence of the Same.* University of California Press.

Lyotard, J.-F. 1984. *The Post-Modern Condition.* University of Minnesota Press.

Lukàcs, G. 1976. *The Young Hegel.* MIT Press.

MacIntyre, A. 1984. *After Virtue.* University of Notre Dame Press.

Magnus, B. 1986. Nietzsche's Philosophy in 1888: The Will to Power and the Übermensch. *Journal of the History of Philosophy* 24, January: 79–98.

Magnus, B., and Higgins, K., eds. 1996. *The Cambridge Companion to Nietzsche.* Cambridge University Press.

Mahler, M., Pine, F., and Bergman, A., eds. 1975. *The Psychological Birth of the Human Infant.* Basic Books.

Mann, P. 1994. *Micropolitics.* University of Minnesota Press.

Marcuse, H. 1960. *Reason and Revolution.* Beacon.

Marcuse, H. 1962. *Eros and Civilization.* Vintage.

Marx, K. 1967. *Writings of the Young Marx on Philosophy and Society*, ed. L. D. Easton and K. H. Guddat. Doubleday.

Marx, W. 1975. *Hegel's Phenomenology of Spirit.* Harper & Row.

May, K. 1990. *Nietzsche and the Spirit of Tragedy.* St. Martin's Press.

McCarthy, T. 1991. *Ideals and Illusions.* MIT Press.

McGinn, R. 1975. Culture as Prophylactic: Nietzsche's Birth of Tragedy as Cultural Criticism. *Nietzsche-Studien* 4: 75–138.

Megill, A. 1985. *Prophets of Extremity.* University of California Press.

Menke, C. 1996. *Tragödie im Sittlichen: Gerechtigkeit und Freiheit nach Hegel.* Suhrkamp.

Messer, S. B., et al., eds. 1988. *Hermeneutics and Psychological Theory.* Rutgers University Press.

Michelfelder, D., and Palmer, R., eds. 1989. *Dialogue and Deconstruction: The Gadamer-Derrida Encounter.* State University of New York Press.

Mills, P. J. 1987. *Woman, Nature and Psyche.* Yale University Press.

Mitchell, S. 1988. *Relational Concepts in Psychoanalysis.* Harvard University Press.

Mitchell, S., and Greenberg, J. 1983. *Object Relations in Psychoanalytic Theory.* Harvard University Press

Mörchen, H. 1980. *Macht und Herrschaft im Denken von Heidegger und Adorno.* Klett-Cotta.

Nagel, T. 1986. *The View from Nowhere.* Oxford University Press.

Nehamas, A. 1985. *Nietzsche: Life as Literature.* Harvard University Press.

Nussbaum, M. 1986. *The Fragility of Goodness.* Cambridge University Press.

Nussbaum, M. 1988. Narrative Emotions: Beckett's Genealogy of Love. *Ethics* 98, January: 225–254.

Nussbaum, M. 1994. *The Therapy of Desire.* Harvard University Press.

Ogden, T. 1989. *The Primitive Edge of Experience.* Aronson.

Oliver, K. 1988. "Nietzsche's 'Woman'": The Poststructuralist Attempt to Do Away with Woman. *Radical Philosophy* 48, spring: 25–29.

Oliver, K. 1994. *Womanizing Nietzsche: Philosophy's Relation to the Feminine.* Routledge.

Ormiston, G. 1994. Traces of Derrida: Nietzsche's Image of Woman. *Philosophy Today* 28: 178–188.

Ottmann, H. 1981. Herr und Knecht bei Hegel. Unmassgebliche Bemerkungen zu einer missverstandenen Dialektik. *Zeitschrift für Philosophische Forschung* 35: 365–384.

Parkes, G. 1994. *Composing the Soul: Reaches of Nietzsche's Psychology.* University of Chicago Press.

Patton, P., ed. 1994. *Nietzsche, Feminism and Political Theory.* Routledge.

Pelczynski, Z. A., ed. 1971. *Hegel's Political Philosophy.* Cambridge University Press.

Peperzak, A. 1960. *Le jeune Hegel et las vision moral du monde.* La Haye.

Pinkard, T. 1988. *Hegel's Dialectic.* Temple University Press.

Pinkard, T. 1994. *Hegel's Phenomenology: The Sociality of Reason.* Cambridge University Press.

Pippin, R. 1989. *Hegel's Idealism: The Satisfactions of Self Consciousness.* Cambridge University Press.

Pippin, R. 1991a. *Modernism as a Philosophical Problem.* Blackwell.

Pippin, R. 1991b. Idealism and Agency in Kant and Hegel. *Journal of Philosophy* 88, no. 10: 532–541.

Pippin, R. 1993. You Can't Get There From Here: Transition Problems in Hegel's *Phenomenology of Spirit*. In *The Cambridge Companion to Hegel*, ed. F. Beiser. Cambridge University Press.

Pippin, R. 1997. *Idealism as Modernism*. Cambridge University Press.

Plato. 1973. *The Gorgias*. Penguin.

Pöggeler, O. 1966. Die Komposition der Phänomenologie des Geistes. *Hegel-Studien* 3: 27–74.

Pöggeler, O. 1973. *Hegels Idee einer Phänomenologie des Geistes*. Alber.

Pöggeler, O. 1980. Hegels Bildungskonzeption im Geschichtlichen Zusammenhang. *Hegel-Studien* 15: 241–269.

Rabinbach, A. 1997. *In the Shadow of Catastrophe: German Intellectuals between Apocalypse and Enlightenment*. University of California Press.

Redding, P. 1996. *Hegel's Hermeneutics*. Cornell University Press.

Ricoeur, P. 1970. *Freud and Philosophy: An Essay on Interpretation*. Yale University Press.

Ricoeur, P. 1992. *Oneself as Another*. University of Chicago Press.

Rickels, L., ed. 1990. *Looking after Nietzsche*. State University of New York Press.

Riedel, M., ed. 1969. *Studien zu Hegel's Rechtsphilosophie*. Suhrkamp.

Riedel, M., ed. 1975. *Metaphysik und Metapolitik*. Suhrkamp.

Ritter, J. 1969. *Metaphysik und Politik: Studien zu Aristoteles und Hegel*. Suhrkamp.

Rockmore, T. 1997. *Cognition: An Introduction to Hegel's Phenomenology of Spirit*. University of California Press.

Rorty, R. 1982. *Consequences of Pragmatism*. University of Minnesota Press.

Rorty, R. 1989. *Contingency, Irony and Solidarity*. Cambridge University Press.

Rose, G. 1996. *Mourning Becomes the Law: Philosophy and Representation*. Cambridge University Press.

Rosen, M. 1982. *Hegel's Dialectic and Its Criticism*. Cambridge University Press.

Rosen, S. 1974a. *G. W. F. Hegel: An Introduction to the Science of Wisdom*. Yale University Press.

Rosen, S. 1974b. Self-Consciousness and Self-Knowlege in Plato and Hegel. *Hegel-Studien* 9: 109–129.

Rosen, S. 1987. *Hermeneutics as Politics*. Oxford University Press.

Rosen, S. 1989. *The Ancients and the Moderns*. Yale University Press.

Rosenkranz, K. 1844. *G. W. F. Hegels Leben*. Duncker and Humblot.

Rosenstein, L. 1970. Foundations of the Metaphysical Theories of Tragedy in Hegel and Nietzsche. *Journal of Aesthetics and Art Criticism* 28, no. 4: 521–533.

Rosensweig, F. 1962. Hegel und die Staat. Nachdr. der. l. Aufl. volumes 1 and 2. Darmstadt.

Ross, A., ed. 1988. *Universal Abandon?* University of Minnesota Press.

Roudinesco, E. 1990. *Jacques Lacan & Co: A History of Psychoanalysis in France, 1925–1985*. University of Chicago Press.

Rovane, C. 1998. *The Bounds of Agency: An Essay in Revisionary Metaphysics*. Princeton University Press.

Royce, J. 1919. *Lectures on Modern Idealism*. Yale University Press.

Safranski, R. 1998. *Martin Heidegger: Between Good and Evil*. Harvard University Press.

Sallis, J. 1991. *Crossings: Nietzsche and the Space of Tragedy*. University of Chicago Press.

Sartre, J. P. 1956. *Being and Nothingness*. Philosophical Library.

Schaberg, W. 1995. *The Nietzsche Canon: A Publication History and Bibliography*. University of Chicago Press.

Schacht, R., ed. 1983. *Nietzsche*. Routledge.

Schacht, R., ed. 1994. *Nietzsche, Genealogy, Morality: Essays on Nietzsche's Genealogy of Morals*. University of California Press.

Schechtman, M. 1996. *The Constitution of Selves*. Cornell University Press.

Schiller, F. 1974. *On the Aesthetic Education of Mankind*. Frederick Ungar.

Schlar, J. 1976. *Freedom and Independence: A Study of Hegel's Phenomenology of Mind*. Cambridge University Press.

Schmidt, J. 1981. Recent Hegel Literature, Part I: The Jena Period and the Phenomenology of Spirit. *Telos* 46, no. 2: 114–147.

Schore, A. 1993. *Affect Regulation and the Origin of the Self: The Neurobiology of Emotional Development*. Analytic Press.

Schrift, A. 1995. *Nietzsche's French Legacy: A Genealogy of Poststructuralism*. Routledge.

Schutte, O. 1984. *Beyond Nihilism: Nietzsche without Masks*. University of Chicago Press.

Schwarz, J. 1938. *Hegels philosophische Entwicklung*. Klosterman.

Segal, C. 1982. *Tragedy and Civilization*. Harvard University Press.

Segal, C. 1986. *Interpreting Greek Tragedy*. Cornell University Press.

Shapiro, G. 1989. *Nietzschean Narratives*. University of Indiana Press.

Shapiro, G. 1991. *Alcyone: Nietzsche on Gifts, Noise, and Women*. State University of New York Press.

Siegel, T. Of Untergang and Übergang: Heidegger, Nietzsche, and the Experience of European Nihilism. Unpublished.

Siep, L. 1974. Der Kampf um Anerkennung. Zu Hegels Auseinander setzung mit Hobbes in den Jenaer Schriften. *Hegel-Studien* 9: 155–207.

Siep, L. 1979. *Anerkennung als Prinzip der praktischen Philosophie*. Alber.

Silk, M. S., and Stern, J. P. 1981. *Nietzsche and Greek Tragedy*. Cambridge University Press.

Simmel, G. 1978. *The Philosophy of Money*. Routledge.

Simmel, G. 1983. "Rodin" in philosophische Kultur. In *Gesammelte Essais*. Wagenbach.

Sklar, J. 1976. *Freedom and Independence: A Study of Hegel's Phenomenology of Mind*. Cambridge University Press.

Smith, G. 1996. *Nietzsche, Heidegger and the Transition to Postmodernity*. Chicago University Press.

Smith, J. H. 1988. *The Spirit and Its Letter: Traces of Rhetoric in Hegel's Philosophy of Bildung*. Cornell University Press.

Solomon, R. 1996. Nietzsche ad hominem: Perspectivism, Personality and Ressentiment. In *The Cambridge Companion to Nietzsche*. ed. B. Magnus and K. Higgins. Cambridge University Press.

Steiner, G. 1961. *The Death of Tragedy*. Hill and Wang.

Steiner, G. 1984. *Antigones*. Oxford University Press.

Stern, D. 1985. *The Interpersonal World of the Infant*. Basic Books.

Stern, J. P. 1979. *A Study of Nietzsche*. Cambridge University Press.

Stillman, P., ed. 1987. *Hegel's Philosophy of Spirit*. State University of New York Press.

Stocker, M., with Hegeman, E. 1996. *Valuing Emotions*. Cambridge University Press.

Stoekl, A. 1992. *Agonies of the Intellectual*. University of Nebraska Press.

Strauss, L. 1991. *On Tyranny*, ed. V. Gourevitch and M. Roth. Free Press.

Bibliography

Strong, T. 1988. *Friedrich Nietzsche and the Politics of Transfiguration,* expanded edition. University of California Press.

Szondi, P. 1974. *Poetik und Geschichtsphilosophie.* Suhrkamp.

Szondi, P. 1986. *On Textual Understanding and Other Essays.* University of Minnesota Press.

Taylor, C. 1975. *Hegel.* Cambridge University Press.

Taylor, C. 1979. *Hegel and Modern Society.* Cambridge University Press.

Taylor, C. 1985. *Human Agency and Language: Philosophical Papers,* volume 1. Cambridge University Press.

Taylor, C. 1989. *Sources of the Self: The Making of the Modern Identity.* Harvard University Press.

Taylor, C. 1992. Inwardness and the Culture of Modernity. In *Philosophical Interventions in the Unfinished Project of Enlightenment,* ed. A. Honneth et al. MIT Press.

Taylor, C. 1995. *Philosophical Arguments.* Harvard University Press.

Taylor, M. 1980. *Journeys to Selfhood: Hegel and Kierkegaard.* University of California Press.

Toews, J. 1993. Transformations of Hegelianism, 1805–1846. In *The Cambridge Companion to Hegel.* ed. F. Beiser. Cambridge University Press.

Tomkins, S. 1995. *Exploring Affect: The Selective Writings of Silvan Tomkins.* Cambridge University Press.

Tronick, E. 1989. Emotions and Emotional Communication in Infants. *American Psychologist* 44: 112–119.

Tucholsky, K. 1960. *Gesammelte Werke.* Rowohlt.

van Dooren, W. 1973. Der Begriff der Bildung in der Phänomenologie des Geistes. *Hegel-Jahrbuch,* 162–191.

Vattimo, G. 1988. *The End of Modernity.* Johns Hopkins University Press.

Verene, D. 1985. *Hegel's Recollection.* State University of New York Press.

Vernant, J. P. 1980. *Myth and Society in Ancient Greece.* Humanities Press.

Vernant, J. P. 1981. *Tragedy and Myth in Ancient Greece.* Humanities Press.

Warren, M. 1987. *Nietzsche and Political Thought.* MIT Press.

Westphal, M. 1979. *History and Truth in Hegel's Phenomenology.* Humanities Press.

White, A. 1987. Nietzschean Nihilism: A Typology. *International Studies in Philosophy* 19, no. 2: 29–44.

White, H. 1973. *Metahistory: The Historical Imagination of Nineteenth-Century Europe.* Johns Hopkins University Press.

Whitebook, J. 1985. Reason and Happiness: Some Psychoanalytic Themes in Critical Theory. In *Habermas and Modernity,* ed. R. J. Bernstein. MIT Press.

Whitebook, J. 1995. *Perversion and Utopia: A Study in Psychoanalysis and Critical Theory.* MIT Press.

Wildt, A. 1982. *Autonomie und Anerkennung.* Klett-Cotta.

Williams, B. 1993. *Shame and Necessity.* University of California Press.

Williams, R. 1992. *Recognition: Fichte and Hegel on the Other.* State University of New York Press.

Williams, R. 1997. *Hegel's Ethics of Recognition.* University of California Press.

Winnicott, D. W. 1965. *The Maturational Processes and the Facilitating Environment.* International Universities Press.

Wood, A. 1991. *Hegel's Ethical Thought.* Cambridge University Press.

Yovel, Y. 1998. *Dark Riddle: Hegel, Nietzsche, and the Jews.* Pennsylvania University Press.

Žižek, Slavoj. 1989. *The Sublime Object of Ideology.* Verso.

Index